The Radical Critique of Liberalism

Anamnesis

Anamnesis means remembrance or reminiscence, the collection and recollection of what has been lost, forgotten, or effaced. It is therefore a matter of the very old, of what has made us who we are. But *anamnesis* is also a work that transforms its subject, always producing something new. To recollect the old, to produce the new: that is the task of *Anamnesis*.

a re.press series

The Radical Critique of Liberalism:
In Memory of a Vision

Toula Nicolacopoulos

re.press Melbourne 2008

re.press

PO Box 75, Seddon, 3011, Melbourne, Australia
http://www.re-press.org

© re.press 2008

This work is 'Open Access', published under a creative commons license which means that you are free to copy, distribute, display, and perform the work as long as you clearly attribute the work to the authors, that you do not use this work for any commercial gain in any form whatsoever and that you in no way alter, transform or build on the work outside of its use in normal academic scholarship without express permission of the author (or their executors) *and* the publisher of this volume. For any reuse or distribution, you must make clear to others the license terms of this work. For more information see the details of the creative commons licence at this website:
http://creativecommons.org/licenses/by-nc-nd/2.5/

British Library Cataloguing-in-Publication Data
A catalogue record for this book is available from the British Library

Library of Congress Cataloguing-in-Publication Data
A catalogue record for this book is available from the Library of Congress

National Library of Australia Cataloguing-in-Publication Data

Nicolacopoulos, Toula.
The radical critique of liberalism : in memory of a vision.

Bibliography.
Includes index.
ISBN 978-0-9803052-5-8 (paper)
978-0-9803052-8-9 (cloth)

1. Liberalism. 2. Political science - Philosophy. I. Title. (Series : Anamnesis).
320.51

Designed and Typeset by *A&R*
Typeset in *Baskerville*

This book is produced sustainably using plantation timber, and printed in the destination market reducing wastage and excess transport.

This publication has been supported by La Trobe University
http://www.latrobe.edu.au

To Alec Hyslop, dear friend and colleague

Contents

Acknowledgements   ix
Abbreviations   xi

Introduction   3

PART I: POLITICAL PHILOSOPHY AND RADICAL CRITIQUE IN THE LIBERAL AGE   13

1. Political Philosophy as Critical Understanding   17
2. What is it to Critique Liberalism?   39
3. Critical Reconstructionism as a Philosophical Methodology   63
4. The Critical Reconstruction of Liberalism   81

PART II: LIBERALISM AS A MINIMAL POLITICAL MORALITY   101

5. Will Kymlicka: Liberalism and Foundational Ideas   105
6. Jeremy Waldron: Liberalism and Consensual Legitimation   121
7. Charles Larmore: Liberalism and Neutral Procedural Discourse   143

PART III: JOHN RAWLS' POLITICAL LIBERALISM   175

8. Political Liberalism as a Minimal Political Morality   179
9. Publicness and Privateness in the Deep Structure of Political Liberalism   195
10. The Relative Superiority of Political Liberalism   219
11. The Radical Critique of the Minimal Political Morality Approach   231

Conclusion: Liberal Theory in Epistemological Crisis   255

Bibliography   260
    About the Author   277

Acknowledgements

I would like to acknowledge the support of La Trobe University for a publication grant and a period of study leave during which I conducted part of the research for this book. A number of people have made this publication possible. First and foremost my deep appreciation to the re.press team for making their vision of open access publications a reality and, in particular, to Paul Ashton for his work on this manuscript and Claire Rafferty for her cover design. Thanks also to Juan Ford for the use of the cover image *An Imminent Silhouette*, 2007 (courtesy of Dianne Tanzer Gallery, Melbourne, Sullivan & Strumpf Fine Art, Sydney and Jan Manton Art, Brisbane); the reviewers of the book, Geoff Boucher and Garry Hall; and to friends and colleagues with whom discussions over the years have helped to clarify my thoughts, and especially to Paul Ashton, Carol Bacchi, Andrew Brennan, Lynda Burns, John Campbell, George Michelakakis, Ross Phillips, Kay Schaffer, George Vassilacopoulos and Robert Young. Finally, thanks to George and Kostas for all their love and patience and to my parents, John and Ekaterini, for their generosity.

Toula Nicolacopoulos

Abbreviations

CPP   Kymlicka, Will, *Contemporary Political Philosophy: An Introduction*, Oxford, Oxford University Press, 1989.

LCC   Kymlicka, Will, *Liberalism, Community, and Culture*, Oxford, Oxford University Press, 1989.

LPL   Larmore, Charles, 'Political Liberalism', *Political Theory*, vol. 18, no. 3, 1990, pp. 339-60.

PL   Rawls, John, *Political Liberalism*, New York, Columbia University Press, 1993.

PMC   Larmore, Charles, *Patterns of Moral Complexity*, Cambridge, Cambridge University Press, 1987.

WJ   MacIntyre, Alasdair C., *Whose Justice? Which Rationality?*, Notre Dame, University of Notre Dame Press, 1988.

The genuine refutation must penetrate the opponent's stronghold and meet him on his own ground; no advantage is gained by attacking him somewhere else and defeating him where he is not.

G. W. F. Hegel, *Science of Logic*

introduction

Introduction

Alasdair MacIntyre poses the question: 'Nietzsche or Aristotle?' If *I* am right, the question is 'Nietzsche or Liberalism?'; and, unless one is a psychopath [...] the answer must be the latter.[1]

When this statement was published in 1990, liberal theorists were still devoted to addressing the abstract question of whether it was possible to justify a liberal social order and its associated values. Today Anglophone political philosophy is generally conducted in the light of the perceived triumph of liberalism. That is, it typically proceeds on the assumption that it is unreasonable, if not irrational or pathological, to resist liberalism, whether as a mode of thought or as a social order. Despite critics' repeated attempts to demonstrate the incoherence of liberal values, these latter appear to have withstood the test of time so much so that engagement with them has become the meeting point of the different political philosophical traditions. Political philosophy's recent 'contextual turn' now attests to a widely shared desire *to be* a world order in the terms that a liberal theoretical framework makes possible.[2] Through this turn Anglophone political philosophy has re-

---

1. Gerald F. Gaus, *Value and Justification: The Foundations of Liberal Theory*, Cambridge, Cambridge University Press, 1990, p. 457 fn. 46.

2. The 'contextual turn' focuses theory on addressing the pressing social problems of the day. See Avigail I. Eisenberg and Jeff Spinner-Halev (eds.), *Minorities Within Minorities: Equality, Rights, and Diversity*, Cambridge, Cambridge University Press, 2005, pp. 3-7, Duncan Ivison, Paul Patton and Will Sanders (eds.), *Political Theory and the Rights of Indigenous People*, New York, Cambridge University Press, 2000, pp. 1-24, Tariq Modood, Judith Squires and Stephen May (eds.), *Ethnicity Nationalism and Minority Rights*, Cambridge, Cambridge University Press, 2004, pp. 1-26. See also the essays devoted to the contextual turn in *Ethical Theory and Moral Practice*, vol. 7, 2004. On the taken for grantedness of a liberal intellectual framework see Duncan Ivison, *Postcolonial Liberalism*, Cambridge, Cambridge University Press, 2002. See also Kymlicka's contributions in Will Kymlicka, Bruce Berman and Dickson Eyoh (eds.), *Ethnicity and Democracy in Africa*, Athens, Ohio University Press, 2004, Will Kymlicka and Bao-

directed its focus to the complexities of historical practice and context within the ethno-culturally diverse societies of today's globalized world, but the solutions to the world's pressing social problems are largely being conceived within the taken for granted parameters of a *liberal* world order.

This situation in turn makes the *radical* critique of liberalism look like (it should be) a thing of the past. The work of John Rawls was of course most influential in this regard. Having succeeded in placing liberal values and institutions at the centre of all *reasonable* political discussion, Rawls' theory of social justice invites further reflection on the question of its application to *particular* areas of social life.[3] This is so irrespective of whether one favours a universalist or contextualist reading of the theory. That is, irrespective of *how far* one thinks that liberal principles of social/global justice justifiably apply across time and within and across cultures, the suggestion is that to reflect *reasonably* on social justice within the western democratic tradition is to elaborate and defend the institutional embodiment of some sort of *liberal* political values. If this position is well founded, then political theory with radical aspirations, that is, with some view of the need for the radical transformation of liberal societies, must be misplaced. To resist liberalism would be *unreasonably* to deny the moral and/or political superiority of (the values governing) liberal societies as compared with their historical and contemporary social alternatives.

But should radical critique justifiably become a thing of the past? In this study I try to develop a certain kind of radical critique of liberalism in order to demonstrate that resistance is not just a *reasonable option*. Contemporary liberal philosophy is fundamentally flawed despite the appeal of its seemingly more grounded orientation to real world cultural differences. However, I also agree with liberal theorists that, on the whole, critiques of liberalism, whether more traditionally Marxist, post-Marxist, feminist, communitarian, postmodern, postcolonial, or some combination of these have proved unsatisfactory. Though I share many of the concerns raised by radical critiques of liberalism coming from such perspectives, I think that they lack a suitable approach to critical philosophical inquiry and a methodology that can produce the necessary results. In the book I aim to elaborate such an approach and methodology and I attempt to demonstrate their validity through the radical critique of four liberal political theories.

My critique of liberalism takes off from Alasdair MacIntyre's conclusion that 'liberalism has become the kind of social and cultural tradition in

---

gang He, *Multiculturalism in Asia*, Oxford, Oxford University Press, 2005; Will Kymlicka and Magdalena Opalski (eds.), *Can Liberal Pluralism be Exported?: Western Political Theory and Ethnic Relations in Eastern Europe*, New York, Oxford University Press, 2001.

3. See, for example, Hsieh Nien-he, 'Rawlsian Justice and Workplace Republicanism', *Social Theory & Practice*, vol. 31, no. 1, 2005, pp. 115-42, p. 142.

which incoherence [...] is at home'.[4] MacIntyre attributes liberalism's incoherence to the co-presence in liberal culture of logically incompatible and incommensurable modern individualist values and the virtues of pre-modern cultural and intellectual traditions, such as competing conceptions of justice and desert.[5] He suggests that this incoherence is socially and politically protected because the survival of the liberal tradition depends on it. Distinguishing between the liberal *intellectual* tradition and the wider *social and cultural* tradition in which the former is embedded, he also suggests that this protection is partly afforded by the liberal *intellectual* tradition, that is, by liberalism's various traditions of inquiry—such as utilitarianism, natural rights theory and contractarianism.[6] Liberal theories reinforce the liberal culture's incoherence when they represent the latter's incompatible commitments and rationally irresolvable disagreements as a set of continuing and ineliminable disagreements about which all should agree to disagree.[7] So, MacIntyre locates liberalism's incoherence at the level of its socio-political culture and institutional embodiments leaving open the possibility that particular liberal traditions of inquiry may themselves be coherent, albeit at the expense of suppressing the incompatible aspects of liberal culture.[8]

In so far as it seeks to identify liberalism's *incoherence* a position like MacIntyre's serves as the starting point for reflecting upon the terms of a radical philosophical critique of liberalism. But MacIntyre's approach does nothing to challenge the liberal *form of thought*, as distinct from liberal political culture, given that on his account theories advanced *within* any of the particular liberal intellectual traditions may nevertheless turn out to be internally

---

4. Alasdair C. MacIntyre, 'A Partial Response to my Critics', in John Horton and Susan Mendus (eds.), *After MacIntyre: Critical Perspectives on the Work of Alasdair MacIntyre*, Cambridge, Polity, 1994, pp. 283-304, pp. 292-3.

5. See ch. 17 of Alasdair C. MacIntyre, *After Virtue: A Study in Moral Theory*, 2nd ed., London, Duckworth, 1985. For a slightly different account of the 'confusion' that liberal societies create in denying that liberalism is the regime of consumers and servicers of consumers, see Ronald Beiner, *What's the Matter with Liberalism?*, Berkeley, University of California Press, 1995, pp. 137-41.

6. MacIntyre, 'A Partial Response to my Critics', pp. 291-4.

7. MacIntyre, 'A Partial Response to my Critics', pp. 291-2. On MacIntyre's analysis, as I understand it, it would be a mistake to think of liberalism only, or primarily, as a principled response to *the fact of value pluralism*, that is, as a way of dealing, socially and theoretically, with the social phenomenon of disagreement about values rather than as a way of explaining its existence and continuation. Because the kind of incoherence he identifies in the culture results from an implicit, if not explicit, commitment to logically incompatible beliefs about value(s) it cannot properly be understood merely in terms of a response to the fact of pluralism.

8. MacIntyre, 'A Partial Response to my Critics', pp. 293-4. For MacIntyre Nozick's and Rawls' theories of distributive justice which give no place to desert claims illustrate this tendency of liberal theory to suppress the elements of liberal culture that produce incoherence. See MacIntyre, *After Virtue*, pp. 249-51.

consistent. Whilst this may well be the case at what I call the *surface level* of liberal theorists' intellectual practice, the conclusion follows only to the extent that philosophical critique also remains on this level. When, however, a radically aspiring critique shifts to what I call the *deep structural level* of inquiry, it becomes possible to see that seemingly divergent liberal theories share certain fundamental commitments that also render *them* incoherent, and not just their cultural and institutional embodiments. Conversely, liberal theories retain a semblance of coherence at a surface level only by failing to follow through the demands set by their own implied view of justification. As we will see, for a radically aspiring critique, an appreciation of the deep structure of liberal theory is crucial for three reasons. Firstly, it reveals an aspect of liberal discourse that is undertaken *by* but not recognized *in* liberal theory. Secondly, it is constituted by a number of equally incoherent ways of dichotomously inter-relating its most basic categories, namely the categories of publicness and privateness. Thirdly, it explains why liberal theories systematically fail to meet the adequacy criteria of their own view of justification.

Along with many other critics of liberalism, MacIntyre has also defended the view, with which I agree despite liberals' arguments to the contrary, that liberal theory presupposes commitment to a misconceived individualist view of persons.[9] MacIntyre attributes this to the liberal conception of practical rationality according to which the individual *reasons as an individual*. This refers to a 'social and cultural artifact' defined by the coming together of a certain psychology of the individual and 'the procedures of the public realm of liberal individualism'. In the former the expression of a preference functions as a prima facie good reason for deciding how one ought to act. In the latter the arenas of public choice are relatedly understood as 'places where bargaining between individuals, each with their own preferences, is conducted' (WJ, pp. 338-9). My aim will be to show that a conclusion like MacIntyre's is best reached by exposing the deep structural commitments of liberal theory since liberal individualism is a product of liberal dichotomous thought and the inconsistencies of this form of thought can only be fully exposed at the level of its *deep structure*. The individualist commitment of liberal theory can and needs to be traced back to the identity of the liberal theorizing subject since, irrespective of how the liberal theorist represents the identity of the theorized subject, the theorist remains *intrinsically private* in his or her own inquiring practices.

So, I will argue that liberal thought cannot sustain itself and, relatedly,

---

9. The objection that liberalism is individualist takes issue with the representation of human beings as self-contained, self-governing choosers. This representation may be discovered in (1) an ethical claim about the just and good life for human beings; (2) a metaphysical claim about human nature; (3) a political ideal; and/or (4) a methodological principle about the ways in which society's basic units of agency are conceived.

that to be a liberal theorist is inescapably to embody liberalism's incoherence at the deep structural level of liberal inquiring practice. It is in this sense that the present work *extends* MacIntyre's assessment of liberalism. This said my argument does not also rely on MacIntyre's negative diagnosis of *modern* culture. This is the thesis that modernity is essentially a corrupting force from which only a few small-scale communities have managed to survive in a less fragmented and distorted way than is generally the case in the (post)modern world.[10] In contrast, my inquiry into liberalism is linked to a larger project aimed at the exploration of the potential of western modernity to realize the human ideal of communal being that is generally associated with western revolutionary thought and practice and is, more specifically, informed by a reading of Hegel's systemic philosophy and, in particular, of the conceptual development of syllogistic reason in *The Science of Logic*.[11]

In Part I of the book I clarify the nature and contemporary significance of my project and the role of radical critique in today's world. I will be suggesting, firstly, that the need for an immanent radical critique of liberal theory arises from the fact that liberalism denies the philosophical significance of *intrinsically public communal being*; and, secondly, that this in turn calls for a certain kind of systemic critical reconstruction of liberal political theories that would otherwise appear to be merely contingently related. Parts II and III work through the theories of prominent liberal theorists, Will Kymlicka, Jeremy Waldron, Charles Larmore and John Rawls. This investigation shows how an adequate appreciation of the deep structural flaws of liberal theory presupposes the employment of a critical philosophical methodology that has the power to reveal the systemic interconnections within and between the varieties of liberal inquiring practices. Then in a forthcoming second volume focused on Ronald Dworkin's writings on liberalism, I show why liberalism cannot consistently be reformulated to avoid its deep structural incoherence.[12]

So, the study as a whole explores the precise character of liberal theory's indirect denial of intrinsically public communal being or, conversely, its constitutive commitment to intrinsically private agency. I try to show why this commitment cannot be justified within a liberal conceptual framework

---

10. See MacIntyre, *After Virtue*, p. 251. Compare Charles Taylor's positive diagnosis of modernity in Charles Taylor, *Sources of the Self: The Making of the Modern Identity*, Cambridge, Cambridge University Press, 1989.

11. G. W. F. Hegel, *Science of Logic*, trans. A.V. Miller, New Jersey, Humanities Press, 1997. See part 1 of Toula Nicolacopoulos and George Vassilacopoulos, *Hegel and the Logical Structure of Love: An Essay on Sexualities, Family and the Law*, Aldershot, Ashgate, 1999. Also see Toula Nicolacopoulos and George Vassilacopoulos, 'The Ego as World: Speculative Justification and the Role of the Thinker in Hegel's Philosophy', in Paul Ashton, Toula Nicolacopoulos and George Vassilacopoulos (eds.), *The Spirit of the Age: Hegel and the Fate of Thinking*, Seddon, re.press, 2008, pp. 252-91.

12. Toula Nicolacopoulos, *In Memory of a Vision, Volume 2*, Seddon, re.press, forthcoming.

and why the rejection of liberalism's commitment to intrinsically private agency calls for a rejection of liberal inquiring practice itself. Such a demonstration is important in two ways. On a substantive level, it shows why the elaboration of a philosophy of intrinsically public communal being is, after all, relevant to our times. On a methodological level, it reveals the potential limitations of the forms of thought that radically aspiring critiques of liberalism sometimes take.

part 1

Political Philosophy and Radical Critique in the Liberal Age

> oh, boundless longing for that which we were never able to enjoy but which was our very life [...]
>
> the beautiful mystery of being alone, the mystery of the two, or the great mystery of the gathering of us all.[1]

In the experience of the communist poet, Tasos Livadites, the 'mystery' of our being as a singular subject who can nonetheless affirm the 'we' is bound up with the reality of the denial of community. Community simultaneously involves hope and recognition of a loss. Whereas the 'great mystery' is the source of inspiration and hope, the 'longing' in question implicitly refers us to the experience of a certain kind of loss. Indeed, as Jacques Ranciere notes in connection with the idea of the 'community of equals', its 'fundamental aspect [...] has to do with the relationship of the idea of community to the idea of loss itself, to what we retain of a loss, or to what takes shape around it'.[2]

For present purposes, this is not the loss associated with some ideal condition that was once enjoyed either collectively, as in previous historical epochs, or individually, as in the psychoanalytic idea of the newborn child's undifferentiated unity with the Mother. The loss in question is the loss of that forward-looking ideal that has traditionally informed Left Anarchist and Marxist revolutionary movements. In this context loss has a double implication: it refers us to the late twentieth century western cultural condi-

---

1. Tasos Livadites, *Small Book for Large Dreams (Greek)*, Athens, Kethros, 1987, pp. 16-7. Translation from the Greek by George Vassilacopoulos and myself.

2. Jacques Rancière, *On the Shores of Politics*, trans. Liz Heron, London, Verso, 1995, p. 64.

tions that failed to give effect to the revolutionary idea of community or solidarity associated with the French Revolution, but it also refers us to the conditions that have resulted in the near abandonment of this idea as *an ideal to be realized*, that is, to the evental retreat of the revolutionary project.[3]

The loss of community in the above sense is directly linked to the lived experience of the limits of individualism that radical critiques of liberalism associate with the conditions of contemporary life in a liberal capitalist world order. In Part I of the book I will begin by outlining a certain view of the relationship between the idea of community understood as a loss and the need for the radical critique of liberalism. In Chapter 1 I will explain how life in the liberal age might give rise to the need for the radical critique of liberalism and introduce the general features characterizing the liberal critic's reflective standpoint. The purpose of Chapter 2 is to specify the object of radical critique and to position my claims in relation to alternative approaches. Chapters 3 and 4 develop more fully my account of the nature of the radical critique of liberalism. In Chapter 3 I will elaborate and defend what I call 'critical reconstructionism'. This is a dialectical philosophical methodology that has the power to systematize liberal theory. In Chapter 4 I rely upon the methodology of critical reconstructionism to engage with the current variety of Anglophone liberal theories with a view to proposing a systemic taxonomy. I will suggest that this systemic way of reconceiving liberal theory has the potential to offer a comprehensive map of liberal discourse that, in turn, gives rise to the possibility of an immanent and dialectical assessment of liberal theory from its least to its most comprehensive formulations.

---

3. Toula Nicolacopoulos and George Vassilacopoulos, 'Philosophy and Revolution: Badiou's Infidelity to the Event', in Paul Ashton, A. J. Bartlett and Justin Clemens (eds.), *The Praxis of Alain Badiou*, Seddon, re.press, 2006, pp. 367-85.

I

Political Philosophy as Critical Understanding

It is true that today's Left is undergoing the shattering experience of the end of an entire epoch for the progressive movement, an experience which compels it to re-invent the very basic co-ordinates of its project.[1]

'Looking ahead' from his extensive survey of contemporary radical social theory in the North Atlantic/North American area, Göran Therborn predicts that Left intellectual creativity will continue, despite the vanishing of the socialist horizon:

> Capitalism still produces and will continue to produce a sense of outrage [...] Twenty-first century anti-capitalist resisters and critics are unlikely to forget the socialist and communist horizons of the past two hundred years.[2]

Yet, Therborn fears that

> the classical Marxist triangle [consisting of a philosophy of dialectics, historical social sciences focused on the forces and relations of production and a revolutionary politics] has been broken and is most unlikely to be restored.[3]

So, what should we make of the likely means and ways of 're-inventing the very basic co-ordinates' of the Left project of whose urgent need Žižek re-

---

1. Slavoj Žižek, 'Introduction: Between the Two Revolutions', in Slavoj Žižek (ed.), *Revolution at the Gates: A Selection of Writings From February to October 1917*, London, Verso, 2002, pp. 1-12, p. 3.

2. Göran Therborn, 'After Dialectics: Radical Social Theory in a Post-Communist World', *New Left Review*, no. 43, 2007, pp. 63-114, p. 113.

3. Therborn, 'After Dialectics: Radical Social Theory in a Post-Communist World', p. 113.

minds us? Therborn suggests 'the existing repertoire of positions [amongst the Anglophone intellectual Left] is unlikely to please everyone, but it does nevertheless include rallying points for nearly everybody on the left'.[4] But if Žižek's observation is well founded then 'rallying points' will not suffice.

I want to begin with the suggestion then that for the intellectual Left a re-invention of basic co-ordinates must begin from the undisputed position of our being at 'the end of an entire epoch' or, conversely, from the self-affirmation of the liberal age in which we live. But, this suggests a critical interest not only in *the social/global order* with which the liberal age is associated but also with its *self-affirming aspects* and this includes liberal theories. In other words, to begin from our being at 'the end of an entire epoch' is to raise the question of the connection between a liberal society/world order (hereafter 'a liberal order') and liberal thought.

However, this still leaves open the question of why a critical interest in a liberal order should lead to an investigation of liberal *political* theory. To answer this question we shall consider a fundamental difference between liberal political theorists and the kind of liberal critic I have in mind. This difference concerns the way we understand the philosophical significance of the liberal age. I will be suggesting that for the alienated social participant the importance of the liberal age lies in the combined facts that we live in it, yet it denies our (potential for) intrinsically public communal being. This calls for a diagnosis of liberal political theory from the reflective standpoint of a theorist who is in but not (yet) of liberalism, a standpoint that in turn calls for the suspension of identification with intrinsically public communal being and reflection in the light of awareness of the cultural force of intrinsically private agency. Such a diagnosis translates into the need for an immanent critique of liberal inquiring practice as a precondition for the justified elaboration of a utopian philosophy of intrinsically public communal being.

1.1 The liberal age and liberal theory

1.1.1 Liberal political theory in the liberal age

Our current reality is overwhelmingly one of *life in the liberal age*. For many liberal *social theorists* ever since the collapse of Euro-socialism and the Soviet Union the events of world history serve to confirm the indispensability of a liberal order, its values and the institutions embodying them. Few today do not presume that 'liberalism of some kind has won' over Marxism.[5] Many accept that some form of liberal order is after all, as Fukuyama claimed in

---

4. Therborn, 'After Dialectics: Radical Social Theory in a Post-Communist World', p. 113.

5. Allan Ryan, 'Liberalism', in Robert E. Goodin and Philip Pettit (eds.), *A Companion to Contemporary Political Philosophy*, Oxford, Blackwell, 1997, pp. 291-311, p. 308.

the early 1990s, the final social paradigm.⁶ Even the most insightful critics of this position now articulate their alternative visions as better or richer understandings of commonly endorsed liberal values. To take just two prominent examples, when Bhiku Parekh advances a postcolonial theory for the management of multicultural societies he does not challenge 'the liberal way of life' but rather seeks to bring it into 'intercultural dialogue' with other ways of understanding and organizing life that also contain commendable insights and values.⁷ Similarly, when post-Marxist theorist, Chantal Mouffe takes issue with a certain misrepresentation of ethico-political values as supposedly being grounded in a universalistic rationality, she does not also challenge the liberal democratic order of their operation.⁸

Of course, there are still the rather negative diagnoses of the liberal age.⁹ Liberal *political theorists* are not necessarily blind to these, often acknowledging the shortcomings of the liberal political culture and institutions that ground such diagnoses. Even so, as Mark Lilla's comparison of Anglo-American and French political philosophy reveals, the 'self-satisfied' air of Anglo-American liberal political philosophy is unmistakable.¹⁰ Characteristically, in his textbook introduction to contemporary political philosophy, Will Kymlicka suggests that liberal philosophy's distinctively *liberal* political principles may have 'radical implications' for traditional liberal political practice and institutions. On this view liberal political theory and liberal political practice have become so 'disengaged' that the latter fails to embody the principles of the former (CPP, pp. 89-90). Yet, Kymlicka's defence of the highly contestable claim that freedom is located in the realm of the social and not the political comes down to the assertion that 'liberalism has simply won the historical debate, and all subsequent debate occurs, in a sense within the boundaries of basic liberal commitments' (CPP, p. 252).

Even when, as for John Rawls, the state of the world has the power to evoke negative emotions, the emphasis is on the rationality of the principles that supposedly *underlie* liberal cultural practices and institutions:

> Political philosophy calms our frustration and rage against the social world by showing us the way in which its institutions, when properly understood from a philosophical point of view, are rational.¹¹

---

6. Francis Fukuyama, *The End of History and the Last Man*, New York, Penguin, 1992.

7. Bhikhu C. Parekh, *Rethinking Multiculturalism: Cultural Diversity and Political Theory*, 2nd ed., Basingstoke, Palgrave Macmillan, 2006, p. 369.

8. Chantal Mouffe, *On the Political*, London, Routledge, 2005, pp. 121-2.

9. Eric J. Hobsbawm, *Age of Extremes: The Short Twentieth Century, 1914-1991*, London, Abacus, 1995. Compare Alain Badiou, *The Century*, trans. Alberto Toscano, London, Polity, 2007.

10. Mark Lilla, *New French Thought: Political Philosophy*, Princeton, Princeton University Press, 1994, p. 16.

11. Cited in Michael O. Hardimon, *Hegel's Social Philosophy: The Project of Reconciliation*, Cambridge, Cambridge University Press, 1994, p. 6.

The implication here is that such rage would be misdirected if it were directed to liberal *values* rather than to their unsatisfactory institutional embodiments.

Nor does the actual assessment of liberal political culture appear to impact upon the self-satisfiedness of the liberal mind-set. For example, for Nancy L. Rosenblum because '[t]he problem with orthodox liberal thought is that some men and women cannot recognize themselves in it' the solution is to reconstruct liberal thought so as to enable it to 'evoke genuine personal affinity' with 'a certain kind of experience' of liberal political practice, namely 'the romantic experience of liberalism'.[12] So despite viewing the affective relationship of political philosophy to liberal political culture very differently to Rawls, Rosenblum's approach equally manifests a self-satisfied liberalism.

Irrespective then of liberals' readings of the historical relationship between liberal theory and liberal practice, liberal *political*, as distinct from social, theory claims to represent the liberal age in its best possible (rational/emotive) light, even if current institutions and practices do not (as yet) give full expression to liberal values. Because of this connection between a liberal order and liberal political theory a critical interest in the former inevitably leads to a critical interest in the latter.

1.1.2 The philosophical significance of liberalism

So what is the appeal of liberal political theory? To be sure, philosophical engagement with familiar liberal ideals is central to Anglo-American thought for radicals and conservatives as well as liberals.[13] Still, I want to suggest that the *philosophical* appeal of Anglophone liberal political theory lies in its representation of a liberal order, and hence of the liberal age, as capable of resolving what we can refer to as *the predicament of modern individual subjectivity*. What is this predicament? As is well known, western modernity is marked by the differentiation of society into distinct political, economic and domestic spheres, a differentiation that gives rise to the question of the degree to, and grounds upon, which these social spheres are to be conceived as integrated.[14] With modernization this task—understanding the normative basis of social integration—increasingly becomes identified as taking place against the background of the disenchantment of the world. It, therefore, becomes a task for the modern *individual subject* conceived as the legitimate

---

12. Nancy L. Rosenblum, *Another Liberalism: Romanticism and the Reconstruction of Liberal Thought*, Cambridge, Harvard University Press, 1987, p. 1.

13. See, for example, Lilla, *New French Thought*, pp. 3-4. Also see ch. 1 of Elizabeth Frazer and Nicola Lacey, *The Politics of Community: A Feminist Critique of the Liberal-Communitarian Debate*, New York, Harvester Wheatsheaf, 1993.

14. See Charles Taylor, 'Invoking Civil Society', in Robert E. Goodin and Philip Pettit (eds.), *A Companion to Contemporary Political Philosophy*, Oxford, Blackwell, 1997, pp. 66-77.

source of the identification of meaning and value; modern western individuals have to invest their social world—not necessarily their actual world but a certain form of social/world organization—with value through autonomous critical reflection upon it in order to then recognize the legitimacy of its institutions' authority over them.

Even contemporary debates about the source of moral value, like that between realists and non-realists, presuppose the predicament of modern individual subjectivity. Such debates take place against the background assumption that the questions they pose are rationally resolvable *without having to appeal to authoritative sources beyond human reason*. No matter where or how one locates the source of value—in the subject (individual person or community) or the object (the independent world)—the problem and the act of locating it, belong to those of us who are prepared to rely on our own reasoning capacities and to be moved by their products.[15]

Thus the modern individual subject faces a distinctively modern western form of the demand for justification, a demand to which western modernity itself gives rise. To quote Habermas,

> Modernity can and will no longer borrow the criteria by which it takes its orientation from the models supplied by another epoch; *it has to create its normativity out of itself*.[16]

From this perspective, to offer a *modern* justification of some institutional order is to generate and satisfy adequacy criteria that are not externally derived. Understood as an all-embracing principle of self-determination, the demand for justification belongs to our times. Indeed, neither the conditions of our economically and communicatively globalized world nor the postcolonial critique of the Eurocentric origins of the predicament of individual subjectivity detract from this general observation.

In so far as liberal theory claims to be capable of meeting this demand (hereafter 'the modern western demand for justification') it claims to estab-

---

15. For very different ways of articulating this point compare Ross Poole, *Morality and Modernity*, London, Routledge, 1991, Gianni Vattimo, *Nihilism and Emancipation: Ethics, Politics and Law*, Santiago Zabala (ed.), trans. William McCuaig, New York, Columbia University Press, 2004. See also Michael Walzer, 'Three Paths in Moral Philosophy', *Interpretation and Social Criticism*, Cambridge, Harvard University Press, 1987, pp. 1-32. Differences aside, modern versions of the three paths in moral philosophical inquiry that Walzer discusses, namely discovery, invention and interpretation, all presuppose the individual's critical reflective agency.

16. Jürgen Habermas, *The Philosophical Discourse of Modernity: Twelve Lectures*, trans. Frederick G. Lawrence, Cambridge, MIT Press, 1992, p. 7. There are, of course, different ways of invoking modernity as a framework for intellectual inquiry. See, Enrique D. Dussel, *The Invention of the Americas: Eclipse of the 'Other' and the Myth of Modernity*, trans. Michael D. Barber, New York, Continuum, 1995. Nevertheless, in so far as we are interested in the standpoint of western modernity, as distinct from the Eurocentric limitations of this standpoint, Habermas best articulates the predicament of modern individuality.

lish the philosophical basis of a liberal order's political legitimacy. Now, if one takes the philosophical significance of liberalism to derive from the fact that *we live in the liberal age*, this, together with a recognition of the predicament of modern individual subjectivity, invites investigation of liberal theory's claims to satisfy the modern western demand for justification, quite apart from whether or not the political philosopher finds any intuitive appeal in particular liberal values.

1.1.3 The problem of communal being as a motivation for resisting liberalism

There is a second philosophically significant feature of life in the liberal age and this motivates *resistance* to liberalism. This, I want to suggest next, is the fact that the liberal age *denies intrinsically public communal being*. I use the term 'intrinsically' here to refer to the non-contingent aspect(s) of the public form or structure of communal identity without wishing to imply that communal being is defined by some specific substantive property.[17] Despite variations in focus, modern political discourse offers many examples of *intrinsically public* forms of being that invoke the '*we* language' of participation, as Benjamin R. Barber puts it.[18] Communal being is *intrinsically public* when the reasoning processes ideally involved in the articulation, and not just in the realization, of communal values are unavoidably (potentially, if not actually) inter-subjective in ways that manifest relationships of mutual responsiveness, responsibility and accountability. In the present context 'responsiveness' refers to a structural feature of the individual subject's self-awareness. In other words, the being of that which is inter-subjectively recognized is not independent of the recognition in question. This means that the subject incorporates in the structure of its self-awareness, not merely the unity of the self that the Cartesian tradition recognizes, but the element of differentiation that is implied in the idea of ongoing processes of mutual recognition between selves. So, the experience of communal being is grounded in the dyadic structure of subjectivity.[19] On this view, in the absence of mutual recognition the self

---

17. This formulation avoids the charge of essentialism that is targeted to theories that posit some universal human or sex-specific essence. See, for example, Elizabeth Groz, 'A Note on Essentialism and Difference', in Sneja Marina Gunew (ed.), *Feminist Knowledge: Critique and Construct*, London, Routledge, 1990, pp. 332-44, Susan Moller Okin, 'Gender Inequality and Cultural Differences', *Political Theory*, vol. 22, no. 1, 1994, pp. 5-24, Shane Phelan, *Identity Politics: Lesbian Feminism and the Limits of Community*, Philadelphia, Temple University Press, 1989.

18. For Barber the participation characteristic of 'participatory citizenship' 'is by its very nature public activity [...] The language of consent is *me* language: 'I agree' or 'I disagree'. The language of participation is *we* language: 'Can we?' or 'Is that good for us?', Benjamin Barber, 'Liberal Democracy and the Costs of Consent', in N. L. Rosenblum (ed.), *Liberalism and Moral Life*, London, Harvard University Press, 1989, p. 65.

19. On the dyadic structure of subjectivity (a) in connection with caring activity see Nel

remains an abstraction.

Nor is communal being necessarily restricted to the social field of interpersonal practices and institutions, the paradigm instances of which might be friendship and other intimate relationships.[20] The intrinsically public character of the experience of communal being may extend to one's world as a whole. As a fundamental orientation to *self and world* communal being may coincide with a holistic worldview in which human society is viewed as an integrated yet differentiated system. In the political institution of society, just as in relationships to the non-human world, the value of solidarity mediates the subject-object relationship. Thus communal being necessarily includes a political dimension, regardless of how one defines the specifics of the structure of the political life of a community.[21]

It follows from this understanding of communal being as intrinsically public that communal being cannot simply be a matter of *my unilaterally choosing* to live or act in a certain way. For, although autonomous choice is necessary, it is not sufficient for community since others, or more precisely, relevant aspects of the world, must also be appropriately responsive. It is *the experience of the absence* of this responsiveness, an absence that may even defy (occasional or habitual) acts of collective will formation, that I referred to earlier as a loss. The experience of the loss of visionary community in roughly the above terms is what I shall mean by 'the (ontological) problem of communal being or community'. As I understand it, then, in the liberal age community is a *problem* and it is a problem *of being* in the sense outlined here.

Not only is the problem of community an ontological one but it also arises *pre-reflectively*. That is, one may identify with intrinsically public communal being (hereafter 'communal being') immediately, that is, without the aid of

---

Noddings, *Caring: A Feminist Approach to Ethics and Moral Education*, Berkeley, University of California Press, 1984, esp. p. 69; and (b) in connection with loving activity see Nicolacopoulos and Vassilacopoulos, *Hegel and the Logical Structure of Love*. See also George Vassilacopoulos, *A Reading of Hegel's Philosophy*, Ph.D., La Trobe University, Melbourne, 1993. Hegel introduces this idea as the simplest form of ethical being in the first moment of 'Ethical Life' (paragraphs 158-180), in G. W. F. Hegel, *The Philosophy of Right*, trans. T. M. Knox, Oxford, Oxford, 1976. See also Darren R. Walhof's reading of the features of 'life together' and 'reciprocal co-perception' in Gadamer's account of friendship and solidarity: Darren R. Walhof, 'Friendship, Otherness and Gadamer's Politics of Solidarity', *Political Theory*, vol. 34, 2006, pp. 569-93.

20. See, for example, Virginia Held, 'Non-Contractual Society: The Post-Patriarchal Family as Model', *Feminist Morality: Transforming Culture, Society, and Politics*, Chicago, University of Chicago Press, 1993, pp. 192-214.

21. Here I have in mind not only the heirs to the Left anarchist and Marxist traditions including eco-philosophers, eco-feminists and communicative ethicists but also theorists influenced by post-modern readings of our current cultural conditions. As Drucilla Cornell has argued, on some readings of postmodern discourses 'the protection and care of difference' is done, not against, but in the name of, the dream of community. Drucilla Cornell, 'The Post-structuralist Challenge to the Ideal of Community', *Cardozo Law Review*, vol. 8, 1987, pp. 989-1022.

a theory of community. But, since in the liberal age this is an experience of *loss*, it also involves a related inability immediately to identify with one's social world. One's affirmative attitude towards one's communal being is thus concretely embodied in the experience of alienation from one's world as a totality and, by extension, from one's activity in it (hereafter 'the experience of total alienation'). The experience of total alienation is a late twentieth century phenomenon associated with the realization that neither the traditionally Marxist, nor the New Left social movements' efforts to create stable revolutionary identities have succeeded.[22] John Dunn sums it up well when he suggests that, following the collapse of Soviet and western European socialism 'what has been deleted from the human future, almost inadvertently but still with remarkable decisiveness, is any form of reasonable and relatively concrete social and political hope'.[23]

Now, it is in this sense of giving rise to totally alienated social participants that the liberal age *denies* communal being. Although the experience of the problem of community is not a widespread phenomenon, it is nevertheless a feature of *modern* life in a philosophically significant way in so far as it points to a negative definition of the modern western actuality as the denial of community. The focus of philosophical reflection thus becomes the normative-ethical question of what to make of the problem of community to which the liberal age has given rise.

1.1.4 Liberal political theorists' response to the problem of community

The response of liberal political theorists to the problem of community has been, implicitly if not explicitly, to represent the liberal age as *justifiably* having set aside all models of communal being. This position relies on the apparent failure of the western intellectual tradition to elaborate a modern *non-liberal* conception of political community that does not privilege society over the individual.[24] Rejecting the choice between non-modern ideals of community that fail to recognize modern individuality and totalitarian notions of the state that subordinate the individual, liberal political theorists advocate (reflection upon) a place for community *in the light of* liberal individualism understood as the attempt to give moral, if not ethical or ontological, priority to the individual.[25] Accordingly, in the liberal-communitarian

---

22. See Ernesto Laclau, 'Introduction', in Ernesto Laclau (ed.), *The Making of Political Identities*, London, Verso, 1994, pp. 1-10, Steven Seidman, 'Identity and Politics in a "Postmodern" Gay Culture: Some Historical and Condeptual Notes', in Michael Warner (ed.), *Fear of a Queer Planet: Queer Politics and Social Theory*, Minneapolis, University of Minnesota Press, 1993, pp. 103-42.

23. John Dunn, *Western Political Theory in the Face of the Future*, Cambridge, Cambridge University Press, 1993, p. 122.

24. See, for example, John Rawls, *Political Liberalism*, New York, Columbia University Press, 1993, p. 206.

25. Some liberals attribute *ontological* priority to individual persons based on the primacy

debates of the 1980s and early 1990s many liberal theorists sought to accommodate the values of individuality and community in non-oppositional terms.[26] Liberal theorists developed three general types of response to the 'new-communitarian' critique of the times.[27] At one extreme those who remained committed to a liberal individualist social ontology argued that in-

---

of human/natural rights. See, for example, ch. 8 of Gaus, *Value and Justification: The Foundations of Liberal Theory*. And ch. 3 of Douglas B. Rasmussen and Douglas J. Den Uyl, *Liberty and Nature: An Aristotelian Defense of Liberal Order*, La Salle, Open Court, 1991. Others claim that 'whatever their metaphysical status, it is only individual agents who matter in the design of socio-political institutions and it is only the interests of individuals that we ought to take into account in devising such arrangements', Philip Pettit and Chandran Kukathas, *Rawls: A Theory of Justice and its Critics*, Cambridge, Polity, 1990, p. 11.

26. See the articles reproduced in Shlomo Avineri and Avner De-Shalit (eds.), *Communitarianism and Individualism*, Oxford, Oxford University Press, 1992. Also the collections of essays in the journals, *Philosophy and Social Criticism*, vol. 14, nos. 3-4; and *California Law Review*, vol. 77, 1989. See also K. Anderson, *et al.*, 'Roundtable on Communitariansim', *Telos*, vol. 76, 1988, pp. 2-32, Allen E. Buchanan, 'Assessing the Communitarian Critique of Liberalism', *Ethics*, vol. 99, no. 4, 1989, pp. 852-82, Simon Caney, 'Liberalism and Communitarianism: a Misconceived Debate', *Political Studies*, vol. 40, no. 2, 1992, pp. 273-89, Clarke E. Cochran, 'The Thin Theory of Community: The Communitarians and Their Critics', *Political Studies*, vol. 37, no. 3, 1989, pp. 422-35, Lyle A. Downing and Robert B. Thigpen, 'Beyond Shared Understandings', *Political Theory*, vol. 14, no. 3, 1986, pp. 451-72, Ralph D. Ellis, 'Toward a Reconciliation of Liberalism and Communitarianism', *Journal of Value Inquiry*, vol. 25, no. 1, 1991, pp. 55-64, David Fisher, 'Crisis Moral Communities: An Essay in Moral Philosophy', *Journal of Value Inquiry*, vol. 24, no. 1, 1990, pp. 17-30, J. P. Geise, 'Liberal Goods', *International Journal of Moral and Social Studies*, vol. 5, no. 2, 1990, pp. 95-115, H. N. Hirsch, 'The Threnody of Liberalism: Constitutional Liberty and the Renewal of Community', *Political Theory*, vol. 14, no. 3, 1986, pp. 423-49, Annas Julia, 'Review: MacIntyre on Traditions', *Philosophy and Public Affairs*, vol. 18, no. 4, 1989, pp. 388-404, Michael Kelly, 'MacIntyre, Habermas and Philosophical Ethics', *Philosophical Forum*, vol. 21, 1990, pp. 70-93, Will Kymlicka, 'Liberalism and Communitarianism', *Canadian Journal of Philosophy*, vol. 18, no. 2, 1988, pp. 181-204, Charles Larmore, 'Review of Michael Sandel's Liberalism and the Limits of Justice', *The Journal Of Philosophy*, vol. 81, no. 6, 1984, pp. 336-43, James W. Nickel, 'Does Basing Rights on Autonomy Imply Obligations of Political Allegiance?', *Dialogue: Canadian Philosophical Review*, vol. 28, no. 4, 1989, pp. 531-44, Timothy O'Hagan, 'Four Images of Community', *Praxis International*, vol. 8, no. 2, 1988, pp. 183-92, William Rehg, 'Discourse Ethics and the Communitarian Critique of Neo-Kantianism', *Philosophical Forum*, vol. 22, no. 2, 1990, pp. 120-38, Kenneth L. Schmitz, 'Community: The Elusive Unity', *Review of Metaphysics*, vol. 37, no. 2, 1983, pp. 243-64, Philip Selznick, 'The Idea of a Communitarian Morality', *California Law Review*, vol. 75, no. 1, 1987, pp. 445-63, John R. Wallach, 'Liberals, Communitarians, and the Tasks of Political Theory', *Political Theory*, vol. 15, no. 4, 1987, pp. 581-611. See also chs. 5-6 in Allan C. Hutchinson and Leslie J. M. Green (eds.), *Law and the Community: The End of Individualism?*, Toronto, Carswell, 1989, Stephen Mulhall and Adam Swift, *Liberals and Communitarians*, Oxford, Blackwell, 1992, Nancy L. Rosenblum (ed.), *Liberalism and Moral Life*, Cambridge, Harvard University Press, 1991.

27. The term 'new communitarianism' was used to refer to post-1980s critiques of liberalism inspired by Aristotle and Hegel rather than Marx. See, for example, Amy Gutmann, 'Review: Communitarian Critics of Liberalism', *Philosophy and Public Affairs*, vol. 14, no. 3, 1985, pp. 308-22, p. 308.

dividual legal and political rights are threatened by models of political association that invoke the concept of community.[28] But liberals who rejected an individualist construction of the nature of human beings developed forms of 'cautious communitarianism', to use Allan Buchanan's phrase.[29] Here, the emphasis was on offering an interpretation of the liberal political community that could acknowledge the value of community for society taken as a whole, including its political sphere, whilst remaining compatible with the liberal principles of freedom and equality. Somewhere between these two extremes, a third type of response held that liberalism's commitment to a form of *moral-political* (though not ontological) individualism was compatible with the development of certain forms of communal association.[30]

In the face of perceived communitarian objections, community-sensitive liberals endorsed some view (a) of the necessary social constitution of individuals; (b) of moral reasoning that recognizes the relational identity of subjects; and (c) of the value of non-individualist conceptions of the good life. (This is not to say that liberals had not addressed such matters prior to the debate.[31] Rather these particular views about liberal social ontology, the nature of moral reasoning and the structure of morality were highlighted in the debates and the positions of participating liberals were thereby clarified or refined.) It is no longer possible to argue against liberalism that it cannot explain political association in terms of a common good or even that it cannot accommodate the communitarian insights of republican thought.[32] Such understandings of political community inform, not only the liberal princi-

---

28. See, for example, Stanley I. Benn, 'Community as a Social Ideal', in Eugene Kamenka (ed.), *Community as a Social Ideal*, London, Edward Arnold, 1982, pp. 43-62, pp. 43-62. Also see George Kateb, 'Individualism, Communitarianism, and Docility', *Social Research*, vol. 56, no. 4, 1989, pp. 921-42, pp. 921-42, Carlos Santiago Nino, 'The Communitarian Challenge to Liberal Rights', *Law and Philosophy*, vol. 8, 1989, pp. 37-52, pp. 37-52, John Rawls, *A Theory of Justice*, Cambridge, Harvard University Press, 1988, pp. 255-62, Bruno Rea, 'Rights and the Communitarian Ideal', *Idealistic Studies*, vol. 18, no. 2, 1988, pp. 107-22, pp. 107-22, Jeremy Waldron, 'When Justice Replaces Affection: The Need for Rights', *Harvard Journal of Law & Public Policy*, vol. 11, no. 3, 1988, pp. 625-47.

29. Buchanan, 'Assessing the Communitarian Critique of Liberalism', p. 860. For an example of this type of response see Ronald Dworkin, 'Liberal Community', *California Law Review*, vol. 77, no. 3, 1989, pp. 479-504, pp. 479-504.

30. See, for example, Charles Larmore, 'Political Liberalism', *Political Theory*, vol. 18, no. 3, 1990, pp. 339-60, Rawls, *Political Liberalism*.

31. For pre-debate examples of the development of the above mentioned positions by liberals see Bruce A. Ackerman, *Social Justice in the Liberal State*, New Haven, Yale University Press, 1980, p. 330, Joseph Raz, *The Morality of Freedom*, Oxford, Oxford University Press, 1986, pp. 267-368.

32. In relation to the common good, see ch. 4 of Rasmussen and Den Uyl, *Liberty and Nature: An Aristotelian Defense of Liberal Order*. In relation to liberal republicanism see Dworkin, 'Liberal Community', pp. 479-504.

ples of distributive justice, but also that of government neutrality.³³

In so far as late twentieth century Anglo-American liberalism was seen as foundationalist in its orientation, at least in its formative years, the communitarian challenge was also read as a challenge to liberalism's universalist aspirations. Thus Raymond Plant represents the liberal-communitarian debate as a disagreement between 'those [liberals] who believe that political philosophy is concerned with providing a basic universal foundation for political judgment and those [communitarians] who think that political philosophy is concerned with a coherent, self-conscious understanding of the political and moral values which suffuse a particular society'.³⁴ At the level of meta-ethical discourse the liberal-communitarian debate did eventuate in various contextualizations of liberalism's universalist aspirations. Let me explain.

Whereas the term 'universalism' marks the scope of a liberal theory's application, whether *across* cultures or (types of) socio-political system(s) or to subjects *within* ideal or actual socio-political systems, 'contextualism' refers to a theory's reliance on the (historically contingent) cultural specificities—like language and social practices—of the time(s) and place(s) of actual people and particular communities.³⁵ Contextualist theories typically propose ideas and ideals without eliminating, or reducing to *one*, the plurality of theorized subjects' situations and reflective standpoints. They are generally contrasted with methodologies that (a) mistakenly take (some aspect of) one social position, situation or reflective standpoint to be shared by all the relevant subjects (eliminating others); or (b) take one socially privileged position to be the only morally relevant one (reducing others to the one). Both these methodological practices engage in what Seyla Benhabib calls 'substitutionalist universalism'.³⁶ Now, at one extreme, a theory may be universalist in the sense of proposing fully non-contextualized ideas and ideals as in the

---

33. See, for example, Peter de Marneffe, 'Liberalism, Liberty, and Neutrality', *Philosophy and Public Affairs*, vol. 19, no. 3, 1990, pp. 253-74, p. 254.

34. Raymond Plant, *Modern Political Thought*, Oxford, Blackwell, 1991, p. 20. For similar interpretations of the debate as being largely about the universalism-contextualism controversy see Alessandro Ferrara, 'Universalisms: Procedural, Contextualist and Prudential', in David M. Rasmussen (ed.), *Universalism vs. Communitarianism: Contemporary Debates in Ethics*, 1st MIT Press ed., Cambridge, MIT Press, 1990, pp. 11-38, David M. Rasmussen, 'Universalism vs. Communitarianism: An Introduction', in David M. Rasmussen (ed.), *Universalism vs. Communitarianism: Contemporary Debates in Ethics*, 1st MIT Press ed., Cambridge, MIT Press, 1990, pp. 1-10.

35. See, for example, Alasdair C. MacIntyre, *Whose Justice? Which Rationality?*, Notre Dame, University of Notre Dame Press, 1988, Susan Moller Okin, *Justice, Gender and the Family*, New York, Basic Books, 1989, p. 42, Michael Walzer, *Spheres of Justice: A Defence of Pluralism and Equality*, Oxford, M. Robertson, 1983.

36. Benhabib compares this idea with 'interactionist universalism' in Seyla Benhabib, *Situating the Self: Gender, Community and Postmodernism in Contemporary Ethics*, Cambridge, Polity Press, 1992, pp. 164-5 and pp. 227-8.

case where liberal political principles are taken to apply to everyone at all places and in all times in virtue of their nature. This is the mode of universalist liberalism that has been the proper object of criticism on the grounds of being a-historical and a-social.[37] At the other extreme, a theory might advocate values that are suitable *only* for the theorist's particular society and its peculiar social and intellectual tradition.[38] Between these two extremes, liberal theorists developed a range of contextualist-universalist approaches enabling their theories to be placed along this continuum depending on the degree of the contextualization of their universalist claims. For example, within such a scheme John Rawls' political liberalism is contextualist in limiting its application to (ideal) *modern liberal democracies* whilst remaining *universalist* both in applying its principles to *all* such societies irrespective of background cultural differences and to *all* persons within such societies.[39] By comparison, Ronald Dworkin's account of liberal equality appears *more* universalist in that it applies to all persons within *all* the societies of the modern world and not just to (ideal) modern liberal democracies.[40]

Despite these significant methodological advances, liberal theorists' responses to the new communitarian challenge showed that even community-sensitive liberal theory was not in a position to address the problem of communal being. In the process of incorporating the perceived strengths of communitarian thought, liberal theorists reformulated (signs of) ideals of communal being and related views about the tasks and methods of political philosophy *in advance of* their assessment; communitarian claims were effectively cut down to fit into a liberal conceptual framework in order subsequently to be assessed and discarded or incorporated as the case may be. In what sense were such insights left out of consideration? I do not mean to suggest that they were not discussed—they were of course. Rather, they were assessed only after having been reformulated in a way that obscured their appeals to forms of communal being in the sense I outlined above (1.1.3). We can illustrate this point by reference to the reception of Alasdair MacIn-

---

37. See ch. 3 of Steven B. Smith, *Hegel's Critique of Liberalism: Rights in Context*, Chicago, University of Chicago Press, 1989. See also Gerald Doppelt, 'Is Rawls's Kantian Liberalism Coherent and Defensible?', *Ethics: An International Journal of Social, Political, and Legal Philosophy*, vol. 99, no. 4, 1989, pp. 815-51.

38. Richard Rorty's bourgeois liberalism may be a case in point, see Richard Rorty, *Contingency, Irony, and Solidarity*, Cambridge, Cambridge University Press, 1989.

39. For an even more contextualist reading of Rawls' *Political Liberalism* see Bruce A. Ackerman, 'Political Liberalisms', *Journal of Philosophy*, vol. 91, no. 7, 1994, pp. 364-86, pp. 375-80. Ackerman thinks that Rawls appeals directly to the actual political practice of his own society and not to the modern western intellectual tradition of thought and inquiry more generally. But see also Mulhall and Swift, *Liberals and Communitarians*, p. 195, Samuel Scheffler, 'The Appeal of Political Liberalism', *Ethics*, vol. 105, no. 1, 1994, pp. 4-22, pp. 20-2.

40. On contextualized universalisms see also Ferrara, 'Universalisms: Procedural, Contextualist and Prudential'.

tyre's analysis of the character of progress within intellectual traditions (see WJ).[41] For example, noting that feminism is and is not a tradition according to MacIntyre's usage, Susan Moller Okin objects that MacIntyre 'gives conflicting accounts of what a tradition *is*':

> at times he describes it as a defining context, stressing the authoritative nature of its 'texts'; at times he talks of a tradition as 'living', as a 'not-yet-completed narrative', as an argument about the goods that constitute that tradition.[42]

However, Okin conflates the different senses of tradition whose relationship MacIntyre discusses. The references to 'authoritative texts' form part of a reconstruction of the stages through which *socio-cultural traditions* pass in order to become *self-evaluating traditions of inquiry*. Thus for MacIntyre traditions of inquiry may operate *within* social-cultural traditions. He also talks of 'textual authority' in the context of discussing language acquisition and usage but this does not conflict with the idea of a tradition as living or, indeed, of the reflective autonomy of its members, since MacIntyre's focus is on something's being *at some point* (as distinct from once and for all) received as authoritative by the participants in a particular cultural and social tradition.[43]

---

41. Another example is the reception of Charles Taylor's analysis of a community in terms of the holistic (expressivist) idea of a 'speech community'. See chs.1, 2, 4 and especially, ch.10, p. 234 of Charles Taylor, *Philosophy and the Human Sciences: Philosophical Papers 2*, Cambridge, Cambridge University Press, 1992. Also see chs 1-4 of Taylor, *Sources of the Self*, Charles Taylor, 'Inwardness and the Culture of Modernity', in Axel Honneth, Thomas McCarthy, Claus Offe and Albrecht Wellmer (eds.), *Philosophical Interventions in the Unfinished Project of Enlightenment*, Cambridge, Mas., MIT Press, 1992, pp. 88-110, Charles Taylor, *Philosophical Arguments*, Cambridge, Harvard University Press, 1995, pp. 79-99. For other examples of the tendency first to reformulate the issues within a liberal framework and then to show how a liberal response to communitarian objections can be given see ch. 8 of Mulhall and Swift, *Liberals and Communitarians*. After having represented the political writings of Taylor, Sandel and MacIntyre as communitarian responses to a Rawlsian theory of justice, the authors argue that Joseph Raz's *communitarian liberalism* ultimately escapes their critique of liberalism. See also the discussion of liberal and communitarian conceptions of the self by Donna Greschner, 'Feminist Concerns with the New Communitarianism', in Allan C. Hutchinson and Leslie J. M. Green (eds.), *Law and the Community: The End of Individualism?*, Toronto, Carswell, 1989, pp. 119-50, pp. 135-45.

42. Okin, *Justice, Gender and the Family*, p. 61.

43. David Miller's discussion of Charles Taylor offers another example of this tendency to leave out of discussion a certain kind of communitarian insight. See David Miller, 'In What Sense Must Socialism Be Communitarian?', *Social Philosophy and Policy*, vol. 6, 1989, pp. 51-73. Miller suggests that in Taylor's view the idea of community has 'no necessary political dimension' and then he suggests that Taylor is inconsistent in endorsing the civic republican view that political participation is an essential part of freedom (see 'In What Sense', p. 65). However, no such inconsistency arises when we read Taylor's political philosophy against the background of his holistic understanding of linguistic community—an understanding that rejects linguistic representationalism and the subject-object dichotomy. See Charles Taylor,

Okin's critique is characteristic of an approach within liberalism that represented non-liberal communitarianism as advocating either individuals' uncritical conformity to (external) communal values or uninteresting, if non-controversial, empirical theses about the nature of human association. Alternatively, from the standpoint of the liberal it appeared that the two sides of the liberal-communitarian debate must have been using different words to advance similar, if not the very same, normative claims about the (theorization of the) individual-society relationship. So, for example, MacIntyre's discussion of the narrative structure of a human life was reduced to an empirical thesis (in the empiricist sense) about the partial social constitution of individuals with non-threatening implications for the ways in which liberal theory addresses normative questions on this issue. Thus, in their introductory remarks on MacIntyre's account of the narrative structure of the self, John Horton and Susan Mendus suggest that 'where liberalism emphasizes our status as choosing and deciding beings, MacIntyre draws attention to the importance of the background circumstances and moral context which inform and make intelligible those choices but which are themselves unchosen'.[44] Here the authors emphasize differences of focus between liberals and MacIntyre respectively on (the capacity for) individual choice and the often-unchosen (moral) context in which such choices are made. Given this reading, an attempt to sensitize liberalism to individuals' different cultural contexts of choice, as in the work of Will Kymlicka, appears as *a solution* to the problem that MacIntyre's view supposedly poses for liberalism.

But if we read MacIntyre's view as developing a specific conception of communal being in the world (in the sense referred to in 1.1.3), then reference to the narrative structure of a life is not reducible to the observation that our choices are made within specific moral-social contexts. This latter is a claim that views the subject-object relationship dichotomously in so far as it sets the subject (individual) up against its object (community) and gives priority to the former. It does not reflect the structure of MacIntyre's claims and not for the reason that MacIntyre reverses the order of priority in favour of the object. Rather, MacIntyre does not view the inter-relationship of subject and object oppositionally. We can see this from his description of what is involved when individuals face the question 'what is *my* good?'. For MacIntyre, 'this they can only succeed in doing *in company* with those others *who participate* with them and with each other in various practices, and who

---

'Overcoming Epistemology', in Kenneth Baynes, James Bohman and Thomas McCarthy (eds.), *After Philosophy: End or Transformation?*, Cambridge, MIT Press, 1987, pp. 464-85, p. 466.

44. John Horton and Susan Mendus, 'After MacIntyre: After Virtue and After', in John Horton and Susan Mendus (eds.), *After MacIntyre: Critical Perspectives on the Work of Alasdair MacIntyre*, Cambridge, Polity, 1994, pp. 1-15, p. 9.

also participate with them in the common life of their whole community'.⁴⁵ So, MacIntyre's commitment to a form of communal being seems to have been lost in the liberal re-presentation of his theses as a set of claims about the narrative structure of the self and the operations of traditions.

Although MacIntyre's communitarianism is informed by the rejection of a representational view of language and of the fact-value distinction, liberal responses to the communitarian critique did not typically address these meta-ethical commitments.⁴⁶ This is not to say that liberal theorists have not taken a position on these issues. For example, Richard Rorty explicitly rejects both the fact-value distinction and a representational view of language.⁴⁷ Yet, liberal political theories seem to be constituted by inquiring practices that preclude or, at least, neutralize the impact of discussion of such meta-ethical issues from what is taken to be *distinctively* liberal discourse. Instead, what is distinctively liberal seems to be the inability to address this issue *as a matter of the operations* of liberal discourse. So, for example, when Rorty opposes the fact-value distinction and challenges representationalism he does not do this qua *liberal* theorist. For him, (private) philosophical inquiry around such issues falls outside the scope of (public) liberal discourse. This mode of dichotomous thought seems to be at the heart of Rortian liberalism. Other liberals will disagree with Rorty's use of this distinction. They might, for example, think in terms that render (private) comprehensive philosophy as falling beyond the scope of (public) political philosophy or in terms that render (private) judgments about such issues as falling beyond the scope of a (public and private) comprehensive liberal philosophy. Still, Rorty's position illustrates the claim that liberal discourse appears to rely on such ways of distinguishing between the public and private aspects of philosophical reflection. If this is correct, then some position on the fact-value distinction and the use of representational language must *define* liberal discourse without also being defined *within* it (or within some privileged aspect of it). As a result, the philosophical significance of *differently structured discourses* would be rendered invis-

---

45. MacIntyre, 'A Partial Response to my Critics', p. 288 (my emphasis). On the subject-object dichotomy and representationalism and see MacIntyre, *Whose Justice?*, pp. 257-8.

46. For their rejections of the fact-value distinction see MacIntyre, *After Virtue*, Charles Taylor, 'Justice After Virtue', in John Horton and Susan Mendus (eds.), *After MacIntyre: Critical Perspectives on the Work of Alasdair MacIntyre*, Cambridge, Polity, 1994, pp. 16-43.

47. See Richard Rorty, *Philosophy and the Mirror of Nature*, Princeton, Princeton University Press, 1986, Selznick, 'The Idea of a Communitarian Morality'. As Richard Rorty's work attests, endorsement of the fact-value distinction is not a shared feature of liberal thought. So whilst an (implicit) endorsement of the fact-value distinction dominates current political thinking, it does not follow that liberal theory stands for the endorsement of the distinction. This is why critiques of liberalism that appeal to such an endorsement fail. See, for example, Elizabeth Frazer and Nicola Lacey (in *The Politics of Community*, p. 4) who mistakenly attribute the failure of liberalism to connect the political realm to social theory to its endorsement of the fact-value distinction.

ible to liberalism. I think that we can understnad the reason for this through an examination of the limits of liberal inquiring practice. So, the hypothesis is that these issues were not merely overlooked in the liberal-communitarian debate. Rather, they fall outside liberalism's discursive field. This is to raise the question of whether there is something about the way liberal inquiring practice relates its most basic categories of analysis that renders such questions invisible within liberalism's field of inquiry.

The point of drawing attention to such misreadings is not to revisit the terms of the liberal-communitarian debate in order to call for a re-assessment of the substantive and methodological issues that were raised. It is rather to inquire into the reflective conditions under which liberalism, and indeed some form of *communitarian* liberalism, could appear to have withstood the new communitarian challenge of the 1980s and 1990s. It is to ask what facilitated this practice of implicitly denying communal being and its associated conceptual presuppositions. For those who accept MacIntyre's thesis that liberalism operates as a (set of) tradition(s) of inquiry, we can explain the state of affairs just described by pointing to liberal theorists' (understandable) failure to appreciate the 'untranslatability' of certain claims that have been put forward from within rival intellectual traditions. (Their failure is understandable to the extent that they do not appreciate the full implications of recognizing the non-neutrality of their own language and standards of inquiry.) In attempting to make sense of such claims using the conceptual resources and modes of argumentation available to the liberal, the Anglophone liberal vocabulary was no doubt enriched but this does not detract from the suspicion that the untranslatable claims of non-liberals were *unavoidably* inadequately represented.[48] Without wishing to imply that a dialectical interchange between traditions is never possible, the fact remains such an interchange did not take place. This, in turn, suggests that a consideration of liberal inquiring practice is needed to explain precisely why liberal theory is limited in this respect. The failure of liberals to address the problem of communal being in the terms we have analyzed so far thus calls into question the nature and adequacy of *their inquiring practice.*

What are the implications of this practice for political theorizing? It seems that even within the conceptual framework of communitarian liberalisms, liberal theory implicitly represents the liberal age as capable of solving

---

48. On MacIntyre's position on the problems of translatability and untranslatability see *Whose Justice?* ch. 19. In 'A Partial Response' (p. 296) he also responds to an objection to the notion of untranslatability on Davidsonian grounds. His comments are concerned with the question of how one can consistently, on the one hand, claim that standards of rationality are internal to traditions and, on the other, deny the relativism of truth and seek to prove the rational superiority of one's views over those of rival traditions. In this context MacIntyre does recognize the possibility of a 'dialectical interchange between rival standpoints', a possibility that presupposes universal truth to be the participants' shared presupposition, 'A Partial Response' p. 297.

the predicament of modern individual subjectivity (by meeting the modern western demand for justification that this predicament raises) *without having to recognize*—as distinct from realize—the intrinsically public view of individuality characterizing communal being. This non-recognition of intrinsically public agency is significant in that it implicitly affirms the cultural force of what I will call *intrinsically private agency*. This refers to a unit of agency that is understood as a singularity and whose identity is *in principle* capable of being defined without the mediation of inter-subjective relationships or processes. (As with the idea of intrinsically public agency, the reference to intrinsicness here is intended to convey the non-contingency of the privateness of the agent's identity. This privateness is, in turn, to be understood as defining the form or structure of the agent's being rather than as one of the substantive properties defining the agent's identity.) A view of justification within liberalism's moral individualist framework, whether communitarian or community-sensitive, at best, not only derives the value of community from, and subordinates it to, that of individuality but it implicitly treats the denial of communal being as having *no* philosophical significance. The point here concerns the view of justification and not whether liberalism can allow communal being some restricted social space in which to test its potential for flourishing. Thus it is this view of justification and not any particular liberal conception of community or any particular methodological claim that marks the meeting point of liberal and non-liberal political theorizing.

So far I have suggested that the fact that the liberal age denies communal being evokes fundamentally different pre-reflective (intuitive) responses in liberal theorists and in those, like myself, who do recognize the problem of community. I turn next to indicate how this fundamental difference in the understanding of the philosophical significance of the liberal age can, in turn, give rise to radically different views of the nature, role and tasks of contemporary political philosophy.

1.2 Political philosophy as critical understanding

1.2.1 The purpose and reflective standpoint of the liberal critic

The relationship between political philosophy and contemporary western political culture or, more specifically, life in a liberal order raises two preliminary issues. The first concerns the purpose of political philosophical inquiry and the second relates to the reflective standpoint from which it should take place. The more popular view is that political theorists work systematically to address questions concerning the nature of democracy, justice, equality, the accommodation of differences, individual and group rights, and so on. These are questions that social participants in general would do well to consider. Thus, the theorist typically takes up the analytic, explanatory and normative dimensions of political theory from the standpoint of *an enlightened citizen* seeking to contribute to the resolution of current social problems. In the post-metaphysical era, in Habermas sense of this phrase, in an era that no longer favours speculative inquiry, political philosophy is generally confined to reflection from the standpoint of practical agents interested in empirically verifiable answers to their questions.[49] But if, contra Habermas—and the dominant trend in contemporary political thought today—the abandonment of speculative inquiry does not mark a progress in the history of the western intellectual tradition, then it is important to retain a critical eye on the limits that the post-metaphysical orientation places on reflection. In this regard, it is worth noting Raymond Plant's assessment of 'the nature of political philosophy in a post-positivist world'.[50] In the aftermath of the linguistic turn Anglophone political philosophy comes to be informed, not only by the endorsement of a representational view of language and a related commitment to the subject-object dichotomy, but also by acceptance of the fact-value distinction.[51] According to Plant, prior to logical positivism's influence on twentieth century political philosophy the foundationalism characterizing the western intellectual tradition—foundationalism in the sense of assuming that questions of political morality can be answered in rational and objective ways that are not reducible to individual preference or desire—gave rise to political theories that (a) claimed to advance fundamental truths regarding the nature and conditions for the realization of the good life and the nature of political right; and (b) supplied a metaphysical ground for these claims supported by some account of cognition. Logical positivism's philosophy of language and epistemology posed a challenge to the purported cognitive basis of political philosophy by rendering emotive rather than cognitive the meaning of normative language.[52] The positivist critique of political theory suggested two approaches to political studies: 'a behavioural science of politics adopting a reductionist meth-

---

49. Jürgen Habermas, 'Life-Forms, Morality and the Task of the Philosopher', in Peter Dews (ed.), *Autonomy and Solidarity: Interviews with Jürgen Habermas*, London, Verso, 1986, pp. 187-211, Jürgen Habermas, 'Philosophy as Stand-in and Interpreter', in Kenneth Baynes, James Bohman and Thomas McCarthy (eds.), *After Philosophy: End or Transformation?*, Cambridge, MIT Press, 1987, pp. 296-318.

50. Plant, *Modern Political Thought*, pp. 20 and esp. pp. 1-2.

51. On a representational view, language offers correct or incorrect representations of an independent order of existence. This view of the relationship of language to the human world presupposes a view of the linguistic subject and his or her object world as ontologically and epistemologically independent of each other. For a critical review of the linguistic turn in philosophy see Rorty's essays 'Ten Years After' and 'Twenty-five Years After' in Richard Rorty (ed.), *The Linguistic Turn: Essays in Philosophical Method*, Chicago, University of Chicago Press, 1992.

52. Plant, *Modern Political Thought*, p. 10.

odological individualism and the logical analysis of political concepts'.[53] The latter theoretical enterprise could serve the former observational and empirical one by clarifying its concepts and advancing morally neutral, scientific ones. The role of political philosophy was thus transformed from its earlier foundational and prescriptive one.

Following the decline in commitment to the positivist program and the rejection of verificationism two positivist presuppositions survived such that the revival of interest in political philosophy continued to be informed by the fact-value distinction and the abandonmnet of speculative metaphysics.[54] So, taking representationalism and the fact-value distinction for granted and having abandoned a speculative approach to philosophy, the dominant tendency in Anglo-American political theorizing conforms to the constraints imposed by such presuppositions about the nature, tasks and methods of its mode of inquiry.

In contrast, I favour a view of political philosophy as *critical understanding* in the tradition of speculative inquiry, a tradition that aspires to reflect upon life without taking for granted the inevitability of the very dichotomies that give rise to the problems being reflected upon. So, I take it to be a legitimate purpose of political theory to aspire to the *understanding* of its subject matter for its own sake rather than for the primary purpose of contributing to social change by supplying theoretically derived solutions to current social problems.[55] The need for political philosophy as understanding can arise when, as in liberalism, the current discourse has no place for the language of communal being.

Moreover, since my inquiry concerns the alienated social participant, in the sense already outlined, it cannot be taken up from the standpoint of

---

53. Plant, *Modern Political Thought*, p. 16.

54. When discussing the positivist legacy, Plant actually refers to 'anti-naturalism' in ethics rather than 'speculative metaphysics' by which he means the grounding of a philosophical account of politics in some view of human nature and the conditions for the realization of the latter's truth. However, the term anti-naturalism can be confusing in this context since critics of the positivist strand of the social and political sciences, like Charles Taylor, attack this strand for its 'naturalism' meaning the tendency to model the social sciences on the practices and methods of the natural sciences. See chs. 1-4 of Taylor, *Philosophy and the Human Sciences*. Also see Charles Taylor, 'Reply to de Sousa and Davis: Human Agency and Language', *Canadian Journal of Philosophy*, vol. 18, 1988, pp. 449-58. For this reason 'speculative metaphysics'—in the sense of metaphysics that does not purport to be merely descriptive and cannot be tested by observation alone—best captures what I think Plant has in mind here.

55. My view about the relationship of theory to political practice is basically Hegelian rather than Marxist. On this question see Hannah Arendt, 'Philosophy and Politics', *Social Research*, vol. 57, no. 1, 1990, pp. 73-103, Richard Rorty, 'The Priority of Democracy to Philosophy', *Objectivity, Relativism, and Truth: Philosophical Papers Volume 1*, Cambridge, Cambridge University Press, 1991, pp. 175-96, Michael Walzer, 'Philosophy and Democracy', *Political Theory*, vol. 9, no. 3, 1981, pp. 379-99, Michael Walzer, 'The Practice of Social Criticism', *Interpretation and Social Criticism*, Cambridge, Harvard University Press, 1987, pp. 33-66.

an enlightened member of society. Here, it is important to bear in mind the significantly different ways in which we may *experience* life in a liberal order. One way of expressing this difference concerns the question of whether or not we are *of* the liberal age and not merely *in* it, to adapt a phrase from Mark Lilla. Lilla draws this distinction in an attempt to explain how French theorists who, since the 1980s have been writing sympathetically about the liberal tradition, differ from their Anglo-American counterparts. Attention to his description of these French intellectuals' writings, though not directly relevant to my discussion, helps to clarify the point I want to make about the reflective standpoint from which to conduct political theory with radical aspirations. Lilla describes the work of the French in this area as by and large diagnostic rather than propositional or programmatic. 'Indeed there is an air of strangeness, or exteriority, accompanying French analyses of liberal society, as if they were *in* liberalism but not yet *of* it.'[56] Unlike their Anglo-American counterparts, the French liberal theorists to whom Lilla refers are not, one might say, imbued with the spirit of liberalism in that they lack confidence in the justifiedness of liberal values, principles and/or institutions. What I want to suggest here is that in order to address the concerns of the alienated social participant through a diagnosis of liberal theory, political philosophy needs to be taken up explicitly from the reflective standpoint of the theorist who is *in but not (yet) of liberalism*, in contrast to the liberal theorist who is both in and of liberalism or, indeed, of the theorist who is neither in nor of liberalism.

What would it mean to take up the reflective standpoint of the theorist who is in but not (yet) of liberalism? Here it is important to bear in mind a tension that is created for one who recognizes *the combined facts* that we live in the liberal age and that this age denies communal being. On the one hand, the liberal age is experienced as an abstraction in the sense of recognizing modern individuality only after having abstracted it from its potentially mutually defining relationship to communal being. On the other, as already explained (1.1.2), recognition of the modern predicament of individual subjectivity calls for an investigation of liberal theory's claim to satisfy the modern western demand for justification without presupposing the universal value of communal being. It follows that such an investigation cannot simply be undertaken from the reflective standpoint of a commitment to communal being without begging the question against liberal theory's ability to formulate and satisfy the demand. For the purposes of the inquiry then the critic must suspend one's pre-reflective identification with communal being. The reflective standpoint of the theorist who is in but not (yet) of liberalism must be understood as that of a subject who is aware of the cultural force of the idea of intrinsically private agency. This would be to differentiate between one's

---

56. Lilla, *New French Thought*, pp. 15-6.

being as a potentially communal being and one's power to think of oneself in the limited terms of an awareness of the abstract idea of intrinsically private agency. This differentiation enables us to specify the theorist's intellectual identity qua critic of liberalism (hereafter 'the radical critic') appropriately to the task of the inquiry to be undertaken.

1.2.2 Why justify the move beyond liberalism?

Now, if liberal theory can be shown incapable of satisfying the modern western demand for justification to which it is committed (1.1.2), the claim that liberalism does indeed involve an objectionable abstraction will have been *justified* and, with this, I will have *justified* the move beyond liberalism to a philosophy of communal being. Why is such a justification necessary? Broadly speaking, the view of justification that accords with modern communal being assigns different roles to the individual in raising the demand for justification and in contributing to its resolution. Like liberal theory, it takes the demand for justification to be a demand *raised by* the individual person. However, unlike liberal theory, it locates the potential *to satisfy* this demand in intrinsically public inter-subjective processes and institutions of collective will formation. In this sense, the political community—the differentiated unity constituted by such processes and institutions—potentially *defines* value as well as supplying the cultural conditions for its realization. Nevertheless, this sort of analysis *presupposes* that the liberal age cannot but be an abstraction in the sense referred to above. This is why the demonstration that liberal theory cannot consistently rely on an intrinsically private view of agency is a necessary first stage in the elaboration of a philosophy of communal being.

This is not to say that one should not develop an alternative vision of communal being independently of such a critique of liberalism. Rather, a pre-reflective commitment to communal being does not explain why we are not, after all, faced with the choice between non-modern conceptions of political community or liberal forms of political association, as the liberal maintains (1.1.4). Moreover, since *the problem* of community is the modern actuality, 'communal being' does not refer to the actuality of modern life, but to a hope, a vision of a radically transformed world. For this reason a philosophy of communal being must be elaborated in a visionary or utopian spirit. But this, in turn, gives rise to the need for a demonstration of its *relevance* to our current reality. This suggests that the development of a modern philosophy of communal being gives rise to a three-stage inquiry. First, a radical critique of liberal theory is needed to reveal the inadequacy of the view that the liberal age has justifiably set aside the ideal of communal being. Such a conclusion establishes the relevance of communal being to the liberal age by showing its indispensability to any effort to satisfy the modern western demand for justification. This result transforms an otherwise pre-reflective identification with communal being into a justified philosophical starting point for the elaboration of a substantive ideal of communal being in what would be a second stage of inquiry. A final stage, offering a theory of social transformation, would give an account of the transition from the reality of life in the liberal age to the ideal of a socially instituted communal being.

So, as a first stage in the development of a utopian philosophy of modern communal being, my inquiry aims to determine whether liberal theorists can justifiably present an ideal liberal order as capable of resolving the predicament of modern individual subjectivity and liberal theory as capable of meeting the modern western demand for justification (1.1.2). If liberal theory can succeed in this, then one would do well to adjust to the conditions of the liberal age and modify one's vision of community accordingly. In short, one should become a liberal in both philosophical and practical life. If, on the other hand, liberal theory fails to meet the modern western demand for justification, then I will have justified the need for the move beyond liberalism to the elaboration of a philosophy of communal being. This issue forms the basis of my view that the radical critique of liberal theory remains an important task of contemporary political philosophy.

2

What is it to Critique Liberalism?

If political philosophy is best conceived in terms of critical *understanding*, what of the mode of *critique* to be employed for the purposes of this understanding? Given the nature of my inquiry (1.2.2) and the reflective standpoint that I attribute to the radical critic (1.2.1), the critique needs to be immanent to liberal theory. That is, it should attempt neither to assess liberal theory from some supposedly neutral standpoint nor to reject it on the ground that it compares unfavourably with some other social alternative using criteria that belong to that alternative. Instead, it should employ liberalism's own terms whilst simultaneously setting these terms up against the conceptual background that they presuppose in order to render visible the conditions of their possibility. For, if liberal theory does indeed (implicitly) depend on abstracting its idea of individuality from this idea's mutually informing relationship to communal being (1.1.3), this abstraction must ultimately be registered in liberal theory, albeit negatively, as the condition of the theory's possibility pursuant to which the idea of communal being remains suppressed. In such a case a *positive* coherent account of liberalism *in liberalism's own terms* should not be possible given that liberal theory does not recognize the philosophical significance of communal being (1.1.4).

So, to investigate this question we need a systematic assessment of liberal theory *as such* in order to bring into focus the conceptual conditions that make liberal theories possible. As *the object* of radical immanent critique, liberal theory renders visible the conditions of its possibility when attention is given to the ways that it is variously structured, that is, to the organized activity of liberal theorizing. For, if liberal theory can satisfy the modern western demand for justification without having to recognize the intrinsically public view of individuality at the heart of communal being, this should be visible not only in what liberal theory has to say *about* human association, that is, about the theorized subject-object relationship, but also in its methods and processes of inquiry. For this reason, the focus of investigation is *liberal inquiring practice(s)* rather than the theories that liberals produce about individuality and community.

If the task of a radical immanent critique of liberal theory is to focus on liberal inquiring practices, this in turn calls for an investigation of the *modes of inter-relationship* of the *basic categories* that structure liberalism as a *discourse*. More specifically, the claim to be investigated is that liberal discourse is constituted by various ways of dichotomously inter-relating the basic categories of publicness and privateness that define the identity of the liberal theorizing subject in his or her relationship to his or her theorized object.[1] Here, we should not restrict our thinking to the so-called public-private dichotomy that feminist research attributes to the liberal organization of society.[2] As we will see below, the feminist critique of liberalism's public-private dichotomy misses its target to the extent that it is directed exclusively to the organization of social life. Rather, in the present context 'a dichotomous inter-relationship' must refer to the relationship that exists between mutually exclusive, mutually exhaustive and hierarchically related categories that are conceived in the abstract. Moreover, we should think of the abstract categories of publicness and privateness as broadly capable of being concretely embodied in the social and intellectual practices of diverse units of agency. Indeed, following Stanley Benn and Gerald Gaus I use the terms 'publicness' and 'privateness' in preference to 'publicity' and 'privacy' to avoid the narrow connotations of the latter.[3] In the present chapter I want to position my approach in relation to the currently held approaches to the critique of liberalism and the feminist critique of liberalism's public-private dichotomy, in particular. My purpose is to show, firstly, why alternative approaches will not suffice and, secondly, why despite pointing to the need for an investigation of the sort I am proposing, the feminist critique of liberalism's public-private dichotomy does not go far enough.

2.1 Alternative approaches to the critique of liberalism

The Anglophone critique of liberalism takes a number of different forms but as Mark Lilla has observed, following the translation into English of the

---

1. Although Mulhall and Swift raise the question of 'the liberal theorist's understanding of his or her own status as a liberal theorist' they do not follow through the implications of this question for understanding the process of theory production. Mulhall and Swift, *Liberals and Communitarians*, pp. 290-1.

2. See, for example ch. 8 of Frazer and Lacey, *The Politics of Community*.

3. Stanley I. Benn and Gerald F. Gaus, 'The Public and the Private: Concepts and Action', in Stanley I. Benn and Gerald F. Gaus (eds.), *Public and Private in Social Life*, London, Croom Helm, 1983, pp. 3-27, p. 3.

works of some major Continental figures of the 1960s, there emerged a split between

> those employing the language of analytic philosophy to treat problems internal to liberalism and those who criticised contemporary liberal societies from a more historical standpoint using other vocabularies, whether those of Marxism, French structuralism, or German critical theory [...] two independent ways of conceiving the tasks and methods of political philosophy have since grown up within the Anglo-American world.[4]

There are, of course, theorists (amongst them Charles Taylor, Richard Bernstein, Richard Rorty, Seyla Benhabib, Drucilla Cornell, Nancy Fraser, Judith Butler, Chantal Mouffe and Ernesto Laclau) whose works have contributed to the bridging of the perceived gap between these two strands of inquiry and the broader question of the relationship between analytic and continental philosophy has received increased attention in recent years.[5] Even so, with some refinement, the identification of 'two independent ways of conceiving the tasks and methods of political philosophy' still serves as a useful point of comparison with my own approach.

2.1.1 The revisionist critique of liberalism

First, 'those employing the language of analytic philosophy to treat problems internal to liberalism' generally offer a revisionist critique in the sense that their line(s) of argument aspire to a more defensible version of liberal theory rather than to its complete rejection.[6] They also often present their

---

4. Lilla, *New French Thought*, p. 5. Within a wider frame than that of the present study, this development would include the now very extensive range of influential works in translation, particularly from the French and German.

5. Benhabib, *Situating the Self*, Richard J. Bernstein, *Beyond Objectivism and Relativism: Science, Hermeneutics and Praxis*, Oxford, Longman Cheshire, 1983, Drucilla Cornell, *The Philosophy of the Limit*, London, Routledge, 1992, Rorty, *Contingency, Irony, and Solidarity*, Richard Rorty, *Essays on Heidegger and Others: Philosophical Papers Volume 2*, Cambridge, Cambridge University Press, 1991, Richard Rorty, *Objectivism, Relativism, and Truth: Philosophical Papers Volume 1*, Cambridge, Cambridge University Press, 1991, Charles Taylor, *Hegel and Modern Society*, Cambridge, Cambridge University Press, 1980, Charles Taylor, *Human Agency and Language: Philosophical Papers 1*, Cambridge, Cambridge University Press, 1992, Taylor, *Philosophy and the Human Sciences*. See also Kenneth Baynes, James Bohman and Thomas McCarthy (eds.), *After Philosophy: End or Transformation?*, Cambridge, MIT Press, 1987, Seyla Benhabib, *Feminist Contentions: A Philosophical Exchange*, New York, Routledge, 1995, Nancy Fraser, *Unruly Practices: Power, Discourse and Gender in Contemporary Social Theory*, Cambridge, Polity Press, 1989, Ernesto Laclau and Chantal Mouffe, *Hegemony and Socialist Strategy: Towards and Radical Democratic Politics*, London, Verso, 1985, Chantal Mouffe, *The Return of the Political*, London, Verso, 1993. In the development of my approach to the critique of liberal theory I have benefited from extensive reading of these works as well as that of Alasdair MacIntyre.

6. The issue of whether the critique of liberalism should aspire to its rejection or revision arose most explicitly with the emergence of the liberal-communitarian debates of the 1980s and 1990s. See Will Kymlicka, *Liberalism, Community, and Culture*, Oxford, Oxford University

arguments by mistakenly (explicitly or implicitly) denying the *tradition-dependence* of their standard(s) of rationality, in the sense given to this idea by Alasdair MacIntyre (WJ, p. 356).[7] According to MacIntyre, when it is in good order, a tradition of inquiry is:

> a coherent movement of thought [...] in the course of which those engaged in that movement become aware of it and of its direction and in self-aware fashion attempt to engage in its debates and to carry its enquires forward (WJ, p. 326).

As already noted above, my approach is to focus on the assessment of 'problems internal to liberalism' in the sense that it employs the (explicit or implicit) terms *of* liberal theory. In this respect it follows the revisionist approaches just referred to.

2.1.2 The radical critique of liberalism

Despite the above mentioned point of similarity, the proposed critique employs standards of rationality that do not pretend to be neutral between competing traditions of inquiry and it is, of course, radical rather than revisionist in its aspirations since what is ultimately at stake is the very social space that is occupied by a liberal order and denied to communal being. Now, radical critics of liberalism who adopt 'other vocabularies' such as the ones Lilla refers to, as well as those of post-Marxist and post-colonial theorists, generally rely on conflict models of social interaction and change to propose (a) alternative ways of thinking critically about socio-political life in a western liberal order or (b) alternative visions of living in the western liberal order.[8]

2.1.2(a)

In the former case, some critics propose methods of localized resistance to

---

Press, 1989. As an example of a revisionist feminist critique see Okin, *Justice, Gender and the Family*. Some of the so-called communitarian criticisms of liberalism also fall into this category. See, for example, Walzer, *Spheres of Justice: A Defence of Pluralism and Equality*. In 'Cross-Purposes' Taylor interprets his own earlier critique of liberalism (in *Philosophy and The Human Sciences*) and that of M. Sandel (*Liberalism and The Limits of Justice*, Cambridge, Cambridge University Press, 1982), as an attack restricted to the dominant strands of liberalism, namely 'individualist' and 'procedural liberalism' and, as an indirect defence of the 'civic humanist' strand of the liberal tradition, see Charles Taylor, 'Cross-Purposes: The Liberal-Communitarian Debate', *Philosophical Arguments*, Cambridge, Harvard University Press, 1995. For similar clarifications by Okin and Walzer that their objections to liberalism are intended to be revisionist in spirit see Susan Moller Okin, 'Humanist Liberalism', in Nancy L. Rosenblum (ed.), *Liberalism and Moral Life*, Cambridge, Harvard University Press, 1991, pp. 39-53; Michael Walzer, 'Liberalism and the Art of Separation', *Political Theory*, vol. 12, no. 3, 1984, pp. 315-30, Michael Walzer, 'The Communitarian Critique of Liberalism', *Political Theory*, vol. 18, no. 1, 1990, pp. 6-23.

7. I take MacIntyre's work, especially in *Whose Justice*, to have demonstrated the correctness of the view that standards of rationality are always tradition-dependent.

8. See also Frazer and Lacey, *The Politics of Community*.

the dominant forms of life or advocate counter-hegemonic projects whereas others seek to identify the factors leading to the formation or ultimate demise of the economic and power structures underpinning such forms.[9] Some others support the development of protected small-scale communities.[10] None of these approaches is suited to the tasks of critical understanding since they either presuppose answers to the very questions that the inquiry into liberalism poses (1.2) or else they are blind to the significance of the questions underpinning the role of radical critique (1.1). Let me illustrate this claim with some examples. Take, firstly, the approach to the critique of liberalism oriented to localized resistance. Here the proposed methods of resistance focus on the transgressive and disruptive practices available to (appropriately positioned) subjects. Judith Butler's recent discussion of the problem of statelessness is a case in point. For Butler, the theorist faces 'the representational challenge of saying what life is like' for those who are subject to various states of dispossession.[11] Moved by 'the demand to find post-national forms of po-

---

9. For examples of approaches that focus on localized resistance and counter-hegemonic projects see Mouffe, *The Return of the Political*. Judith Butler's contribution in Judith Butler and Gayatri Chatravorty Spivak, *Who Sings the Nation-State?: Langauge Politics Belonging*, Calcutta, Seagull Books, 2007, Elizabeth Frazer, 'Politics, Culture and the Public Sphere: Toward a Postmodern Conception', in Steven Seidman and Linda J. Nicholson (eds.), *Social Postmodernism: Beyond Identity Politics*, Cambridge, Cambridge University Press, 1995, pp. 287-312, Iris Marion Young, *Justice and the Politics of Difference*, Princeton, Princeton University Press, 1990. I would include Tariq Modood's conception of 'civic multiculturalism' in this group since, although it proposes a liberal democratic 'political conception', it is not revisionist in spirit given Modood's view that 'multiculturalism could not get off the ground if one totally repudiated liberalism: but neither could it do so if liberalism marked the limits of one's politics: Tariq Modood, *Multiculturalism: A Civic Idea*, Cambridge, Polty Press, 2007, p. 8. See also Julia Kristeva, *In the Beginning Was Love: Psychoanalysis and Faith*, New York, Columbia University Press, 1987. For a post-colonial critique that addresses the global hegemonic power of liberal capitalism by focusing on Eurocentrism and the coloniality of power see Anibal Quijano, 'Coloniality of Power, Eurocentrism and Latin America', *Nepantla: Views from the South*, vol. 1, no. 3, 2000, pp. 533-80. Gayatri Chatravorty Spivak's 'critical regionalism' is another orientation that falls within this group, see Butler and Spivak, *Who Sings the Nation-State?: Langauge Politics Belonging*. For a contemporary North American example of an 'end of the liberal-capitalist order thesis' that focuses on the dimensions of the breakdown see Immanuel Maurice Wallerstein, *The Decline of American Power: The US in a Chaotic World*, London, New Press, 2003. Perhaps we could also include within this general category the approaches of radical critics of the liberal age such as Alain Badiou, Slavoj Žižek and Michael Hardt and Antonio Negri that Göran Therborn includes under the heading of 'Europe's theological turn' in order to highlight their use of religious examples in their political philosophies in response to the loss of a future vision (Therborn, 'After Dialectics: Radical Social Theory in a Post-Communist World', pp. 80-2).

10. The classic example here is Alasdair MacIntyre's critique of liberalism in *Whose Justice?* See also his description of the role that the critique of liberalism plays in his work as a whole: Alasdair C. MacIntyre, 'The Spectre of Communitariansim', *Radical Philosophy*, no. 70, 1995, pp. 34-5, p. 35.

11. Butler and Spivak, *Who Sings the Nation-State?: Langauge Politics Belonging*, pp. 41-2.

litical opposition', Butler invokes her analysis of the possibilities of performative contradiction to locate a moment of insurgency when in 2006 illegal residents demonstrating on the streets of Los Angeles asserted the irreducibility of difference and translation by singing the US and Mexican national anthems in Spanish.[12] Even if, as Butler maintains, performative contradiction is the precondition of radical politics of change, since such politics do not depend upon the theorist's meeting the 'representational challenge' *she* sets herself, the role of a theoretical discourse thus oriented remains at the very least unclear, if it is not superfluous.[13]

Chantal Mouffe also aspires to articulate an 'approach which will enable us to grasp the challenge with which democratic politics is today confronted' but her aim is to render visible the relationship of the (concept of the) political to our ontological conditions.[14] So, on the face of it, she addresses the role of theory by focusing on the question of the *ontological* possibilities of radical democratic politics. However, in analyzing the political in terms of the antagonism that she claims is constitutive of human societies—the 'we/they distinction' that is the condition of possibility of formation of political identities—Mouffe's approach presupposes a certain answer to the very question concerning the problem of communal being in the liberal age (1.1.3). This presupposition informs her objection to liberalism as a philosophical discourse, that liberal theory problematically presupposes the rational/reasoned elimination of the we/they distinction—read as the antagonistic friend/enemy relation in which the 'enemies' share no common ground. For Mouffe, the point is rather to engage with the question of democratic politics about how to establish agonistic forms of the distinction. In this latter case, 'adversaries' confront the permanent antagonistic dimension of their relation through democratic practices and institutions that recognize a 'common bond' of 'belonging to the same political association' and 'sharing a common space within which the conflict takes place'.[15] Now, in my view if we were to conceptualize the fundamental we/they relationship, upon which Mouffe claims all collective political identities are grounded, without appealing to some formulation of communal being we would inevitably be relying upon a liberal conceptual framework, despite Mouffe's assertions to the contrary.[16] On the other hand, if Mouffe's approach must in-

---

12. Butler and Spivak, *Who Sings the Nation-State?: Langauge Politics Belonging*, pp. 58-65.

13. In the history of Greek-Australian political activism we find similar instances of defiant resistance to the nation's monolingualism dating back to the early 1940s, long before the theorization of such actions. See Toula Nicolacopoulos and George Vassilacopoulos, *From Foreigner to Citizen: Greek Migrants in White Australia and Social Change 1897-2000 (Greek)*, Melbourne, Eothinon Publications, 2004.

14. Mouffe, *On the Political*, p. 9.

15. Mouffe, *On the Political*, see esp. pp.10-14 and p.20.

16. I develop this argument in 'Radicalism Without Vision: Chantal Mouffe's Affiliation to

deed appeal to a form of communal being at the ontological level of her we/they distinction, then for the reasons already explained (1.2) the approach in question cannot serve the demands of a radical critique of liberalism. In recognition of the philosophical significance of being in liberalism, radical critical inquiry must proceed from the suspension of any identification with communal being, whether substantive or formal.

We can make a similar point about the case where the critique of liberalism seeks to uncover the impact of the liberal socio-cultural tradition on some alternative form of explicitly *non-liberal* small-scale substantive community. As in the case of Alasdair MacIntyre, the critique of liberalism may form only an incidental part of a different sort of inquiry into the cultural spaces of the contemporary world but this sort of outsider's interest in liberalism is limited in its radical critical orientation in so far as it relies upon a developed *substantive* notion of communal being. Like the approach of an otherwise very illuminating Latin American post-colonial critique of liberal capitalism, this mode of critique at best addresses the question why one should *remain* not of (western Eurocentric) liberalism.¹⁷ That is, the inquiry proceeds from the standpoint of one who *already is not* of liberalism. So, despite significant differences in approach and orientation, the mode of radical critique discussed so far is no less ineffective for the sort of critical inquiry that I undertake. To repeat, given that liberalism is negatively constituted by its denial of communal being (1.1.3), we need an assessment of the *justifiedness* of its total rejection from the standpoint of one who is in but not (yet) of liberalism.

2.1.2(b)

In the case of critique oriented to the elaboration of some alternative to the dominant western liberal order, there are those focused on the comparative assessment of western liberalism with an alternative western vision, like socialism, communism or some form of anarchist society. Here I have in mind theoretical approaches that have been influenced by Marx's theory of worker exploitation under liberal-capitalism.¹⁸ Such radical critique often locates the material conditions necessary for radical social transformation in a certain form of social group conflict and opposes liberal theory by claiming to represent the true or valid interpretation of social reality but more often than not such critique also relies on dichotomous thinking. Within feminist theory, for example, opponents of liberal feminism generally find fault with it for its failure to recognize some critical aspect of the true reality of wom-

---

Liberal Democracy' working title of review article in progress.

17. See, for example, Quijano, 'Coloniality of Power, Eurocentrism and Latin America'.

18. See, for example, John E. Roemer and Erik Olin Wright, *Equal Shares: Making Market Socialism Work*, London, Verso, 1996, Erik Olin Wright (ed.), *Approaches to Class Analysis*, Cambridge, Cambridge University Press, 2005.

en's lives in liberal-capitalist-patriarchal orders.[19] The assumptions here are, firstly, that the liberal age somehow gives rise to a master-opposition, a conflict that is generated within liberal societies yet has radical transformative power and, secondly, that radical critical theory can articulate and mobilize this opposition in the interests of social change.[20] Even André Gorz's theory, that greatly broadens our understanding of the potential agent of revolutionary transformation with his very inclusive concept of a *non-class of non-workers* seeking free time, still does not manage to escape the presupposition of a master opposition. This is because it remains non-all-inclusive at the level of practice since 'free time' is a concept that, in being defined in relation to the time taken up in paid employment, does not apply in the same way to the living conditions of the long-term unemployed.[21] For those who remain committed to a conflict model and to the transformative power of critical theory, to give up the oppositional model would be to give in to the dichotomous reality of structural social domination. Yet the tendency has been for such alternative traditions to challenge the dichotomous terms of liberal discourse at the expense of invoking another set of dichotomies.

Critical comparisons of the dominant form of western liberalism with alternative visions that are articulated in 'other vocabularies' typically rely on premises and standards of rationality that do not operate within the conceptual framework of the former. This renders such rivals logically incommensurable even when they profess to be uncovering another suppressed version of liberalism from within the western intellectual tradition. For example, when Charles Taylor opposes the dominant 'procedural' strand of liberal thought by appealing to his preferred civic republican alternative

---

19. On Marxist, dual-systems and psychoanalytic feminisms see Rosemarie Tong, *Feminist Thought: A Comprehensive Introduction*, London, Unwin Hyman, 1989. For a discussion of the conceptual problems that have historically emerged within such critical discourses see Iris Marion Young, 'Gender as Seriality: Thinking About Women as a Social Collective', in Steven Seidman and Linda J. Nicholson (eds.), *Social Postmodernism: Beyond Identity Politics*, Cambridge, Cambridge University Press, 1995, pp. 187-215. See also Tina Chanter, *Gender: Key Concepts in Philosophy*, London, Continuum, 2006, pp. 8-55. For a recent review of second wave visionary yet simultaneously ambivalent relationship to the liberal state see Nacey Fraser, 'Mapping the Feminist Imagination: From Redistribution to Recognition to Representation', *Constellations*, no. 12, 2005, pp. 295-307, p. 297.

20. See, for example, Andrew Collier, *Socialist Reasoning: An Inquiry Into the Political Philosophy of Scientific Socialism*, London, Pluto Press, 1989, Milton Fisk, *The State and Justice: An Essay in Political Theory*, Cambridge, Cambridge University Press, 1989. To the extent that it aspires to the radical critique of liberal theory a portion of literature focused on establishing the link between social movements' claims for recognition and redistribution would fall under this heading. One prominent example, is the debate between Nancy Fraser, who relies upon a Weberian notion to advocate a 'status model' of recognition, and Axel Honneth who, according to Fraser, elaborates a Hegel inspired 'identity model'. Nancy Fraser, 'Rethinking Recognition', *New Left Review*, no. 3, 2000, pp. 107-20, Nancy Fraser and Axel Honneth, *Redistribution or Recognition?: A Political-Philosophical Exchange*, London, Verso, 2003.

21. André Gorz, *Critique of Economic Reason*, London, Verso, 1989.

that takes political participation to be an essential or constitutive element of freedom, for reasons already explained (1.1.4), despite posing a serious challenge to the methodological, substantive and ontological positions that his opponents rely upon, liberal discourse does not register Taylor's communitarian insights.[22] This tendency of liberal theorists to read Taylor's political claims in abstraction from his (a-liberal) epistemology and social ontology continues in relation to Taylor's more recent work in which he elaborates an account of multiculturalism and the politics of recognition to advocate what we might call a more *self-aware* liberalism—one whose awareness of its own cultural specificity positions it to accommodate the good of cultural survival—as an alternative to the procedural liberalism he critiques for its misrepresentations of neutrality and its failure fully to appreciate public goods.[23] In so far as they rely upon standards that are internal to their own tradition yet *external* to the *liberalism* they oppose critiques such as Taylor's provide an analysis of *already* being in but not of the western liberalism that serves as the object of their critique. Despite the seeming theoretical advances and their extension of our intellectual landscape, some post-colonial theories of multiculturalism suffer from precisely the same sort of limit when considered as an approach to the radical critique of liberalism. Conversely, when radical aspirations explicitly give way to the desire to expand western liberalism's receptivity to non-western forms of social organization, we might say that such critique aspires to be *in and of an other non-western liberalism.*[24]

As I hope to show in Parts II and III, radically motivated critiques of liberalism often make important and sound critical observations—they identify problems such as inconsistencies in liberal theories—yet to the extent that they lack the resources fully to explain precisely why the theoretical problems they identify arise in liberal theories they do not ensure that their own approaches escape similar limitations. Without the aid of a deeper un-

---

22. Taylor, 'Cross-Purposes'. This said, I don't wish to attribute to Taylor some sort of general anti-liberal conviction for this would be to neglect his history of progressive retreat from readings of his critique of liberalism as aspiring to a wholesale rejection. See for example, Charles Taylor, 'Charles Taylor Replies', in James Tully and Daniel M. Weinstock (eds.), *Philosophy in an Age of Pluralism: The Philosophy of Charles Taylor in Question*, Cambridge, Cambridge University Press, 1994, pp. 213-57, pp. 250-1. Here Taylor explains that the target of his critique is a 'single principle neutral liberalism' in favour of a view of the plurality of goods that the ascription of the label 'communitarian' does not make plain. Nevertheless, we can link the radical aspiration in Taylor's work to the desire to articulate an *other* liberalism.

23. Charles Taylor, 'The Politics of Recognition', in Amy Gutmann and Charles Taylor (eds.), *Multiculturalism: Examining the Politics of Recognition*, Princeton, Princeton University Press, 1994, pp. 25-73. For an argument that reads Taylor's appeal to the inter-subjective character of self-hood as warranting a rejection of his call for a politics of recognition see Brenda Lyshaug, 'Authenticity and the Politics of Identity: A Critique of Charles Taylor's Politics of Recognition', *Contemporary Political Theory*, vol. 3, no. 3, 2004, pp. 300-20.

24. The strongest articulation of such an approach is perhaps that of Parekh, *Rethinking Multiculturalism*.

derstanding of the deep structural logic of liberalism such arguments at best show that the liberal theories they critique warrant some modification, in spite of being proposed in a radical rather than revisionist spirit.[25] If my observations are correct, they lend support to the claim that in order to understand the limits of liberal theory it will not be enough for the radical critic to look merely to the surface level of liberal claims and argue that some substantive value or other has been under-valued or ignored or to challenge some methodological assumption or other by presupposing criteria internal to another language. The radical critic needs to look closely at *the systematic operations* of liberal inquiring practice in order to draw from this activity an understanding of the identity of liberal theorizing using criteria internal to the theory in question.

Is this sort of inquiry misguided? We can anticipate a response in the affirmative from authors such as Bikhu Parekh who believe that such a focus goes hand in hand with a 'spirit of intolerance':

> To ask whether a writer or a theory is liberal is to take in one form or another an essentialist (monist?) view of liberalism and to assume that there is only one true way of being a liberal.[26]

For Parekh:

> the question whether someone is a consistent liberal [...] implies that one must have an unambiguous doctrinal identity [...] and that this identity involves an unswerving and exclusive commitment to a fixed set of principles which one must not corrupt or dilute by mixing with some others.[27]

Parekh suggests that to speak instead in terms of selective 'liberal values' and 'the liberal way of life' is to avoid liberalism's 'overtones of essentialism, closure, system building and intellectual rigidity.'[28]

Now, there are two points we can make in response to this sort of concern. The first is that Parekh's preferred alternative is in fact only available to one who is already either sufficiently *in and of* liberalism in the sense already discussed (1.2.1) or is interested in incorporating ideas associated with liberalism into some other framework or tradition with which one identifies (2.1.2). As it happens Parekh presents himself as proposing a theory of multiculturalism that is 'liberal in its orientation' at the same time as seek-

---

25. To the extent that liberal critics adopt a reflective standpoint characteristic of Michael Walzer's rendition of the 'marginal social critic', I think that my critique will also indirectly show that Walzer's description of the difference between 'internal' and 'external criticism' is too simple. Walzer, 'The Practice of Social Criticism'.
26. Parekh, *Rethinking Multiculturalism*, p. 367.
27. Parekh, *Rethinking Multiculturalism*, p. 368.
28. Parekh, *Rethinking Multiculturalism*, p. 369.

ing to advance intercultural dialogue with non-western ways of life.[29] So, for the radical critic the question of the meaning and implications of any relation to that to which one *may become* oriented still remains. Second, the question of the identity of liberalism no doubt harbours all the dangers that Parekh envisages when one thinks in the narrow terms of a *doctrinal* identity and radical critique that remains at a surface level of discourse will face a challenge in attempting to answer Parekh's charge. Nevertheless, as I hope to show, the question of liberalism's identity is more complex than Parekh would have us believe.

2.2 Publicness and privateness in liberal discourse

2.2.1 Complex-structured concepts and liberalism's public-private dichotomy

Before turning to a consideration of the feminist critique of liberalism's public-private dichotomy, let us take note of the ways in which liberals understand the operations of the categories of publicness and privateness. Liberal theorists recognize the centrality of the categories of publicness and privateness for the way(s) in which the liberal social world is ordered. Liberal social scientific explanations employ these categories and they also underlie philosophical representations of liberal society and constructions of liberal social ideals. In a survey of the liberal concepts of publicness and privateness Stanley Benn and Gerald Gaus find that:

> '[p]ublicness' and 'privateness' [...] are particular concepts by which our western liberal society organizes such areas of social life as involve ascriptions of access agency and interest. Though they are not universal or necessary concepts, they are profoundly important ones in western societies. [...] The liberal social world [...] evinces a strong tendency to split itself into two distinct parts: what is public and what is private. And from this split it draws a multitude of consequences for action.[30]

Benn and Gaus make two important observations about the liberal categories of publicness and privateness, the first concerning the internal relations amongst the various meanings that belong to each of the categories and the second concerning the inter-relationship of the two categories. They point out, firstly, that in order to make sense of the continuities that underlie the different senses of publicness and privateness respectively, these categories should be understood as 'complex-structured concepts'. According to the authors, in complex-structured concepts the relations obtaining among their different senses are systematic rather than bearing a family resemblance. Using the example of a publicly funded library that is open to all, they draw

---

29. Parekh, *Rethinking Multiculturalism*, p. 370.
30. Benn and Gaus, 'The Public and the Private: Concepts and Action', p. 25.

attention to the 'strong presumption that facilities financed by the community at large should be open to all'. The authors observe further,

> that something is or is not public in one sense [...] is often seen as a reason why it should or should not be public in another sense. [...] Embedded in a culture and its language are principles or presuppositions that account for the continuity of the various senses of 'public'.

Whilst the relations of continuity to which the authors refer are 'internal semantic relations', the 'principles or presuppositions' that explain the connections between these relations are, nevertheless, 'ideological' in so far as their explanations rely on 'beliefs about the natures of societies and of individuals, of collective agents and collective actions, etc, rather than on purely logical entailments.'[31]

Secondly, Benn and Gaus maintain that liberal conceptions of the relationship between the categories of publicness and privateness tend to favour a view of them as dichotomous rather than continuous. That is,

> the domain to which they apply is divided sharply so that, in principle, every case can be allocated to one or the other category instead of allowing for degrees of publicness or privateness.[32]

Furthermore,

> [l]iberalism exhibits strong theoretical pressures towards a bi-polar view of social life, tending as it does to assimilate [...] deviant cases [those in which explanation in terms of bi-polarity breaks down ...] to one or the other of the two poles.[33]

Significantly, the authors suggest that this bi-polar inter-relationship of the categories of publicness and privateness applies *universally*. That is,

> the distinction between publicness and privateness applies to the life of every member of the society. This is the strength of the bi-polar structure [...] there is no antithesis except this one that the liberal employs universally, structuring his concept of *anyone's* social life.[34]

Let us take a moment to distinguish the analysis that Benn and Gaus offer about liberal theorizations of the categories of publicness and privateness from explanations of the socio-historical emergence of the distinctively modern-liberal public and private social spheres consisting of capitalist production, market exchange and bureaucratic administration, on the one

---

31. Benn and Gaus, 'The Public and the Private: Concepts and Action', pp. 4-5.
32. Benn and Gaus, 'The Public and the Private: Concepts and Action', p. 14.
33. Benn and Gaus, 'The Public and the Private: Concepts and Action', p. 17. I will return to the authors' discussion of deviant cases and their implications for the application of the ideas of publicness and privateness to particular contexts in Chapter 3.3.2.
34. Benn and Gaus, 'The Public and the Private: Concepts and Action', p. 17.

hand, and personal and domestic life, on the other.[35] Such explorations of the liberal public and private spheres are partly motivated by an interest in their impact on and relationship to theoretical constructions of public and private life. In contrast, Benn and Gaus identify and explain a certain tension between some recognizably liberal *ideals*. On the one hand, liberal theory gives a central place to the ideals of private (mental) life and privacy and, on the other, it relies on ideals of the public interest and of citizens' participation in political life in non-official capacities. These ideals, they maintain, respectively derive from two distinct models of publicness and privateness that, though internally consistent, are nevertheless based on different and perhaps incompatible conceptions of the individual-society relationship. The *individualist model* is generated by a methodological principle that gives logical primacy to individual persons and recognizes (a) private categories in conformity with a principle of differentiation that pertains to the specific person exclusively and (b) public categories in conformity with a principle of differentiation that pertains to the non-specific. For this reason it cannot recognize notions of the public interest and participation in political life that cannot be framed in terms of the non-specific. The *organic model* is generated by a methodological principle that gives logical primacy to social groups and recognizes (a) private categories in conformity with a principle of differentiation that pertains to the particular taken apart from its character as a member of an organized body and (b) public categories in conformity with a principle of differentiation that pertains to an organized body. For this reason it cannot recognize the atomic notions of persons' private (mental) lives and privacy.[36] Contemporary liberal theories respond to these models and the categories that they respectively generate in one of three possible ways. The first is to remain wholly committed to the limits of the individualist model, as do liberal individualist theories. The second is to apply the organic model to explanatory social theory questions and the individualist model to normative political theory questions justifying the switch on moral individualist grounds. Finally, one may appeal to a third model that is gener-

---

35. See, for example, Jürgen Habermas, *The Structural Transformation of the Public Sphere: An Inquiry into a Category of Bourgeois Society*, Cambridge, MIT Press, 1989. See also Ross Poole whose account of the 'particular structure of exclusion and subordination that marks the modern form of the distinction between public and private spheres of social existence' is careful to point out (a) the way in which this distinction 'maps on to a masculine-feminine distinction', Poole, *Morality and Modernity*, pp. 45-50.

36. Stanley I. Benn and Gerald F. Gaus, 'The Liberal Conception of the Public and Private', in Stanley I. Benn and Gerald F. Gaus (eds.), *Public and Private in Social Life*, London, Croom Helm, 1983, pp. 31-65. Michael Monohan has recently argued that liberalism's individualistic ontological foundations preclude a coherent notion of public goods and public interest, but he fails to acknowledge that an organic model also operates in liberal thought. See Michael Monohan, 'Private Property and Public Interest', *Philosophy in the Contemporary World*, vol. 12, no. 2, 2005, pp. 17-21.

ated by a methodological principle that recognizes both individual persons *and* social groups as basic units of agency.[37] Despite their differences these models do not address the liberal categories of publicness and privateness in their relationship to *the theorizing subject*. For this reason, the differences that these models represent regarding liberal theorists' treatments of the social embodiments of the categories of publicness and privateness (for example, public opinion, public agencies, private agencies, private interests and so on) are of secondary importance in an analysis of liberal inquiring practice. Indeed, to discern the character of an inquiring practice is to focus on the categories of publicness and privateness at an even higher level of abstraction. Let us turn now to the feminist critique of liberalism's public-private dichotomy in order to see why such a focus is necessary.

2.2.2 Carole Pateman's feminist critique of the public-private dichotomy

Whilst relatively little has been made of the claim that the liberal categories of publicness and privateness function as complex-structured concepts, attention to the role of the public-private dichotomy in liberal theory has been at the basis of wide-ranging criticisms by feminist political theorists. They have argued that, along with other major traditions in modern political theory such as the Marxist, liberalism's reliance on a public-private dichotomy has produced a politics of exclusion of women (and other subordinate groups) from philosophical discourse, from access to political and economic power and from the more highly valued social roles, all of which contribute to the maintenance of their social subordination.

Feminist challenges to the liberal public-private dichotomy fall into two broad groups. First, those within the liberal feminist tradition do not take the dichotomy as such to be problematic but the gender divisions that have been historically associated with it, that is, the association of the public social sphere with men and masculinity and that of the private with women and femininity. Within the framework of this sort of analysis the challenge to liberalism's public-private dichotomy amounts to a call for the *degendering* of social spheres. This call for degendering takes any of three forms: (1) ensuring women's equal access to public life; (2) ensuring women's equal formal treatment; and (3) ensuring that the different values governing the public and private spheres ought not be grounded on claims regarding (natural) sexual difference.[38] In addition to calling for the degendering of the public

---

37. Charles Taylor's notion of social holism is a case in point, see Taylor, 'Cross-Purposes'.

38. We find classic expositions of these views in the works of Harriet Taylor Mill, 'Enfranchisement of Women', in Alice S. Rossi (ed.), *Essays on Sex Equality*, Chicago, University of Chicago Press, 1970, pp. 89-121, John Stuart Mill, *The Subjection of Women*, London, Dent, 1985, Mary Wollstonecraft, *A Vindication of the Rights of Woman*, London, Dent, 1985. See also Okin, *Justice, Gender and the Family*.

and private social spheres, the second group, radical critics of liberalism, also draw attention to the fundamental inadequacy of relating the categories of publicness and privateness dichotomously. Whereas a central issue for the first group of critics concerns the problem of where to draw the line between public and private areas of life, the second group sees the need for a reconceptualization of the relationship between public and private areas of life in non-dichotomous terms. The discussion that follows will focus on this second group of feminist critics of liberal theory.[39]

Radical feminist critiques of liberal theory's public-private dichotomy have attempted to show that the dichotomy presupposes the dichotomous inter-relationship of the categories of masculinity and femininity that are, in turn, typically embodied in the respective lives of men and women. In this way they argue that the liberal public-private dichotomy renders liberalism *essentially patriarchal*. This is the view that has been defended most forcefully by Carole Pateman.[40] The general idea is that liberal patriarchal thought (a) *privatizes* the family in a way that puts it beyond the reach of public-political scrutiny and (b) *masculinizes* the realm of public life and so puts it beyond the reach of the feminine and women.

This critique of the liberal public-private dichotomy forms part of a wider feminist challenge to modern western political thought and the modern western intellectual tradition more generally. The challenge focuses on the operation of a so-called masculine bias in the concepts of reason and rationality. This kind of claim does not reduce to the suggestion that men have been disproportionately active in the production of knowledge or that because male thinkers have had opportunity to place value on their (understandings) of their public world they have neglected to give due consideration to the domestic sphere and to women's experiences of public life. The point is rather that such failures have to do with a certain conceptual association of domestic life with woman, nature and the emotions. The claim that there is a masculine bias in the construction of conceptions of reason and ra-

---

39. In the present context 'radical feminism' refers to critique in the sense discussed in 2.1.2 and not in feminist theory's narrower sense of endorsing the view that men dominate women *as a class*. See chs. 5 and 9 of Alison M. Jaggar, *Feminist Politics and Human Nature*, Brighton, Rowman & Littlefield, 1983.

40. Carole Pateman, 'Feminist Critiques of the Public/Private Dichotomy', in Stanley I. Benn and Gerald F. Gaus (eds.), *Public and Private in Social Life*, London, Croom Helm, 1983, pp. 281-303, Carole Pateman, *The Sexual Contract*, Cambridge, Polity, 1988. Reprinted in Carole Pateman, *The Disorder of Women: Democracy, Feminism and Political Theory*, Cambridge, Polity Press, 1989. See also ch. 3 of Jean Bethke Elshtain, *Public Man Private Woman: Women in Social and Political Thought*, Princeton, Princeton University Press, 1981, Linda J. Nicholson, 'Feminist Theory: The Private and the Public', in Carol C. Gould (ed.), *Beyond Domination: New Perspectives on Women and Philosophy*, Totowa, Rowman & Allanheld, 1984, pp. 221-32, Marion Tapper, 'Can a Feminist Be a Liberal?', *Australasian Journal of Philosophy*, vol. 64, 1986, pp. 37-47.

tionality draws attention to a kind of thinking that occurs in terms of the systematic hierarchical ordering of conceptual dualisms. In this ordering activity (a) the concept of woman or the feminine is defined as the inferior of man and (b) the concept of the human is substituted for the concept of man given that whatever differentiates woman from man is transcended in the process of the movement from man-woman to the category human.[41]

Pateman traces liberalism's commitment to a sexual division underlying the separation of the family from the public-political sphere to Locke's endorsement of the natural subordination of women (wives) to men in the family. She maintains that political theorists' references to *individuals*, rather than to men, merely obscure the fact that 'from the period when the social contract theorists attacked the patriarchalists, liberal theorists have excluded women from the scope of their apparently universal arguments'.[42] The liberal individual is implicitly masculine given the conceptualization of the public-private social division as gendered.[43] Once we recognize that the contrast between the private family and public political society depends on the natural subordination of women to men in the family, it becomes clear both that women 'are excluded from the status of 'individual' and so from participating in the public world' and that the two spheres 'are grounded in opposing principles of association which are exemplified in the conflicting status of men and women; natural subordination stands opposed to free individualism'. Thus,

> the public world, or civil society, is conceptualised and discussed in liberal theory [...] in abstraction from, or as separate from, the private domestic sphere.[44]

Pateman claims further,

> because liberalism conceptualises civil society in abstraction from [...] domestic life, the latter remains 'forgotten' in theoretical discussion. The separation of public and private is thus re-established as a division *within* civil society itself, within the world of men [...] in *this* version of the separation of private and public, one category, the private, begins to wear the trousers.[45]

Following the exclusion of the concept of the family from political theory

---

41. See Lorraine Code, *What Can She Know? Feminist Theory and the Construction of Knowledge*, Ithaca, Cornell University Press, 1991, Genevieve Lloyd, *The Man of Reason: 'Male' and 'Female' in Western Philosophy*, London, Methuen, 1984, Val Plumwood, *Feminism and the Mastery of Nature*, London, Routledge, 1993.

42. Pateman, 'Feminist Critiques of the Public/Private Dichotomy', pp. 283-4.

43. Pateman, *The Sexual Contract*, pp. 41-3. See also, Okin, *Justice, Gender and the Family*, pp. 8-14.

44. Pateman, 'Feminist Critiques of the Public/Private Dichotomy', p. 284.

45. Pateman, 'Feminist Critiques of the Public/Private Dichotomy', p. 285.

the liberal category of the private is given moral priority. So too are its referents within the masculine world: private individuals as opposed to the state; private individuals as opposed to civil society; or private civil society as opposed to the state. In this way, Pateman's argument draws attention to the fact that the phrase 'liberal public-private dichotomy' does not just refer to a mutually exclusive and exhaustive relationship between these categories, as Benn and Gaus claim. It also refers to a *hierarchy* and, since the relations in question are implicitly gendered, this is a *gendered* hierarchy.

Pateman's discussion also illustrates how the liberal public-private dichotomy is generated in two distinct moves. The first, which, according to her, abstracts civil society from feminine domestic life, thereby constituting the former as part of a masculine public world, involves what we might call *an initial act of exclusion*. The second, that on her analysis reconstitutes the privileged domain of the private within the already constituted masculine world of civil society, serves to *prioritize* the private.

As already suggested, the above sort of analysis is intended to demonstrate the *inherently patriarchal* character of liberal dichotomous thought *in general*. Pateman defines *modern* patriarchy as involving fraternal, rather than paternal right, that is, men's right of sexual access to women's bodies, a right that effectively strips women of the status of equal participant in a social contract. She suggests that on this account current patriarchal practices should not be understood as lingering remnants of an older political order but as constituting a distinctively modern form of patriarchy.[46] So the question regarding the connection between patriarchalism and liberal theory in general can be framed as a question about whether such theory presupposes an unacknowledged principle of fraternal right. Pateman's reply is in the affirmative. She suggests that even in late twentieth century liberal thought, which would deny women's natural subordination to men, it is simply 'taken for granted' that 'liberal social life can be understood without reference to the sphere of subordination, natural relations and women'.[47]

---

46. Pateman, *The Sexual Contract*, Carole Pateman, 'The Fraternal Social Contract', *The Disorder of Women: Democracy, Feminism and Political Theory*, Cambridge, Polity Press, 1989, pp. 33-57.

47. Pateman, 'Feminist Critiques of the Public/Private Dichotomy', p. 286. For example, Pateman objects to Rawls' version of the social contract for positing sexless reasoners in the 'original position', the place of deliberation about the fundamental principles of a just society, while at the same time introducing 'real, embodied male and female beings' in the course of the argument. 'Before ignorance of "particular facts" [such as sex] is postulated Rawls has already claimed that parties have "descendants" (for whom they are concerned) and Rawls states that he will generally view the parties as "heads of families". He merely takes it for granted that he can, at one and the same time, postulate disembodied parties devoid of all substantive characteristics, and assume that sexual difference exists, sexual intercourse takes place, children are born and families formed. Rawls' participants in the original contract are simultaneously, mere reasoning entities and "heads of families" or men who represent their wives', Pateman, *The Sexual Contract*, p. 43.

2.2.3 A liberal reformulation of the public-private distinction

Even if Pateman's analysis of particular liberal theories is sound, there appears to be nothing in her argument—or in other feminist objections to liberalism's depoliticization of the family—to indicate why liberalism *need be* committed to a view of the family as private. Indeed liberal theorists have not only incorporated the concept of the family in liberal theories of social justice,[48] they have also reformulated—or in their view clarified the liberal formulation of—the public-private distinction to which liberalism remains committed. For example, Will Kymlicka argues that in the two conceptions of the public-private distinction that do operate in liberalism, the line between public and private cuts across the public-domestic distinction.

> There are in fact two different conceptions of the public-private distinction in liberalism: the first, which originated in Locke, is the distinction between the political and the social; the second, which arose with Romantic-influenced liberals, is the distinction between the social and the personal. Neither treats the family as wholly private (CPP, p. 250).

In accordance with the first of these conceptions, he claims that in an effort 'to free society from political interference' (CPP, p. 252)

> liberalism expresses its commitment to modern liberty by sharply separating the public power of the state from the private relationships of civil society, and by setting strict limits on the state's ability to intervene in private life (CPP, p. 251).

Kymlicka replies to Pateman's objection—that through its exclusion from the liberal conception of civil society the family is rendered private and, consequently, non-political—by insisting that liberalism's state-civil society distinction does not presuppose a view of the family as private. Instead, he suggests that male philosophers, and not only liberals, must have endorsed the domestic-public distinction, and with this the exclusion of the family from their political theories' discussions of civil society, for entirely self-interested reasons (CPP, p. 253). So, liberalism is not unavoidably patriarchal, as Pateman claims, even if some of its exponents have been sexist.

In any case, Kymlicka suggests, feminists would do well to accept the liberal view of the relationship between the state and society because the alternative would be to view politics as a higher form of life, a view that presupposes a hierarchical nature-culture dualism that devalues women's work (CPP, pp. 253-5). But the feminist critique of liberalism's public-private dichotomy does not deny the need for the identification of normative limits to state interference in other areas of social life. Nor does it imply such a de-

---

48. This is not only true of liberal feminists like Okin but also of the theorists that Pateman criticizes like Rawls, who locates the family as one of the institutions which form the subject matter of his account of social justice, the basic structure of society.

nial or a denial of the modern differentiation of social life into distinct political, social and domestic spheres. The point has been to contest the methods and/or political effects of liberal conceptualizations of the distinctions in question. [49]

2.2.4 The need for an investigation of the dichotomously related abstract categories of publicness and privateness

Despite the fact that Pateman's argument does not show, as she means it to, that liberalism is *essentially* patriarchal, I want to show why there is some basis for investigating the claim that liberal theory necessarily involves certain inadequacies in the inquiring practices that inform its reliance on the public-private dichotomy. Contemporary liberal theories exemplify the tendency to employ the categories of publicness and privateness dichotomously, in Pateman's sense of relating them oppositionally *and* hierarchically, but this is not primarily, or necessarily, evident in their references to, or omissions concerning, women and the feminine. It is rather to be identified in the reflective processes involved in posing as well as addressing the questions of liberal theory.

Consider why and how it is that Kymlicka's reply to Pateman appears to have critical force. Note, firstly, that it looks for some reason *beyond* liberal theories themselves, like a theorist's self-interest and sexist prejudice, to explain why liberals have excluded the concept of the family from their analyses of civil society. This is enabled by Kymlicka's reformulation of 'the problem'—the liberal theorist's exclusion of the family from civil society—as incapable of stemming from liberalism's view of the *private* family. This, he suggests, is because 'the problem here is precisely that it [the family] is not viewed as part of the private realm [civil society], which is the realm of liberal freedom'. Secondly, note that this reformulation of the problem to be resolved is made possible only by ignoring that part of Pateman's analysis that suggests that the liberal public-private dichotomy is generated by *two* moves with different effects, the first exclusionary and the second prioritizing.

If we were to take seriously the full implications of the suggestion that liberal theories engage in a double act of privatization with different effects at different moments in their inquiring practice, then Kymlicka's way of representing 'the problem', to which, as already explained, he finds an an-

---

49. See Seyla Benhabib, 'Models of Public Space', *Situating the Self: Gender, Community and Postmodernism in Contemporary Ethics*, Cambridge, Polity Press, 1992, pp. 89-120, Frazer and Lacey, *The Politics of Community*, Anna Yeatman, 'The Personal and the Political: A Feminist Critique', in Nancy Fraser and Paul James (eds.), *Critical Politics: From the Personal to the Global*, Melbourne, Arena Publications, 1994, pp. 35-58, Iris Marion Young, 'Politics and Group Difference: A Critique of the Ideal of Universal Citizenship', *Ethics: An International Journal of Social, Political, and Legal Philosophy*, vol. 99, 1989, pp. 116-21. Nevertheless, the racial character of white feminism's critique of the public-private dichotomy has in turn been the subject of much criticism. On this see Chanter, *Gender: Key Concepts in Philosophy*, pp. 17-22.

swer in particular theorists' illiberal sexist prejudices, does not even arise.[50] Yet Pateman's analysis seems to *leave open* the possibility of a reformulated view of the public-private distinction, such as Kymlicka's. His is a reformulation that not only avoids *the substance* of the first exclusionary move identified by Pateman's analysis—the treatment of the family as non-political. It also avoids the very idea of there being *any initial act of exclusion whatsoever* in the constitution of the liberal public-private distinction.

To illustrate this last point, consider how Kymlicka formulates and discusses the liberal view of individuals' privacy *within* civil society. This is the view that defines the second of Kymlicka's two conceptions of liberalism's public-private distinction referred to above, that between 'the social and the personal'. He claims that:

> modern liberalism is concerned not only to protect the private sphere of social life but also to carve out a realm *within the private sphere* where individuals can have *privacy*. Private life, for liberals, now means both active involvement in the institutions of civil society, as classical liberals emphasized, and personal retreat from that ordered social life, as Romantics emphasized (CPP, p. 258).

Note that (despite the fact that 'ordered social life' is supposed to represent the *public* side of the social-personal distinction) this assertion implicitly denies that civil society constitutes a *public* sphere given that it is represented as 'the private sphere' and the categorical relations are mutually exclusive. Kymlicka's view amounts to a *reformulation* of liberal theory to this extent and it obviously avoids the idea of there being any kind of initial act of exclusion in the constitution of the liberal public-private distinction. Pateman's analysis *leaves open* this possibility because, although it correctly identifies what I referred to as an initial act of exclusion of the family—the aspect of liberal inquiring practice which renders the family private and non-political—in a number of liberal theories, it does not investigate in sufficient depth the double acts of excluding and prioritizing the private as *characteristic practices* of liberal theorizing. This is because her discussion, like that of liberal theorists, is confined to the assessment of theories merely as *theorized objects* and not as *theorized objects in relationship to the identities of their theorizing subjects where the latter are defined by their practices of inquiry*. This is why it is open to Kymlicka to redefine the liberal public-private distinction (in terms of his formulation of the social-personal distinction) without implying the exclusion of anything private.

Even more revealing is Kymlicka's discussion of the formal right to pri-

---

50. Kymlicka makes little attempt to assess the view that the privatization and de-politicization of the family plays *more than* an incidental role in liberal theories, such as Locke's, where the public-domestic dichotomy does clearly operate. See, for example, Nancy J. Hirschmann, *Rethinking Obligation: A Feminist Method for Political Theory*, Ithaca, Cornell University Press, 1992, esp. pp.44-52.

vacy taken as a social embodiment of the liberal social-personal distinction. He acknowledges that, as recognized by the U.S. Supreme Court, this view of the public-private distinction has effectively 'immunized the domestic sphere' from public political intervention, something that has also been subject to feminist criticism. Yet, he attributes the decisions of the U.S. Supreme Court, which often interpret the formal right to privacy as a family-based right, to the 'lingering influence of pre-liberal ideas about the naturalness of the traditional family' (CPP, pp. 260-1).

> While the court invokes the language of a liberal public-private distinction, it is in fact invoking an illiberal public-domestic distinction, one which subordinates individual privacy to family autonomy (CPP, p. 261).

Here Kymlicka agrees with feminist critics' statement of *the problem*—the Court's interpretation of the right to privacy renders the family private. However, whereas feminists claim that 'the protection of domesticity is entailed by the liberal ideal of privacy' Kymlicka counter-asserts 'the protectors of domesticity have adopted the language of liberalism' (CPP, p. 261). For present purposes I need not defend either side of this disagreement. My point is rather that both explanations raise, without satisfactorily addressing, the question of the character of liberal *discourse*. That is, they presuppose competing unexamined views about whether or not 'the language of liberalism' plays a constitutive role—in this case whether it constitutes the domestic sphere as a realm of sexual subordination. Kymlicka's argument presupposes that 'the language of liberalism' is a neutral instrument that can be put to the service of both patriarchal and non-patriarchal purposes. The radical feminist argument presupposes the contrary view that liberal language is necessarily defined by the patriarchal uses to which it is put.

Despite its limitations, the radical feminist critique of liberalism's public-private dichotomy is on the right track in so far as it raises questions about the inter-relationship of the abstract categories of publicness and privateness and attempts to explain *how liberal categories function*. Together with liberal theorists' attempts to justify the liberal public-private dichotomy, this critique points in the direction of an investigation, firstly, of the complex-structured abstract notions of publicness and privateness as basic categories of liberal inquiring practice; secondly, of the claim that *the inter-relationship* of these basic categories is constituted in oppositional and hierarchical terms; thirdly, of the view that the question of the inter-relationship of the basic categories of liberal inquiring practice is distinct from the related question of what such practice *produces* in terms of substantive theoretical positions, such as the depoliticization of the concept of the family.

2.3 Conclusion

In suggesting that liberalism's commitment to a public-private dichotomy needs to be traced back to the theorizing subject's inquiring practices, we need not assume that the meanings of publicness and privateness remain constant in (the history of) liberal thought. The point is rather that in some senses, to be specified in Chapter 4, they are always fundamental to the structuring of liberal thought irrespective of its specific subject matter at any given moment. This said, if liberal theory is to satisfy the modern western demand for justification then no aspect of the process involved in meeting this demand should invoke *intrinsically public* agency. It follows from this that it is not only the idea of the individual person to which liberal theory attributes moral priority (the theorized subject) that must avoid invoking the idea of intrinsically public agency. Rather, the liberal theorist qua *theorizing* subject must also consistently avoid having to invoke it as a constitutive part of his or her own identity. This is why the liberal theorist's intellectual identity forms an indispensable part of the object of an immanent radical critique. (This holds irrespective of what view liberal theorists take on the relationship between theory production and the theorist's own identity.)

Now, given (a) the liberal theorist's implicit denial of the philosophical significance of intrinsically public agency (1.1.4) and (b) the relationship between such a denial and the affirmation of intrinsically private agency (1.2.2), the liberal theorist's own identity must give expression to the cultural force of the idea of *intrinsically private* agency (1.2.2). Accordingly, the radical critic should expect to find the liberal theorist's identity to be constituted by a certain kind of interplay between the category of intrinsically private agency and that which this category excludes, namely intrinsically public agency. Since the ideas of intrinsically public and intrinsically private agency relate as mutually exclusive and mutually exhaustive, this relationship suggests that the radical critic should also expect the liberal theorist's identity to embody the abstract categories of publicness and privateness in a dichotomous inter-relationship.

Finally, one should expect to find that a dichotomous inter-relationship of the abstract categories of publicness and privateness does not just define the identity of the liberal theorizing subject (as if this identity were taken in abstraction from the basic structure of his or her theorized object), but that this defining feature belongs both to the liberal theorist's identity and to liberal theory. Together the liberal theorizing subject and his or her theorized object (the subject-object relationship of the theory) reveal the most basic categories of *liberal discourse*. Here I use the phrase 'liberal discourse' to highlight the liberal theorizing subject's formative and transformative participation in her communicative practices of inquiry that are, in turn, enabled by the system of categories making up her social reality, namely the liberal age in the terms already discussed (1.1.2 to 1.2.2). By 'the most basic categories of liberal discourse' I mean to refer to the categories that, in shaping the liberal theorizing subject's identity, can also invoke the very moment of discourse itself (and not just to the ways in which the theorizing subject views his or her reality). Such categories are basic in the sense of having the power to explain the fundamental structure of liberal theory (the object that liberal discourse makes possible) *and* liberal theorizing practice. In so far as they define the liberal theorist's identity (the speaking subject of liberal discourse) they do not need themselves to be explained by appeal to some other, more basic categories.

If this understanding of the non-representational nature of the relationship between the liberal theorist and his or her theory is correct, then the radical critic should expect to find the fundamental structure of liberal theorizing revealed in what this practice produces. That is, a detailed investigation of the ways in which liberal theory is structured in accordance with the abstract categories of publicness and privateness should make possible an understanding of how these categories function in the liberal theorist's inquiring identity. (Here I am referring to an inversion in the order of *investigation* given my derivative interest in liberal theory as explained in Chapter 1, but not to any view about the causal relations that might operate between theorist and theory in liberal discourse.) Because the character of liberal theorizing should be revealed in what it produces, an investigation of how liberal theory gives effect to a public-private dichotomy can reveal the dichotomous identity of the liberal theorist.

3

Critical Reconstructionism as a Philosophical Methodology

In Chapters 1 and 2 I indicated that liberal political theory, as distinct from liberal political practice, is the proper object of our inquiry since it defends or presupposes the view that as modern individuals we are justified in endorsing some form of liberal social order. If this view is correct, then liberalism has the potential resources to respond to what I described as the predicament of modern individual subjectivity. I also indicated how an interest in what I termed a 'critical understanding' of this issue derives from the combination of two concerns. The first is a pre-reflective identification with a certain kind of ontological condition that I explained in terms of the valuing of communal being. The second concern is that the *justified* elaboration of a philosophy of communal being presupposes the radical critique of liberalism. If modern individuals have good reason to become liberal-minded and this, in turn, requires the abandonment of any commitment to the value of intrinsically public communal being—though not to every view of the value of community—then so be it. This is the broad philosophical background that informs our inquiry. This background gives rise to a critical reflective standpoint that is suited to the purposes of the critical understanding of liberalism. The standpoint in question is constituted by an awareness of the cultural force of intrinsically private agency. I have suggested that precisely because we require an *immanent* critique of liberal theory in order to identify the nature and limits of liberal inquiring practice the radical critique of liberalism needs to be undertaken from the standpoint of intrinsically private agency rather than from a yet to be justified commitment to the value of intrinsically public communal being. Chapter 2 ended with the defence of the view that attention to liberal inquiring practice calls not only for an assessment of the liberal theorizing subject's identity as this is constituted by liberal discourse but also for an appreciation of the fundamental categories that define this discourse at the most abstract level.

My purpose in this chapter is to advance the claim that a certain view of what I call *critical reconstructionism* is best suited to the radical immanent critique of liberal theory. I will begin by reformulating more precisely *the problem* to which liberal theory must offer an adequate response. I will present what we may refer to as *the problem of liberalism's definition* in section 1, having regard to what liberal theorists have had to say about the meaning of liberalism and, in section 2, having regard to the radical critic's question of what it would mean for liberal theory to give a positive coherent account of liberalism in its own terms. Section 3 will outline the phases of a critical reconstructionist method of inquiry and will explain the special merits of this method. The first of these is its ability to recognize the internal complexity and relative diversity of specific accounts of liberalism. The second is its ability to assess two distinct levels of liberal discourse, the *surface* and *deep structural* levels. The assessment of both these levels of discourse is indispensable to an adequate understanding of the nature and limits of liberal inquiring practice and of its consequent inability to solve the problem of liberalism's definition. Section 4 will offer a comparative defence of critical reconstructionism and an elaboration of its criterion for ordering particular liberal theories.

3.1 The Problem

How have liberals addressed the question of the meaning of liberalism? Liberal theorists acknowledge that for historical reasons the political ideals of their intellectual tradition—liberty, freedom, personal autonomy, equality, government neutrality—cannot neatly be distinguished from those of its conservative or socialist alternatives. Indeed, as a political ideology, liberalism has been said to lack any definitive (common and peculiar) characteristics, being likened instead to 'an extended family' with a history of considerable 'intermarriage'.[1] It has even been likened to a 'quarrelsome family' whose members disagree over far more than they actually share.[2]

What is particularly noteworthy in the *philosophical* discourse is the extent to which the term 'liberal' appears without any apparent need to specify its intended meaning. Some understanding of a *distinctively* liberal philosophy is implied by the popular view that a community-sensitive *liberalism*

---

1. Jeremy Waldron, 'Theoretical Foundations of Liberalism', *Philosophical Quarterly*, vol. 37, no. 147, 1987, pp. 127-50, pp. 127-8. See also Parekh, *Rethinking Multiculturalism*, p. 368.

2. Thomas A. Spragens, Jr., 'Reconstructing Liberal Theory: Reason and Liberal Culture', in Alfonso J. Damico (ed.), *Liberals on Liberalism*, Totowa, Rowman & Littlefield, 1986, pp. 34-53, pp. 36-7. But see Ralph D. Ellis, 'Toward a Coherent Definition of Liberalism', *Southwest Philosophical Review*, vol. 7, no. 2, 1991, pp. 31-46.

emerged triumphant after having absorbed the insights of its communitarian critics.³ Yet, as Thomas Nagel observes, 'liberalism' does mean different things to different people.⁴ To be sure some ease with the commonsense or pre-reflective meanings of liberalism is understandable in an intellectual climate that privileges philosophical debates centred on the question of the (best) way(s) to be liberal, rather than whether to become liberal. Moreover, the taken for grantedness of this meaning tends to conceal the fact that contemporary liberals' failure to agree on or produce a consensus over a self-definition based on a commitment to some fundamental (set of) substantive or procedural value(s) or idea(s) has historically given rise to some concern.⁵

Some forty years ago North American discussions about the nature and meaning of liberalism arose as a skeptical thesis about liberalism's very *existence*. For example, Ronald Dworkin introduced his first attempt to define the essence of liberalism as follows.

> In this essay I shall propose a theory about what liberalism is. But I face an immediate problem. My project supposes that there is such a thing as liberalism, and the opinion is suddenly popular that there is not.⁶

When this essay was first published in 1978 Dworkin was motivated to give a principled account of liberalism in response to the political developments of the time that posed a challenge to the perception that liberalism was a 'fundamental political theory' capable of generating a 'package of liberal causes' such as the New Deal.⁷ No doubt Dworkin was seeking to counter the pejorative uses of the term 'liberal' in U.S. politics at the time.⁸ But for our purposes the noteworthy point is that the question of the meaning of the fundamental feature(s) of liberal philosophical thought was taken up as what

---

3. This is reflected in the repeated call to view theories of community as supplementing and not substituting liberalism. See Amy Gutmann, 'Communitarian Critics of Liberalism', in Shlomo Avineri and Avner De-Shalit (eds.), *Communitarianism and Individualism*, Oxford, Oxford University Press, 1992, pp. 120-36, Stephen Newman, 'Challenging the Liberal-Individualist Tradition in America: "Community" as a Critical Ideal in Recent Political Theory', in Allan C. Hutchinson and Leslie J. M. Green (eds.), *Law and the Community: The End of Individualism?*, Toronto, Carswell, 1989, p. 274. See also Nancy L. Rosenblum, 'Repairing the Communitarian Failings of Liberal Thought', *Another Liberalism: Romanticism and the Reconstruction of Liberal Thought*, Cambridge, Harvard University Press, 1987, pp. 152-86.

4. Thomas Nagel, 'Rawls and Liberalism', in Samuel Freman (ed.), *The Cambridge Companion to Rawls*, Cambridge, Cambridge University Press, 2003, pp. 62-85.

5. For a discussion of explanations for this failure of agreement see Ryan, 'Liberalism'. See alos Ronald Dworkin, 'Liberalism', *A Matter of Principle*, Oxford, Oxford University Press, 1986, Douglas MacLean and Claudia Mills, 'Introduction', in Douglas MacLean and Claudia Mills (eds.), *Liberalism Reconsidered*, Totowa, Rowman & Allanheld, 1983, p. ix.

6. Ronald Dworkin, *A Matter of Principle*, Oxford, Oxford University Press, 1986, p. 182.

7. Dworkin, *A Matter of Principle*, p. 183.

8. On this usage see Beiner's comments in Beiner, *What's the Matter with Liberalism?*, p. 8 fn. 4.

we may describe as an *internally* raised concern, thought not in the sense of attempting to produce an internally coherent account of what are admittedly liberal claims. Rather, for the liberal this internally raised concern makes possible the question of what it is about some (set of) claim(s) that gives them their status as genuine products of a distinctively *liberal* thought or intellectual practice. Indeed the early challenge to liberalism's existence drew the liberal theorists' attention to the question of the essence of liberalism as a philosophical *discourse*. Accordingly, attention to the standpoint of liberal theory's internally raised concerns need not limit an inquiry to the liberal character of its *theorized objects*. Significantly, it makes possible consideration of the liberal character of the *theorizing subject's* identity as well. I will call this problem of providing an account of liberalism's distinctive inquiring practices 'the problem of liberalism's definition'.

3.2 Investigating liberal approaches to the problem

How should the radical critic proceed to address the problem of liberalism's definition? One might think that since liberals (and their critics) evidently use expressions like 'the liberal state', 'liberal society', 'liberal institutions and practices' and 'the liberal way of life' meaningfully, the failure to produce a consensus or agreement that I referred above is confined to *the justificatory grounds* of the commonsense or pre-reflective understanding of liberal socio-political arrangements and the norms that regulate them. Indeed the question of the defensibility of liberalism is often presented in these terms so that differences amongst liberals come to be presented as commitments to different arguments for some specified set of universal principles. For example, John Gray presents liberals as divided over their support for three basic types of argument—consequentialist, contractarian and perfectionist—in favour of a set of principles that they take to be universally valid.[9] But we should not take it for granted that the problem of liberalism's definition can be reduced to that of providing *philosophically defensible* principles of socio-political organization. The philosophical elaboration of a political morality is one way in which liberals may attempt to deal with the problem of liberalism's definition but whether or not it is (a) the best available way and (b) adequate to the task is a matter to be addressed by our inquiry.

The above observation—that we cannot just assume that liberalism's answer to the problem of its definition is to be given in the form of providing arguments for its political principles—calls attention to the need for some suitable method of identifying and ordering possible approaches to the problem. Two initial considerations are relevant to the task of adopting a suitable method. On the one hand, given liberalism's poor track record when it

---

9. John Gray, 'Postscript: After Liberalism', *Liberalisms: Essays in Political Philosophy*, London, Routledge, 1991, pp. 239-66.

comes to the elaboration of a philosophical account of liberalism, one should not expect to advance too much in the project of accounting for liberalism if one were simply to take liberals' own statements of its meaning at face value. On the other hand, the object of investigation is indeed the ability of liberal discourse to give a satisfactory account of itself. The aim, as already explained in Chapter 1, is to arrive at an *immanent* critical understanding of liberal inquiring practice. This aim directs us away from framing our investigation as a matter of appealing to liberal theorists' own characterizations of liberalism. This is because, as I suggested in Chapter 1.2.1, we should not conflate an investigation of the question of the nature of liberal inquiring practice and, relatedly, of what it is to be liberal, from the standpoint of the theorist who is in but not (yet) of liberalism with that of a self-satisfied liberalism. It also leads us away from an investigation of developments in liberalism's long social and intellectual history or of its comparative strengths and weaknesses. Rather, because the arrangement of the material to be examined should enable liberal theory to *speak for itself*, we must pay attention to liberal theorists' explicit claims about the nature of liberalism and the form of liberal inquiring practice without assuming that the two converge in the case of any particular theorist. That there may well be discrepancies between what a liberal says *about* liberalism and what (s)he *does* as a liberal theorist should not be surprising if it is correct that (1) liberal theory generally lacks the *self-awareness* characteristic of a well developed tradition of inquiry; and (2) one of the things liberal theorists characteristically *do not do* is raise *their own* doubts about what it is to be liberal. Even Ronald Dworkin's attention to the question of liberalism's existence (3.1), arose in response to a skeptical challenge *from the outside*, so to speak.

How then should we proceed? I want to suggest that in order for liberal theory to speak for itself, it would need fully to view itself as a tradition of inquiry in the sense given to this phrase by Alasdair MacIntyre. According to MacIntyre, when in good order, a tradition of inquiry is

> a coherent movement of thought [...] in the course of which those engaged in that movement become aware of it and of its direction and in self-aware fashion attempt to engage in its debates and to carry its enquires forward (WJ, p. 326).

We can draw upon MacIntyre's work in this area in order to adapt some of his ideas to our own needs. MacIntyre offers an explanation of how it is possible for traditions of inquiry, given that their standards of rationality are internal to them, to make rational progress and prove the rational superiority of their claims over those of rival traditions.[10] In this context he develops

---

10. I leave aside objections to MacIntyre's account of the rational superiority of a tradition on grounds that it is culturally imperialist since I do not rely on his views to defend the rational superiority of any tradition. For the elaboration of this objection see Richard J. Bernstein,

the idea that the rationality of the inquiring practices of a tradition of inquiry is 'a matter of the kind of progress which it makes through a number of well-defined types of stage'. Roughly, these stages characterize the degree of questioning, (re)formulation and re-evaluation of the traditions' commitments concerning their reality (WJ, pp. 354-8).[11] Three features of this account of the possibility of rational progress are especially relevant. First, relatively well-developed traditions may reach a point in their history at which those engaged in inquiry 'may find occasion or need to frame a theory of their own activities of inquiry' (WJ, p. 359).[12] Second, although specific traditions move differently through the stages of development characterizing their rational progress, they may also share some features. These include the establishment of 'requirements for successful dialectical questioning' that enables a tradition to move forward through the consideration and resolution of inconsistent commitments (WJ, p. 359). Elsewhere MacIntyre clarifies that 'what inconsistency always presents to those engaged in enquiry is a *problem*, that of how to reconcile whatever truth two inconsistent sets of beliefs may each possess in such a way as to arrive at a consistent view'.[13]

> The identification of incoherence within established belief will always provide a reason for enquiring further, but not in itself a conclusive reason for rejecting established belief, until something more adequate because less incoherent may be discovered (WJ, p. 359).

Third, an 'epistemological crisis' may occur at some point in the history of a tradition. Such a crisis is marked by 'the dissolution of historically founded certitudes' and by the sterility of the available methods of inquiry so that rational progress ceases. The successful resolution of an epistemological crisis requires the framing of new theory and the discovery or invention of concepts that are new to the tradition. MacIntyre specifies three requirements that such concepts must satisfy. Briefly, they must: (1) provide a solution to the problems that have previously proved intractable; (2) account for the previous sterility and/or incoherence of the tradition; and (3) ensure fundamental continuity between the old and the new conceptual structures (WJ, pp. 361-2).

Now, I propose to use these characteristic features of the development of traditions of inquiry in a creative way. That is, by combining them with a certain Hegelian reading of the dialectical movement of conceptual think-

---

The New Constellation: The Ethical-Political Horizons of Modernity/Postmodernity, Cambridge, MIT Press, 1991, pp. 59-67.

11. It is worth noting that this view of the rational progress of a tradition is 'anti-Cartesian' due to its beginnings in 'the contingency and positivity of some set of established beliefs', MacIntyre, *Whose Justice?*, p. 360.

12. MacIntyre illustrates this point by reference to attempts by adherents of the traditions he discusses to give an account of truth.

13. MacIntyre, 'A Partial Response to my Critics', p. 291.

ing, they will constitute *guidelines* for the organization and discussion of liberal theories.[14] My claim is that we can read liberal theories by tracing a progressive movement of liberal thought through a number of stages constituted by the formulation, questioning, evaluation and reformulation of liberal inquiring practice. Adapting MacIntyre's language we can (1) *frame a theory of liberal theory's own activities* by identifying a number of views of justification that function in liberal inquiring practice pursuant to its commitment to the public-private dichotomy that was discussed in Chapter 2.2; (2) trace the specifics of the movement of liberal theory by engaging in a process of *dialectical questioning* that will serve to identify *incoherence within the theory* that will, in turn, provide the reason for further inquiry into a reformulated theory; and (3) identify a moment of epistemological crisis in the development of liberal theory and assess its ability to solve the crisis.

Before attempting to elaborate these claims it is worth clarifying why it is that MacIntyre's ideas can be used as guidelines for our inquiry even though his critique of liberalism purports to have demonstrated the need for a narrative history of liberalism and I have no intention of proposing such a history (see WJ, p. 349). That is, in attempting to allow liberal theories to speak for themselves as they would were they to view liberalism as a tradition of inquiry the organization and discussion of liberal theories may be more or less informed by discussions within the *historical* tradition, but their contributions to an actual history of the development of liberal doctrines is not at issue here. This might be thought to give rise to a problem that we can best put in the form of a question. Why investigate what liberals *would say* about their theory (were they in a position to do so) using as guidelines features that purportedly belong to historical traditions in virtue of what they *have said*? Indeed, why not focus on liberal theories that have recognized liberalism as itself being tradition-bound? I will take up this second question first.

As MacIntyre points out, liberals have increasingly recognized the tradition-dependence of the standards of rationality that their theories employ, standards that are 'contingently grounded and founded'. He also notes that liberals (can) give this recognition without being inconsistent.[15] I want to suggest, however, that, it is one thing to recognize (the implications of) the contingency of a tradition's origins and quite another to take seriously the correctness of MacIntyre's thesis that liberalism is the sort of tradition *that*

---

14. On this Hegelian reading of the movement of conceptual thought see part I of Nicolacopoulos and Vassilacopoulos, *Hegel and the Logical Structure of Love*.

15. This is so, according to MacIntyre, despite liberals' understandable reluctance to do so in the light of the history of the development of universalist liberal doctrines. He cites Rawls, Rorty and Stout as examples, MacIntyre, *Whose Justice?*, pp. 345-6. Rawls presents his theory of justice as a response to a tension between the interplay of freedom and equality derived from Locke and Rousseau and his project purports to 'complete and extend the movement of thought that began three centuries ago', Rawls, *Political Liberalism*, pp. 5 & 154.

characteristically does not recognize itself as a tradition. Such a lack of self-awareness on the part of the tradition must inevitably restrict the degree to which liberal theorists can *adequately* position themselves as participants in a tradition of inquiry that is 'in good order', to use MacIntyre's words. For example, when John Rawls recognizes the tradition-dependence of the standards of reasoning employed in his theory what this amounts to is the appreciation that such standards do not constitute neutral criteria by which to assess the competing claims of socio-political cultures other than the western liberal democratic tradition.[16] The intended universalistic *application* of his claims is, accordingly, contextualized. Its application is restricted to the lives of all persons within liberal democratic societies (1.1.4). Yet nothing else about the theorist's operative reasoning practices and methods of inquiry need be affected by this limited, albeit significant, recognition.

Stephen Mulhall and Adam Swift also recognize that 'the liberal theorist tends to think of himself or herself as essentially tradition-free'. However, they claim 'there can be no reason for thinking that there is any fundamental contradiction between the content of a liberal theory of justice and an explicit acknowledgment of the elementary truth that this theory (like any other product of human intellectual endeavour) emerged from a tradition of inquiry. To think otherwise is simply to commit a version of the genetic fallacy, to conflate the question of a theory's origins with that of its content'. In this way they think they dispense with the claim that 'the liberal theorist cannot consistently acknowledge this truth about herself'.[17] Mulhall and Swift thus imply that liberal theorists' mistaken historical denial of their tradition-dependence can simply be remedied by theorists' 'owning up' to the fact. They take it for granted that the theorist's awareness of her theory's tradition-dependence plays no *constitutive* role in the construction of its content.

By way of contrast, I am interested in determining what else liberal theory would have to confront were it to become *more fully self-aware* as is the mark of a well-developed tradition of inquiry. This brings us to the first question raised above. In reply, I want to suggest that if it is indeed a characteristic feature of the liberal intellectual tradition that it does not take itself to be a tradition, then this *practice of the denial of (an aspect of) its identity* should somehow be capable of being rendered visible. If my claim is correct, it should be possible to make sense of this aspect of the practice of liberal theorizing subjects. Our inquiry, therefore, should try to formulate an account of what liberals *would* say were their tradition of inquiry to be more fully self-aware since this is a way of identifying what, as a matter of history, they *have not said*

---

16. See John Rawls, 'Law of Peoples', in S. L. Hurley and Stephen Shute (eds.), *On Human Rights: The Oxford Amnesty Lectures*, New York, BasicBooks, 1993, pp. 41-82, Rawls, *Political Liberalism*.

17. Mulhall and Swift, *Liberals and Communitarians*, pp. 291-2.

in saying what they have said.[18] This is what I mean when I suggest that an immanent critique should assess liberal theories in the terms that they would employ were they fully to view themselves as a tradition of inquiry, that is, as belonging to a self-aware movement of thought that aspires to coherence.

3.3 A reconstructive method of inquiry

The above considerations suggest a *reconstructive method* that recognizes (1) the internal complexity of specific accounts of liberalism as well as any patterns of convergence and divergence emerging from the variety of alternative accounts; and (2) the operation within specific liberal theories of two distinct yet related *levels* of liberal discursive practice. In response to the first of these requirements, the reconstruction of liberal theories requires a taxonomy of approaches to the problem of liberalism's definition in order subsequently to examine a number of specific accounts as exemplary versions of the kind of approach to which each one of them belongs. I will undertake the first of these two tasks in Chapter 4 but first we should turn to an account of liberalism's two levels of discursive practice and of their methodological implications for a radical critical method of inquiry.

3.3.1 The surface and deep structural levels of liberal discourse

The second requirement mentioned above can be met by differentiating between a particular theory's *surface level of inquiry* and its *deep structure*. The former refers to the claims and arguments put forward by liberal theories as well as to their substantive and methodological presuppositions. So, for example, it includes a theorist's formulation of a problem, such as whether gov-

---

18. Compare Rosenblum's reconstruction of the romantic experience of liberalism that, although non-historical, focuses on achieving *psychological* coherence, Rosenblum, *Another Liberalism*, p. 3. On the other hand, Luce Irigaray's deconstruction of Freud's account of female sexuality (in Luce Irigaray, *Speculum of the Other Woman*, Ithaca, Cornell University Press, 1989.) focuses on Freud's philosophical concepts. By turning his psychoanalytic methods on his own texts Irigaray adopts the role of the analyst in relation to the texts. She effectively aids Freud in a rewriting of his texts with her probing questions. These are questions to which the texts themselves give rise but in unself-aware fashion have left unsaid. In this way Irigaray renders Freud's texts on female sexuality 'truer' to themselves by bringing to the surface the conceptual incoherence that their writer could not recognize whilst still writing and endorsing what he wrote. Having drawn this limited parallel with Derrida's deconstructive method in the hands of Irigaray, I wish to emphasize, firstly, that I make no claim to be applying such a method, see Jacques Derrida, *Of Grammatology*, Baltimore, Johns Hopkis University Press, 1976. Secondly, even though from the standpoint of Derrida's theory of meaning the terms of my inquiry as set out in Chapter 1 arguably render it *logocentric* in that it remains motivated by a recognition of the philosophical significance of the identity of intrinsically public communal being, nevertheless, from the radical critical standpoint that I wish to develop, it might be possible to argue that Derrida's critique of the metaphysics of presence itself fails sufficiently to appreciate that liberal societies are premised on the suppression of this very identity. The development of this critique falls beyond the scope of the present work.

ernment should be perfectionist or neutral, (the defence of) some answer to it *and* the treatment of whatever assumptions the theory makes about social ontology and methodology, its forms of argument and criteria for assessing its claims, its role and relationship to other areas of (philosophical) inquiry, etc. My taxonomy of approaches to the problem of liberalism's definition will draw upon aspects of liberal theory at this surface level.

In contrast, the deep structure of a liberal theory concerns the way in which it inter-relates the basic categories characterizing the inquiring practice to which it gives unrecognized expression. As already suggested in Chapter 2, the view to be investigated is that liberal inquiring practice is discursively constituted by the dichotomously related complex-structured abstract categories of publicness and privateness. I will propose a taxonomy of the variety of formulations of the public-private dichotomy that operate at the deep structural level of liberal theory—rather than merely at the level of the representation of the division of the social world into public and private spheres of activity—in order to investigate the claim that different formulations of the dichotomy *parallel* the proposed taxonomy's different surface level approaches to the problem of defining liberalism. (Hereafter, unless otherwise indicated, references to 'the public-private dichotomy' are to this operation of the categories of publicness and privateness at the abstract level of a theory's deep structure.)

What is the relationship between the surface and deep structural levels of any particular liberal theory? First, I want to suggest that the deep structure of a theory frames its surface level discourse by supplying the conditions of its possibility. Yet this organizing role—in the sense of the role of a constitutive principle that makes the theory what it is—is itself unrecognized by the liberal theorist; the deep structure is not itself *articulated in* liberal discourse but is that which enables the *articulation of* liberal discourse.

Second, regarding the status of the relationship between the surface and deep structural levels, my hypothesis is that the deep structure of a liberal theory explains (1) the limits of its surface level claims and (2) the position of the theory in a rational progression from less to more advanced formulations and responses to the problem of liberalism's definition. That is, the idea of a deep structure functions as an explanatory hypothesis in the absence of which it is not possible to identify the source of a particular theory's surface level inadequacies or to give a coherent account of liberal theory in developmental terms.

Third, rather than proceeding from the assumption that there *exists* a deep structure of liberal theories and attempting to follow through the implications of its existence, the starting point for the examination of particular theories is always their own surface level claims. That is, the discussion should move from a consideration of the surface level of a theory to the reconstruction of its deep structure and not the reverse since to do the latter would be to introduce into liberal theory unwarranted considerations that are external to it. (In Chapter 2 I explained why avoiding reliance on the truth of considerations that are external to liberal theory is one of the features of the kind of radical critique of liberalism that I want to develop.)

3.3.2 Critical reconstructionism

How should the radical critic's investigation of the relationship between the surface and deep structural levels of specific liberal theories proceed? My inquiry will adopt what can be referred to as a *critical reconstructionist method*. Critical reconstructionism undertakes three moves in the investigation of each theory: the first is expository, the second, reconstructive and the third, critical. I will outline these in turn and, at the same time, introduce some technical terms that will be employed in the extensive analyses of Parts II and III of the book.

First, the *exposition* of a particular theory addresses the theory at its surface level of inquiry with three tasks in mind. To begin with, it will identify 'the theory's own adequacy criterion'. This is the criterion that the theory puts forward, whether implicitly or explicitly, as that by which to judge the success of its inquiry. It, therefore, reveals the view of justification that the liberal theorist employs in relation to his or her own practice of inquiry. The second objective of the exposition is to set out precisely how the particular theory purports to meet its own adequacy criterion in order to give the reader sufficient basis for an assessment of the theory's achievements in this regard. The third objective is to report enough of the theory's specifics to give the reader sufficient basis for a consideration of the question of what the theory would take itself to be doing were it aware of itself as offering a response to the problem of liberalism's definition. It is worth noting that this task does not assume that the theory is, albeit unaware, trying to solve the problem of the definition of liberalism. For one thing, as the difference in the reflective standpoints of the radical critic and the liberal theorist attests (Chapter 1.2.1.), the task of addressing the problem of liberalism's definition is one that the radical liberal critic has set *herself*. For another, this task assumes that in so far as a particular liberal theory is a *liberal* theory pursuant to its employment of liberal reasoning practices it implicitly offers some response to the question of what it is about its claims that gives them their status as genuine products of distinctively liberal thought. Thus, every particular liberal theory implicitly offers what I will be referring to as 'its account of liberalism'. From a theory's specifics it will also be necessary to take note of the claims and presuppositions that will prove useful for the attribution of a public or private character to its surface level ideas. Accordingly, the exposition of a theory will not be limited to an outline of some of the theory's claims taken in abstraction from the role that they are supposed to play in the theory as a whole.

The second aspect of the critical reconstructionist method, the *reconstruction* of a particular theory, addresses each theory at the deep structural level. The first objective is to render visible a theory's deep structural commitments in the light of a consideration of its specific surface level claims and presuppositions, including those regarding the publicness and privateness of its ideas. In this regard, the reconstruction should begin by identifying the categories that a theory constitutes as public and private, paying attention to the precise way(s) in which the surface level discourse effects the assimilation of, what Stanley Benn and Gerald Gaus call, 'deviant cases' to its bi-polar view of social life. According to these authors, 'deviant cases' are those in which explanation in terms of bi-polarity breaks down due to the context in which the issue of publicness or privateness arises. Their survey of liberal theories suggests that this occurs despite the fact that bi-polarity breaks down in a way that is systematically related to the dimensions of access, agency and interest thereby giving rise to some important presumptions for the application of the categories of publicness and privateness.[19] These presumptions are, firstly, that publicness is usually the residual category with respect to access so that

> to call something private in respect of access is to give a ground of a particular sort for withdrawing it from the range of the publicly accessible.[20]

Still, 'within a context that from a particular standpoint is itself private, there can be further distinctions between what is private and what is not, and then the residual category will not be public but will relate to that particular [private] context'.[21] Secondly, in the dimensions of both agency and interest,

> the presumption is generally the other way around from that of access. A person will be taken to 'own his action' simply as a private agent, unless there is a reason for looking at it differently.[22]

Similarly,

> in liberal thinking, private interest is residual, in the sense that it is taken to provide the most general explanatory motive for action, and, in the absence of overriding reasons, to be a legitimate motive too.[23]

---

19. Benn and Gaus, 'The Public and the Private: Concepts and Action', pp. 15-6. In drawing on the work of these theorists to elaborate my methodology I do not wish to attribute to them any endorsement of the claim concerning the operation of distinct surface and deep structural levels of liberal discourse.

20. Benn and Gaus, 'The Public and the Private: Concepts and Action', p. 15.

21. Benn and Gaus, 'The Public and the Private: Concepts and Action', p. 15.

22. Benn and Gaus, 'The Public and the Private: Concepts and Action', p. 16.

23. Benn and Gaus, 'The Public and the Private: Concepts and Action', p. 17. Compare Frazer and Lacey, *The Politics of Community*, p. 73. These authors make a similar observa-

To reconstruct is to observe the extent to which the presumptions that Benn and Gaus identify are operative, whether explicitly or implicitly, at the surface level of a particular theory. This assists in the elaboration of a theory's deep structural commitments. To identify a theory's deep structural commitments any findings concerning the operation of the presumptions just mentioned need to be combined with an elaboration of the precise way in which a theory inter-relates the basic categories. This exercise brings to the surface the theory's specific formulation of the public-private dichotomy. The features that constitute a theory's specific formulation of the public-private dichotomy (hereafter its 'deep structure') will be referred to as its 'suppositions'.

A second objective of reconstruction is to draw attention to the relative complexity and superiority of different formulations of the public-private dichotomy in order to demonstrate, by way of a comparison of specific theories, that (some formulation of) the public-private dichotomy plays the organizing role within each particular theory.

The third, critical component of critical reconstructionism involves two tasks, one negative and the other positive. The main objective of the negative aspect of the critique is to place the theory's surface level claims alongside its deep structural commitments in order to expose the theory's incoherence. This can be established by showing: (1) that the theory's deep structural commitments are inconsistent; (2) that the theory fails to satisfy its own adequacy criterion; and (3) that the failure of the theory to satisfy its own adequacy criterion is due to the theory's inconsistent deep structural commitments.

The inconsistent commitments of a particular theory's deep structure results in what I will refer to as 'the collapse' of its model of the public-private dichotomy. This collapse refers to a breakdown in the operative logic, that is, to the failure of the deep structure of a theory fully to conform to the requirements of its suppositions. The collapse of a model of the public-private dichotomy can be established by a demonstration of the reliance at the theory's surface level on views that remain unacknowledged at the deep structural level. The 'unacknowledged views' of a theory's deep structure refers to positions that cannot consistently be acknowledged.

Showing that a particular theory fails to satisfy its own adequacy criterion establishes the negative claim that the theory fails as a response to the

---

tion about the liberal attribution of privateness adding that a political effect of this privacy discourse is that 'women's oppression is not only constituted and maintained, but also and most damagingly, rendered apolitical'. Despite their attempts to identify the political impact of attributions of publicness and privateness, something which Benn and Gaus neglect, I nevertheless rely on Benn and Gaus' analysis because in failing to differentiate between the dimensions of access, interest and agency, Frazer and Lacey's discussion lacks the same level of clarity and precision.

problem of liberalism's definition. However, the critique also has a positive side in revealing the conditions of what would constitute a more adequately formulated theory. These conditions serve to identify a relatively superior response to the problem of liberalism's definition until all possible formulations are exhausted.

Critical reconstructionism thus provides a way of revealing: (1) the source of the surface level inadequacies of any account of liberalism, and by extension, of the sort of approach it exemplifies; and (2) an account's position in a rational progression and, in one particular case, its position as the most advanced. Importantly, it does so without having to appeal to considerations external to the particular account, considerations that may themselves form the subject matter of yet another surface level dispute. It therefore, also accords with the requirement that the critique proposed be immanent to liberal theory.

3.4 The advantages of critical reconstructionism

A successful application of critical reconstructionism and, in particular, of its surface level *exposition* of liberal theories, also serves indirectly to show that the limitations of some alternative methods of political criticism need not be accepted. Ian Shapiro neatly sums up such methods and their 'attendant dangers' when he introduces his alternative to so-called 'neo-Kantian political theory' out of views that 'share a basic antipathy toward [this] style and content of political thinking':[24]

> In this book I analyse and compare various arguments as part of a discursive attempt to incorporate what is useful in each into an alternative view. The author of any such work confronts a basic choice between either characterizing arguments in general terms and discussing them without worrying much about attributing them to anyone in particular, or intensively discussing the views of particular authors that he takes to be representative of the arguments with which he is concerned. [...] Both methods have their advantages and their attendant dangers: the first allows one to cover a great deal of ground, but it often provokes charges that no one actually holds the view in question so that critical discussion of it exhibits a straw or artificial quality. The second approach invites more intensive analytical discussion of particular views, but it frequently triggers the response that other formulations are more powerful than the one discussed or that the author examined was concerned with a narrow class of problems and that one cannot, therefore, legitimately generalise much from a discussion of those views. I have adopted the second method of analysis, although in deference to the spirit of the first all the authors I have chosen to discuss have substantially influenced

---

24. Ian Shapiro, *Political Criticism*, Berkeley, University of California Press, 1990, p. 11.

debates about politics in the past decade.[25]

An approach that really has the strength attributed to the first that Shapiro describes, namely that 'it allows one to cover a great deal of ground', presupposes that its critical exposition can incorporate a suitable explanation of the relationship of the arguments it characterizes 'in general terms' to the specific views that presumably make up this 'ground'. Such an explanation cannot be given about the relationships of particular views to the characterization of 'arguments in general terms' if, by this, one has in mind certain inductive generalizations. The latter abstract from the characteristics peculiar to particular theories and it is due to this sort of abstraction that they acquire the 'artificial quality' about which complaints may justifiably be made. As described by Shapiro, and as exemplified by some authors, the first approach lacks genuine critical force and is best avoided given that it has only the appearance of covering considerable ground.

Like Shapiro I adopt a critical approach that involves detailed analysis of the views of specific authors. However, rather than merely focusing on authors who are influential, thereby leaving unexplained why the conclusions drawn from critiques of *them* should be taken to have a much broader application, my selection of authors is determined by a criterion that assists in avoiding the usual responses that Shapiro correctly attributes to the second of the approaches he describes. This criterion is the inclusion of the most explicit accounts of liberalism across the full range of relevant theories. The most explicit version(s) of each kind of approach has a form that facilitates the elaboration and defence of its presuppositions. If liberalism has an adequate answer to the problem of its definition, one should expect to find it amongst its more explicit views. Accordingly, the sufficiency of the breadth of the 'class of problems' with which any particular author is concerned should itself be one of the reasons for choosing to examine one author's views rather than some other's. At the same time, since the views to be

---

25. Shapiro, *Political Criticism*, pp. 15-6. According to Shapiro, 'Volume one of Roberto Unger's *Politics* and Alasdair MacIntyre's *After Virtue* embody the first approach; Jürgen Habermas's *The Philosophical Discourse of Modernity* and Michael Sandel's use of Rawls as the central target for a critique of modern liberalism exemplify the second, Shapiro, *Political Criticism*, p. 16. Even within theoretical approaches that share substantially more than the above authors one finds both approaches taken up often with disappointing results. For example, we find both these approaches in feminist critiques of liberalism. The first approach is exemplified in the work of Moira Gatens, *Feminism and Philosophy: Perspectives on Difference and Equality*, Cambridge, Polity, 1991, see ch. 3. Others, like Alison Jagger (*Feminist Politics and Human Nature*) and Carole Pateman (*The Sexual Contract*), adopt the second approach but then face problems trying to show how and why their arguments have any broader application than to the specific works with which they deal extensively. Amongst defences of multiculturalism we find a similar difference. For example, compare the general approach of Tariq Modood, *Multiculturalism*, to Bikhu Parekh who focuses on the work of three liberals 'because they are among the most influential, stress different liberal principles and concentrate on different kinds of diversity': Parekh, *Rethinking Multiculturalism*, p. 80.

examined are taken to cover the full range of conceptual possibilities available to liberalism, if an adequate answer cannot be found amongst them, any claim that 'other formulations are more powerful' would need to raise objections at a fundamental level. In particular, in order to appeal to further formulations one would need to demonstrate that there is a *fundamental* flaw or omission in the proposed taxonomy of either or both the surface and deep structural levels of liberal discourse.

Unlike the approach Shapiro adopts, critical reconstructionism seeks to explain how its aspirations to conclusions that are general in scope can be realized. Since the criterion it employs—that used to select the specific theories that should form part of the reconstruction of liberalism's response to the problem of its definition—refers to *the full range* of available approaches, the satisfaction of this criterion can also supply critical reconstructionism with a sound basis for taking its conclusions to have sufficiently broad application.

It is this aspect of the methodology I adopt that differentiates my work from that of critics such as John Gray who argues that liberalism is self-defeating by generalizing from an examination of the views of a number of liberal theorists.[26] For the radical critic the possibility of drawing certain *inescapable* conclusions about the limits of liberal thought are very significant. Let me illustrate this point by reference to William Galston's response to an approach to critique like Gray's. Even though Galston accepts Gray's argument that liberalism cannot consistently endorse the priority of negative liberty and respect for value pluralism, no questions about the radical implications of this conclusion need be raised. Instead, it is open to Galston to defend a comprehensive view of 'liberal pluralism' by reformulating the liberal conception of negative liberty and showing how it may complement value pluralism.[27] The radical critic may well agree with Emanuela Ceva's review of Galston's reformulation that because it still relies on a 'liberal understanding of pluralism', it 'never goes beyond the safe boundaries of liberal thought'.[28] Nevertheless, the fact remains that a surface level critique such as Gray's does not produce compelling conclusions in so far as it leaves unexposed the deep structural dimensions of these 'safe boundaries'.

This brief discussion of the advantages of critical reconstructionism assumes that a successful challenge to liberalism—of the kind which argues that the problem of its definition cannot be resolved within its own conceptual terms as defined by its deep structure—should, and can, be advanced in the light of the full range of the conceptual approaches available to lib-

---

26. See John Gray, *Liberalisms: Essays in Political Philosophy*, London, Routledge, 1991.

27. William A. Galston, *Liberal Pluralism: The Implications of Value Pluralism for Political Theory and Practice*, Cambridge, Cambridge University Press, 2002.

28. Emanuela Ceva, 'Liberal Pluralism and Pluralist Liberalism', *Res Publica: A Journal of Legal and Social Philosophy*, vol. 11, no. 2, 2005, pp. 201-11.210.

eralism. In the next Chapter I will turn to a consideration of the purported scope of the idea—in the dual sense of concept and conception—of liberalism in order to determine this range.[29] However, I note here that should my argument fail to convince the reader of its strong claim to (be able to) cover the full range of approaches to defining liberalism, it may still prove of interest in so far as it covers an important range of approaches. The reconstruction of liberal theory 'in the form of a learning process', to adapt a phrase from Axel Honneth,[30] provides a different sort of grounding for such an admittedly weaker claim.

---

29. On the dual sense of an idea as concept and conception see Rawls, *Political Liberalism*, p. 14 fn. 5.

30. Honneth describes his own project of providing 'a reconstruction of the history of critical theory' in these terms in, Axel Honneth, *Critique of Power: Reflective Stages in a Critical Social Theory*, Cambridge, M.I.T. Press, 1991, p. xv.

4

The Critical Reconstruction of Liberalism

My aim in this chapter is to propose a taxonomy of liberal theories that meets the requirements set out in the previous chapter. To this end sections 4.1 and 4.2 respectively outline and defend the classification of liberal theories into three surface level approaches to defining liberalism. The three approaches are differentiated in accordance with the degree of complexity that they attribute to the idea of liberalism understood as a complex-structured concept. Section 4.3 sets out three basic claims regarding the dichotomous inter-relationship of the liberal abstract categories of publicness and privateness. These claims serve as principles for the parallel classification of liberal theories at the deep structural levels corresponding to the three surface level approaches to defining liberalism. After explaining the relationship between the respective deep structures of the three approaches to defining liberalism I will conclude this chapter with a few words about the selection of works that will be the focus of Parts II and III of the book.

4.1 Three approaches to the problem of liberalism's definition

At the surface level, liberal theorists' accounts of liberalism may differ in two related but distinct respects that have to do with the purported scope of the idea. The first concerns what is presented as the appropriate *subject matter* of liberalism. The object of liberal philosophical inquiry (hereafter 'the theorized object') is sometimes taken to be the nature of political relations between human beings qua contractors, rights bearers or sources of moral value (hereafter 'the theorized subject'). At other times more weight has been placed on determining the role and powers of specific institutions like government or on the question of the nature of the justifiedness of the basic structure of political society. For example, in order to escape the objection that his principles of justice do not adequately reflect persons' moral outlook, Rawls insists that his theorized object is not individual persons but the basic institutional structure (PL, Lecture VII). These are differences of focus that may well be crucial for the defence or critical evaluation of a specific theory but they are not particularly useful as a guide for ordering approaches to the problem of liberalism's definition. This is because accounts of liberalism are not necessarily given in terms of their *exclusive* focus on the subject matter discussed. Indeed, liberal theorists sometimes re-describe the subject matter that their account of liberalism addresses while remaining essentially committed to one account. The reason for this is that an account of liberalism given in terms of a thesis concerning one of the above mentioned points of focus may involve a corresponding thesis concerning another in terms of which the account might also have been given. Ronald Dworkin's work on liberalism is a case in point.[1]

The second respect in which attempts to deal with the problem of liberalism's definition may differ concerns a different aspect of the purported scope of the idea of liberalism. This has to do with the complexity of the structure given to the meaning of the idea itself as distinct from the range of social phenomena to which the idea purports to relate. Now, if we take the idea of liberalism to be a 'complex-structured concept' in the sense explained in Chapter 2 (2.2.1), then we should treat the relationships obtaining among the different senses of such concepts as systematic rather than bearing a family resemblance. Leaving open the question of the precise nature of the relationship between the idea of liberalism and the social phenomena to which it is related—in Chapter 1.1.4 we saw that liberal theorists differ on whether or not they endorse or, at least, implicitly work with a representational view of language—we can specify differences in the complexity of the structure given to the meaning of the idea of liberalism by describing three basic approaches to defining liberalism. For this description we will draw upon and reformulate some of the claims that liberal theorists have made about liberalism without at the same time ascribing to any of them either an express attempt to address the problem of liberalism's definition or a commitment to the three distinct approaches. It is also worth noting here that the three proposed surface level approaches to defining liberalism cut across other distinctions as between liberals/libertarians; liberal individualists/communitarian liberals; and individual/group rights advocates.[2]

---

1. See Nicolacopoulos, *In Memory of a Vision, Volume 2*.

2. On the first distinction see Philip Pettit, *Republicanism: A Theory of Freedom and Government*, Oxford, Oxford University Press, 1997, p. 10. On the latter two distinctions see Will Kymlicka (ed.), *The Rights of Minority Cultures*, Oxford, Oxford University Press, 1995, pp. 1-30, Will

4.1.1 The limited political thesis approach to defining liberalism

Let us begin with the least complex of the three concepts that define the idea of liberalism. This is what I will call 'the limited political thesis approach to defining liberalism'. We can begin to formulate this approach by drawing on Allen E. Buchanan's definition of liberalism 'as a minimal political philosophy or, more precisely, as a single thesis about the proper scope and limits of the power of the state'.[3] Buchanan presents this focus on state power as a 'strategy' for responding to the communitarian critiques of the time. He suggests that if we identify the distinguishing feature of liberalism as a political thesis about state power taken apart from its possible 'justificatory frameworks', then liberalism's potential appeal to both individualists and communitarians is assured.[4] As will become evident below, to distinguish so generally between political theses, on the one hand, and their justificatory grounds, on the other, is to conflate two further approaches to defining liberalism both of which include justificatory frameworks. Still, Buchanan's isolation of a *political thesis* captures something important about the idea of liberalism. A commitment to some number of specific political positions is often associated with liberalism, whether as characteristics attributable to liberals or to their theories. For example, in one of his best essays on liberalism, Ronald Dworkin identifies liberals as being predisposed to deplore great inequalities of wealth, to think of rights to civil liberties as 'trumps' and to be tolerant concerning matters of personal morality. In other words, they value equality, liberty and tolerance or official neutrality. Dworkin suggests that amongst liberals these are 'instinctive' commitments; they are 'aspects of character as well as habits of thought'.[5] In a similar vein, Thomas Nagel identifies two moral impulses amongst liberals. One is to look favourably on placing limits on governmental restrictions to the liberties of individuals and the other is hostility to the state's imposition of status inequalities.[6] John Rawls explains that his conception of justice is 'broadly liberal in character' meaning three things:

> first, it specifies certain basic rights, liberties, and opportunities (of the kind familiar from constitutional democratic regimes); second, it assigns a special priority to these rights, liberties, and opportunities, especially with respect to claims of the general good and of perfectionist values; and third, it affirms measures assuring all citizens adequate all-purpose

---

Kymlicka and Wayne Norman (eds.), *Citizenship in Diverse Societies*, Oxford, Oxford University Press, 2000, pp. 1-44.

3. Buchanan, 'Assessing the Communitarian Critique of Liberalism', p. 853.

4. Buchanan, 'Assessing the Communitarian Critique of Liberalism', p. 853.

5. Ronald Dworkin, 'Foundations of Liberal Equality', in Grethe B. Peterson (ed.), *The Tanner Lectures on Human Values*, vol. 11, Salt Lake City, University of Utah Press, 1990, pp. 1-119, pp. 9-10.

6. Nagel, 'Rawls and Liberalism'.

means to make effective use of their basic liberties and opportunities (PL, p. 223).[7]

Whilst characterizing liberalism in something like the above terms is necessary for what I have called a limited political thesis approach, it is not sufficient. What is distinctive about this approach is that in confining the idea of liberalism to a certain thesis consisting of a (number of) proposition(s) it thereby *excludes* from the scope of the idea the reasons that might be given in support of such proposition(s). It, therefore, claims to be neutral on the question of the kinds of justificatory frameworks that might accompany liberalism qua a set of political theses. This is not to say that the approach entails that the merits of different proposed justifications cannot be assessed. The point is only that on this approach to undertake this sort of evaluative exercise is independent of what liberalism *is* and, consequently, so too are the products of such an exercise. So, the limited political thesis approach to defining liberalism implicitly treats *differently structured justificatory grounds* as being on a par vis a vis the definition of liberalism.

Taken as a whole neither the work of Rawls nor that of Dworkin exemplifies the limited political thesis approach given that each offers its interpretation of the propositions referred to above in the light of an elaboration of what the theorist takes to be *the appropriate kind* of justificatory grounds.[8] In contrast to these two writers, even though he does not present his view of liberalism in these terms, Richard Rorty's idea of 'post modernist bourgeois liberalism' and his view of a 'liberal utopia' inhabited by 'liberal ironists' exemplify the limited political thesis approach. By eschewing any reference to a theoretical justification of liberalism *within* liberal political discourse,[9] Rorty's view of liberalism is thereby restricted to its political theses. Notice that I am not claiming that the limited political thesis approach merely *denies* the need for justificatory grounds. Instead, to advocate this denial, as Rorty's account of liberal discourse does, constitutes the *most explicit* way of excluding justificatory grounds from the idea of liberalism. In other words, Rorty's denial satisfies the requirement of exclusion in the most vivid terms.

4.1.2 The minimal political morality approach to defining liberalism

The limited political thesis approach expresses the least complex of the pos-

---

7. See also Kymlicka who describes liberalism as giving priority to the basic liberties where the basic liberties are understood as the standard civil and political rights recognized in liberal democracies and priority refers to the restriction of liberty only for the sake of liberty. For Kymlicka's list of what he takes to be distinctively liberal propositions see Will Kymlicka, *Contemporary Political Philosophy: An Introduction*, Oxford, Oxford University Press, 1989.

8. I demonstrate this claim in connection with Rawls in Part III of the book and in connection with Dworkin in *In Memory of a Vision, Volume 2*.

9. Rorty, *Contingency, Irony, and Solidarity*, p. xv. See also Richard Rorty, 'Postmodernist Bourgeois Liberalism', *The Journal Of Philosophy*, vol. 80, no. 10, 1983, pp. 583-9.

sible structures that may be attributed to the idea of liberalism. The second approach that I will call 'the minimal political morality approach' builds on the structure of the first one. It incorporates into the scope of its view of liberalism *moral grounds* in support of its political theses. In this context moral grounds are to be understood, firstly, as *reasons concerning the appropriate treatment of persons by moral agents*, that is, concerning the needs, ambitions and interests they all have in their capacity *as persons*. Moral grounds are to be understood as referring to reasons that have *categorical force* but they do not include what I will be referring to as 'ethical reasons'. These are reasons concerning determinate conceptions of well-being such as specific self-interested preferences and ideals of living well.[10]

Although more complex than the limited political thesis approach, in that it is not confined to the mere specification of a political thesis, this second approach nevertheless also restricts the scope of the idea of liberalism. However, it does so by being selective about the type of moral ground that can be included in a definition. In particular, the minimal political morality approach distinguishes in a distinctive way between *public and private morality* and confines the scope of liberalism to specific claims concerning what it treats as matters of public morality. Notice that this is not the same as saying that the minimal political morality approach is defined by a commitment to what is usually referred to as the priority of the right over the good, the view, as Dworkin puts it, that 'liberalism itself takes no view about what a good life is but only stipulates the principles of a just society, leaving it to other theories or disciplines to imagine what living well in such a society would be'.[11] To be sure, some versions of liberalism that defend an interpretation of the priority of the right over the good exemplify this approach in so far as they treat the idea of the good as a matter of private morality and, in doing so, place it beyond the scope of the idea of liberalism. Even so, the exclusionary aspect of the minimal political morality approach need not be expressed in terms of a priority relation between the ideas of rightness and goodness. For

---

10. On the distinction between moral and ethical reasons see Dworkin, 'Foundations of Liberal Equality', pp. 8-9 & 23-5. Here, Dworkin also draws a distinction between broad and narrow uses of the term 'ethics'. The former refers to both moral questions about how to live well and to questions of well-being, namely 'how we should live to make good lives for ourselves'. The latter is restricted to matters concerning *well-being*. I will follow Dworkin in the usage of these terms indicating narrow and broad senses of 'ethics' when appropriate. Throughout the book I assume neither that ethical theory is prior to normative political theory (and to the political organization of society) nor that the latter is a relatively autonomous sphere of reflection. Since, as Robert P. Wolff has demonstrated (in his 'Introduction' to Robert Paul Wolff (ed.), *Political Man and Social Man: Readings in Political Philosophy*, New York, Random House, 1966, pp. 10-1.), both these positions about the relationship of ethics to normative political theory are historically represented in liberal thought, I assess theories that endorse each of them, without assuming the correctness of one of them.

11. Dworkin, 'Foundations of Liberal Equality', p. 4.

example, Rawls advocates the priority of certain liberties but he also maintains that his conception of political liberalism rests on a *political* idea of the good (PL, p. 176).

This said, there are two different ways in which the minimal political morality approach's incorporated moral ground(s) may be constituted as public: (1) through the elaboration of some foundational idea grounding liberal political morality; or (2) through the elaboration of a political morality made up of acceptable/reasonable, as distinct from true, propositions. As we will see in Parts II and III of the book, a number of prominent accounts of liberalism fall within this group. These include Will Kymlicka's foundationalism, the contractualism of Jeremy Waldron and the versions of political liberalism proposed by Charles Larmore and John Rawls.[12]

4.1.3 The comprehensive approach to defining liberalism

Both the minimal political morality approach and the limited political thesis approach to defining liberalism have at least in part emerged in response to what have been perceived to be the weaknesses of liberalism understood as a 'comprehensive approach'. It is worth noting, however, that although the versions of liberalism that exemplify this third approach are more often attributed to classical and nineteenth century liberalism as well as to critics of liberalism, a number of contemporary liberal theorists maintain that only some version of a comprehensive view of liberalism is ultimately defensible. Ronald Dworkin's account of liberalism in the *Tanner Lectures* is a case in point.[13]

We can present a clear statement of what the comprehensive approach involves by drawing on John Rawls' general discussion of comprehensive conceptions in *Political Liberalism*. Of course, Rawls is not interested in defining liberalism as a comprehensive conception. Rather he discusses the general nature of comprehensive conceptions in order to distinguish from them the moral grounds underpinning his own version of liberalism. Still, his comments are instructive. For Rawls a moral conception is comprehensive:

> when it includes conceptions of what is of value in human life, and ideals of personal character, as well as ideals of friendship and of familial and associational relationships, and much else that is to inform our conduct, and in the limit to our life as a whole. A conception is fully comprehensive if it covers all recognized values and virtues within one rather precisely

---

12. See Larmore, 'Political Liberalism', Rawls, *Political Liberalism*, Waldron, 'Theoretical Foundations of Liberalism'. Taken in abstraction from his later work in his *Tanner Lectures*, Dworkin's early statements of 'liberal equality' falls into this category as well. Compare Dworkin's 'Liberalism' and 'Why Liberals Should Care about Equality' (chs. 8 & 9) in Dworkin, *A Matter of Principle*.

13. For further examples see: William A. Galston, *Liberal Purposes: Goods, Virtues, and Diversity in the Liberal State*, Cambridge, Cambridge University Press, 1991, Galston, *Liberal Pluralism*, Rasmussen and Den Uyl, *Liberty and Nature: An Aristotelian Defense of Liberal Order*.

articulated system (PL, p. 13).

So, a comprehensive moral conception need not be confined to a *public* morality and it may deal with ethical questions in the broad sense of this term.

Rawls also distinguishes comprehensiveness from *generality* of application, that is, from 'the range of subjects to which a conception applies'. Whereas a 'moral conception is general if it applies to a wide range of subjects, and in the limit to all subjects universally', the 'subjects' in question may range, as is the case with the principle of utility, 'from the conduct of individuals and personal relations to the organization of society as a whole as well as to the law of peoples'. Linking the 'content' of a conception with what is required by the breadth of the range of subjects to which it applies, Rawls suggests further that the more *general* a conception is, in the above sense, the more *comprehensive* it is likely to be. He does this in the context of making the point that while many 'moral doctrines' aspire to both these dimensions of scope, it is possible for a moral conception, such as his own idea of 'political liberalism', to be neither general nor comprehensive (whether relatively or fully) (PL, p. 13).

This description of *comprehensiveness* is useful in explaining what is involved in a comprehensive approach to defining liberalism. However, two clarifications are in order. First, it is not necessary to associate the idea of a comprehensive view of liberalism with Rawls' suggestions regarding the relationship between comprehensiveness and generality. As I am presenting it, the comprehensive approach to defining liberalism leaves open the possibility that some version of liberalism may be both general, in Rawls' sense, and a version of the minimal political morality approach rather than of the comprehensive approach. Indeed, I want to proceed on the working hypothesis that the relationship between an account's specification of its subject matter and the level of complexity that it implies about the idea of liberalism is not a strict one. In other words, specific instances of all three approaches to defining liberalism—the limited political thesis, minimal political morality and comprehensive approaches—may or may not be general with respect to their subject matter. Second, we should not understand the references to 'values' and 'ideals' as limiting the scope of liberalism to the *moral* domain narrowly understood. In other words, the comprehensive approach should be taken to leave open the possibility that the values and ideals that make up some particular version of liberalism may be prudential or strategic, and that ontological, as well as moral and ethical, claims may be involved. So, the comprehensive approach to defining liberalism places no restrictions on the kinds of justificatory grounds it deems to fall within the scope of the idea of liberalism. In this respect it is potentially all-inclusive.

4.2 Determining the full range of approaches

The arrangement and examination of accounts of liberalism in accordance with the above three approaches is intended to ensure that we are in a position to address the full range of conceptual possibilities. The approaches are distinguished by reference to different theories' understandings of the *internal structure* of liberalism as a complex-structured concept. This structure refers both to the ways in which various (kinds of) ideas are included and inter-related in a theory as well as to the rationale underlying any exclusion of ideas. Each of the three approaches to defining liberalism is identified by reference to the degree of complexity it requires for the structure of the idea of liberalism and together the three approaches cover the spectrum from least to most complex. Thus accounts of liberalism grouped together as exemplifying any one approach share a basic internal structure, as distinct from merely adopting a similar position on (one of) the themes with which the theories may be concerned and the three approaches are inter-related so as to cover the full range of possibilities.

To illustrate the difference just mentioned—between a taxonomy that relies on the identification of the internal structure of theories and an arrangement of different theories in accordance with their treatment of some theme(s)—compare the taxonomy I propose to William Galston's apparently similar observations about the current variety of approaches to liberalism:

> Broadly speaking, three quite distinct approaches to liberalism have emerged in the past generation. At one end of the spectrum we find *perfectionist* liberalism—the thesis that liberalism finds its justification, and its point, in a distinctive vision of the human good. [...]
>
> At the other end of the spectrum lies what may be called *pragmatic* liberalism—the thesis that liberalism can be understood as an agreement struck by symmetrically situated, self-interested individuals animated solely by prudential or strategic considerations. [...]
>
> Between these two views lies what Charles Larmore has called *political* liberalism. [... To quote Larmore's summary, political liberalism] 'is a conception at once *moral* and *minimal*. It holds that the liberal principle of political neutrality toward controversial ideals of the good life finds its justification in certain moral commitments. But it also claims that these commitments are themselves compatible with a wide range of ideals of the good life'.[14]

On the face of it, there is some similarity between Galston's scheme and the one I have proposed. For instance, both describe an approach to liberalism mid-way across the spectrum that each identifies (partly or wholly) by refer-

---

14. Galston, *Liberal Purposes*, pp. 98-9.

ence to the role played by certain kinds of moral reasons in theories exemplifying that approach. Indeed, the minimal political morality approach includes what Galston, following Larmore, calls *political liberalism*.

However, points of overlap aside, the two schemes illustrate quite different organizational methods and this is evident on closer examination of the way in which the spectrum to which Galston refers is worked out. Notice, firstly, differences in views as to the role that moral and ethical ideas play in liberal theories determine his presentation of the approaches to liberalism, the two extremes of the spectrum being respectively characterized by the presence and absence of a determinate vision of the human good. Thus Galston's description of the three approaches to liberalism says nothing about the nature and/or proper role of metaphysical assumptions in liberal theories. As it stands, it leaves unclear their significance, if any, leaving open the possibility that differences amongst liberal theories on these questions are not relevant to an understanding of liberalism. It also does not mention those versions of liberalism that exemplify the limited political thesis approach. Such versions do not appeal to moral considerations yet they also cannot easily fall in with Galston's description of the *pragmatic* approach given that their view of liberalism in terms of a strictly political thesis equally excludes from their frame of reference strategic and self-interested reasons.

The point here is not to reject Galston's scheme since focusing on a particular theme over which liberal discourse has been divided may well be adequate to Galston's purposes.[15] Rather, I want to highlight the inadequacy of any such scheme for a critical reconstructive project that has radical aspirations of the kind I outlined in the previous chapters. One reason for this is the fact that we might draw upon any one of a number of themes in liberal discourse for the purposes of identifying differences amongst liberals. For example, we might just as easily order liberal theories in accordance with the view they take on the relationship between the ideals of individual freedom and the proper role of government. One could place theories that conceive of individual freedom and the role of government in negative terms at one extreme and those that conceive of freedom as an expression of a genuine ethical order at the other extreme thereby enabling other possibilities, such as the combination of a view of freedom from inhibiting circumstances or a positive view of freedom with a view of (limited) government interventionism, to occupy the middle ground. Another way of identifying the

---

15. In *Liberal Purposes* Galston reviews current approaches to liberalism as part of his attempt to elaborate a conception of liberalism that represents what he describes as a 'third way' of dealing with the themes that have emerged in the liberalism-antiliberalism debates about the role of theories of the human good in defences of a liberal order. He describes this 'third way' as 'a nonneutral, substantive liberalism committed to its own distinctive conception of the good, broadly (though not boundlessly) respectful of diversity and supported by its own canon of the virtues', Galston, *Liberal Purposes*, pp. 43-4.

spectrum might be to focus on different formulations of a commitment to the value of equal respect.[16] Yet another way is to focus on liberals' different formulations of the division of the social order in terms of spheres of limited (public) government and of an extensive (private) society.[17] In an inquiry of the kind I am proposing, if we were to organize the theories to be investigated in accordance with one theme, the availability of a number of such 'theme-centred' ways of identifying the variety of approaches to liberalism would inevitably give rise to the irresolvable problem of producing a non-arbitrary criterion for prioritizing one of them. This is because liberal writings are typically theme-centred.

In contrast to any scheme derived from theme-centred thinking, the scheme I have proposed faces no such methodological problems. In addition, it is able to identify some important lines of continuity amongst theories that a theme-centred scheme renders invisible. These are continuities underlying the sorts of differences to which Galston's scheme draws attention and the former can be expressed without having to ignore the latter. For example, in so far as they explicitly rely on some (different) view of human nature to ground their respective claims, theories that fall under the headings of *pragmatic* and *perfectionist* liberalisms, the two extremes of Galston's scheme, would instead fall into respective sub-groups within the broader, comprehensive approach to liberalism that I have identified. My scheme is able to highlight the fact that such (otherwise very different) versions of liberalism share in, and implicitly endorse the appropriateness of, the tendency explicitly to appeal to metaphysical claims. It also highlights the fact that they do not presuppose the exclusion of certain types of reason from those with which the idea of liberalism is, can or should be concerned.

4.3 The deep structure of approaches to the problem of defining liberalism

Parallel to the three surface level approaches to defining liberalism just outlined, there are three corresponding deep structural formulations of the public-private dichotomy. Each of the formulations offers what I will be referring to as a 'basic claim'. The basic claim (hereafter 'BC') of the deep structure corresponding to each of the three approaches to defining liberalism represents the mode of the inter-relationship of its basic categories, publicness and privateness, in the form of a principle. In the case of each basic claim, this principle represents the mode of the inter-relationship of the basic categories *within* the domain, in the sense of a field of operation, given by the scope of the idea of liberalism, as this scope is determined at the surface

---

16. See, for example, Douglas MacLean and Claudia Mills (eds.), *Liberalism Reconsidered*, Totowa, Rowman & Allanheld, 1983, p. ix.

17. Thomas A. Spragens Jr., for one, takes a commitment to this division to unite liberals, see Spragens, 'Reconstructing Liberal Theory: Reason and Liberal Culture', p. 38.

level. Yet the principle also defines *the boundaries* of this domain by the exclusions it implies. In this section I will explain these ideas by outlining the specifics of the basic claim of the deep structure corresponding to each of the three approaches to defining liberalism in turn. I will then outline the relationship *between* the basic claims in order, firstly, to indicate how and why they can be placed in an order of progression from less to more adequate formulations of liberalism's deep structural commitment to the public-private dichotomy; and, secondly, to outline how the idea of intrinsically private agency runs through them and why uncovering the role of this idea can ultimately result in the justified rejection of liberal theory and, with it, of the inquiring practice that generates it.

4.3.1 The basic claim that publicness is the only basic category

First, the basic claim of the deep structure corresponding to the limited political thesis approach represents the mode of the inter-relationship of its basic categories in terms of the principle that *there is only one basic category, the public*. Let us call this principle 'LBC' to represent the link between BC, the basic claim, and the limited political thesis approach. This principle gives expression to the *dominance* of the category of publicness within the domain given by the scope of the idea of liberalism. Even though it refers to only one of the basic categories, it still offers a formulation of the mode of their *inter-relationship*. This is because in defining the boundaries of its domain in terms of the category of publicness, the principle implies that the relationship of the basic categories is one in which privateness is altogether excluded. Accordingly, LBC is no less a principle specifying the public-private dichotomy.

4.3.2 The basic claim that one basic category plays the defining role in their inter-relationship

Second, the basic claim of the deep structure corresponding to the minimal political morality approach represents the mode of the inter-relationship of its basic categories in terms of the principle that *one basic category plays the defining role in their inter-relationship*. This principle, let us call it 'MBC', gives expression to the basic categories' relationship of *primacy* within the domain given by the scope of the idea of liberalism. (I will refer to this simply as 'categorial primacy'.) The idea of categorial primacy refers to an oppositional relationship between the two basic categories in which (1) they are both mutually exclusive and mutually exhaustive; and (2) one of them is positively defined whilst the other is defined only in its (negative) relationship to the first. One of the two categories is, therefore, given priority over the other in their definition. Accordingly, within the domain given by the scope of the idea of liberalism the basic categories are hierarchically related in virtue of the positive defining role of one category over the other. MBC is, therefore, open to a range of interpretations depending on which of the basic categories is positioned as primary and how this is secured. In defining the boundaries of its domain in terms of categorial primacy, the principle also implies that the inter-relationship of the basic categories is one that altogether excludes non-dichotomous categorial inter-relationships. Accordingly, MBC is a principle that champions the public-private dichotomy.

4.3.3 The basic claim that whereas the basic categories appear as dichotomously related, they are mutually defining.

Finally, the basic claim of the deep structure corresponding to the comprehensive approach represents the mode of the inter-relationship of its basic categories in terms of the following principle: *whereas the basic categories appear as dichotomously related, they are mutually defining*. This principle, let us call it 'CBC', gives expression to the *appearance* of the basic categories' relationship of primacy within the domain covered by the scope of the idea of liberalism. However, CBC also gives expression to the basic categories' inter-relationship in the supposed non-dichotomous terms of *complementarity* that their mutually defining roles indicate. Accordingly, within the domain given by the scope of the idea of liberalism the basic categories are supposed to be symmetrically related in virtue of their mutual defining roles and they have only the appearance of a categorial relationship of primacy. In defining the boundaries of its domain in terms of categorial complementarity, the principle also implies that the inter-relationship of the basic categories is (potentially) an all-inclusive one given that the basic categories are still mutually exclusive. Accordingly, CBC is a principle that dissolves the public-private dichotomy in favour of a relationship of difference.

4.3.4 The relationship between the three basic claims

The above remarks suffice to introduce the basic claim characterizing the deep structure of each of the three approaches to the problem of defining liberalism. If my explanatory hypothesis is sound—if liberal theories function on both the surface and deep structural levels as outlined—each formulation of the basic claim offers a way for liberal theory, were it fully self-aware, to frame a theory of its own activity of inquiry. As we saw in the previous chapters, this is a requirement of *immanent* radical critique. Each of the three formulations of the basic claim offers a view of the public-private dichotomy that, in turn, suggests a different way of understanding liberal inquiring practice. In the first, the dichotomy *marks the boundary* of the domain of the idea of liberalism; in the second the dichotomy is *located within* this domain; and in the third it constitutes *the appearance* rather than the complete reality of this domain.

Whilst each formulation of the basic claim offers a different account of liberal inquiring practice, these formulations do not represent equally defensible ways of engaging in this practice. Whereas MBC offers a richer understanding of liberal dichotomous thought as compared to LBC, the same can be said for CBC as compared to both MBC and LBC. Indeed the transition from one principle to the next can be shown to accord with the successful resolution of an epistemological crisis faced by what amounts to a relatively inferior, because too restrictive, principle.[18]

As my earlier outline of the critical reconstructionist method would suggest (3.3), a demonstration of the relative inferiority of LBC and MBC could be achieved by showing that the deep structures of theories embodying their respective principles collapse due to their inconsistent commitments. What is the significance of such a demonstration? Here it is worth bearing in mind that if the explanatory hypothesis is sound, then it is the, albeit unrecognized, *co-presence* of the two levels of discourse that will expose the incoherence of particular liberal theories. Yet I do not want to suggest that the demonstration of incoherence, and its related critique of the limits of a theory's deep structure, might lead *the liberal theorist*—one who engages in inquiry only at the surface level without recognizing this to be one of two distinct levels of liberal discourse—to abandon commitment to liberalism's familiar surface level inquiries. For the liberal, acceptance of the critique of a particular theory may result in attempts at more defensible reformulation(s) of liberalism's surface level response to the problem of its definition in accordance with the liberal theorist's surface level view of justification. This is because the explanatory hypothesis that is tested in an inquiry of the kind undertaken in Parts II and III of the book does not assert that liberal theory fails *merely contingently* to recognize that the deep structure of liberal inquiring practice plays an organizing role, or even *some* role, in liberal theory. Instead the hypothesis to be explored is that this non-recognition is itself a constitutive feature of liberalism. If the specific characteristics of the deep structure of liberal theories derive from the pre-reflective intrinsically private identity of the liberal theorist—a claim that we must attempt to assess—and, regardless of the degree of their contextualism, universalizing liberalisms deny that the theorist's identity is implicated in the theory then, even when the deep structure of a particular liberal theory is rendered visible and the theory's incoherence exposed, the liberal theorist *qua liberal* cannot fully recognize the presence and role of its deep structure.

It follows from the above that the assessment of LBC, MBC and CBC and, indeed, their treatment in a line of rational progression will have significance from the standpoint of the radical critic. As explained in Chapter 1, this standpoint is constituted by an *abstract* awareness of the cultural force of intrinsically private agency and this is the standpoint from which to address the question of whether liberal theory can coherently embody such

---

18. I defend this claim in Nicolacopoulos, *In Memory of a Vision, Volume 2*.

awareness. This awareness informs the dialectical questioning that I undertake in the inquiry as a whole. Now, even if the deep structure of a particular liberal theory can be shown to collapse due to its inconsistent reliance on an unacknowledged view of intrinsically private agency, the question of liberal theory's potential adequately to embody the awareness of intrinsically private agency is not thereby resolved. Unless *the very idea* of intrinsically private agency is also exhaustively assessed this idea cannot justifiably be abandoned along with the theory's particular mode of deep structural dichotomous thought. This is because from the outset of the inquiry the radical critic has the abstract notion in mind rather than any one of its concrete articulations as might be discovered in particular liberal theories. The abstract idea of intrinsically private agency supplies the critic's rationale for continuing the inquiry into more adequate forms of its representation in liberal theory. This process of inquiry ends justifiably when the negative assessment of some particular theory also exhausts the possibilities for a reformulated account of the concrete embodiment of intrinsically private agency.

We can now formulate the central substantive thesis of my critique of liberalism as follows. Irrespective of the differentiated modes of liberal dichotomous thought—LBC, MBC and CBC—the liberal theorist's unacknowledged and ultimately unjustifiable privileging of intrinsically private agency is what constitutes liberal inquiring practice. The purpose of our examination of liberal theories then is to determine whether the practice of unjustifiably privileging intrinsically private agency at a deep structural level is what makes liberal theory liberal and, relatedly, what makes the liberal theorist, liberal (hereafter 'the main argument of the study').

4.4 Selecting exemplary versions of the three approaches to defining liberalism

In the previous chapter I suggested that in order to recognize the internal and comparative complexity of specific accounts of liberalism a critical reconstruction of liberal theory calls, firstly, for a taxonomy of approaches to the problem of liberalism's definition and, secondly, for the use of this taxonomy as a basis for developing a critique of exemplary versions. Having proposed a taxonomy, we are now in a position to address the second of these tasks, the defence of the main argument of the study through the detailed examination of exemplary versions of the three approaches. To this end Parts II and III of the book are devoted to just such an examination of exemplary versions of the minimal political morality approach to defining liberalism. *In Memory of a Vision, Volume 2* assesses this approach in association with the other two approaches to defining liberalism and demonstrates the claim that together the three approaches embody the three modes of liberal dichotomous thought, LBC, MBC and CBC, representing a logical progression from the least to the most complex. This said, are there any methodological implications flowing from the fact that we begin the critique of exemplary versions of the three approaches with the minimal political morality approach, the approach that is neither the least nor the most complex of the three identified? The decision to present the critical evaluation of the minimal political morality approach ahead of the limited political thesis approach has no troubling methodological implications since the critique of each approach must rely upon criteria of adequacy that are not merely internal to liberal theory generally but must be specifically internal to the specific approach under consideration, as well as to the specific account of liberalism within the approach in question.

Indeed, the demands of an immanent critique in the terms we have outlined extend to the very question of determining the relative superiority of each of the three approaches. Let me illustrate this point by reference to the minimal political morality approach. Its adherents typically claim that their theories are particularly suited to the aspirations of universalist liberal philosophy (in the sense explained in Chapter 1) under the modern conditions of pluralism. That is, they purport to supply a way of demonstrating the justifiedness of a liberal order without ignoring the nature and implications of a pluralist culture. Indeed, John Rawls goes so far as to apply a 'principle of toleration' to political philosophy itself and, by implication, to the presence of competing approaches to the problem of defining liberalism as well (PL, p. 10). If Rawls' theory can withstand the test of radical critique, then it should be possible for the minimal political morality approach that his theory exemplifies to account for and accommodate the other two approaches. Part III of the book aims to put the minimal political morality approach to this test via an exploration of the capacity of Rawls' theory to meet its own adequacy criteria. This said, in conformity with the demands of the main argument of the study (4.3), Volume 2 aims to show just how the dialectical relationship between the three approaches works to reveal the ways in which each relatively more complex approach can be represented as a response to the epistemological crisis that the relatively less complex approach faces.

Now, the radical critique of the minimal political morality approach to defining liberalism is necessary, even if not sufficient, for the main argument. That is, assuming for the moment that, taken as a whole, Ronald Dworkin's work on liberalism does indeed exemplify the comprehensive approach, we could not still focus exclusively on this theory presupposing that it represents the most advanced version of liberalism. For no matter how successful the critique of any comprehensive view of liberalism might be, it would not demonstrate that the minimal political morality approach to defining liberalism must also be flawed. The success of the argument calls no less for a demonstration of the *relative inferiority* of the least complex approach. The same holds not only for each of the three approaches but, as we will see in Part II, for the distinct *versions* of the minimal political morality approach—the versions arising from the range of interpretations available for MBC depending on the positioning of the basic categories (4.3.2).

Let us turn finally to the selection of material. Why focus specifically on the textual material selected? Published in the latter half of the previous century, the texts that I will examine represent works that belong to a formative period in the development of late twentieth century Anglophone liberalism. They largely precede works that contextualize the themes of liberalism by raising such questions as the nature of multicultural citizenship, the accommodation of cultural diversity and even liberalism's relationship to questions of global justice. There are two reasons for concentrating on this work. My focus on the development of liberal ideas in the post-World War II period is the result of a deliberate attempt to allow for the legacy of logical positivism. I take the view that due to its influence on Anglophone liberal theorizing it is no longer possible to take it for granted that political philosophy should or needs to be informed by some view of human nature or of human flourishing. The questioning of the relationship, if any, between metaphysical claims and the elaboration of political ideas has been facilitated by the logical positivist legacy as explained in Chapter 1.2.1. It is this questioning that has, in turn, facilitated the emergence and identification of exemplary versions of the three approaches to defining liberalism. Accordingly, I make my selection of particular theories from within what we can call the post-logical positivist period.

At the same time, the most explicit formulations of the three approaches (and the distinct versions within these) emerge at a time in this formative period when the question of liberalism's ability to accommodate the value of community is also at issue. Whilst the theories that I will be examining are variously (potentially) community-sensitive, I did not select the material based on whether or not it addresses the value of community. The reason for selecting material that accords with a broadly communitarian liberalism but does not deal at all with what liberals have to say about the relationship of individuality to community has already been suggested in Chapter 1.1.4. Since community-sensitive liberalisms purport to accommodate the values of community and individuality in non-oppositional terms, if any one of them satisfactorily resolves the problem of liberalism's definition then it should have the conceptual resources to offer a defensible communitarian discourse (in a way that liberal individualism will not). Whether or not a theory is capable of offering a defensible view of community depends in part on whether it can offer a satisfactory answer to the problem of liberalism's definition. But this relationship of dependence cannot be reversed. Whether or not a theory can offer an adequate solution to the problem of liberalism's definition cannot be made to depend on an assessment of a theory's specific conceptualization of community without falling into the general problems faced by those who aspire to the radical critique of liberalism. (On this recall the relevant discussion of Chapter 2.1.) With these words of clarification I now turn to the detailed investigation of the minimal political morality approach to defining liberalism.

part II

Liberalism as a Minimal Political Morality

Part II of the book is devoted to an examination of three exemplary versions of the minimal political morality approach to defining liberalism. We find these in a selection of works by prominent liberal theorists, Will Kymlicka, Jeremy Waldron and Charles Larmore. Each of the selected works exemplifies a *distinct* version of the minimal political morality approach as well as a different interpretation of the basic claim that one of liberalism's basic categories plays the defining role in their inter-relation at a deep structural level. Together with John Rawls' account of political liberalism, the fourth version of the minimal political morality approach that is the focus of Part III of the book, these theories represent four different responses to the problem of liberalism's definition.

This raises the question why is it necessary to examine four exemplars of the same approach? Why not concentrate on the theory judged to be the most sophisticated amongst these? The need to consider all four derives from the fact that the specific grounds for rejecting each one of them play a role in establishing the main argument of the study. That is, we need to establish that, despite variations in the surface level claims of the theories and in their corresponding formulations of the public-private dichotomy, a commitment to the theorizing subject's intrinsically private identity not only remains constant throughout but also cannot coherently sustain itself. Although, as we will see, Rawls' theory exemplifies the most complete model of four possible *interpretations* of MBC, I could not defend my claim regarding the incoherence of the minimal political morality approach by going directly to a detailed assessment of the version that Rawls' theory exemplifies. Since the relative superiority of Rawls' theory rests on its explicit recognition of the distinct presence of the theorist in the process of theory construction, the critique I develop against Rawls should be capable of being repeated against other liberal theories that embody *the same* interpretation of MBC. But the fundamental flaw that my critique attributes to this version of the minimal political morality approach does not have any critical force whatsoever against the other available interpretations of MBC. This is why I need to demonstrate that these other versions constitute *relatively inferior* interpretations of this formulation of the public-private dichotomy. In the absence of this demonstration it is still open to the liberal theorist who defends a version that insists on the theorist's completely detached and disinterested reflective standpoint to claim that Rawls creates problems for the minimal political morality approach in so far as he mistakenly insists on situating the theorizing subject in relation to the theorized object.

5

Will Kymlicka: Liberalism and Foundational Ideas

Amongst the theories that take liberalism to be defined by a commitment to some foundational idea those focusing on the value of personal liberty or autonomy could understandably be considered as the most likely candidates for our assessment. Joseph Raz, amongst others, endorses the view that liberalism's 'specific contribution [...] to political morality has always been its insistence on the respect due to individual liberty' (hereafter 'the standard view').[1] In spite of the historical association between liberalism and the value of personal liberty, the inadequacy of the standard view has been well documented at the surface level. For example, Jeremy Waldron has argued convincingly that:

> to say [...] that a commitment to freedom is the foundation of liberalism is to say something too vague and abstract to be helpful, while to say that liberals are committed fundamentally to a particular conception of liberty is to sound too assured, too dogmatic about a matter on which, with the best will in the world, even ideological bedfellows are likely to disagree (TFL, p. 131).

Waldron draws this conclusion from two observations. On the one hand, the abstract claim (a) can be difficult to sustain as a generalization in the light of the view held by some liberals that liberalism is more deeply committed to the ideal of equality than to that of liberty, and (b) is too vague in the light of its implications when applied to different areas of social life. For example, 'liberty in economic life is an uncharacteristic concern of modern liberalism'—since liberalism can be said to be concerned with the 'equal

---

[1]. Raz, *The Morality of Freedom*, p. 2.

freedom of everyone in the economic domain' and this is not assured by advocating an ideal of economic liberty—yet in politics liberals are committed to a number of freedoms. On the other hand, the debate within the liberal tradition over the adequacy of a number of specific conceptions of freedom suggests at the very least that liberals are unlikely to be united in their commitment to one such conception (TFL, pp. 129-31).[2] Not surprisingly, a conception of liberalism based on the universal value of individual liberty or freedom would reflect the limitations of drawing on one complex notion to articulate another relatively complex idea. The result would be that the complexity of the notion relied on to do the interpretive or explanatory work (in this case, liberty or freedom) would have to be ignored.

One response to the problem of philosophical reflection on the character of liberalism has been to abandon the standard view, that is, to turn attention away from the idea of individual *freedom* to *that which motivates* a commitment to freedom. For example, in her survey of proposed definitions of liberalism, Susan Mendus suggests that:

> liberalism [...] begins from a premise of individual diversity: each person has his own unique conception of what makes life worth living and is entitled to pursue that conception to the best of his ability.[3]

Though Mendus is right to suggest that liberal philosophical thought sometimes begins from such a 'premise of individual diversity', the focus, nonetheless, on the value of *individual diversity* as distinct from *individual freedom* as the central idea grounding liberalism's political morality is more reflective of the individualist strand in the liberal philosophical tradition since it invokes a multiplicity of irreducibly different conceptions of the good life.[4] Mendus herself offers a number of arguments to suggest that this premise cannot consistently be converted into a statement of liberalism's philosophical foundations, but in proposing it as liberalism's initial premise her position fails to acknowledge that liberal theorists have sought to develop their arguments in order to allow for the possibility of a non-individualistic conception of the moral foundations of liberalism.[5] As already suggested in Chapter 1, a number of liberals have insisted that liberalism need not presuppose an individualistic ethic in the narrow sense of referring to well-being.[6] For present pur-

---

2. See also Dworkin, *A Matter of Principle*, p. 189, Susan Mendus, *Toleration and The Limits of Liberalism*, Basingstoke, Macmillan, 1989, pp. 71-4.

3. Mendus, *Toleration and The Limits of Liberalism*, p. 75.

4. The idea of value pluralism as suggested by Mendus' reference to the existence of each person's 'unique' conception of the good life is distinct from the broader claim that people disagree about the nature of the good life since the latter claim leaves open the question of whether people's different conceptions of the good are *irreducibly* different. I will examine an attempt to rely on the broader idea in Chapter 7.

5. See Chapters 4 and 5 of Mendus, *Toleration and The Limits of Liberalism*.

6. For example, both Charles Larmore and Allen E. Buchanan, claim that liberalism can

poses it will be sufficient to understand by the claim that liberalism should allow for the possibility of a non-individualistic conception of its foundations *either* that it should not assume as part of the specification of its foundational aspect that individual persons are the only sources of moral value (moral individualism) *or else*, if its moral ontology recognizes only individual persons, that it should not also assume that such persons' conceptions of the good are formed pre-socially or a-socially (abstract individualism).

Now, Will Kymlicka, offers an account of the basis of liberalism's political morality that, at the surface level, is a variation and improvement on both the standard view and Mendus' premise of individual diversity in so far as it tries to escape the problems associated with presupposing the correctness of individualism whilst also focusing on the rationale underlying liberals' traditional interest in the value of personal liberty or freedom. In *Liberalism, Community and Culture* Kymlicka maintains, like Mendus, that liberal political arrangements (seek to) serve people's interest in pursuing their own conception of a worthwhile life, but he does not imply that each person's conception is unique or irreducibly different. Instead, like Raz, he characterizes liberalism's foundation in terms of a *single, abstractly specified* human ideal, albeit a different one, namely, the value of *leading an objectively good life*. Given that it obviously appeals to the value of well-being, does Kymlicka's account appeal to an idea that falls beyond the scope of a minimal political morality approach? (Recall my claim in Chapter 4 (4.1.2) that conceptions of liberalism that exemplify the minimal political morality approach confine the scope of the idea of liberalism to narrowly construed moral claims and exclude claims regarding ethics.) It is important to bear in mind here that in Kymlicka's account of liberalism the idea of leading a good life merely stands for the unspecified needs and ambitions of citizens, however they define these, and so, as we will see in the analysis that follows, it functions as a moral, rather than an ethical, idea in the sense explained in Chapter 4.

This chapter will examine the role that the idea of leading an objectively good life plays in Kymlicka's theory. I aim to demonstrate that, even though at the surface level the idea of an objectively good life supplies a more defensible account of liberalism as compared with the views referred to above, it cannot solve the problem of liberalism's definition due to the form of its deep structure. To do this I will advance three main claims. The first expository claim holds that in order to meet its own adequacy criterion Kymlicka's theory must give an account of the justifiedness of a liberal political order which appeals to an understanding of the meaning of an objectively good life that is not effectively reduced to that of a merely subjectively defined good life. The second reconstructive claim holds that Kymlicka's account of liberalism rests on a deep structure that embodies a model of the public-private

---

remain silent on this question. See Buchanan, 'Assessing the Communitarian Critique of Liberalism', Larmore, 'Political Liberalism', pp. 343-5.

dichotomy that attributes a defining role to the category of publicness. The third critical claim holds that this form of the dichotomy collapses due to the unacknowledged defining role that is played by the category of privateness, and this explains why the theory's adequacy criterion cannot be met at the surface level.

To establish these expository, reconstructive and critical claims I will begin in section 1 by outlining Kymlicka's position in keeping with its significance at the surface level in order to identify its own adequacy criterion. The next section will reconstruct those aspects of the theory that will bring to view its deep structural commitments. This exercise should show that the model of the public-private dichotomy I attribute to the deep structure of Kymlicka's account of liberalism does indeed belong to it. Section 3 will offer a critique that demonstrates how rendering this model visible reveals the fundamental flaw in the theory and how this flaw prevents it from meeting its own adequacy criterion. The chapter will end with the identification of a positive outcome of my assessment of Kymlicka's theory. This concerns the direction of the further investigation of the minimal political morality approach to defining liberalism.

5.1 Will Kymlicka's account of liberalism

5.1.1 Leading an objectively good life

Kymlicka's account of liberalism's moral foundation distinguishes between 'leading a good life in fact' and 'leading the life we *currently believe* to be good' and maintains that the basis of liberal political morality is its commitment to the former as 'our essential interest' (LCC, p. 10).[7] Kymlicka explains the idea of *leading a good life in fact as distinct from the one we currently believe to be good* by distinguishing it from our mere pursuit of the satisfaction of our current preferences:

> Preferences [...] do not define our good. [...] We want to have those things which are worth having, and our current preferences reflect our current beliefs about what those worthwhile things are. But it is not always easy to tell what is worth having, and we could be wrong in our beliefs. [...] people want to have or to do the things which are *worth* having or doing, and this may be different from what they *currently prefer* to have or do (CPP, p. 15).

Since the goodness of one's life is not reducible to one's preferences or subjective standpoint, Kymlicka's view is that our essential interest is in leading, what I will refer to, throughout this chapter as, an *objectively* good life. Kymlicka also takes the view that the goodness of an objectively good life

---

7. See also Will Kymlicka, *Multicultural Citizenship: A Liberal Theory of Minority Rights*, Oxford, Oxford University Press, 1995, pp. 80-2.

lies neither in the capacities one shares with no one else nor in those that one shares with all human beings. Instead, as a 'liberal culturalist' he thinks that it is tied to the cultural practices one shares with others in the cultural community with which one identifies as a member. He suggests that one chooses from amongst the meaningful options about how to live well that are supplied by one's cultural community. Indeed, he takes the view that the best way to conceive of this community is in terms of what he calls a 'societal culture', that is 'a territorially-concentrated culture, centred on a shared language which is used in a wide range of societal institutions, in both public and private life'. In this sense the members of a cultural community may share a 'common culture' in only a thin sense that allows for significant differences in matters such as religion, personal and familial values or life style choices (CPP, p. 203).[8]

Whilst an objectively good life is not *reducible* to that which an agent currently believes to be good, it, nonetheless, *includes* one's subjective standpoint. Kymlicka claims that, since the objectively good life cannot be imposed and since individuals can be mistaken about what they believe to be the good,

> we have two preconditions for the fulfillment of our essential interest in leading a life that is in fact good. One is that we lead our life from the inside, in accordance with our beliefs about what gives value to life; the other is that we be free to question those beliefs, to examine them in the light of whatever information and examples and arguments our culture can provide (LCC, pp. 12-3).

Kymlicka presents these two aspects of what I will refer to as 'critical willing' as the universal preconditions for the realization of an objectively good life by citizens. The idea is that irrespective of the great variety of cultural differences to be found in pluralist societies, all citizens are owed the support necessary for exercising their critical willing. Although in his early work he concluded that the best way to serve citizens' critical willing is 'to endorse a neutral state' and to distribute resources without aiming to enforce any particular way of life (CPP, p. 205), following his more recent sociological turn,[9] Kymlicka endorses the view that citizens' critical willing is best served by liberal states whose nation-building practices protect and reinforce the actual societal cultures that citizens' happen to rely upon at any given time and place. He not only acknowledges but incorporates into his defence of national minority rights an argument concerning the propriety and significance of Western liberal states' multi-nation-building practices on the grounds that a 'nation-building model' of the liberal democratic state more accurately re-

---

8. See also Will Kymlicka, *Politics in the Vernacular: Nationalism, Multiculturalism and Citizenship*, Oxford, Oxford University Press, 2001, p. 25.

9. See Sujit Choudhry, 'National Minorities and Ethnic Immigrants: Liberalism's Political Sociology', *Journal of Political Philosophy*, vol. 10, no. 1, 2002, pp. 54-78.

flects the historical practices of 'promoting a common language, and a sense of common membership in, and access to, the societal institutions based on that language'.[10]

5.1.2 Liberalism's foundational idea

So, Kymlicka ultimately grounds a multi-nation-building model of the liberal order on peoples' essential interest in leading an objectively good life because this order supposedly aids citizens' critical willing and critical willing, in turn, serves this interest. A liberal political morality—a theory of the nature and proper role of government—can, in turn, be understood as a theory concerning the public domain of society that seeks to ensure for citizens the liberties and resources that they require to engage in the critical willing presupposed for the realization of their essential interest in leading an objectively good life (LCC, p. 13). The idea that we have an essential interest in leading an objectively good life thus functions as a *foundational* idea in the sense that it is the ultimate ground of political values and institutions. This interpretation of Kymlicka's approach is also supported by his endorsement of the view that 'modern political theories do not have different foundational values [...] every plausible political theory has the same ultimate value which is equality', the latter being the abstract idea that each person matters equally (CPP, p. 4). According to Kymlicka, the best way to understand modern political theories is not to see them as differing according to their endorsement of competing values. Instead, they should be understood to differ according to their *interpretation* of the foundational idea of equality and, relatedly, to their commitment to their own interpretation as the most coherent and attractive view (CPP, p. 5). On his view, liberalism is best understood as a political theory that (a) interprets the abstract foundational idea of equality in terms of the idea that we have an essential interest in leading an objectively good life and (b) defends this interpretation as the most coherent and attractive (LCC, p. 13).

Arguably, the potentially global appeal of Kymlicka's foundational idea has something to do with the abstractness of its specification and its association with the exercise of critical willing. Critical willing cuts across, rather than relies upon, the substantive specificities—particular convictions, cultural values and so on—to be found in the variety of cultures globally. Moreover, the idea of leading a *revisable* worthwhile life *from the inside* is the mark of what Hegel identified as the ethical heart of the modern principle of formally free subjectivity.[11] Indeed, Kymlicka's defence of his foundational idea draws attention to the fact that it supposes (a) that we can know the good; (b) that goodness is not reducible to our arbitrary preferences and beliefs about the good; and (c) that one must work out what it means to live well in the

---

10. Kymlicka, *Politics in the Vernacular: Nationalism, Multiculturalism and Citizenship*, p. 27.
11. Hegel, *The Philosophy of Right*.

course of one's life *in society* and, in particular, in one's societal culture. So, if liberal political morality can be understood as derived from his foundational idea it would appear to escape the charge of presupposing the correctness of moral skepticism and, indeed, of subjectivist forms of moral relativism. It would also appear to be sufficiently culture-sensitive to escape the problems typically associated with presupposing the correctness of an atomistic ontology, including being incompatible with non-western cultures.[12]

5.1.3 The theory's adequacy criterion

From the elaboration and defence of the foundational idea just sketched we can derive the adequacy criterion immanent to the theory: an adequate liberal theory should give an account of the justifiedness of a liberal order as necessary for the realization by individuals of an objectively good life where an objectively good life is understood as something that is knowable, is more than the mere satisfaction of subjective preferences and beliefs and is worked out by individuals themselves in their societal cultures. Satisfaction of this adequacy criterion requires that the operative notion of an objectively good life should not be effectively indistinguishable from that of a merely subjectively good life.

5.2 *A model of the public-private dichotomy in which publicness plays the defining role*

As already mentioned, according to my reconstructive claim, the deep structure of Kymlicka's formulation of liberalism's foundational idea—the idea that we have an essential interest in leading an objectively good life—embodies a model of the public-private dichotomy in which the category of publicness plays the defining role. In order to make out this claim I will demonstrate the following: (1) the notion of an objectively good life functions as a public category; (2) that of a life merely believed by a subject to be good functions as a private category; (3) these categories are defined in opposition to each other; and (4) the public category is supposed to play the defining role. I will begin by identifying the key elements of Kymlicka's formulation of liberalism's foundational idea with a view to rendering visible their treatment as public or private and then to examine the way in which these categories are combined.

Note, firstly, that the interest in question, 'our essential interest', is presented as a universal interest of persons. That is, in respect of it persons are identical. So, if 'A' stands for *the person who has an interest in leading an objectively good life*, A represents us all equally. The subject as theorized here constitutes a *singularity* in that the single interest attributed to it would not (need to) be

---

12. See Kymlicka, *Contemporary Political Philosophy*, pp. 199-237, Kymlicka, *Liberalism, Community, and Culture*, pp. 13-8 & ch. 8, Kymlicka, *Multicultural Citizenship: A Liberal Theory of Minority Rights*, pp. 33-48, Kymlicka, *Politics in the Vernacular: Nationalism, Multiculturalism and Citizenship*, pp. 39-66.

revised were it to be discovered upon empirical investigation that, as it happens, there is only one person in existence. In the light of the role that a societal culture plays in the theory, such a discovery would affect only what an advocate of Kymlicka's approach would want to say about that person's limited or non-existent *practical* opportunities for her to define and to realize her essential interest in leading an objectively good life. Now, the noteworthy point about the subject, A, is that A has the capacity to critically will something for A's life. In addition to this, there is reference to the particular life, let us say, 'P', that A in fact pursues in critically willing something. Finally, there is appeal to the life that is *objectively* good, that which it is in A's essential interest to lead. Call this 'U'.

U and P represent categories that function respectively as public and private categories. P stands for a life that is *private* not merely in the sense that it is A's own life but also in the sense that others do not mediate between A and A's *reasons* for critically willing what she does for P. The category of privateness is thus constituted by the idea of a good life as *merely* subjectively understood. In contrast, U stands for a life that has a *public* dimension in so far as the life to which it refers must be so constituted as to be a potential object of choice for *any* subject (with access to the specific cultural community's options) and not just for some specific subject. This follows from the facts (a) that the goodness of the life to which U refers is not reducible to a specific subject's reasons for choosing to lead that life and (b) that it is capable of being known to be good not just by the subject who chooses it. The category of publicness is thus constituted by the idea of a good life as a potentially *universal object*. Notice, however, that these two categories do not just mark distinctions. They define an oppositional relationship. The public category, the idea of an objectively good life, is understood to refer to that which is not merely subjectively good, whilst the private category is defined as the *merely* subjectively good. The categories of publicness and privateness are, therefore, related as mutually exclusive and mutually exhaustive.

Finally, note that the foundational idea attributes a defining role to the category of publicness. By viewing persons' interest in leading an objectively good life, and not a merely subjectively good life, as the essential interest that grounds a liberal order, the foundational idea gives moral priority to this public category thereby rendering the foundational idea's reflective standpoint as public. At the same time, the foundational idea subordinates the private to the public category. That is, the value of persons' interest in leading the life they currently believe to be good derives from its contribution to the realization of an objectively good life. These observations indicate that the deep structure of the foundational idea conforms to a form of the public-private dichotomy that supposes the category of publicness to play the defining role. Call this model MBC1.

5.3 *The collapse of the model of the dichotomy in which publicness plays the defining role*

I turn now to the elaboration and defence of the critical claim that bringing to view the deep structural logic of MBC1 shows why this logic breaks down and, relatedly, why the theory's adequacy criterion cannot consistently be met at the surface level. Let us begin by asking what is required in order for the theory to meet its adequacy criterion in the light of its now visible deep structural commitments? At the surface level, P and U represent in a merely formal way the difference between a life that is merely subjectively good and one that is objectively good. This difference would have to be distinguishable, in more than such a merely formal way, if the notion of an essential interest in leading an objectively good life is to function as the foundation of liberalism's political morality as Kymlicka's theory claims. At the same time, our reconstruction of the theory (5.2) has shown that the foundational idea renders its reflective standpoint as *public*. It therefore should be possible to differentiate P and U from this standpoint. In what follows I will show that P and U respectively represent private and public categories that are related in such a way as to be incapable of being publicly differentiated in any single application. Due to this ineffectiveness of the category of publicness, MBC1 collapses and this collapse in turn explains why the foundational idea fails to satisfy its own adequacy criterion.

To see that P and U are incapable of being differentiated when embodied in a subject's life choice, consider the following argument (hereafter 'the formal argument').

1. When a person engages in critically willing something for her particular way of life that she values as objectively good (in Kymlicka's sense that its goodness does not merely reside in her believing it to be valuable), she seeks to realize her essential interest in leading an objectively good life.
2. A person, A, critically wills something for her life, x, where 'x' represents a *specific* lifestyle, as one out of a range of lifestyles, projects or activities that she might critically will in pursuing her particular life, P.
3. In critically willing x, A leads a life that she values as *objectively* good, that is, as U.
4. A is therefore engaged in realizing her essential interest in leading an objectively good life.

This argument is implied by, or at least consistent with, Kymlicka's account (though it does not represent a restatement of it). Premise 1 sets out the connection between critical willing and realizing the interest of leading an objectively good life. Premises 2 and 3 are derivable from Kymlicka's outline of this interest in non-skeptical, non-relativist, non-individualist terms. The proposition expressed in the conclusion (4) represents an application of Kymlicka's formulation of the foundational idea to the life activity of any single person.

Now, I do not want to deny that we could differentiate x from U by formally assigning a negative value to x or that A could do so on the basis of some revised private reasons. Rather, since Kymlicka's foundational idea requires that such assignments be made from the public reflective standpoint on which it relies, it takes for granted that there is a publicly available criterion (in the sense of a criterion available to any subject due to the constitution of the object) on the basis of which to make such assignments. The claim is that the foundational idea lacks a criterion on the basis of which to make the necessary differentiation. Since this can be demonstrated when we consider the case where A happens in fact not to be mistaken about x, suppose that x is objectively good and that the conclusion is correct.

What is the relevance to it of the fact that it was x that was critically willed as indicated in premise 2? On the face of it, it looks as if x should play an important role in the determination that A is engaged in realizing U. After all, if the nature of the good is neither pre-socially determined nor arbitrary on this view, and leading a good life requires making some correct decisions, then goodness has to be a property of x. But if it is as we have supposed, there is no way of confirming this from the public standpoint favoured in the deep structure of the foundational idea. This is because x is singled out from amongst the range of P only in virtue of A's choice. (Even though in making her choice A does not think x valuable just because she values it, her reasons as already explained in 2, are constituted as private.) Had A critically willed not-x and—for A could (have) critically will(ed) any one of an indefinite number of alternatives—it would not be possible to draw any other conclusion than that drawn in 4. It follows that although A must critically will *something* for her life in order that the conclusion be correct, that it was x, the specific lifestyle, that was willed is of no special significance to a determination by an advocate of Kymlicka's theory that the conclusion is correct. There is no way of assessing the conclusion without taking up A's subjective position.

Nor can the determining factor be the fact that *A* has critically willed *something* for this would be to treat the fact of critical willing as sufficient and not merely as necessary for, or enabling, A to realize U. This would be to collapse the distinction between the objectivist idea of leading a good life and that of leading a life that is merely currently believed to be good. Kymlicka's position would thus favour a subjectivist and, hence, objectionable form of moral relativism (despite his and A's attempts to avoid subjectivism). Critics have highlighted the lack of clarity in Kymlicka's account of the relationship between individuals' choosing and the options that their societal cultures make available.[13] My analysis suggests that these surface level problems arise precisely because Kymlicka invokes but cannot give effect to the public reflective standpoint that the deep structural analysis renders visible.

What of the statement in premise 3 that A critically wills that which she values *as objectively good*? Can the conclusion in 4 be drawn in the light of the recognition that the reflection from A's subjective standpoint appeals to U? The problem here is that, even though in critically willing x A takes herself to will U and *not merely* P, from the public standpoint favoured in the foundational idea, there is no way of confirming that she is critically willing U since the idea of *leading a life that is objectively good* is indeterminate due to the fact that the theory lacks (the ability to supply) a criterion for determining objective value. Even though Kymlicka holds that the objectivity of value is tied to the cultural practices of one's community he does not want to specify objective goodness. Nor could he without inappropriately appealing to ethical reasons in the sense already discussed (4.1.2). Alternatively, one could say that U is determinate only in so far as it is indistinguishable from P; the determinateness of U *depends on* its being indistinguishable from P.

So, if the conclusion of the above-stated formal argument is correct, as we have supposed, the conclusion must be accepted, not merely independently of the co-presence of the facts represented by premises 2 and 3, but in virtue of something that is unspecifiable within the conceptual framework of MBC1. If this is correct, then Kymlicka's account of liberalism's foundational idea relies on an inadequately conceived distinction between its basic categories of publicness (represented in terms of the objectively good life) and privateness (represented as that which is merely believed by a subject to be good). Because the foundational idea requires but cannot supply an independent public criterion for differentiating U from P, it remains too indeterminate and fails to do any real conceptual work.

One might respond to the above argument that the problem to which I have drawn attention arises because I have mistakenly assumed that Kymlicka's account contains some *argument in support* of his foundational idea whereas the account begins from the supposition that this idea is correct and selectively discusses those implications of its endorsement that are relevant to the justification of political arrangements. To put the same point in another way, one could say that in order for the formal argument I presented above to be complete and consistent with Kymlicka's account a further unstated premise would need to be inserted, namely that *A satisfies the further conditions for realizing her essential interest in leading an objectively good life, whatever they might be.* This response could be developed by pointing out that the absence of an independent way of determining U does not necessarily imply that U

---

13. See, for example, Choudhry, 'National Minorities and Ethnic Immigrants: Liberalism's Political Sociology', pp. 60-5, John Tomasi, 'Kymlicka, Liberalism, and Respect for Cultural Minorities', *Ethics*, vol. 105, no. 3, 1995, pp. 580-603, p. 591.

and P are incapable of being publicly distinguished, as I have argued above. The point could be made that U is deliberately left indeterminate because the attempt to define it falls beyond the scope of liberalism's foundation. In other words, U appears as indeterminate, not because it is rendered necessarily indeterminate by MBC1, but because it does not need to be, indeed should not be, presented in its determinateness. The liberal's aim is to provide a justification for the liberal order and this will be achieved by showing that its institutions *make possible*—as distinct from give effect to—the realization of people's essential interest in leading an objectively good life. Recall that according to Kymlicka's account a liberal political order is justified in so far as it can be shown to facilitate the critical willing constituting the preconditions for realizing persons' essential interest whereas what it is to lead an objectively good life is left to people to work out for themselves in their own ways. As we already noted (5.1.2), the aspiration to secure an appropriate space for individual reflection and judgment is after all the mark of distinction of the tradition of modern western thought to which the philosophy of liberalism belongs.

The above response to my criticism of Kymlicka's account of liberalism rests on some misunderstandings that are worth examining not only for the purposes of defending my position but also in order to illustrate how the collapse of MBC1 ultimately explains why Kymlicka's foundational idea fails to satisfy its own adequacy criterion. Firstly, note that I am not questioning the correctness of the substantive claim expressed by the foundational idea as either a full or partial account of persons' essential interests. My objection is directed to the suitability of such an idea to play the foundational role that Kymlicka attributes to it. It is supposed to be the non-individualist, non-skeptical, non-relativist ground of a liberal political morality. In order to show that liberal institutions *make possible* the realization of people's interest in leading an *objectively* good life, it is necessary to be able to distinguish such a life from the *merely* subjectively good so as to account for that possibility from within the public reflective standpoint favoured by the foundational idea. Accordingly, my criticism would not be met either by an argument in support of the correctness of the view that we have an essential interest in leading an objectively good life or by the recognition that the articulation of the necessary and sufficient conditions for realizing that interest fall beyond the scope of Kymlicka's task.

Secondly, and perhaps more importantly for present purposes, the response misunderstands the conclusion that we should draw from my demonstration that, contrary to first appearances, it is not possible within the framework of MBC1 publicly to distinguish U from P. The response takes the issue to be a question of deciding *to whom* it should be left to decide the nature of U. Invoking the two aspects of critical willing outlined above (5.1.1) it emphasizes that this should be done from people's own perspectives in their own ways, that is, from the subject's perspective. This sort of response engages with an objection like the one Margaret Moore raises against Kymlicka. Moore argues against Kymlicka's assertion that paternalistic intervention is counter-productive, that it can be an effective strategy when both its motivation and likely effect are the elimination of perceived corrupt influences.[14] However, the point of my argument is not to dispute Kymlicka's claim that life must be lived from the inside as a safeguard against counter-productive paternalism. Indeed, premise 3 of the formal argument I outlined earlier takes it for granted that it is *the individual subject* who makes the distinction between U and P and investigates the implications of doing so. Rather, the point of my argument is that the ability to make the distinction from the subject's reflective standpoint alone will not suffice for a justificatory idea that appeals to a public reflective standpoint precisely because the theory thereby inadvertently constitutes the theorized subject's reflective standpoint as private. By way of contrast let us consider another argument that Margaret Moore raises against Kymlicka's position. Moore complains that Kymlicka's appeal to the fact that we can be mistaken about our values does not justify his differential treatment of persons' 'private' and 'public' decisions. By this she means that he has no good reason for suggesting that, whereas a person's decisions about one's personal life can be based on considered ethical beliefs, decisions about 'the organization of one's community' should not.[15] But this objection leaves it open to Kymlicka to respond by pointing to the disanalogous features of decisions that can be revised by the individual person at will and those that depend on favourable multi-person decision procedures. The reason is that it fails to appreciate the deep structural flaw underlying the role that Kymlicka's theory attributes to the difference between a public reflective standpoint and persons' private reflective standpoints. My deep structural analysis suggests that, rather than simply being unable to find convincing reasons for the exclusion of ethical reasoning from public policy decision procedures, Kymlicka's theory suffers from the deep structural flaw of having *no effective way* of securing the result that it takes to be desirable.

Within the framework of MBC1 the theorized subject's private differentiation of U from P, as in premise 3 above, is unavailable to a public reflective standpoint because it is made from the excluded standpoint of an *intrinsically private* agent in the sense explained in Chapter 1.1.4. That is, the exclusion is due to the definition of the categories of publicness and privateness as mutually exclusive and the reflective standpoint is one of an intrinsically private agent due to the constitution of the subject as a singular identity within the limits of this conceptual framework. In thus constituting the

---

14. Margaret Moore, *Foundations of Liberalism*, Oxford, Oxford University Press, 1993, pp. 148-9.

15. Moore, *Foundations of Liberalism*, pp. 149-51.

theorized subject as a singularity the account retains an element of abstract individualism, albeit not in the sense rejected by Kymlicka on the surface level of his theory. Even though Kymlicka asserts that peoples' conceptions of the good life are reliant on their societal culture in that they are formed in their cultural communities, *the liberal theorist's attribution* to people of an interest in leading an objectively good life—Kymlicka's reliance on the foundational idea—is itself pre-social or a-social in that this attribution is not presented as either derived from or informed by the social, that is, by (the nature of) inter-subjective interaction or by (the nature of) participation in social institutions or cultural practices. Nor is the attribution of *this* interest informed by the recognition of the nature and inter-relationship of any other interests that persons might have, whether essential or local.[16] Whilst at the surface level the theory claims the opposite to the proposition *that* people form their conceptions of the good a-socially, at the deep structural level, the person is still being *thought of* a-socially, that is, by reference to a single interest of the individual that is abstracted from everything else about her including her relationships and institutional positioning. So, even though Kymlicka's account envisages that people develop what they can know to be correct conceptions of leading a worthwhile life *in their cultural community* it still represents their interest in doing so in a problematically abstract way. The theory treats individuals as intrinsically private persons and in doing so their judgments about the nature of objective value appear as intrinsically private judgments.

It follows that even though the foundational idea purports to exclude a *merely* subjective standpoint, since the only way to differentiate U from P is precisely from this standpoint, the articulation of the foundational idea inevitably relies upon reflection from an intrinsically private subjective standpoint. Because in the absence of an unjustified reliance on the judgments of intrinsically private agents the notion of an objectively good life is indistinguishable from that of a merely subjectively good life, the theory fails to satisfy its own adequacy criterion. At the same time, the conflation of the operation of the intrinsically private and the public reflective standpoints and the effective reliance on the former in the name of the latter constitutes what we can refer to as the inherently colonizing tendency of this form of liberal discourse, the discourse that is, of a *would-be public* intrinsically private agency.[17]

---

16. Indeed, to the extent that Kymlicka attempts to redress this problem whilst remaining within the conceptual parameters of his liberal discourse, he renders his approach vulnerable to the charge of having made a problematic sociological turn. On this see Choudhry, 'National Minorities and Ethnic Immigrants: Liberalism's Political Sociology', pp. 65-72.

17. I discuss the implications of the above analysis for our understanding of current debates surrounding the globalization of liberal pluralism and its models for managing ethnic-cultural minorities in Toula Nicolacopoulos, 'What's Wrong with "Exporting Liberal Pluralism"?

5.4 The desiderata for a second model of the public-private dichotomy

I have shown that, contrary to the model of the public-private dichotomy on which the foundational idea rests, the category of privateness, rather than publicness, is, after all, the one that plays a defining role. At the deep structural level Kymlicka's account of liberalism treats merely subjective, intrinsically private choices as having public, objective value in spite of its insistence that *only* the latter ground a liberal order. For this reason MBC1 collapses.

In addition to this negative outcome of the critique, there is also a positive outcome. In revealing the unacknowledged defining role that is played by the category of privateness the discussion points to the need for the consideration of a theory whose deep structure gives a defining role to the category of privateness in its model of the public-private dichotomy.

At the surface level, rejecting Kymlicka's attempt to construe liberalism's moral foundation in terms of an appeal to the abstract notion of an essential interest in leading an objectively good life, may lead the liberal theorist to propose a liberal *ethics* (an account of the good life) as an essential part of liberalism's self-definition. This would amount to recognizing that the scope of the idea of liberalism is broader than the minimal political morality approach admits. But there is another response that remains within the confines of the approach presently under consideration. This response warrants investigation, especially since the grounds for rejecting Kymlicka's account of liberalism do not also tell against an account that focuses on *private* agents' capacity critically to will something for themselves. The liberal theorist's response to the critique undertaken in the present chapter may be to drop the reference to persons' interest in leading an objectively good life and to focus instead on the *implications* of the claim that we have certain rational and volitional *capacities*.

I turn next to the view defended by Jeremy Waldron that liberalism can be construed in terms of the idea of individual consent or agreement, an idea which attempts to ground liberal political institutions on human beings' rational and volitional powers. This surface level variation on liberalism's purported foundational idea will be examined together with its parallel variation in the form of liberalism's deep structure.

On the Radical Self-denial of Contemporary Liberal Philosophy', *Philosophical Inquiry*, vol. XXIX, no. 1-2, 2007, pp. 89-111.

6

Jeremy Waldron: Liberalism and Consensual Legitimation

In this chapter I will argue that whilst there are considerable and rather obvious differences between the views endorsed by Jeremy Waldron and Will Kymlicka on the surface level, in one significant way the deep structure of Waldron's inquiring practice is similar to that of Kymlicka. It constitutes a variation of the idea that one category is supposed to play a defining role in the dichotomous inter-relationship of the abstract categories of publicness and privateness. Whereas in Kymlicka's account of liberalism's foundation this defining role is supposed to be played by the category of publicness, in Waldron's account[1] it is taken up by the category of privateness.

As in the previous chapter, I will begin in section 1 with an outline of Waldron's account of liberalism in order to identify the theory's adequacy criterion. After reconstructing the theory, in section 2, to render visible its deep structure, section 3 will proceed to defend the critical claim that this model of the public-private dichotomy also collapses this time due to the unacknowledged defining role of the category of publicness. Having revealed the limitations of the theory's deep structure, I will elaborate and defend the critical claim that the theory cannot meet its adequacy criterion due to its

---

1. In attributing to Waldron commitment to a foundational idea as the ground of liberalism this chapter focuses exclusively on the argument in 'Theoretical Foundations'. My aim is to draw from this essay an exemplary version of the approach I wish to examine without however denying Waldron's wider contribution to liberal theorizations of justice, and in particular his critique of judicial review and elaboration of a procedural account of democratic legitimacy. For reviews of the latter see David M. Estlund, 'Jeremy Waldron on Law and Disagreement', *Philosophical Studies: An International Journal for Philosophy in the Analytic Tradition*, vol. 99, no. 1, 2000, pp. 111-28, Keith E. Wittington, 'In defence of Legislatures', *Political Theory*, vol. 28, no. 5, 2000, pp. 690-702.

deep structural limitations. The chapter will conclude with some observations about the constructive implications of my critique.

6.1 Jeremy Waldron's account of liberalism

6.1.1 The liberal thesis

As a response to the surface level problem of characterizing liberalism, Waldron's approach may seem promising given the historical connection between the development of liberal ideas and the social contract tradition.[2] He claims that liberalism aims to reconcile personal freedom with the demands of social cooperation by emphasizing 'the capacity of human agents to determine for themselves how they will restrain their conduct in order to live in community with others' (TFL, p. 133). What matters about human agents is that they be in a position, firstly, to scrutinize the arrangements under which they are to live 'as they [human beings] are in ordinary life', that is, from the standpoint of their 'occurrent subjective experience' (TFL, p. 132) and, secondly, 'to choose to live under a social order, to agree to abide by its restraints' (TFL, p. 134).

So, according to Waldron, liberalism can be conceived as proposing a theory of political *legitimation*, as distinct from political *obligation*, that appeals to the notion of *individual consent*:

> The thesis I want to say is fundamentally liberal is this: a social and political order is illegitimate unless it is rooted in the consent of all those who have to live under it; the consent or agreement of those people is a condition of its being morally permissible to enforce that order against them [hereafter 'the liberal thesis'] (TFL, p. 140).

Three clarifications are in order here. First, the liberal thesis advocates a form of consent theory that focuses on *original* consent that creates the social contract. As Benjamin R. Barber points out, this is the weakest form of liberal consent theory in comparison to two other types of consent theory within the social contract tradition. One of these, 'periodic consent' requires some 'periodic rehearsals of consent most often through the election of representatives' and the other, 'perpetual consent' is the most demanding given that it calls for 'consent to each and every collective act'.[3] The idea of original consent, given once and for all, is thus the least demanding

---

2. The social contract theories of Locke and Rousseau have been subject to much discussion and criticism that is either revisionist or radical in spirit in the sense given to these two terms in Chapter 2.1. Waldron's particular version of the social contract argument seems to by-pass the two main objections to social contract theories, namely that appeals to a state of nature (a) presuppose abstract individualism (the problem I raised in Chapter 1) and (b) contain a masculine bias (see Hirschmann, *Rethinking Obligation*, Pateman, *The Sexual Contract*.)

3. Barber, 'Liberal Democracy and the Costs of Consent', pp. 57-8.

of the three forms.[4]

Second, although social contract theory offers *one kind* of contractarian moral theory (applied to the political institution of society), in the present chapter we will not be concerned with the broader question of the relationship between liberalism and contractarian moral theory in general. Instead because there are significant deep structural differences to be found in different liberal contractarian theories (and indeed between liberal and non-liberal uses of contractarian ideas) we must consider these separately.[5]

Third, within the social contract tradition consent theory often serves to address two problems simultaneously. These are the problems of *political legitimacy*, the legitimacy of interference with individual freedom by political agencies, and the problem of *political obligation*, the question of whether persons who find themselves within the territories of some government (whether citizens, residents or aliens) have obligations to obey its laws. Waldron takes the view that although consent may have a bearing on both questions, the first of these issues can, nevertheless, be treated separately.

> Sometimes, when I give my consent to an arrangement, I make it permissible for other people to do what it would otherwise be impermissible for them to do; and sometimes my agreement also makes it impermissible for me to do what it would otherwise be permissible for me to do. (For example, the first but not the second idea is involved when I consent to a surgical operation.) (TFL, p. 136)

So, for Waldron 'a regime may be morally legitimate even though disobedience to its laws is not always morally wrong' (TFL, p. 139). Since, as we will see, Waldron relies on hypothetical consent in the sense of cognitive agreement to the legitimacy of a liberal order as such, it will not be necessary to consider the implications of the liberal thesis for the problem of political obligation.[6] There is also the view that the idea of a hypothetical contract typically plays an *evaluative*, rather than *legitimating*, role since only an actual or implied contract is taken to be of an appropriate pedigree.[7] As we will see

---

4. For a useful schematic representation of differences in understandings of the nature and roles ascribed to the contract by contemporary contractarian political theory see Chandran Kukathas and Philip Pettit, *Rawls: A Theory of Justice and its Critics*, Cambridge, Polity Press, 1992, pp. 26-35.

5. Chapter 7 will consider the kind of liberal contractarianism that focuses on the *discursive procedures that produce agreement* rather than on the abstract notion of consent and Part III examines Rawls' use of hypothetical consent as a *representational device*.

6. In the present context, we can disregard arguments like the one that Joesph Raz advances in *The Morality of Freedom* whereby 'consent to a political authority entails a promise to obey it (as well perhaps as an obligation to support it in other ways)' (p. 83) since this analysis of consent confines the notion to 'the performative sense of agreement' and holds that hypothetical consent theories that in fact are only concerned with cognitive agreement do not therefore discuss consent' (pp 80-81.).

7. Kukathas and Pettit, *Rawls: A Theory of Justice and its Critics*, pp. 26-7.

below in section 6.1.3, Waldron's model purports to address the problem of political legitimacy by combining a hypothetical situation with persons' *actual* motivations.

6.1.2 The theory's adequacy criterion

For Waldron, consent confers political legitimacy. The consent of individuals makes it permissible for political agencies like the state to interfere with their lives, something that would otherwise be impermissible. In this way they can benefit from social co-operation without being denied their freedom in the sense of their 'individual need for control' (TFL, p. 137). Accordingly, universal subjective consent constitutes the theory's adequacy criterion. A theory that can give an account of the legitimacy of the liberal political order as grounded in the consent of all its subjects will meet the adequacy criterion of the liberal thesis in Waldron's terms.

Notice that this formulation of the theory's adequacy criterion in terms of a single idea—universal subjective consent—conforms to the demands of the minimal political morality approach in that it represents a certain moral ground in support of a political thesis as characteristically liberal. So, even though we may agree with Charles Larmore that taken as a whole Waldron's work on liberalism represents a comprehensive approach in so far as it endorses an individualist view of human nature, the textual account we are focusing on does not rely upon any specific reading of the (ideal) ends of human life.[8]

In fact, Waldron proposes an interpretation of the liberal thesis by linking liberal thought to the Enlightenment demand for justification according to which the world 'must be understood by the individual mind':

> Liberals demand that the social order should in principle be capable of explaining itself at the tribunal of each person's understanding (TFL, p. 149).

> Society should be a *transparent* order, in the sense that its workings and principles should be well-known and available for public apprehension and scrutiny (TFL, p. 146).

> Like his empiricist counterparts in science, the liberal insists that intelligible justifications in social and political life must be available in principle for everyone (TFL, p. 140).

Waldron's rather loose references to 'social and political life', to 'society' and to 'the social order' suggest that the object of justification with which his theory is concerned should be understood broadly as the liberal order in the sense of the basic coercive and regulatory institutions and practices of a

---

8. See Charles Larmore, 'The Moral Basis of Political Liberalism', *Journal of Philosophy*, vol. 96, no. 12, 1999, pp. 599-625, p. 623. Larmore cites Waldron's *Liberal Rights*.

modern society rather than more narrowly in terms of the particular political decisions of governments.

Moreover, for Waldron, whilst the liberal thesis holds that the justifiedness of a liberal order requires the consent of all its subjects, this thesis is taken to accord with a wider interest of modern individual subjects. In the Enlightenment vision this is an interest in *critically understanding* one's world. It belongs to subjects qua *individuals* and is met when their social order supplies *intelligible justifications* rendering its rationality *transparent*.

6.1.3 The hypothetical consent strategy

The above association of the liberal thesis with the Enlightenment demand for justification, combined with a recognition of the insurmountable theoretical problems faced by an account of political legitimacy that requires citizens' actual consent, lead Waldron to conclude that the best formulation of the liberal thesis is *rationalist* rather than *voluntarist* (TFL, pp. 140-3).[9] He appeals to hypothetical consent theory which shifts attention away from the will, that is, from claims regarding what people actually accept, to what would be accepted under certain conditions, that is, 'to the *reasons* that people might have for exercising their will in one way or another' (TFL, p. 144).

Thus Waldron endorses a justificatory strategy in which the choice *situation* is hypothetical whilst the motivational basis giving rise to the demand for consent remains actual. Explaining this distinction, James S. Fishkin notes that this type of justificatory strategy represents one of four types of thought experiment used in liberal theory. In it 'the situation of choice is an imaginary one, held to be morally relevant but not the situation in which those who must abide by the principles must live together as an on-going enterprise' whilst the motivation underlying consent is taken to be that of the person as she is in ordinary life.[10] By relying on the combination of a *hypothetical* situation and individuals' *actual* motivations for requiring consent, Waldron's theory is immune to the general surface level objection that hypothetical consent theory is forced to depend on essentially contestable philosophical theories of human nature.[11] Moreover, Waldron by-passes the

---

9. For critical discussions of the voluntaristic aspect of social contract theory see Carole Pateman, *The Problem of Political Obligation: A Critical Analysis of Liberal Theory*, New York, Wiley, 1979, A. John Simmons, *Moral Principles and Political Obligations*, Princeton, Princeton University Press, 1979, pp. 57-74. But see Hirschmann, *Rethinking Obligation*, pp. 80-8. She argues that both Pateman (in this work) and Simmons fail to appreciate the significance of consent theory's reliance on a-contextual notions of individuality and consent.

10. James S. Fishkin, 'Liberal Theory: Strategies of Reconstruction', in A. J. Damico (ed.), *Liberals on Liberalism*, New Jersey, Rowman and Littlefield, 1986, pp. 54-66, p. 54 & category II, Fig. 3.1, p. 55.

11. For one version of this kind of objection see Alison M. Jagger, 'Taking Consent Seriously: Feminist practical Ethics and Actual Moral Dialogue', in E. R. Winkler and J. R.

strongest objections associated with the notion of hypothetical consent[12] by arguing that they work against theories of political *obligation* and not against theories of political *legitimacy*. He suggests further that, even though 'there are limits on how far hypothetical consent can confer legitimacy on what would otherwise be wrongful interferences', 'hypothetical consent at least *makes a difference* to the wrongness of interference'. Even in situations where we think interference wrong, we think it *less* wrong to treat someone in a way that they would have agreed to had they been asked than if we think that, even hypothetically they would not have agreed (TFL, pp. 138-9).

So, on Waldron's rationalist formulation of liberalism's fundamental thesis the legitimacy of a liberal order derives from the moral reasons in its favour that the social order offers to all citizens. It is in this sense that the liberal thesis can be satisfied in relation to *all* the citizens of a liberal order. Accordingly, the theory's adequacy criterion—universal subjective consent—is supposed to be met using the hypothetical consent strategy.

6.1.4 The gap between ideal and real liberal societies

Having reached this conclusion, Waldron acknowledges that his account of liberalism ultimately involves a cost to liberalism in that it must abandon 'any claim about the "neutrality" of politics' as regards different conceptions of the good life.'[13] His reason is that the gap between citizens' hypothetical and actual assessments of the liberal order is such that it could only be bridged by unjustifiably making certain 'minimal assumptions of "reasonableness"'. These assumptions are not only that human beings share certain relevant underlying interests and beliefs like

> the basic needs of nature, certain desired objects that are means to the pursuit of any ideal, common general beliefs about how the world works, similar modes of argument and reason [...] But in addition to that liberals must assume that all ethical commitment has a common form: that there is something like *pursuing a conception of the good life* in which all people, even those with the most diverse commitments, can

---

Coombs (eds.), *Applied Ethics: A Reader*, Oxford, Blackwell, 1993, pp. 69-86 pp. 76-7. Because Jagger fails to distinguish between theories such as Waldron's and those that represent both the motivation giving rise to the demand for consent and the choice situation in hypothetical terms, she mistakenly attributes the problem she identifies to hypothetical consent theory in general.

12. For a brief outline and discussion of the general problems of 'indoctrination' and 'jurisdiction' faced by the different types of justificatory strategies that appeal to consent see Fishkin, 'Liberal Theory: Strategies of Reconstruction', pp. 54-9. See also Dworkin, 'Foundations of Liberal Equality', pp. 24-6, Jagger, 'Taking Consent Seriously: Feminist practical Ethics and Actual Moral Dialogue', pp. 77-81.

13. For a recent discussion of the idea of political neutrality see Morten Ebbe Juul Nielsen, 'Limited Neutrality', *SATS: Nordic Journal of Philosophy*, vol. 6, no. 1, 2005, pp. 110-27. See also Robert E. Goodin and Andrew Reeve, *Liberal Neutrality*, London, Routledge, 1989.

be said to be engaged (TFL, p. 145).

Do these 'assumptions of reasonableness' relate to questions of well-being and so render Waldron's account incompatible with the requirements of a minimal political morality approach? Notice that Waldron raises these issues only in connection with the unacceptability of liberalism's claim to political neutrality in the *implementation* of the liberal vision, a vision that is nevertheless *defined by moral considerations* about persons' proper treatment of each other.

Now Waldron gives a number of reasons for rejecting the universal applicability of these claims about the reasonableness of human beings. These are that 'people in fact exhibit different basic wants and needs, [...] beliefs about the world, and [...] modes of reasoning'; that 'some people's commitments are so overwhelming that they appear to swamp the basic human concerns' whilst the commitments of others 'are so inextricably bound up with their sense of themselves that they find it impossible to abstract from them'. Finally, Waldron notes 'some may find themselves with commitments so fervent that they cannot be pursued *except through the endeavour to impose them on others*' (TFL, p. 145). He concludes:

> [...] the liberal has a hard choice. Either he concedes that his conception of political judgment will be appealing only to those who hold their commitments in a certain 'liberal' spirit. Or he must look for a form of social order in which not only those with different ideals, but those with different views about the legitimacy of imposing their ideals, can be accommodated. Since the prospects for a social order of this kind are not very promising, the former more robust response seems the only one available (TFL, pp. 145-6).

Here we are given a picture of actual life in a liberal order in which, on the one hand, there are the liberal-spirited citizens, those whose political judgment coincides with the exercise of the 'liberal reason' (TFL, p. 146) that supplies the rationalist contractarian justification of a liberal order. For them there is no (inevitable) gap between the hypothetical reasons justifying a liberal order and their actual reasons for consenting to it. On the other hand, there are the non-liberal-spirited citizens for whom there is an inevitable gap between the hypothetical reasons justifying a liberal order and the actual reasons constituting their own assessment of it. Their reflection does not conform to Waldron's specification of the 'minimal standards of reasonableness'. That is, their wants, needs, beliefs, self-sense or commitments happen to be such as to render their political judgment incompatible with the exercise of liberal reason (hereafter 'non-reasonable citizens').

Waldron points out the political or practical implications of this observation about the application of the theory to the reality of life in a liberal order:

> [t]he liberal will have to concede that he has a great many more enemies

(real enemies—people who will suffer under a liberal dispensation) than he has usually pretended to have (TFL, p. 146).

So, in reality the liberal order cannot embody the principle of political neutrality since this order must be *imposed* on some of its citizens. Waldron thinks that the liberal can acknowledge the imposition of a liberal order on such citizens as a mere *practical* limitation on the application of the theory to reality presumably because such *non-liberal spirited* citizens are non-reasonable. He does not also conclude from the observation that there exist non-reasonable citizens in liberal societies that the liberal order is not justifiable *to them*. On the contrary, he thinks he has already shown how the liberal thesis can be satisfied when the social order supplies appropriate justificatory reasons in its favour. The personal failure or inability of some citizens—such as the unreasonable people who want to impose their conception of the good life on others—to accept them cannot undermine this conclusion.

6.2 *The model of the dichotomy in which privateness plays the defining role*

In this section I want to draw attention to the form of the deep structure of Waldron's account of liberalism as the first step in the development of my argument to show why taking this line cannot solve the problem of liberalism's definition. As already indicated, my reconstructive claim is that the deep structure of Waldron's intellectual practice takes the category of privateness to play the defining role. I will demonstrate precisely how the category of privateness is supposed to define publicness and what the significance of this is for their inter-relationship, that is, for the model of the public-private dichotomy that they constitute.

6.2.1 Private individuality

Once again, the first step in making out my reconstructive claim is to identify the key elements of Waldron's account with a view to bringing to the surface their treatment as either public or private. These elements are to be found in Waldron's formulation of the liberal thesis since it functions as a *foundational* idea, in the sense explained in section 1 of the previous chapter and, accordingly, grounds liberal thought. Focusing on its specifics it should be noted, firstly, that the concept of individuality and, in particular, consenting individuality, is implicitly treated as a private category. Individuals are thought of as appropriately being in control of their lives themselves. Just as in Kymlicka's theory the merely subjective power to define one's good constitutes this idea as private (5.2), here too the subjective power of decision over one's life (6.1.1) is constituted as private. Indeed individual persons are constituted as *intrinsically private* agents given that they are represented as capable of exercising their power of rational decision in their singularity (6.1.2). This is why the justificatory project to which the foundational idea refers emerges as the need to rebut the presumed illegitimacy of the state's interference with individuals' lives. Recall that a presumption in favour of private agency operates on the surface level of liberal discourse (3.3.2). Consistent with this, as Benjamin Barber explains, 'one of the effects of liberalism's reliance on consent theory is the construction of the sphere of political interaction in terms of conflicting private spaces which give rise to political demands of the form "Stay off my turf!"'[14]

6.2.2 Public agents potentially consenting to a public order

Secondly, the public categories are supposed to be defined in the light of this conception of private individuality. It is not just that the question of the legitimacy of the power of the theorized object, the public order, arises pursuant to the theory's recognition of intrinsically private agency (6.2.1). It is also the case that the publicness of the theorized subject's identity, the identity individuals share, is itself constituted by abstracting one property from this understanding of them as intrinsically private agents. This property is their capacity rationally to consent to the liberal order that in turn defines the individual as a universal subject. All other subjective characteristics continue to be rendered as private. These include subjects' needs, wants, modes of reasoning and modes of interaction (6.1.4) other than the capacity rationally to consent. So, in the rationalist formulation of the foundational idea persons are narrowly conceived of in terms of this one shared aspect of their identity as citizens (hereafter 'potentially consenting agents'). The category of publicness is thus constituted through the ideas of a public socio-political order and of the citizen as a universal potentially consenting agent.

6.2.3 A fully public foundational idea

Once private individuality defines the public identity of citizens in terms of their potentially consenting agency, this inter-relationship of public and private categories explicitly excludes everything else about private individuality from the scope of the rationalist interpretation of the foundational idea. On the one hand, this has the effect of constituting the domain of liberalism's foundational idea as *fully public* in the sense that all the foundational idea's elements are now restricted to the public dimensions of the subject-object relationship with which it deals, the relationship between citizen and

---

14. Barber, 'Liberal Democracy and the Costs of Consent', p. 59. Compare Michael Freeden's argument (in connection with the assertion of a right) that intervention can just as well be viewed as a positive aspect of human beings' necessary developmental process rather than as something that should be presumed to have a negative effect on them unless the reverse can be shown, Michael Freeden, *Rights*, Milton Keynes, Open University Press, 1990, pp. 64-5. For a surface level defence of the view that, contrary to the common assumption that 'interference in somebody else's activities needs to be justified', 'a claim *not* to be interfered with needs justification', see R. E. Ewin, 'The Presumption of Non-Interference', *Liberty, Community and Justice*, New York, Rowman and Littlefield, 1987, pp. 13-35.

liberal order. That is, firstly, the rationalist interpretation of the foundational idea proposes a *public* justification as the ultimate ground of a liberal order in that its requirement of consent is taken to be universally applicable to all the citizens of a liberal order. Secondly, the foundational idea's rationalist notion of citizens' consent to a liberal order is proposed as fully satisfying the requirement of a public justification because the hypothetical reasons that are supposed to ground citizens' consent are taken to be supplied by the liberal order: they function as *public* reasons, in the sense of reasons not derived from different modes of reasoning specific to particular individuals but as reasons derived from the objective character of a liberal order. (The publicness of the reasons grounding consent to a liberal order is rendered visible by their objective source in the liberal order in much the same way that the availability of options from which to choose an objectively good life renders such options public in Kymlicka's account of liberalism (5.2).) Thirdly, as public reasons in this sense, the reasons grounding consent to a liberal order explicitly function to the exclusion of all other reasons on the basis of which people might actually assess a liberal order. Hence, whatever their specifics, the latter *private* reasons are excluded.

6.2.4 The defining role of privateness

On the other hand, in contrast to the model of the deep structural dichotomy Kymlicka's theory embodies, the model of the dichotomy that Waldron's hypothetical consent theory embodies gives defining priority to the category of privateness. Significantly, in the case of the latter theory the constitution of the foundational idea as fully public (6.2.3) *results from* the actual situation of what are taken to be intrinsically private agents. This is because the justificatory strategy of hypothetical consent emerges from a motivational structure that remains actual (6.1.3) and belongs to intrinsically private individuals (6.2.1). It is in this sense that the category of privateness is supposed to play the defining role in the inter-relationship of the basic categories.

So Waldron's rationalist formulation of the foundational idea exhibits a model of the public-private dichotomy in terms of the above observations about the interplay of publicness and privateness. Call this model MBC2. MBC2 opposes that which is constituted as private to that which is constituted as public. In this opposition the considerations that come into play in the satisfaction of the requirement of a public justification—the provision to all citizens of public reasons on the basis of which they might rationally consent to a liberal order—function in abstraction from the excluded considerations that, in turn, appear as irrelevant to the justificatory strategy, though not to the issue of how the problem of justification arises. So, at the heart of Waldron's theory is an underlying conception of intrinsically private citizens whose private identities that give rise to the problem of justification, are defined through the exclusion and opposition of their public identity. Their public identity, constituted as their rational consenting potential, is in turn invoked in the justificatory strategy to the exclusion of their private identities.

6.2.5 The gap between citizens' public and private identities

The final point to note is that in Waldron's discussion, the private identities of citizens are supposed to come back into play only after the theory's adequacy criterion has been satisfied—through the elaboration of the rationalist interpretation of the foundational idea—when consideration is given to the practical-political implications of the application of Waldron's account to the reality of a liberal order. The possibility of there being a conflict between citizens' public and private reasons emerges at this point. It follows that, when Waldron recognizes the existence of non-reasonable citizens by denying the universality of the minimal conditions of reasonableness that he discusses (6.1.4), he is not merely acknowledging that citizens of a liberal order may, or may not, actually give their consent to that order. He is also implying that regardless of their actual reasons for doing so, withholding consent, or active dissent, is *unreasonable* given the public reasons in favour of a liberal order. This is an implicit characterization of *all* non-liberal spirited citizens as unreasonable, rather than merely non-reasonable, and not merely of fanatics who would impose their view of the good life on others. Amongst them would be included all who support the radical transformation of the liberal order in which they live such as anarchists, Marxists, civic humanists and non-liberal feminists. Accordingly, no matter what the actual reasons of dissenters are, the gap existing between them and the hypothetical reasons supplied by the liberal order has to be explained away as a matter of the former being unreasonable. Through the elaboration of the critical argument that follows I will show why this sort of explanation is unsatisfactory given Waldron's own terms and, consequently, why Waldron's justificatory strategy cannot supply a public justification as is required by his adequacy criterion.

6.3 The collapse of the model of the dichotomy in which privateness plays the defining role

By rendering visible MBC2 we are in a position to expose the account's *theoretical* limits, as distinct from the merely practical problem of the theory's application that Waldron acknowledges. That is, Waldron's concession that a liberal order must be imposed on some of its citizens is not a mere practical consequence of the existence in the real world of non-reasonable citizens (6.1.4). The gap between the operation of reasons in reality and as conceived in the rationalist formulation of the foundational idea is generated by the theory's deep structural commitment to MBC2. My critical argument will show why MBC2 collapses and, consequently, renders the liberal thesis an inadequate conception of justification. In this way the collapse of MBC2 will explain why the theory cannot satisfy its own adequacy criterion. More specifically, I will argue, firstly, that a fully public justificatory strategy, in the sense explained in 6.2.3 above, must rely on an unacknowledged deep structural denial of *active* reflective agency on the part of the theorized subject whose public and private identity is, after all, determined by the category of publicness as embodied in the theorized object. This deep structural analysis will be supported by showing how, on the surface level, (1) *giving* consent ultimately amounts to *receiving* the liberal order's public reasons; (2) the liberal citizen's public identity is unjustifiably redefined from that of a potentially consenting agent to that of a (willing) object of interference; and (3) the private identities of non-consenting citizens are unjustifiably redefined from being non-reasonable to being unreasonable.

6.3.1 The unacknowledged defining role of privateness

I argued above (6.2.3) that Waldron's rationalist interpretation of liberalism's foundational idea constitutes this idea as fully public in the sense that it appeals only to the public dimensions of the subject-object relationship (citizen-liberal order) with which it deals. Political legitimacy requires that, private identities aside, all citizens might exercise their capacity rationally to consent to interference by the liberal order in accordance with their public identity. This consent can be given when the liberal order, in turn, reveals its rationality and supplies them with the reasons for doing so (hereafter 'the reflective standpoint of the liberal order'). Of the two public reflective standpoints to which MBC2 gives rise, those of the theorized subject and object as embodied respectively in the potentially consenting citizen and the liberal order, the former is supposed to be the *active* one. This is because the liberal order's rationality is made transparent in order that it be subjected to the scrutiny of potentially consenting agents.

Despite this, the reflective standpoint of the theorized subject qua potentially consenting agent becomes inactive in contradiction to MBC2's own supposition. This is due to the inter-relationship of MBC2's basic categories. On the one hand, having abstracted the single property constituting citizens' public identity (6.2.2) and having placed it in an exclusive and oppositional relationship to the features constituting their private identities (6.2.4), MBC2 renders the theorized subject's public identity as merely formal and devoid of any content of its own. That is, since all that the theorized subject has to rely on is the rationality defining the power of consent, in encountering the theorized object's rationality the theorized subject has only formal structures of rationality to rely on. On the other, it is the mere exposure of the theorized subject's public identity to the *theorized object's* public rationality (in the sense of consistent public reasons) that brings the two together and gives content to the former. Accordingly, the fully public subject-object relationship that MBC2 recognizes effectively denies the theorized subject's supposed active agency.

One implication of the above deep structural analysis is that contrary to MBC2's supposition, the category of publicness, rather than privateness, defines the public dimensions of the theorized subject-object relationship. This follows from the deep structure's constitution of the theorized object as public (6.2.2). Second, the unacknowledged defining role played by the category of publicness also extends to the definition of that which is constituted as private. This is because MBC2 lacks the deep structural conceptual resources to limit the effects of its denial of the theorized subject's active reflective agency. Since this denial is *unacknowledged* within MBC2, this model of the public-private dichotomy cannot limit the effects of its denial to the public dimensions of the theorized subject-object relationship.

Bringing to the surface MBC2's unacknowledged deep structural commitments results in the collapse of this model of the dichotomy since its attribution of the defining role to the category of privateness can be shown to be incomplete. I turn next to the surface level assessment of Waldron's theory in the light of these deep structural considerations.

6.3.2 *Giving* consent or *receiving* the liberal order's public reasons

Given MBC2's deep structural commitments it would seem that on the surface level the task of an enlightened citizen, such as the liberal theorist, is to construct the hypothetical situation in which the public reasons in favour of the liberal order might be made transparent to citizens' formal reason. In fact, however, such a task requires the theorist to abandon the reflective standpoint of the citizen in favour of that of the liberal order itself and this, in turn, renders the citizen's critical reflective standpoint inactive.

To see that this unacknowledged shift in the liberal theorist's critical standpoint is required (when the construct of hypothetical consent is used to render transparent the rationality of the liberal order) consider the surface level conditions under which hypothetical consent may have justificatory force. These are, firstly, that individuals benefit from the interference, regardless of whether or not they consent to it and, secondly, that the liberal order's mode of interference (its particular coercive and regulatory institutions and practices) does indeed supply the benefit.

To see that these conditions characterize Waldron's own reasoning consider an example he introduces to explain why hypothetical consent can make a difference to the wrongness of interference (6.1.3). He suggests that if a surgeon hypothesizes that his unconscious patient would consent to life-saving surgery were he in a position to do so, 'the operation may be morally legitimate, even though, as it happens the patient never recovers and is unable to ratify the agreement given on his behalf' (TFL, pp. 138-9). It is worth noting here that Waldron does not offer the imaginary case of the surgeon's relationship to an unconscious patient in need of life-saving surgery as an argument by analogy that finds its parallel political relationship in a case where circumstances do not permit a government to consult the citizenry about some specific decision that will extraordinarily interfere with citizens' lives, such as a declaration of war. Instead, the doctor-patient relationship serves to illustrate some of Waldron's general claims concerning the legitimacy of the liberal institutional order as a totality. Now if hypothetical consent makes a moral difference in the imaginary case this presumably has to do with the patient's objective medical condition, on the one hand, and the doctor's ability to perform the necessary operation, on the other. These two conditions take for granted the existence of a relationship of provider (surgeon) and recipient (patient) of the benefit (life-saving surgery).

Similarly, the justificatory force of citizens' hypothetical consent to the liberal order rests on the assumption that the liberal order's mode of interference is objectively beneficial to them. That is, in order that hypothetical consent serve as a strategy for justifying the political legitimacy of the liberal order the liberal theorist must already presuppose that the liberal order's mode of interference is in fact beneficial to individuals. In presupposing this relationship of provider (liberal order) and recipient (citizen) of the benefit (the liberal order's mode of coercion and regulation) the liberal theorist effectively adopts the reflective standpoint of the liberal order whose role, as already explained, is to supply the public reasons in its favour (6.1.3 and 6.2.3). Taking it for granted that the liberal order's mode of interference is objectively beneficial puts the liberal theorist in the position of *advocate* for the liberal order; having become its mouthpiece, so to speak, the theorist takes up the role of making the liberal order's rationality transparent.

Now, there are two significant features of this understanding of the liberal theorist's role in adopting the hypothetical justificatory strategy. One is that the advocacy role just referred to sets the liberal theorist's role apart from the critical role that Waldron's theory attributes to the citizen. Recall that citizens are supposed to subject the social order to *critical scrutiny* (6.1.1) and it is for this reason that their consent to a social order is supposed to have the power to confer political legitimacy on it (6.1.2). The other significant point is that the reflection in the hypothetical situation, the theorist's act of rendering transparent the liberal order's rationality is not after all directed to the hypothetical citizen. Just as in the doctor-patient case mentioned above, the question of the legitimacy of intervention is a matter for the doctor and not the patient, so too, the problem of the liberal order's political legitimacy becomes a question of how the liberal theorist is to represent the liberal order to himself qua advocate rather than critic.

It follows from that above that in the liberal theorist's intellectual exercise of hypothesizing, the liberal institutional order's advocate, rather than the citizen, turns out to be the active agent of reflection. Therefore, Waldron's hypothetical justificatory strategy renders the citizen's critical reflective standpoint inactive.

One might object to the above argument that the liberal order's advocate merely acts or reflects *on behalf of* its citizens. In much the same way as the doctor imagines a situation in which *the patient* instructs him to operate, in the hypothesis the liberal institutional order takes it that *its citizens* give it the go ahead to impose restrictions on them. The problem with this response is that it ignores the effect on the constitution of the rational citizen of the fact that the hypothesizing is taken up from the reflective standpoint of the social order. I turn next to this issue.

6.3.3 The redefinition of the citizen's public identity from that of a potentially consenting agent to that of a (willing) object of interference

In section 6.3.1 above I argued that at the deep structural level of Waldron's theory, the category of publicness, rather than privateness, defines the public dimensions of the theorized subject-object relationship, even though MBC2 does not acknowledge this. I have already introduced some surface level evidence in support of this claim by showing how in Waldron's elaboration of the hypothetical consent strategy the liberal order, which is constituted as public, plays the *active* reflective role through its advocate, the liberal theorist (6.3.2). (In what follows all references to the role of the liberal theorist should be understood as relating to the theorist's role as advocate or mouthpiece for the public liberal order in the sense already explained in 6.3.2.)

Now I want to explore further *the effect* of the operation of the liberal order's active reflective role on the constitution of the citizen's public identity. I will argue, firstly, that this identity undergoes an unacknowledged redefinition when the liberal theorist invokes the hypothetical consent strategy and, secondly, that the surface level effect of this redefinition is to deny Waldron's conception of consent its supposed legitimating power. The demonstration of the first of these claims will lend support to the deep structural claim that Waldron's theory attributes an unacknowledged defining role to the category of publicness. The second will show why, due to this deep structural limitation, Waldron's surface level argument lacks a form suited to the satisfaction of its own adequacy criterion.

Recall from section 6.3.1 above that the citizen's public identity is defined by the power to consent to a social order whose public reasons conform to the formal structures of the citizen's rationality. Now, in hypothesizing, the liberal theorist invokes the public identity of citizens after having taken for granted the objectivity of the benefit to them of the social order's interference. So, the operative conception of the citizen's public identity must implicitly be restricted from the outset by the kind of justification that the liberal order is capable of supplying. That is, if the liberal order's reasons are to be acceptable, the citizen's public identity must first be understood as that of a *potential willing object of the relevant mode of interference*. Only then can the citizen's public identity be hypothesized specifically as the identity of a *willing* object of interference.

Notice, however, that in this kind of intellectual exercise, the view that the citizen's public identity should be understood as a potential object of interference does not form part of that which the theory's model of justification can address, the construct of hypothetical consent. Whereas the justification of the liberal order's mode of interference is an issue for the liberal theorist/order, the justification of citizen's specific object status is not. Yet this object status does not form part of, nor is it entailed by, the definition of citizen's public identity in terms of their power of rational consent. Moreover, a surface level revision of Waldron's theory could not simply introduce citizens' object status as constitutive of their public identity by rendering it a further property that is abstracted from the view of private individuality with which Waldron's theory begins. This is because, as we will see shortly, to recognize citizens' object status would be to deny the primacy that Waldron's theory tries to give to individuals' status as agents with the legitimating power of consent.

If the above analysis is correct, then Waldron's reliance on the hypothetical consent strategy does not merely put citizens' private identities aside in order to rely only on their power of rational consent. Significantly, it involves an unacknowledged redefinition of the citizen's public identity from that of *potentially consenting agent* to that of a mere *object of interference* (hereafter 'individuals' object status'). Because the liberal theorist who has adopted the role of *the public order's advocate* is the one who plays this defining role, it is the category of publicness that plays an unacknowledged defining role after all.

This unacknowledged re-definition of citizens' public identity, whose deep structural source is the unacknowledged defining role played by the category of publicness, can also explain why Waldron's surface level argument lacks a form suited to the satisfaction of the adequacy criterion implied by the liberal thesis. Recall that to meet the criterion of universal subjective consent Waldron's theory should give an account of the legitimacy of the liberal political order as *grounded* in the consent of all its subjects (6.1.2). Satisfaction of this adequacy criterion calls for an argument in roughly the following form.

1. Individuals' hypothetical consent confers political legitimacy on a social order.
2. Individuals hypothetically consent to a liberal order.
3. Therefore, a liberal order is politically legitimate.

Now, Waldron's argument does not merely face the problem of failing to give adequate support for premise 2 above. Rather, when we bring to the surface the unacknowledged deep structural commitments of MBC2 (6.3.1) they suggest that his surface level argument takes the following form instead.

1. A rational order is politically legitimate.
2. A legitimate order should be the object of individuals' consent.
3. A liberal order is a rational order.
4. Therefore, a liberal order should be the object of individuals' consent.

Because Waldron's hypothetical justificatory strategy redefines citizens' public identity as a potential object of interference, contrary to Waldron's assertions hypothetical consent cannot *confer* political legitimacy on the liberal order. At best, in hypothetically receiving the liberal order's public rationality and thereby becoming its willing objects of interference, liberal citizens can be viewed as consenting to a social order whose political legitimacy must be already and otherwise established. Interestingly, when Waldron denies that consent theory necessarily relates questions of political *legitimacy* to questions of political *obligation* he implicitly rejects versions of consent theory that base political legitimacy on obligation deriving from consent. Yet in attempting to employ hypothetical consent theory to address the question of political legitimacy alone, he ends up putting forward a version of consent theory that bases consent on the state's legitimacy which then needs to be otherwise established, contrary to his own assertions.[15] Now we can see from the deep structural analysis why, even though Waldron's strategy of treating questions of legitimacy and obligation separately initially looks to be an advance on classical consent theory, it nevertheless succumbs to the deep structural limitations of theories that adopt this version of a minimal political morality approach.[16]

6.3.4 The redefinition of citizens' private identities from non-reasonable to unreasonable

My deep structural analysis of MBC2's limitations argued that the unacknowledged defining role that the category of publicness plays also extends to the redefinition of that which is constituted as private (6.3.1). In this final part of my critique I will show that by playing an *unacknowledged* defining

---

15. On the distinction between the use of consent as a basis of obligation *grounding* political legitimacy and as something that *follows from* the state's legitimacy in the works of Locke and Rousseau see Hirschmann, *Rethinking Obligation*, pp. 87-8.

16. Of course, supporters of liberal contractarianism may avoid focusing on consent as the ground of justification. For example, Gerry Gaus favours a 'deontologically constrained teleology' in, Gaus, *Value and Justification: The Foundations of Liberal Theory*, pp. 328-67. This more sophisticated version of contractarianism is beyond the scope of our present discussion since it exemplifies a comprehensive approach to defining liberalism.

role, the category of publicness, as embodied by the liberal order also *unjustifiably* redefines that of privateness that is in turn embodied by the surface level notion of individuality.

We can find surface level evidence of this effect in the theory's treatment of the gap between non-liberal spirited citizens' hypothetical and actual assessments of the liberal order. Recall that Waldron's account attributes this gap to the fact that there exist, not only unreasonable people who want to impose their views on others but also, *non*-reasonable individuals (6.1.4). Recall also that the deep structural analysis of Waldron's theory showed that when individuals' private identities are supposed to come back into play in a consideration of the theory's application to the reality of life in a liberal order—once the hypothetical grounds of consent have been constructed—the private identities of *all* non-liberal-spirited individuals must be implicitly treated as *unreasonable* despite Waldron's surface level claims (6.2.5). What we have here is a reversal in the order of explanation of the phenomena with which the theory is concerned. Whereas individuals are initially said to withhold their consent because they are non-reasonable, in the end (non-liberal) individuals appear to be unreasonable because they withhold their consent.

Now I want to show that in the absence of its reliance on this unjustified reversal in the order of its explanation Waldron's theory cannot meet its own adequacy criterion. The reason for this is that when citizens' object status is taken for granted, as it is in the theory's model of justification (6.3.3), their private identities must also be understood in a way that does not permit them to question the attribution to them of an object status, since it is their private identities that give rise to the demand for justification (6.1). To allow for such a possibility would be to recognize the limits of the theory's justificatory model. Accordingly, on the surface level, Waldron's theory needs to rely on an unjustified classification of individuals' private identities into *reasonable* ones that do not question their object status and the remainder that must be relegated to the unreasonable. So, such non-liberal-spirited individuals' private identities are themselves redefined as unreasonable in the light of the theory's unacknowledged attribution to all citizens of an object status.

Yet non-liberal spirited citizens' unwillingness to conceive of themselves in terms of this formulation of their public identity is not necessarily a matter of unreasonably rejecting the liberal order's public reasons. An unwillingness to embrace the object status to which Waldron's rationalist interpretation of the foundational idea reduces citizens' public identity does not straightforwardly involve a mere failure to abstract the power of rational consent from the constituents of one's private identity as the theory requires. It may instead derive from a reasonable resistance to the taken for granted constitution of the individual's public identity in the terms of an object of the liberal order's interference as discussed above. Left anarchist theory probably supplies the best example of political philosophy that does not set up the problem of the state-citizen relationship in terms of the justification of some mode of state interference but we can also find other examples of political philosophy that might reasonably reject the theory's attribution of an object status to citizens from approaches (rightly or wrongly) associated with the republican tradition. For instance, on Philip Pettit's characterization, republicanism views the state-citizen relationship as one of trustee and trustor(s) and, on the version of republicanism he defends, its central value is the ideal of freedom as non-domination, a condition that may exist both in the presence and in the absence of state interference.[17] Precisely because the attribution to individuals of an object status is what enables Waldron's theory to ignore this republican ideal and to focus exclusively on the question of the legitimacy of state *interference* in citizens' lives, the republican might *reasonably* question the starting point of Waldron's theory. At the same time, if, as Pettit maintains, the approach of populists (who, in advocating a direct democracy, have been misidentified as republicans) 'represents the people in their collective presence as master and the state as servant', then they too could not reasonably accept citizens' object status as their background assumption.[18]

It follows that without its unjustified redefinition of the private identities of all non-liberal-spirited individuals as unreasonable, only liberal-spirited individuals can be said to identify their public identity in the terms of a potential object of the liberal order's interference. At the same time, at least some non-liberal-spirited individuals prove to be neither unreasonable nor are they given good reasons to view themselves as the potential objects of the liberal order's interference.[19] Since universal subjective consent requires the rational consent of *all* citizens to the liberal order's mode of interference (6.1.2), the theory fails to satisfy its own adequacy criterion.

---

17. Pettit, *Republicanism*, pp. 8 & 21-7.

18. Pettit, *Republicanism*, p. 8.

19. Waldron's reference to the benefits of social cooperation (6.1.1) do not in themselves supply good reasons to accept the liberal formulation of the state-citizen relationship. It explains its emergence but does not give a normative justification for it. The view that takes the legitimacy of interferences to depend on whether those who find themselves within the liberal state's jurisdiction have thereby benefited merely takes for granted the liberal thesis' implicit formulation of the state-citizen relationship by focusing on *when* the liberal order's interference is justified rather then *whether* interference is justifiable. For example, Rawls' principle of fairness holds that in 'a mutually advantageous cooperative venture' in which 'persons restrict their liberty in ways necessary to yield advantages for all' 'those who have submitted to these restrictions have a right to a similar acquiescence on the part of those who have benefited from their submission', Rawls, *A Theory of Justice*, p. 112. Here, participants are taken to be (willing) objects of beneficial interference within the already given framework of a 'mutually advantageous' cooperative venture.

6.4 The desideratum for a new model of the public-private dichotomy

The negative outcome of the above critique is the collapse of MBC2. The category of *privateness* cannot successfully constitute the starting point of an account of liberalism that seeks to give a *public* justification. The argument has shown that a theory whose deep structure purports to give defining priority to the category of privateness does not fare any better than one that, as we saw in the previous chapter, attributes this role to the category of publicness. Indeed, in both cases, whereas one of the categories is supposed to play the defining role, this role is effectively taken up by its opposite in a way that remains unacknowledged within the frameworks of both MBC1 and MBC2.

This said, there is also a significant difference in the outcome of the assessment of these two models. Whereas in MBC1 the category of publicness failed to play a defining role due to its inability effectively to differentiate between that designated as public and private as required by its foundational idea, in MBC2 *both* the categories of publicness and privateness play some defining role, albeit consecutively. Indeed the conceptual problems emerge precisely because MBC2 cannot recognize the defining role that is *also* played by the category of publicness. These observations lead to the formulation of a new desideratum for the best interpretation of the principle that either publicness or privateness plays the defining role. We need to consider the adequacy of a model of the public-private dichotomy that, on the one hand, takes the category of publicness as the starting point of its theory construction (in order to avoid the limitations of relying on the category of privateness for this purpose), and, on the other, creates the space within its framework for some defining role to be played alternately by each of the categories.

The discussion so far has also demonstrated the link between the inadequate models of the public-private dichotomy and attempts at the surface level to give an account of liberalism in terms of some *foundational idea*. Whilst the arguments have shown that liberalism cannot be successfully defined by reference to hypothetical consent theory or to any of the substantive ideas considered in the previous chapter, the important conclusion is that, differences aside, these theories all fail as accounts of liberalism because they overburden the foundational ideas on which they rely to do the necessary explanatory or interpretive work. This is so regardless of differences in the content of the theorists' respective claims. So a revised account of liberalism that continues to insist on restricting the scope of the idea of liberalism to some foundational idea will be similarly flawed given that at the level of its deep structure this approach relies on what have been shown to be problematic models of the public-private dichotomy.[20]

---

20. This conclusion applies to theories that conform to the deep structural logic under

Still, it has only been established that limiting the scope of the idea of liberalism to some *foundational* idea does not work. As indicated in the introduction to the previous chapter, the second sense in which liberalism may be viewed as a minimal position is that which takes liberalism to consist of a complete political morality worked out by reference to some *acceptable or reasonable*, rather than true, *common ground*. The accounts of liberalism that take this form are developed in the light of a recognition of the presence in modern societies of reasonably held diverse and opposed metaphysical and ethical ideas. This recognition gives rise to the view that the grounds of an adequate political morality should not rely on such ideas. In order to avoid reliance on controversial ideals some have focused on singling out a neutral deliberative and discursive *procedure*. In the version of this sort of account that Charles Larmore has developed this procedure is defined by the norms of rational dialogue and equal respect. This is the view that we will assess in the next chapter. As we will see, Larmore's account of liberalism embodies a third model of the public-private dichotomy characterizing the deep structure of accounts of liberalism that conform to the minimal political morality approach. This model warrants further investigation because it meets the desideratum identified above.

---

consideration irrespective of their surface level claims. It applies, for example, to the account of liberalism's foundations that Graham Long proposes in *Relativism and the Foundations of Liberalism* because at the deep structural level Long's account of the moral relativist foundations of liberalism can be shown to conform to MBC2 (see Graham M. Long, *Relativism and the Foundations of Liberalism*, Exeter, Imprint Academic, 2004.). Because the relativist justificatory standards that he derives from the methodology of reflective equilibrium conform to a structuring logic according to which the category of privateness is supposed to play the defining role, we can expect to find surface level evidence of the same deep structural flaw that operates in Waldron's account as well.

7

Charles Larmore: Liberalism and Neutral Procedural Discourse

Charles Larmore focuses liberalism on a certain deliberative and discursive procedure that is defined by the norms of rational dialogue and equal respect. In this way his account of liberalism avoids appeal to too abstractly formulated ideas such as that of individuals' consent to a liberal order (Waldron) or of persons' interest in leading an objectively good life (Kymlicka). Nor does it suffer from the limitations of confining the scope of the idea of liberalism to some *foundational* idea. By contrast with the theories discussed in the previous chapters, the definition of liberalism in terms of political principles derivable from a discursive procedure enables the development of a liberal political morality from a public reflective standpoint that is based on *acceptable*, as distinct from true, propositions.

Despite these very significant differences at a surface level, I will defend the reconstructive claim that the deep structure of Larmore's theory is similar to that of Waldron's and Kymlicka's theories in so far as it too embodies an interpretation of the principle that one category plays the defining role in the public-private dichotomy. At the same time, the model of the dichotomy that Larmore's theory embodies is more sophisticated than those examined so far since it supposes each of the two basic categories to play a defining role within their separate designated domains. My critical claim will be that this model of the public-private dichotomy nevertheless contradicts the above supposition due to its unacknowledged bias in favour of ideas whose form remains intrinsically private. This results in the collapse of the model of the public-private dichotomy to which the theory's deep structure conforms. The collapse of the dichotomy, in turn, explains why the theory fails to satisfy its adequacy criterion at the surface level.

In section 1 I will outline Larmore's account of liberalism with the aims, firstly, of demonstrating precisely how it exemplifies the minimal political morality approach to defining liberalism; and, secondly, revealing the theory's own adequacy criterion. In section 2 I will reconstruct the theory to bring to the surface its deep structural suppositions. In the remaining sections I will develop a deep structural critique of the account I attribute to Larmore and explore the surface level implications of this critique.

7.1 Charles Larmore's account of liberalism

7.1.1 Liberalism's two problems

According to Larmore, liberal thought seeks a solution to two basic problems: first, 'to fix some moral limits to the powers of government' based on the idea that 'there is a common good which government ought to recognize and promote' and, second, to specify the terms of political association in light of 'the increasing awareness that reasonable people tend to differ and disagree about the nature of the good life' (hereafter 'modern subjective conditions') (LPL, pp. 339-40).[1] In this context 'reasonableness' refers to 'thinking and conversing in good faith and applying the general capacities of reason that belong to every domain of inquiry' (LPL, p. 340). Such 'good faith and common reason' are taken in themselves to be insufficient as a basis for selecting between rival conceptions of the good life that involve 'different structures of purposes, significances and attitudes' (LPL, p. 342).

> To solve both problems together, [liberalism's] aim has been to circumscribe the role of the state by means of a *minimal moral conception* (LPL, p. 340-1).

Larmore believes that a solution to the two problems can be found only when liberals abandon attempts to ground political principles on a theory of human flourishing or on substantive ideals of the human good (hereafter 'ideals of the person' or 'personal ideals'). Liberalism should focus instead on a moral conception that is minimal in the sense that it is 'less comprehensive than the views of the good life about which reasonable people disagree' (LPL, p. 341; also PMC, p. 51). Accordingly, his approach restricts the scope of the idea of liberalism to political principles based on a certain type of moral reason that can play the role of supplying liberal political morality with its justificatory grounds.

---

1. Also reproduced in Charles Larmore, *The Morality of Modernity*, Cambridge, Cambridge University Press, 1996, pp. 121-51. All page references hereafter are to the journal publication. I focus on this piece in preference to other work by Larmore, such as *Patterns of Moral Complexity*, (especially chapters 3 and 4), not on the ground that it best represents Larmore's position, or indeed that of defenders of political liberalism, but for the reason that it offers a clear statement exemplifying a distinctive version of the minimal political morality approach.

7.1.2 The principle of political neutrality as a minimal moral conception

Larmore argues that the idea of *neutrality* provides just the sort of minimal moral conception that is called for under modern subjective conditions. By asserting the discursive procedural principle that 'in a liberal political order, political principles are to be 'neutral' with respect to controversial ideas of the good' (hereafter '(the principle of) political neutrality'), the idea of neutrality is said to provide a way of

> devis[ing] political principles expressing some idea of the common good [via] a conception that as many people as possible can affirm, despite their inevitable differences about the worth of specific ways of life (LPL, p. 341).

Larmore clarifies that this principle of political neutrality is a *moral* conception because, whilst 'it serves as a common ground' for basing political principles, it neither relies on moral skepticism nor is it a purely formal notion:

> [...] neutral principles are the ones we can justify without appealing to the controversial views of the good life to which we happen to be committed. Of course, the neutral ground on which we thus shall reason must continue to have some moral content. Otherwise, it cannot yield moral limits to the role of the state (LPL, p. 341).

(Larmore also points out that the principle of political neutrality is a procedural ideal and that it 'involves a "neutrality of aim" in virtue of which political principles are not intended to favour any controversial view of the good life [...] But it does not include the additional requirement ("neutrality of effect") that political principles have an equal influence on all permissible ways of life' (LPL, p. 358 fn. 4).[2]) By relying on the idea of neutrality in the above sense of 'a [minimal] moral principle stipulating the conditions on which political principles can be justified' (LPL, p. 342), Larmore's theory exemplifies a minimal political morality approach to defining liberalism that restricts the moral grounds it relies on to *acceptable*, as distinct from true, propositions.

7.1.3 A neutral justification for political neutrality

According to Larmore, in order that liberalism be understood as a commitment to the principle of political neutrality as a minimal moral conception (7.1.2) it itself requires a *neutral justification*. First, Larmore acknowledges that the principle of political neutrality is not the only *reasonable* response to the problem of reasonable disagreement (LPL, p. 342) and that liberalism cannot simply be understood as a commitment to the principle of political

---

2. See also Will Kymlicka, 'Liberalism, Individualism and Liberal Neutrality', *Ethics*, vol. 99, no. 4, 1989, pp. 883-905. For a good discussion of the problems associated with the use of this distinction for the purposes of overcoming objections to the liberal value of neutrality see chapter 5 of Galston, *Liberal Purposes*.

neutrality *whatever* the reasons for this. Indeed, the suggestion that it might stand for such a commitment would constitute a version of the limited political thesis approach. Instead it stands for a commitment to this principle *on the basis of a neutral justification* (LPL, p. 345; PMC, pp. 52-3).

Second, because the principle of political neutrality is in need of justification under modern subjective conditions (7.1.1), this justification must be provided in a way that ought to be acceptable to those who could otherwise reasonably disagree about the justificatory ground(s) for the principle of neutrality. Accordingly, the neutral justification of the principle of political neutrality appeals to 'core' elements that are 'common' to different moralities rather than to a single comprehensive morality (LPL, p. 347).[3]

7.1.4 The theory's adequacy criterion

The *neutrality* of the justification counts in favour of understanding liberalism in the above terms (7.1.3) if we accept Larmore's opening suggestion regarding liberalism's self-definition—the claim that 'the best approach [to distinguishing liberalism from other forms of thought] lies in keeping in mind the two basic *problems* that have motivated liberal thought' (7.1.1)—and we interpret this as a criterion of adequacy for any proposed view of liberalism. He claims at the outset that

> [s]ome versions of liberalism will then appear more appropriate than others in that they take the problems seriously and construct liberal thought around them (LPL, p. 339).

So, for Larmore, the provision of a neutral justification (7.1.3) for the principle of political neutrality (7.1.2) will have the merit of (a) supplying political neutrality with a moral ground at the same time as (b) taking the problem of reasonable disagreement seriously (7.1.1). For this reason, Larmore claims that, whilst he does not hold a 'neutral justification to be the only justification for neutrality', he does 'consider it the only mode of justification fully within the liberal spirit' (LPL, p. 68). (Hereafter references to a 'neutral justification' are to a neutral justification of the principle of political neutrality.) To supply a neutral justification is to meet both aspects of the criterion of adequacy by which Larmore's theory asserts that rival versions of liberalism should be assessed.

7.1.5 Two inadequate models of justification

Larmore presents his account of a *neutral justification* initially by way of con-

---

3. For a surface level argument that the idea of a neutral justification does not support the principle of political neutrality see de Marneffe, 'Liberalism, Liberty, and Neutrality'. More recently, de Marneffe has argued that there is no authoritative account of the distinction between neutral and non-neutral reasons. See Peter de Marneffe, 'The Slipperiness of Neutrality', *Social Theory and Practice: An International and Interdisciplinary Journal of Social Philosophy*, vol. 32, no. 1, 2006, pp. 17-34.

trast with some inadequate alternatives. He argues that neither Kant's nor Mill's respective appeals to the personal ideals of autonomy and individuality can function as an adequate justification since they fail to take seriously the second of the two basic problems liberalism addresses, the problem of reasonable disagreement (7.1.1). According to Larmore, the central insight of their appeals to the ideals of autonomy and individuality is the view that:

> we should always maintain only a contingent and never a constitutive allegiance to any substantial view of the good life, that is, to any concrete way of life involving a specific structure of purposes, significances and activities [...] Such forms of life can be truly valuable, according to Kant and Mill, only if they are chosen from a position of critical detachment, in something like an experimental spirit (LPL, p. 343).

His point is in effect that individualism, the term he uses to refer to the central insight just outlined, is a moral principle about which reasonable people, such as those who defend the so-called 'Romantic ideas' of belonging and custom, can and do disagree. ('Romantics' includes reference to communitarian thinkers such as MacIntyre and Sandel as well as the German Romantics such as Herder and Hegel. Larmore sometimes also refers to 'traditionalists'. I will refer to both groups as 'non-individualists' (PMC, ch. 5)). So, to rely on a controversial ideal like individualism as a moral justification for the principle of political neutrality would be arbitrarily to exclude non-individualist positions from what might be considered 'common ground' (LPL, pp. 342-5; also PMC, pp. 51-2).

On the other hand, Larmore argues, a basically Hobbesian approach is equally unsatisfactory. To base political neutrality on agreement that supposedly results from 'solely strategic considerations', such as the need to accommodate persons who are 'roughly equal in power', will not suffice for at least two reasons. Such an arrangement is inherently unstable 'since it is hostage to the shifting distribution of power' whilst the 'special authority of moral principles'—their categorical force—cannot be explained in terms of mere prudence (LPL, p. 346). Larmore's solution is to substitute a discursive procedure for the personal ideals that people hold as justifications for political principles in order to provide a neutral, moral justification of the principle of political neutrality.

7.1.6 The norms of rational dialogue and equal respect

A neutral justification occupies the space somewhere between the above 'two extremes'. The best such justification, according to Larmore, 'relies on the two norms of rational dialogue and equal respect' (hereafter 'the norms'). According to the first, the appropriate response to disagreement in discussions for the purpose of problem resolution—in particular, that of devising principles of political association—is to 'retreat to neutral ground, to the beliefs [the participants] still share' and to proceed to a solution from this 'common ground' either by resolving the disagreement in favour of one of the initially disputed positions or by by-passing such positions altogether (LPL, p. 347; also PMC, p. 54). Larmore explains further,

> a justification is a proof directed at those who disagree with us to show them that they should join us in believing what we do. It can fulfill this pragmatic role only by appealing to what they already believe, thus to what is common ground between us (LPL, p. 347).

To seek to justify one's beliefs to others is implicitly to adopt the norm of rational dialogue since Larmore claims, firstly following Habermas, that

> to put forward our claim to others in the actual conversation as a claim backed up by good reasons is to assert, in effect, that these good reasons should command the assent of others (PMC, p. 55).

Secondly, he maintains that no matter how one understands the ideal epistemic conditions under which agreement can be reached, the norm of rational dialogue is invariant (PMC, pp. 58-9). Thus the universal applicability of this norm is objectively grounded in the necessary form of communicative action.

Whereas the first norm 'tells us what to do *if* we want to talk together about what political principles to establish', the second, equal respect for persons, 'demands that we go on talking' in the event of disagreement; it prohibits 'resting compliance [with political principles] only on force' (LPL, p. 348). More precisely, this norm claims that persons—that is, those with 'simply the capacity of thinking and acting on the basis of reasons'—be treated as ends in the narrow sense that 'coercive or political principles be as justifiable to [them] as they are to us' (LPL, p. 349; also PMC, pp. 61-4). The norm of equal respect specifies a moral obligation to explain one's actions to others who are affected by them. So, it restates the value that, as we saw in the previous chapter, Waldron refers to as the Enlightenment demand for justification. But whereas in the elaboration of his conception of liberalism Waldron appeals to a rationalist interpretation of this demand, Larmore's dialogical interpretation of the demand rests on a critique of the rationalist view of justification that he thinks has resulted in 'the crisis of Enlightenment ethics' (LPL, p. 349; also PMC, pp. 41-64). Larmore also suggests that the norm of equal respect corresponds to what Ronald Dworkin calls 'the treatment of others as equals' (PMC, p. 62). As we saw in Chapter 5, Kymlicka also invokes the abstract idea of treating others as equals but whereas Kymlicka's account of liberalism consists of a certain interpretation of *the implications* of the abstract idea, Larmore's account appeals only to *the attitude to others* that is expressed in the abstract idea.

According to Larmore, the duty to explain one's actions to persons affected is owed to everyone equally in virtue of their capacity to form their 'own view of the world' (PMC, p. 64). So, liberalism's neutral justification of political neutrality is universalist in that it applies to 'everyone' (that is, within the society or jurisdiction of the political system) in virtue of the objective universality of the norms.[4]

7.1.7 Political liberalism's public-private social division

Larmore terms his account of the neutral justification of the principle of political neutrality, 'political liberalism', in order to signify that it is a reformulation of liberalism as 'strictly a political doctrine' and not a 'general philosophy of man', not a 'comprehensive moral ideal' capturing the whole of life (LPL, pp. 345 & 353). By limiting the application of the norms to the political realm consisting of government and its bureaucracy (PMC, pp. 41-2) (hereafter 'public agencies'), political liberalism is able to endorse the view that

> the individualist treatment of persons as separate from the substantial ideals they may share with others is a strictly political norm, applicable to persons in their role as citizens (LPL, p. 353).

In addition to confining the application of individualism to the treatment of citizens by public agencies, political liberalism treats individualism as 'overriding within the political realm'.

Even so, according to Larmore, since it is not committed to a 'general' individualism concerning the whole of people's lives (LPL, pp. 351-2) this 'shows that Romantics can also be liberals' (LPL, p. 354). They can endorse the principle of political neutrality in the political realm whilst continuing to endorse their preferred ideals of the person, whether individualist or non-individualist, outside of it.

By recognizing 'the heterogeneity of the 'public' (political) and the 'private' (citoyen and homme)' (PMC, p. 124), political liberalism accords priority to the principle of political neutrality in the public realm and to people's attachment to their personal ideal in their private life (PMC, p. 73). This understanding of the modern separation of social spheres views the political order as a 'modus vivendi' understood as a moral 'means of accommodation among individuals sharing different conceptions of the good life', and not as an order that expresses their 'personal ideals' (PMC, p. 91).[5]

Political liberalism thus *explains* its reliance on a hierarchically structured division of public and private categories, a division that gives moral

---

4. For an objection to Larmore's claim that the norms are objectively universal see Richard J. Arneson, 'Neutrality and Utility (Religious and Other Forms of Tolerance by the State)', *Canadian Journal of Philosophy*, vol. 20, no. 2, 1990, pp. 215-40, pp. 223-5.

5. For surface level critiques of the modus vivendi view of liberalism see Rawls, *Political Liberalism*, pp. 145-50. See also Moore, *Foundations of Liberalism*, pp. 126-32, Caney Simon, 'Consequentialist Defences of Liberal Neutrality', *The Philosophical Quarterly*, vol. 41, no. 165, 1991, pp. 457-77, pp. 471-3.

priority to the former whilst also allowing the latter to take priority in their restricted domain. It explains the difference in the moral priority of values operating in the public and private social realms in terms of the embodiment of people's commitment to the norms for the purposes of public discourse. Political liberalism, therefore, treats individualism as the overriding value of the public social realm pursuant to which public agencies should view citizenship in the light of common ideals and, so, in abstraction from controversial ideals of the person. Controversial ideals of the person, in turn, take moral priority in the private social realm (hereafter 'liberalism's public-private social division').

7.1.8 Political liberalism's ideal citizens

Larmore advances the argument for political liberalism against the background of two explicit assumptions. The first appeals to what can be referred to as the subjective universality of the norms. It holds that

> the argument really applies to the ideal case in which everyone in the society already accepts the norms of rational dialogue and equal respect.

Second, it applies only to those who share a 'common life' in terms of '[g]eography, a common language and a common historical experience', and in relation to which they 'are indeed interested in devising principles of political association' (LPL, pp. 351-2). In short, the norms of rational dialogue and equal respect 'are assumed to enjoy a general mutuality' amongst those who 'think of themselves as engaged in this common project' (hereafter 'ideal citizens') (LPL, p. 352).

These two background assumptions combine to restrict the application of Larmore's theory to socio-political orders whose members already happen to endorse the norms and who share, and are willing to continue sharing, a political life. These constitute the subjective conditions under which political neutrality is neutrally justified and, in turn, embodied in the organization of society in accordance with liberalism's view of the public-private social division (7.1.7).

7.1.9 The requirements of a public justification

The argument concludes that the two norms provide 'the terms in which a liberal state ought to *announce publicly* the basis of its legitimacy' and they are 'a more fitting response to the basic problems that liberalism has sought to solve' (LPL, p. 347) because they *combine* an objective and subjective universality. On the one hand, they have 'the special authority of moral principles' (LPL, p. 347):

> in political liberalism [...] the norms of rational dialogue and equal respect, as well as the principle of neutrality they justify, are understood

to be correct and valid norms and not merely norms which people in a liberal order merely believe to be correct and valid (LPL, p. 353).

On the other hand, 'political liberalism is to be understood as a correct moral conception and not just as an object of consensus' but the reasons for taking it to be correct do not function as *the ground* for its 'rational acceptability'. Its rational acceptability remains independent of such a condition in order to take seriously the problem of reasonable disagreement in 'a continuing controversy about what the correctness of a moral conception consists in' (LPL, pp. 354-6).[6] The rational acceptability of political liberalism depends, instead, on its meeting 'a condition of relevance' to modern Western thought (LPL, p. 356). The norms satisfy this condition, according to Larmore, not because they are 'implicitly contained in the bare notion of reasonableness', but because they have been 'central elements in Western thought' that have been held by individualists and non-individualists alike (LPL, pp. 347 & 357).

> It is true that political liberalism aims to occupy a common ground between the champions of individualism and the defenders of tradition. But what makes this common ground an appropriate basis for principles of political association is not the mere fact that it is common ground, an object of agreement. It is rather the fact that this common ground includes the norms of rational dialogue and equal respect (LPL, p. 353).

In so far as he insists on citizens' actual willingness to adopt the norms and share a political life, Larmore's account of liberalism differs significantly from Waldron's that, as we saw in the previous chapter, relies unsuccessfully on hypothetical consent theory. Larmore insists that we should read the subjective universality of the norms in a voluntarist rather than merely rationalist way. At the same time, it by-passes the problems usually associated with actual consent theory given that the object of consent is not the political order as such but the specific procedural norms constituting all public discourse under the subjective conditions of modernity.

7.2 A model of the public-private dichotomy in which each basic category plays a defining role

7.2.1 Public reasoning

The first point to note about the deep structure of Larmore's account is that the norms (7.1.6) are supposed to take the place of ideals of the person (7.1.5) for the purposes of *public* reasoning. Reasoning for the purposes of devising political principles is constituted as *public* both because it seeks to proceed

---

6. As it turns out, Larmore, himself, can offer 'no ready answer' to the question of what reasons should be given in support of the view that the norms are indeed objectively correct, Larmore, 'Political Liberalism', pp. 356-7.

from common ground between the theorized subjects, the participants in political discourse, and because its object is restricted to the political realm conceived as the public social sphere. In contrast to the form of the deep structure characterizing Waldron's intellectual practice, public reasoning as characterized by the norms constitutes the theorized *object* and is not defined solely in terms of individuals' capacity to reason. Recall from section 7.1.9 that the norms are not 'implicitly contained in the bare notion of reasonableness'. Nor is this conception of public reasoning defined in explicit opposition to persons' private reasoning; it does not presuppose the exclusion of all appeals to ideals of the person. Instead, the norms constitute public reasoning as a discursive procedure that dialogically differentiates personal ideals that are common and controversial.

7.2.2 The discursive differentiation of public and private ideals

Second, the dialogical procedure renders the common ideals operative in the public-political realm and excludes ideals that are found to be controversial due to reasonable disagreement (7.1.7) thereby rendering them private. In this way, the differentiation of public and private ideals—the question of where to draw the line—is supposed to emerge out of the actual discursive procedure in which the norms are exercised. Unlike Kymlicka's and Waldron's theories which implicitly or explicitly begin by excluding that which is constituted as private from the domain of public reason, in Larmore's argument that which is constituted as private is supposed to result from, rather than be presupposed by the exercise of public reason (7.1.7). Since the attribution of publicness or privateness to any personal ideal is taken to flow from the procedure of public discourse, prior to the operation of this procedure personal ideals are supposed to be essentially neither public nor private (hereafter 'the supposed initial neutrality of ideals').

7.2.3 Public and private personal ideals

The third point to note is that the substitution of the norms for the ideals that people hold as justifications of political principles withdraws from the latter any public justificatory force only in the event that they turn out to be controversial. Personal ideals are, therefore, not inevitably constituted as private and when rendered public they can justifiably be invoked in the public social domain.

7.2.4 The basic categories alternate defining roles

Fourth, the social division between people's public and private ideals supposedly does not require people to abandon their personal ideals in the event that they cannot be rendered public. Rendering ideals private merely restricts the space in which they may be pursued to the domain designated as private (7.1.7). So, political liberalism's public-private social division is supposed to ensure an alternative space in which the category of privateness can play a defining role without thereby contradicting the defining role played by the category of publicness. Call this model of the public-private dichotomy MBC3.

7.2.5 The neutral justification's public existence

Finally, since the appropriateness of the characterization of public reasoning in terms of the two norms rests on their subjective universality and not just their objective universality (7.1.8), the norms are attributed a public existence in the sense of being the shared properties of ideal citizens. Furthermore, since the norms are taken to supply a public justification (7.1.9) MBC3 gives rise to a public justification that is attributed a public existence in the above sense.

This being the case, it becomes of crucial significance not simply that the norms can be represented as the core of alternative comprehensive moralities but that *they have in fact* functioned in the way that Larmore claims. If this supposed core morality is an appropriate basis for the principle of political neutrality it is because, as a matter of historical fact, it constitutes the common ground between rival positions within the modern western intellectual tradition and culture. This is supposed to be the reason why 'both parties to the dispute about individualism and tradition' can affirm the norms as a basis for justifying political neutrality (7.1.7) and, given their willingness to engage in a common project (7.1.8), endorse liberalism's principle of political neutrality.

7.3 The collapse of the public-private dichotomy in which the basic categories alternately define the content of ideas

The subjective universality of the norms (7.1.8) is difficult to dispute when applied to the participants in liberal societies that are *modern* western thinkers.[7] As an argumentative strategy, the norm of rational dialogue is familiar and seems wise given the pragmatic objective of reaching agreement (7.1.6) and, since the norm of equal respect restates the Enlightenment demand for justification (7.1.6), one can agree that it too has been central to modern western political thought and widely endorsed (by enlightened citizens) within liberal societies. However, this observation will prove to be beside the point once we consider Larmore's account of the *application* of the norms in the light of the above analysis of the theory's deep structure. As already indicated, MBC3 supposes that ideals of the person are in themselves neutral

---

7. We can leave to one side Larmore's treatment of racist fanatics, Charles Larmore, *Patterns of Moral Complexity*, Cambridge, Cambridge University Press, 1987, p. 66. On this see Moore, *Foundations of Liberalism*, p. 136. Here I will not be suggesting that the norm of equal respect is limited because it does not require liberals to justify coercive principles to fanatics on grounds that the latter can accept.

as regards their publicness or privateness (7.2.2). My analysis will show, however, that at the same time as proposing a model of discourse that takes the publicness or privateness of personal ideals to be the outcome of public discourse the theory rests on an unacknowledged view of the intrinsically private *form* of personal ideals. The 'form of personal ideals' refers to the way in which their bearers relate them to their other beliefs and it includes the reasoning processes through which their bearers come to endorse them. I will argue in section 7.3.1 that the theory's deep structure treats all personal ideals as having an intrinsically private *form*, regardless of whether or not their *content* is rendered as public or private. Bringing this unacknowledged view to the surface results in the collapse of MBC3.

I will also argue that this fundamental flaw in the theory's deep structure explains why it cannot satisfy its own adequacy criterion at the surface level. First, because Larmore's model of discourse fails to recognize the existence of ideals whose form is intrinsically public his account of political liberalism cannot satisfy the second aspect of the theory's adequacy criterion, that of taking reasonable disagreement seriously (7.1.4). I will demonstrate in section 7.3.2 that political liberalism's appeal to the norms as its defence of the principle of political neutrality is not neutral with regard to controversial questions concerning the form and the role of personal ideals. Consequently, contrary to Larmore's claims, some reasonable people, namely those who hold personal ideals whose form is intrinsically public, are required to *give up* their ideals of the person as well as their beliefs about the best way to engage in the task of political theorizing.

Secondly, bringing to the surface MBC3's suppositions will show why the theory's idea of public reasoning is an empty category. Because personal ideals with an intrinsically private form define the form rather than merely supply the content of public discourse as the theory supposes the categories constituted as private play a defining role beyond their designated domain (7.2.4). I will demonstrate in section 7.3.3 that *they* play the defining role in the domain where the theory attributes this role to supposedly public categories. Consequently, the theory is unable to satisfy the first aspect of its own adequacy criterion, that of relying on justificatory grounds with the special authority of moral principles (7.1.9).

7.3.1 The form of personal ideals

Recall that Larmore's account is not supposed to discriminate between the individualist and non-individualist ideals of the person that exist within the modern western cultural and intellectual tradition (7.1.5). So, at the surface level, it would appear that people may raise all sorts of ideals for public discussion and possible inclusion in the common ground governing the public social realm.[8] Given that the public discursive procedure places no prior re-

---

8. In this regard Larmore's theory is immune to the sort of objection that Seyla Benha-

strictions on the sorts of modern personal ideals that might be included in public discussion, it ought to be the case that this observation holds for both the content and the form of personal ideals where 'the form of an ideal' refers to the way in which its bearer relates it to other ideas including the reasoning processes leading to its endorsement.

Furthermore, to avoid reliance on controversial claims the theory should remain neutral on the question of the form of personal ideals. Yet, even though it is silent on this issue it does not remain neutral. On the contrary, the theory is biased in favour of ideals of the person whose form is *intrinsically private* in the sense of being represented as the ideals of intrinsically private agents. Recall that the distinguishing feature of persons understood as intrinsically private agents is that they may in principle define their ideals in their singularity, whether or not they happen to pursue them in groups. The theory's bias is due to the fact that, in purporting to be neutral on the question of the character and moral status of personal ideals, the discursive procedure recognizes each person as a bearer of her ideal prior to, and independently of, the process of differentiating common and controversial ideals. Accordingly, ideals enter into the discourse as the properties of private agents. Once ideals are thought of as prima facie the properties of private agents it makes sense to treat them as *privately formed*. Yet, as Brian Barry has argued, to treat certain kinds of moral convictions as if they were matters of *private* belief or *private* preference is to rely on a distorted view of how they function in the belief systems and valuings of non-liberals. Barry makes this point to show that the principle of political neutrality cannot be neutrally justified since, in treating certain kinds of moral convictions as private, it presupposes 'a liberal outlook'.[9] On Larmore's account all such ideals, no matter what their form as understood by their bearer, enter into the discursive procedure as the intrinsically private ideals of intrinsically private agents. In the present context the notion of a private agent may refer to groups of persons (such as the family or other social unit) and not exclusively to human beings. What is significant is that in entering into public discourse participants are recognized in their singularity. Even if their ideal is one that they understand in terms of a goal *to be shared* with other participants, since the discursive procedure recognizes it as their ideal prior to and indepen-

---

bib raises, correctly in my view, against Bruce Ackerman's account of public discourse. In 'Models of Public Space' she argues that Ackerman's model of conversation restraint presupposes that participants know their disagreements before entering into the conversation in which case the issues to be left off the public agenda are pre-determined. This has the effect of denying the 'contestatory elements of public discourse' involving political struggles to redefine and expand the public agenda, Benhabib, *Situating the Self*, pp. 95-103. See also B. Thigpen Robert and A. Downing Lyle, 'Liberalism and the Neutrality Principle', *Political Theory*, vol. 11, no. 4, 1983, pp. 585-600.

9. Brian Barry, 'How Not to Defend Liberal Institutions', *British Journal of Political Science*, vol. 20, no. 1, 1990, pp. 1-14, pp. 6-11.

dently of public discourse, publicness cannot inform the ideal.

The public discursive procedure's bias in favour of viewing the form of all personal ideals as intrinsically private determines the shape of the possible outcomes of public discourse. On the one hand, if the content of an ideal turns out to be controversial, its privateness is discursively affirmed and the scope of appeals on its behalf is restricted to the private social realm. On the other hand, should the content of an ideal turn out to be common to participants and, accordingly, rendered public this discursively attributed public status still does not affect the unacknowledged intrinsically private character of that ideal's form. This is because, as the reconstructive analysis of MBC3 has shown, (a) by being rendered public an ideal becomes one that public-political decisions can justifiably invoke (7.2.3); and (b) in order to be rendered public all that is required is that it be held in common (7.2.2). (Of course, this does not preclude there being more to an ideal qua public ideal. My point is precisely that MBC3 sets inappropriate limits to what the discursive procedure can *recognize* as public.) What matters in Larmore's model of the public discursive procedure is that participants have and offer their reasons and arguments to each other, not that they make each other's reasons their own. Other than that they comply with the constraints of the norms, there are no requirements on the actual reasoning processes that lead each of the participants to endorse the personal ideals that are ultimately rendered public. The model, therefore, treats such reasoning processes as matters of *private* reasoning even when the content of some ideal is rendered public. Accordingly, taking some ideal to be a common ground of political principles does not affect the operation of the unacknowledged view that personal ideals are to be defined by private agents.

So, contrary to MBC3's suppositions, rather than transforming ideals that are initially fully neutral as regards their publicness or privateness into one or other kind (7.2.2), the public discursive procedure merely determines their field of operation in the light of the extent of participants' *endorsement of their content*. This is not to say that by entering into a dialogue with others one cannot exchange views about the form of personal ideals, change the content of one's beliefs and even be convinced to share some ideal with others thereby rendering its content public in the sense that Larmore's account is able to recognize. The point is rather that, no matter what one's commitments end up being and regardless of whether their contents are rendered private, because controversial, or public, in that they are also held by others, the public procedure of discourse cannot alter the taken-for-granted intrinsically private character of their form. This is because the only public requirement concerning the form of ideals is compliance with the two norms.

Now, to take the form of ideals of the person to be intrinsically private is to fail to acknowledge in the model of public discourse the existence of personal ideals whose form is *intrinsically public*. The form of an ideal is intrinsically public when the reflective activity it involves must be conducted with the participation of others in order to be conducted at all (hereafter 'intrinsically inter-subjective reflection'). Thus an idea with an 'intrinsically public form' refers to one that people can only define using intrinsically inter-subjective reflection. If the analysis so far is correct, Larmore's model of discourse must treat personal ideals whose form is intrinsically public as if their form corresponds to that of intrinsically private ideals. By failing to acknowledge the existence of personal ideals whose form is intrinsically public, MBC3 denies citizens' capacity and will to engage in public-political discourse aimed at the recognition of personal ideals such as that of citizen solidarity. William Galston argues correctly, in my view, that Larmore's model of discourse is 'excessively rationalistic' given that its norm of rational dialogue fails to recognize the role of 'shared experiences' in the formulation of evaluative judgments.[10] However, left at this, Galston's critical observation justifies a *modification* of Larmore's model rather than the rejection of it as a view of pragmatic justification. In contrast by revealing the deep structural limits of Larmore's model—in particular its denial of the existence of ideals that are intrinsically public in form—my critique can explain why it could not be consistently modified to recognize the role in public discourse of shared experiences in the sense outlined in Chapter 1.1.3.

So what is at stake here is not a mere matter of adding an item such as this to the public agenda—Larmore's model of discourse could well accommodate this demand. Instead, what is at stake is a re-definition of the public discursive space—as distinct from subjective (re)definitions by private agents of what they understand to be their identity as citizens—since it is this that necessitates the treatment of all personal ideals as having an intrinsically private form. If my deep structural analysis is correct, then MBC3 recognizes only a *content differentiation* between public and private ideas.

It is worth noting here how the point I am making differs from objections, like the one that Seyla Benhabib raises against liberalism's model of public space. Of course, Benhabib's critique is based in an alternative model of discourse ethics and for discourse ethics the publicness of an issue is produced as an effect of discourse where discourse is always, itself, public. From this perspective, Benhabib focuses on controversiality as a basis for excluding issues from the public agenda. However, this does not meet the demands of an immanent critique given that for liberalism the publicness or privateness of discourse is determined by the presupposed publicness or privateness of some issue and, accordingly, discourse can itself be rendered as either public or private. This is why my concern with Larmore's treatment of con-

---

10. Galston, *Liberal Purposes*, pp. 105-6. Compare Moore, *Foundations of Liberalism*, p. 134. She also objects to Larmore's formulation of the norm of rational dialogue but only on the ground that he overlooks the role of a 'shared understanding or conception of the subject in question'.

troversial issues centres on the precise way in which the theory's deep structural conceptual framework secures the exclusion of certain types of ideals precisely when the model of discourse supposes everything to be a potential object of public discourse.[11]

7.3.2 The requirement of taking reasonable disagreement seriously

The discovery that Larmore's theory cannot acknowledge the existence of personal ideals whose form is intrinsically public can show why it cannot meet the second requirement of its adequacy criterion, that of taking reasonable disagreement seriously. Recall that the theory aims to achieve this by insisting that political principles rest only on common personal ideals and that they remain neutral as regards controversial ones (7.1.5). What is the significance of the discovery at the level of the theory's deep structure that MBC3 recognizes only a *content differentiation* between common and controversial ideals? I will argue next that it explains why at the surface level the questions of *the appropriate form* of personal ideals and of *their role in the practice of political theorizing* must unjustifiably appear as matters about which there cannot be reasonable disagreement. In the absence of making the unjustified assumption that these matters fall beyond the scope of reasonable disagreement Larmore's account can be forced to acknowledge: (1) that the answers to these questions have been the subject of reasonable disagreement within the modern western intellectual tradition even amongst theorists who endorse the norms and (2) that political liberalism's appeal to the norms to justify the principle of political neutrality is, therefore, not neutral as regards these controversies about personal ideals. The demonstration of (1) and (2) will support the conclusion that the theory fails to satisfy its adequacy criterion of taking reasonable disagreement about personal ideals seriously.

7.3.2(i)(a) Reasonable disagreement about the form of personal ideals

Firstly, the appropriate form of personal ideals, as distinct from their mere content, is a matter about which there is reasonable disagreement within the modern western intellectual tradition amongst theorists who would, nevertheless, also endorse the norms (though not necessarily the way in which Larmore claims that these are to be applied). The theorists I have in mind defend the view that ethical reflection about the character of political life should, at one and the same time, constitute reflection on the nature of the good life. Within this tradition, non-individualists have advanced the view that a notion of citizenship abstracted from personal ideals whose form is intrinsically public, like that of citizen solidarity mentioned above, cannot

---

11. See Benhabib, *Situating the Self*, p. 46. On the reflective process that privatizes and consequently eliminates controversial ideals from public discourse see Chantal Mouffe, 'Political Liberalism: Neutrality and the Political', *Ratio Juris: An International Journal of Jurisprudence and Philosophy of Law*, vol. 7, no. 3, 1994, pp. 314-24, pp. 320-2.

yield adequate answers to the modern problem of specifying the terms of political association. In doing so, some have challenged the very assumption of the necessity of a hierarchical relationship between the values governing the political and ethical aspects of peoples' lives. So, rather than according priority to the good over the right, as is sometimes suggested, this position proposes a reconceptualization of the relationship between the political and ethical dimensions of social life.[12]

Larmore needs to show that this sort of understanding of ethical-political life falls beyond the scope of what his theory counts as the subject matter of *reasonable* disagreement. This is because to admit the possibility of reasonable disagreement about personal ideals that, due to their form, cannot be privately defined is to admit, contrary to the theory's supposition, that it does indeed require the abandonment of certain kinds of reasonably held personal ideals. As I indicated in the development of my reconstructive claim, MBC_3 supposes that personal ideals that do not become public through discourse do not have to be abandoned but are, instead, rendered private and, consequently, are to be pursued in the private domain (7.2.4).

One way to deny that the ideal in question is the subject matter of reasonable disagreement is to reinterpret the situation and to claim that what initially appears to be a reasonable disagreement is based on an unfortunate misunderstanding on the part of non-individualist theorists. Although Larmore does not directly address the problem that I have raised, in Chapter 5 of *Patterns of Moral Complexity* he argues that theorists like Herder, Hegel, Marx and more recently, Sandel, developed their accounts of the political domain in the light of their personal ideals because they were all victims of the same misunderstanding. These theorists, Larmore claims, were strong critics of social atomism and rightly rejected it. However, they also endorsed a version of social holism and pursuant to their holistic vision of society they each relied on controversial personal ideals to justify their political principles. Larmore suggests that these theorists took this unfortunate path, even though social holism invokes a crude notion of society as an undifferentiated unity, because they failed to realize that their rejection of social atomism does not imply a holistic view of society. He cites Niklas Luhmann's non-atomistic model of society as an example of a preferred alternative to social holism. The implication is that had they had access to such a model of society they would not have thought it necessary to defend an alternative to the liberal ideal of political individualism.

Now, quite apart from the objections that we could make against Larmore's reading of the thought of non-invidualists generally, the important point for present purposes is that we are not compelled to accept that such political theories rest on a misunderstanding of the implications of reject-

---

12. See chapter 7 of Vassilacopoulos, *A Reading of Hegel's Philosophy*.

ing social atomism. (One could argue, for example, that Larmore assumes that social holism inevitably denies differentiation. Even though he accuses non-individualists of 'reliance upon a simple dichotomy', that of society as 'an organic whole' or as 'fragmented and anomic', his own arguments rely on another unsubstantiated dichotomy (PMC, p. 93). They take for granted that society must be understood as a non-organic *differentiated* system or else it is misunderstood to be an organic *undifferentiated* whole. So, he fails to consider seriously the possibility that Hegel had in mind a model of society as an organic yet *differentiated* system.[13]) Indeed, the idea of personal ideals whose form is intrinsically public offers a different sort of explanation for why the non-individualist might seek to develop political principles on the basis of personal, albeit controversial, ideals. This reason, as already suggested, is connected to an effort to formulate an entirely different, yet not necessarily non-modern, conception of the inter-relationship of the ethical and political dimensions of social life so as to accommodate the value of citizen solidarity.[14] Regardless of what the liberal ultimately makes of values like solidarity, she cannot deny that discussion about them constitutes a source of *reasonable* disagreement. Accordingly, Larmore's theory cannot show that the question of the form of personal ideals falls beyond the scope of *reasonable* disagreement by reinterpreting opposed intellectual traditions as having been generated by an unfortunate misunderstanding.

7.3.2(i)(b) Reasonable disagreement about the method of political theorizing

Secondly, although Larmore's account purports to take seriously reasonable disagreement about the *content* of theories that invoke different ideals of the person as justifications of political principles, I want to argue that it cannot consistently recognize that the question of the best *method* of political theorizing, a question that includes consideration of the proper role of personal ideals, is itself subject to *reasonable* disagreement. There is ample evidence within the modern western intellectual tradition of theorists' continued development of strong arguments to establish the futility of avoiding resting political principles on personal ideals. Others advance the weaker claim that the attempt to remain neutral at this level is not the most reasonable approach to take.[15] Whether or not these arguments are compelling is beside

---

13. On this interpretation see Vassilacopoulos, *A Reading of Hegel's Philosophy*.

14. See chapters 1-3 of Nicolacopoulos and Vassilacopoulos, *Hegel and the Logical Structure of Love*.

15. See for example Kurt Baier, 'Justice and the Aims of Political Philosophy', *Ethics*, vol. 99, no. 4, 1989, pp. 771-90, pp. 778-9, Beiner, *What's the Matter with Liberalism*, Benhabib, *Situating the Self*, Jean Hampton, 'Should Political Philosophy be Done Without Metaphysics?', *Ethics*, vol. 99, no. 4, 1989, pp. 791-814. For an example of the first type of argument (which is directed against Rawls' account of political liberalism) see Bellamy Richard and Hollis Martin, 'Liberal Justice: Political and Metaphysical', *The Philosophical Quarterly*, vol. 45, no. 178,

the point since, whatever their ultimate merit, what they do show is that the methodological issues they raise remain reasonably controversial.

Given (a) the challenge that these arguments pose to the adequacy of the role that a theory like Larmore's attributes to personal ideals and (b) the theory's strategy of rendering private—and, thus, eliminating from the public domain—ideals that prove to be controversial (7.3.1), Larmore needs to show that the question of whether or not political ideals should be supported by personal ideals is itself beyond reasonable controversy. He needs to show that these *methodological issues* about personal ideals can be detached from disputes about personal ideals that constitute the subject matter of reasonable disagreement.

In order to place such methodological issues beyond the scope of what is to count as reasonable disagreement, Larmore would have us believe that they are based on yet another misunderstanding, namely a failure to imagine that a moral justification of political principles might be given without invoking personal ideals.[16] He could develop this argument to claim that the success of his account of political liberalism should be proof enough to put these methodological disputes to rest. He takes his account to show that political ideals need not be supported by controversial personal ideals because the norms can be substituted for personal ideals in public discourse. At the same time, the account restricts the role of personal ideals—only those that the procedure of discourse renders private are excluded from the public social domain—pursuant to the application of the norms whose public existence is in turn derived from their subjective and objective universality (7.2.5). Larmore could, perhaps, appeal to the results of this understanding of the relationship between the norms and people's personal ideals to suggest that under modern subjective conditions (1.1) the *only* successful method of developing political principles proves to be that proposed by political liberalism. This result, it could be suggested, is what places other philosophical methodologies beyond the scope of reasonable disagreement.

The problem with this sort of reply is that it relies on an over-simplified understanding of the relationship of the norms to people's personal ideals. Precisely because, as I have already argued, the theory's deep structure only recognizes content differentiation (7.3.1), it fails to acknowledge that the norms might relate differently to *differently formed* personal ideals. By this I mean that the way in which one might apply the norms depends on whether or not one treats the form of one's personal ideal as intrinsically private or intrinsically public. Notice that I am concerned here with a question of the

---

1995, pp. 1-19. For an example of the second type of argument (also directed against Rawls' account of political liberalism) see Berys Gaut, 'Rawls and the Claims of Liberal Legitimacy', *Philosophical Papers*, vol. 24, no. 1, 1995, pp. 1-22, p. 17.

16. He attributes this failure to both German and neo-Romantics (MacIntyre and Sandel) in Larmore, *Patterns of Moral Complexity*, p. 121.

application of the norms *given* their endorsement by ideal citizens. Whether people should adopt the norms is not a matter which Larmore's model of public discourse need address since the effect of assuming the norms to be subjectively universal (7.1.8) is that public discussion must be framed by participants' commitment to them. However, this still leaves open the possibility of reasonable disagreement as to what the norms call for in specific discursive contexts.

To see the different effects that differently formed personal ideals can have on the application of the norms consider how the following questions might be answered. What does the norm of rational dialogue call for in the light of ideal citizens' commitments to personal ideals whose form is intrinsically private? Consistently with Larmore's account as interpreted through my reconstruction of its deep structure, one should reply that the norm or rational dialogue calls upon ideal citizens to look for personal ideals whose content is common and to restrict ideals whose content is controversial to the private social domain. What does the norm of rational dialogue call for in the light of (at least some) ideal citizens' commitments to personal ideals whose form is intrinsically public? The answer to this question is not as straightforward as the first. The application of the norm of rational dialogue—the demand that ideal citizens retreat to neutral, common ground in the face of disagreement about their personal ideals—is complicated by the fact that, as I have already argued, the model of discourse cannot recognize ideals whose form is intrinsically public (7.3.1). This failure generates the need for citizens exposed to it to find a solution to the problem of this lack of recognition. When the supposedly public discursive procedure does not acknowledge the existence of one's intrinsically public ideals one's attention is directed away from the task of differentiating ideals whose content is public, to a questioning of the suitability of the discursive model to supply public justificatory grounds for which it has been designed. The answer to the second question shows that the application of the norm of rational dialogue inevitably leads some ideal citizens to question the very adequacy of the model of public discourse and its supposition regarding the initial neutrality of the form of ideals (7.2.2).

7.3.2(ii) Personal ideals that must be abandoned

Consider next why, contrary to the theory's supposition that controversial ideals need not be abandoned (7.2.4), Larmore's model of public discourse inevitably forces citizens to abandon their personal ideals when their form is intrinsically public. Larmore thinks that he has an answer to the objection that his theory requires people to abandon their controversial personal ideals. This is an objection that he anticipates non-individualists would raise against liberalism's endorsement of political individualism (7.1.7). He considers the case of a conflict arising between the demands of the norms and 'the furtherance of our ideal of the good life' and argues that when this sort of conflict arises political liberalism holds that the requirements of the norms take precedence over those of our ideal of the good life. One could give an example of the type of conflict that Larmore has in mind by adapting his discussion of this relation of precedence. Suppose members of the Catholic Church were inclined to burn heretics (to further their ideal of the good life). What they should do instead is excommunicate them (in order to adhere to the overriding norms) (LPL, p. 150). Larmore suggests that since the norms are also a 'constitutive commitment'—they constitute the core of our comprehensive morality (7.1.3)—ranking them higher does not thereby result in the abandonment of our ideal of the good life. The individualism that is overriding within the political realm does not affect 'internal, extra-political affairs [organized] according to "illiberal" principles' given political liberalism's confinement of its commitment to individualism to the public social realm (LPL, pp. 349-50). Nor is it a problem, according to Larmore, that 'political liberalism must encourage [citizens] to reflect critically upon [... commitments regarding the good life] from the impartial standpoint involved in those two norms'.[17] Since the 'impartial standpoint' should be adopted to examine whether our ideal of the good life conflicts with our overriding commitment to the norms—and not to assess the value of this ideal—it need not involve 'any special affinity for individualist views of the good life' (LPL, pp. 350-1).

These two arguments are based on a serious confusion. They involve a slide from the theory's initial interest in citizens' as *the objects of the reflection of public agencies* to an interest in them as *subjects of reflection*. Recall that, according to Larmore, the problem to which his theory is supposed to offer a solution is how to set limits to the powers *of government*. (7.1.1) This is a question of how public agencies are to treat citizens rather than a question of how citizens are to conduct themselves when they are engaged in political action. This is to conflate the reflective standpoints of private citizens and public agencies.

Furthermore, having conflated these two reflective standpoints the above arguments shift their emphasis from the claim that the norms constitute the common core of the comprehensive moralities that are affirmed by liberals and non-individualists and, so, can be viewed as the overriding commitment of *public agencies*, to the further claim that *within* comprehensive moralities the norms require the exercise of an *impartial, distanced* critical perspective in all cases of political reflection. However, even if one accepts that public discourse as defined by the norms leads to the conclusion that state action should be limited in accordance with the principle of political neu-

---

17. The non-individualist concern is expressed as the worry 'that constitutive commitments to some substantial ideal of the good life, whose value cannot be manifest to an impartial, distanced point of view, must be undermined', Larmore, 'Political Liberalism', pp. 350-1.

trality, one can still reasonably reject the view that citizens active in political life (in a non-official capacity) should also adopt an impartial distanced, critical perspective. Indeed the question of whether or not they should do so is, itself, the subject matter of reasonable disagreement in liberal societies and in the modern western intellectual tradition more generally. Even amongst liberals with similarly undemanding conceptions of political activity on the part of citizens in their non-official capacity, there is disagreement as to the appropriate reflective standpoint from which politically active citizens should make their decisions, when voting, or participating in political parties and the like.[18]

Why does Larmore's account conflate the reflective standpoint of private citizens with the standpoint that they are supposed to attribute to public agencies? One explanation is that MBC_3 allows for the operation of only one form of reason in the public-political domain and this form of public reason is exhaustively but inadequately defined by reference to the norms. (I will discuss the effects of the inadequacy of the norms as a definition of the form of public reason in section 7.3.3.)

Enough has been said about the confusion upon which Larmore's arguments rest. Now, consider the suggestion that nothing stops people from defining and pursuing their personal ideals privately given that political liberalism's commitment to individualism—a commitment to the view that public agencies should treat citizens in abstraction from views about the worth of specific ways of life—is confined to the public social domain (7.1.7). In the case of citizens whose personal ideal is intrinsically public in form, this argument appears to miss the point of the objection, as does the example of (prohibiting) heretic burning. Since their personal ideals, like that of citizen solidarity, involve a necessary public dimension they cannot be defined and pursued privately. The liberal public-private social division cannot meet their needs. Therefore, contrary to Larmore's claim that political liberalism requires people to abandon the belief that their personal ideals constitute adequate justificatory grounds for political principles (7.1.5) but not their belief in the ideals themselves (1.7), at least some ideal citizens are required to abandon their personal ideals. It follows that even though they endorse the norms they cannot justifiably recognize the liberal public-private social division as the embodiment of the norms.

Daniel Weinstock has also criticized Larmore for taking for granted an over-simplified view of the relationship between people's personal ideals, such as those that derive from membership of private associations, and their status as citizens of a political society. He observes that 'membership in pri-

---

18. For example, Rawls and Dworkin give conflicting yet equally reasonable—in Larmore's sense of this term (7.1.1)—responses to this question. See Dworkin, 'Liberal Community', Rawls, *Political Liberalism*, p. 215. In *Liberal Purposes* (p. 114), Galston argues in favour of using arguments based on sectional interests.

vate associations often centrally involves a commitment to sets of views on matters pertaining to the political sphere'. In other words, the personal ideals that Larmore thinks can be neatly confined to the private social domain often include a *public* dimension. For Weinstock Larmore's assessment of the happy co-existence of political liberalism's social ethic (its endorsement of political individualism) and community values (expressed in personal ideals) does not give much assistance in resolving the difficult problem of when the state should interfere in illiberal practices.[19] My argument goes one step further and explains the deep structural source of the difficulty that liberals face, especially in relation to dealing with non-liberal practices understood as practices that do not accord with the *liberal* public-private social division in Larmore's terms.

Still, for the purposes of this argument it is not necessary to settle the issues of disagreement between liberals and non-individualists. What the discussion shows is that, even when the norms are endorsed their demands may be interpreted in different ways depending on the personal ideals one holds and, in particular, on whether or not the form of such ideals is intrinsically private or intrinsically public. So, the question of the way in which the norms might function within differently *formed* comprehensive moralities remains an unresolved controversial issue.

7.3.2(iii) Ideal citizens' intrinsically private and intrinsically public ideals

Why does Larmore's account fail to acknowledge that the question of how the norms inter-relate with people's personal ideals differs according to the form attributed to people's personal ideals? It is worth noting that none of the problems with Larmore's model of public discourse emerge from the standpoint of ideal citizens who view themselves as intrinsically private agents. They neither have reason to doubt the adequacy of the discursive procedure as a model of *public* discourse nor are they required to give up their personal ideals since, being intrinsically private ideals, they lose nothing when the scope of their ideals is restricted to the private social domain. Indeed, as long as the enlightened citizen/liberal theorist identifies with the theory's unacknowledged commitment to intrinsically private agency the question of how the norms are to be applied appears to admit one universally valid answer and the issues about which there is otherwise ample evidence of reasonable disagreement within the modern western intellectual tradition fade from critical view.

However, the discussion so far has also shown that a different intellectual identity, that of the ideal citizen who applies the norms in the light of her intrinsically public personal ideals, comes into view as a result of bringing to the surface the theory's deep structure. Once we engage with Lar-

---

19. Daniel M. Weinstock, 'Modernité et morale (Book Review)', *The Journal Of Philosophy*, vol. XCIII, no. 1, 1996, pp. 41-8, p. 47.

more's proposed model of public discourse from the reflective standpoint of this intellectual identity it becomes clear that the model's apparent success as judged by reference to its own adequacy criterion derives from Larmore's unjustified treatment of a particular intellectual identity as if it were universally valid. Without this unjustified imposition of his theory's implicit understanding of the liberal intellectual identity, the theory cannot meet the second aspect of its adequacy criterion.

Have the arguments of this section overlooked an important proviso of Larmore's theory? Why should it be a requirement on Larmore's account that it does accommodate those whose reflective standpoint is intrinsically public? By insisting that ideal citizens share a 'common project' Larmore takes into account that his theory applies only to those who have *enough* in common. So, perhaps, this proviso should be seen as ruling out the application of the theory to people who hold personal ideals whose form is intrinsically public. In Larmore's words, the argument for political liberalism

> applies only to people who are indeed interested in devising principles of political association. It assumes that they share enough to think of themselves as engaged in this common project and that they understand these bonds as setting them off from other people, since their aim is supposedly to live with one another, and not also with everyone else, in political association. In short, the people to whom it applies must already think of themselves as 'a people'. They must already have a common life *before* they can think of organising their political life according to liberal principles (LPL, p. 352).

Notice, however, that the common life necessary for the project to which he refers, as we have already seen, purports to extend only to geography, language and historical experience. At this point, Larmore conflates two types of person to whom his argument might be addressed and this has the effect of rendering invisible the fact that the question of how the norms are to be applied itself constitutes a matter about which there is reasonable disagreement. He refers on the one hand, to those seeking 'to live with one another [...] in political association', that is, to people who want to be active participants in the determination of the political principles governing their society (a society identified by reference to its geography, language and history). On the other hand, he refers to those seeking to articulate the grounds for recognizing the value of a liberal order, and 'organizing their political life according to liberal principles', that is, to liberals. Whilst these two may coincide, they need not. For instance, nothing in the first characterization excludes those who are willing to share a political life and have a vision of this life as ideally constituted by certain intrinsically public ideals. So, I may see myself, and may appropriately be characterized, in the first way, but if I do not also hold the further individualist commitments of political liberalism, the latter characterization will be inappropriate. It is worth bearing in mind that since Larmore's account must meet a condition of relevance and not merely truth (1.9), reconstruction from true premises is not relevant here. Nor does rejection of Larmore's defence of *political* individualism amount to a rejection of the unobjectionable view that each individual may have her own ideals independently of the consideration she may give to shared substantial ideals. The issue is whether Larmore's model of public discourse can recognize intrinsically public ideals that are subject to reasonable disagreement or whether the theory reduces them to private ideals. I can endorse the norms, participate in a 'common life', in Larmore's sense, and be interested in the project about which Larmore offers an interpretation—devising modern principles of political association—without at the same time accepting *the terms of the project as he interprets them* (7.1.1). Accordingly, in taking it for granted that the norms are held universally (7.1.8) Larmore also mistakenly presupposes that the commitments characterizing his account's deep structure cannot give rise to matters about which there is *reasonable* disagreement amongst people who wish to share a political life.

In this section we have seen that attention to the form and role of personal ideals renders them controversial in Larmore's sense. Furthermore, because the question of how the norms relate to differently formed personal ideals is also controversial, one cannot justifiably rely on a particular way of applying the norms—one that takes it for granted that the form of personal ideals is intrinsically private—as the universally valid way. Larmore's theory fails to take seriously reasonable disagreement about the form and role of personal ideals and about their relationship to the norms. Consequently, political liberalism's appeal to the norms does not supply a neutral justification of the principle of political neutrality and it forces some people to abandon their personal ideals. These problems stem from the model of the public-private dichotomy that the theory's deep structure embodies. They are due to this MBC3's inability to acknowledge personal ideals whose form is intrinsically public. So Larmore's solution to giving limited defining space to the category of privateness does not work.

7.3.3 The requirement that justificatory reasons have the special authority of moral principles

According to MBC3, personal ideals are supposed to play a defining role in the public domain only when they have been discursively rendered as public. However, the discussion in 7.3.1 has shown that, on the one hand, the discursive differentiation of public and private ideals affects only the content and not the form of personal ideals and, on the other, the form of personal ideals is treated as intrinsically private, albeit without this being acknowledged. It follows from this analysis that in the public social domain the defining role is played by personal ideals that are constituted as public due to their shared content and as private due to their unacknowledged form.

What is the effect at the surface level of the discovery that personal ideals whose form is intrinsically private constitute the real ground of liberal political principles and public policy? I want to argue that this discovery explains why the theory cannot satisfy the first aspect of its adequacy criterion, that of supplying justificatory grounds with the special authority of moral principles (7.1.4 and 7.1.9). Whenever personal ideals are relied on in the public social domain, their unacknowledged intrinsically private form effectively displaces the supposed moral authority of public reasoning that is grounded in the objective universality of the norms. This is because the norms are an empty category; whereas *they* are supposed to define the form of the public reasoning that generates political principles, the effect of MBC3's unacknowledged reliance on ideals whose form is intrinsically private is that the form of reasoning characterizing personal ideals plays the defining role in the public domain.

I argued in section 7.3.1 that because ideal citizens' reasoning in support of some ideal remains intrinsically private, the discursive procedure renders a common belief as public only in the limited sense of having a public content. Whilst such ideals supply the *formed content* of liberal political morality their form remains independent of the public discursive procedure in the sense that they are the outcome of the deliberations of private agents. So, even though Larmore claims that such ideals supply liberal political morality with its moral content, in so far as they are privately formed, public personal ideals may or may not have a distinctively *moral* content. For example, as a participant in the discursive procedure I may endorse the application of the principle of political neutrality on pragmatic grounds alone.[20] I may be willing to accept that others do not endorse what I take to be the morally correct ideal of human flourishing, an ideal whose form I view as intrinsically public. My endorsement of political neutrality will thus be a mere strategic compromise made in the light of what I perceive as the unfortunate subjective conditions of modernity. Such non-moral, pragmatic grounds for endorsing political principles must nevertheless be treated by the theory as if they were grounds with the special authority of moral principles, since the definition of public reasoning in terms of the norms makes no other requirements on the form of public reason.

At the surface level of the theory we can find evidence that intrinsically private reasoning plays a defining role beyond its delimited domain when we look to Larmore's response to the objection that the 'neutral ground' supposedly supplied by the norms 'offers too weak a basis for devising any political principles that assign basic liberties and distribute wealth'. As well as emphasizing that political neutrality is a 'relative' idea requiring neutrality only with respect to personal ideals that are 'actually disputed in the soci-

---

20. On the surface level significance between the pragmatic and moral construal of Larmore's political liberalism see Weinstock, 'Modernité et morale (Book Review)', pp. 47-8.

ety', Larmore claims that when relative neutrality is an insufficient basis for political principles due to the extent of disagreement, the enlightened liberal should make necessary political decisions bearing in mind 'the spirit of neutrality'. That is, when a controversial personal ideal must be relied on to justify political principles this should be done in the belief that 'admitting it will constitute the least restriction of neutrality necessary' as judged by reference to the 'beliefs that are least central to anyone's idea of the good life' or, alternatively, to the 'beliefs that the least number of people do not hold' (PMC, pp. 68-8).

In practice, then, the norms cannot be relied on to generate liberal political principles unless, of course, citizens actually happen to share enough personal ideals. But the theory relies on the assumption that they do not share very much since it appeals to the modern subjective conditions of reasonable disagreement (7.1.1) in order to call on people to substitute the norms for the personal ideals that they would otherwise take to justify political principles (7.1.5). On the other hand, when the norms appear to be most needed, in the event of reasonable disagreement about which personal ideals to invoke and how, the account effectively allows personal ideals to determine political principles even when such ideals prove to be neither public, because shared, nor publicly judged to be correct. For, the criterion of admitting a controversial personal ideal when it is judged to be the least restrictive of neutrality necessary ultimately favours majority opinions irrespective of whether or not it has the special authority of moral principles.

This is so irrespective of whether we are dealing with a bare majority or an overwhelming one, but consider also an example that Richard J. Arneson uses to show why Larmore's model of public discourse can produce unfair policy outcomes even when it relies only on common ideals.

> Smith values art, music, and horse-racing (in that order, with horse-racing very much least favoured) and believes that all three activities should be subsidized by the state, Jones values music and horse-racing (in that order) and believes these two activities should be subsidized by the state, and Johnson values horse-racing alone and believes only it should be subsidized by the state. [21]

Arneson concludes that

> a government policy founded on the uncontroversial judgment that horse-racing is a constituent of the good life for humans would seem to be permissible, whatever the implications of state policy tailored to the judgment for the comparative well-being of citizens depending on the relative centrality of racing in their conceptions of the good. [22]

---

21. Arneson, 'Neutrality and Utility (Religious and Other Forms of Tolerance by the State)', pp. 226-7.
22. Arneson, 'Neutrality and Utility (Religious and Other Forms of Tolerance by the

Although Arneson is correct in his reading of Larmore, notice that his argument will appeal only to those who share his intuition that such an outcome is, after all, *unfair*. By way of contrast my deep structural analysis depends on no such intuitions. It suggests instead that the problem with the sort of policy outcome that Arneson correctly identifies is that even though it is based on a common *content*—horse-racing is valued by everyone in the society—the same cannot be said of the different *forms* of reasoning that Smith, Jones and Johnson employ. Even though their reasoning remains intrinsically private in form, because Larmore's model of discourse fails to recognize this, the public policy is after all based on an ideal that is *not publicly judged* to be morally correct but must be treated as if it were. This outcome clearly contradicts the first requirement of the theory's own adequacy criterion that political principles be based on grounds with this authority (7.1.9).

We can find further evidence of the theory's failure to satisfy this aspect of its adequacy criterion in the account's implied response to citizens who would withdraw their allegiance to their political society. Let us follow through the implications of Larmore's analysis of the objective universality of the norm of equal respect for the handling of secessionist movements. In *Patterns* Larmore points out that the norm of equal respect explains why we should continue the discussion not only with those for whose views we have sympathy or who have power but also with 'the strange and the weak': we have a moral obligation to explain ourselves to those who would be affected by the implementation of our proposals (PMC, pp. 61-2 & 75). Accordingly, one would expect the theory to attribute to secessionists who endorse the norms a moral obligation to refrain from withdrawing their political allegiance and, in Larmore's words, continue the conversation with the other members of their political society. This follows from the observation that amongst persons who share a political life the decision of one group to withdraw its political allegiance would inevitably affect others. Yet Larmore also insists, not only that ideal citizens already endorse the norms but that they be willing to continue sharing a political life (7.1.8) as the *preconditions* of the application of his theory. This effectively neutralizes the supposed objective universality of the norm of equal respect. That is, the force it is meant to have due to being attributed the special authority of a *moral* principle becomes a mere formality in the face of people's subjective desires to withdraw their political allegiance for whatever reasons happen to move them.

7.4 *Desiderata for a fourth model of the public-private dichotomy*

If the above interpretation and critique of Larmore's account of liberalism is correct, it does not merely show that such an account fails as an adequate statement of liberalism and as an attempt to show non-individualists why they too can be liberals. More importantly, it invites further investigation of the claim that what is distinctively *liberal* is to be found at the level of the deep structure that characterizes liberal thought. The collapse of MBC3 was due to its differentiation of public and private categories on the basis of their content alone. The partial defining role that was attributed to the category of privateness was not capable of being sustained within this model of the dichotomy. On the one hand, some supposedly private ideals would have to be abandoned, rather than merely restricted. On the other, the private form of reason characterizing ideals with a public content plays the defining role in the domain reserved for public categories.

At the same time, however, the collapse of MBC3 gives rise to the desiderata of a new, more sophisticated interpretation of MBC. It suggests that in defining both the categories of publicness and privateness so as to give each a defining role, the category of publicness should recognize the role of different *forms* of reasoning and not just of differences in the content of a single form. Recall that the failure to acknowledge the possibility of different forms of public reason seems to have led Larmore to conflate the critical standpoints of public agencies and private citizens.

So, the analysis of this chapter points the way for the further investigation of the adequacy of MBC, the claim that one basic category plays the defining role. Part III will argue that the deep structure of John Rawls' version of political liberalism also embodies a model of the public-private dichotomy that takes publicness to define both categories in such a way as to allow each to play an alternate defining role. However, the constitution of public categories involves a differentiation of forms of reasoning and not just of the contents of personal ideals.

At the surface level, the liberal who, thus far, remains unconvinced by the book's central argument might respond as follows. Although Larmore's account of political liberalism fails, this failure is due to his endorsement of the notion of a *neutrally justified* commitment to the principle of neutrality. In *Political Liberalism* Rawls explicitly distinguishes his version of political liberalism from procedurally neutral views like that developed by Larmore (LPL, pp. 191-2, esp. fn. 24). Instead of proposing a neutral procedure of justification as the common ground of its political principles, Rawls insists: 'this common ground is the political conception itself as the focus of an overlapping consensus' (LPL, p. 192). It remains to be seen whether Rawls' more sophisticated version of political liberalism lends support to the minimal political morality approach to defining liberalism.

part III

John Rawls' Political Liberalism

John Rawls' account of 'political liberalism' forms that part of his theory of social justice that explains the nature of philosophical inquiry aimed at deriving substantive morally justified political principles for the regulation of a just society.[1] According to Rawls, political liberalism specifies the conditions under which it is possible for 'a just and stable society of free and equal citizens' to exist despite being profoundly divided over 'reasonable religious, philosophical and moral doctrines' (PL, p. 4). These conditions are set out in terms of three basic propositions:

> First, the basic structure of society is regulated by a political conception of justice; second, this political conception is the focus of an overlapping consensus of reasonable comprehensive [i.e. religious, philosophical and moral] doctrines; and third, public discussion when constitutional essentials and questions of basic justice are at stake, is conducted in terms of the political conception of justice (PL, p. 44).

To characterize political liberalism in terms of these three propositions is to place the idea of *a political conception* at its centre. Moreover, the two principles that define Rawls' account of 'justice as fairness', the account associated with *A Theory of Justice*,[2] exemplify a political conception. Justice as fairness, in turn, supplies principles of justice that are taken to be justified because it first formulates such principles from 'due reflection' upon 'the fair terms of social co-operation' using 'the device of an original position' in its 'political constructivist' procedure and, then, using the idea of 'an overlapping con-

---

1. Unless otherwise indicated, throughout Part III I will use 'political liberalism' to refer specifically to the account that Rawls presents in Rawls, *Political Liberalism*.

2. In *Political Liberalism* (pp. 5-6), Rawls explains that 'justice as fairness' refers explicitly to the substantive conception of justice developed in *A Theory of Justice*.

sensus of reasonable comprehensive views', it demonstrates how a 'well-ordered society', that is, a society regulated by the principles of justice, can be unified and stable.[3] This way of defending a conception of social justice aims to secure its 'full public justification' that, in turn, grounds the liberal ideals of citizenship and political legitimacy.

Rawls' theory has been subject to considerable and wide-ranging criticism over the years. So, it is worth noting from the outset how Part III of the book aims to contribute to, and make use of, this literature. One line of response to Rawls reflects upon the relationship between *Political Liberalism* and *A Theory of Justice* and/or assesses Rawls' progressive revisions of the ideas contained in *A Theory of Justice* in his later essays.[4] In this context one of the main issues of comparison concerns the question of whether the early Rawls, who can be read as offering a comprehensive defence of liberal values, is to be preferred over the later Rawls. These questions fall beyond the scope of our discussion. For one thing, the exploration of interpretive issues about the relationship of the later to the early Rawls is unnecessary in the light of my interest in the later Rawls as exemplary of the minimal political morality approach to defining liberalism. But if we were to read Rawls' account of liberalism as a *comprehensive* approach then, in my view, the early Rawls presents as a less suitable object of radical critique by comparison with the later Ronald Dworkin whose work I examine in *In Memory of a Vision, Volume 2*.

Critical responses to Rawls' political conception fall into three broad categories. One type of criticism takes for granted the basic soundness of the above mentioned conceptual framework for justice as fairness but it disputes the details of its substantive claims, like the specification of the content of the principles of justice or their extension to issues such global justice and international relations.[5] Rather than advocating some adjustment of its details

---

3. For ease of reference I will use 'the principles of justice' to refer specifically to the two principles of justice that define justice as fairness. When referring more broadly to as yet unspecified principles or principles that are in the process of being formulated for this purpose I will use the phrases 'the principles regulating the basic structure' and 'the regulatory principles'.

4. On such questions see Ackerman, 'Political Liberalisms', Brian Barry, 'John Rawls and the Search for Stability', *Ethics*, vol. 105, 1995, pp. 874-915, Kukathas and Pettit, *Rawls: A Theory of Justice and its Critics*, Mulhall and Swift, *Liberals and Communitarians*, pp. 170-91, L. Wenar, 'The Unity of Rawls' Work', in T. Brook and F. Freyenhagen (eds.), *The Legacy of John Rawls*, New York, Continuum, 2005, pp. 22-33. Larmore compares the notion of publicity in *A Theory of Justice* to that of the later Rawls in Charles Larmore, 'Public Reason', in S. Freeman (ed.), *The Cambridge Companion to Rawls*, Cambridge, Cambridge University Press, 2003, pp. 368-93.

5. An example of the former is Rawls' own reformulation in *Political Liberalism* of the content of the principles of justice to meet H. L. A. Hart's objections to the principles that were specified in *A Theory of Justice*. See Rawls, *Political Liberalism*, pp. 5, f.3. Another example is the revision T. W. Pogge, proposes in Thomas W. Pogge, *Realizing Rawls*, Ithaca,

in the light of the (implied) adequacy of this framework, a second type of revisionist criticism seeks to modify the conceptual framework itself.[6] A third, radical type of criticism rejects the very terms in which justice as fairness is framed viewing these as wholly inadequate to the tasks of philosophical inquiry into the nature of social justice.[7] Here the very idea of a political conception, and not just the substantive claims advanced by justice as fairness, can become the focus of radical critique.

My critique of Rawls' theory aims to contribute to this third type of criticism. By assessing the surface level adequacy of Rawls' idea of a political conception I aim to show the limitations of the approach to the problem of defining liberalism that it exemplifies, namely the minimal political morality approach. This means, firstly, that the assessment of the specifics of the principles of justice is unnecessary since, as Rawls suggests, a variety of specifications of the principles may well be in contention *within* the terms of inquiry given by a political conception (PL, p. 226).

Secondly, because it is the adequacy of the idea of a political conception as such that concerns us, it is especially important that we have regard to the precise details of Rawls' process of elaborating such a conception as a whole.

Cornell University Press, 1989. Here I would also include the extensive tradition of social egalitarian inspired critiques of Rawls' distributive principle. On the latter see Simon Caney, 'Cosmopolitanism and the Law of Peoples', *Journal of Political Philosophy*, vol. 10, no. 1, 2002, pp. 95-123, C. Naticchia, 'The Law of Peoples: The Old and the New', in T. Brook and F. Freyenhagen (eds.), *The Legacy of John Rawls*, New York, Continuum, 2005, pp. 177-94, David A. Reidy, 'Rawls on International Justice: A Defense', *Political Theory: An International Journal of Political Philosophy*, vol. 32, no. 3, 2004, pp. 291-319.

6. Attempts to sensitise Rawls' theory to the effects of gender and cultural differences fall into this category. One early example of this type of revision can be found in ch. 5 of Okin, *Justice, Gender and the Family*. Here Okin's main concern is to show how Rawls formulates the device of the original position without adequate regard to the gendered structure of modern societies but she thinks that the device of the original position can be reformulated and put to feminist use. See also E. Brake, 'Rawls and Feminism: What Should Feminists Make of Liberal Neutrality?', in T. Brook and F. Freyenhagen (eds.), *The Legacy of John Rawls*, New York, Continuum, 2005, pp. 67-84, C. McKeen, 'Gender, Choice and Partiality: A Defence of Rawls on the Family', *Essays in Philosophy*, vol. 7, no. 1, 2005, pp. 1-15. Another is W. Kymlicka's attempt in *Liberalism, Culture and Community*, to incorporate into a Rawlsian theory of social justice an explicit role for the values generated by cultural communities. See also R. G. Peffer's attempt to defend Rawls' theory of justice as capable of accommodating the concerns of economic socialists in R. G. Peffer, 'Marxist and Leftist Objections to Rawls' *Theory of Justice*: A Critical Review', *Marxism, Morality, and Social Justice*, Princeton, Princeton University Press, 1990, pp. 361-415.

7. MacIntyre's critique of Rawls' theory in *After Virtue* falls into this category as does M. J. Sandel, *Liberalism and the Limits of Justice*, Cambridge, Cambridge University Press, 1992. See also Benjamin Barber, 'Justifying Justice: Problems of Psychology, Politics and Measurement in Rawls', in Norman Daniels (ed.), *Reading Rawls: Critical Studies on Rawls' A Theory of Justice*, Oxford, Blackwell, 1975, pp. 292-318, Thomas Nagel, 'Rawls on Justice', in Norman Daniels (ed.), *Reading Rawls: Critical Studies on Rawls' A Theory of Justice*, Oxford, Blackwell, 1975, pp. 1-15, Plant, *Modern Political Thought*, pp. 98-106.

Accordingly, Chapter 8 is devoted to an extensive exposition of Rawls' account of political liberalism that aims to establish a number of points crucial for the theory's critical reconstruction. These are, firstly, to demonstrate that Rawls' theory accords with the features of a minimal political morality approach to defining liberalism; secondly, to identify the theory's own adequacy criterion; and, thirdly, to supply enough textual support for the reconstruction that will follow. The chapter is written without assuming the reader's familiarity with the details of Rawls' account.

Chapter 9 will propose a reconstruction of the theory in order to reveal the model of the public-private dichotomy to which its deep structure conforms. Here I will show that the deep structure of Rawls' theory accords with a model of the public-private dichotomy that meets the desiderata identified at the conclusion of Part II. In Chapter 10 I will go on to argue that the deep structure of Rawls' theory offers a complete interpretation of MBC and I will demonstrate its relative superiority. This part of the argument seeks to establish that the minimal political morality approach to defining liberalism stands or falls with a theory whose deep structure conforms to that of political liberalism.

In Chapter 11 the radical critique of Rawls' theory will proceed in much the same way as in Part II of the book. I will seek to draw out the fundamental flaw in the model of the public-private dichotomy to which the deep structure of Rawls' theory is committed. I will then argue that the exposure of this deep structural flaw shows why the theory cannot meet its adequacy criterion at the surface level. If the argument succeeds then this critique will not only show why Rawls' theory fails to supply an adequate solution to the problem of liberalism's definition. It will also demonstrate that liberalism cannot consistently remain within the self-imposed limits of a minimal political morality approach due to the collapse of the theory's deep structure. The collapse of MBC produces an epistemological crisis in the sense explained in Chapter 3.2. Chapter 11 will conclude by indicating how the question of the resolution of this crisis demands investigation of the comprehensive approach to the problem of liberalism's definition and its corresponding model of the public-private dichotomy.

8

Political Liberalism as a Minimal Political Morality

This chapter sets the groundwork for a radical critique of Rawls' theory. My objective is to demonstrate that the theory exemplifies the minimal political morality approach to defining liberalism. To this end I will begin by analyzing the meaning of a political conception as Rawls presents it. This discussion reveals the precise nature of the theory's self-imposed limits. With these in mind, I will be in a position to address the second objective, namely to identify the theory's own adequacy criterion. Here, attention will be given to the notion of justification that the theory relies upon. I will consider the precise terms of the theory's inquiry, the nature and standpoint of the reflection that goes into the elaboration of political liberalism's regulatory principles and its model of justification. I will conclude with a discussion of one of the theory's outcomes, namely its ideals of liberal citizenship and political legitimacy in order to identify the main characteristics of the kinds of reasoning permitted within a well-ordered society's public-political domain. For reasons that I will explain later, these characteristics become a focus of the radical critique of political liberalism.

8.1 *The meaning of a moral political conception*

Rawls describes justice as fairness as both a *moral* and *political* conception. Referring to a conception as moral in this context means that 'its content is given by certain ideals, principles and standards; and that these norms articulate certain values, in this case, political values' (PL, p. 11 & p. 11 fn. 11). Rawls' two principles of justice are moral principles in this sense as are the political virtues that define Rawls' liberal ideal of citizenship (PL, p. 224).

Because they are moral values the political values of the conception of justice are presented as having categorical force.

Rather than using it in any ordinary sense, Rawls gives the phrase, 'a political conception', a special meaning in terms of three features. First, as the focus on principles to regulate the basic structure of society suggests, a political conception is 'worked out for a specific kind of subject' (PL, p. 11). It offers an account of 'the way in which the major social institutions fit into one system' to form a modern constitutional democracy. According to Rawls, 'the political constitution, the legally recognized forms of property, and the organization of the economy, and the nature of the family, all belong to the basic structure' of society (PL, p. 258). Second,

> [it] is presented as a freestanding view [...] we must distinguish between how a political conception is presented and its being part of, or as derivable within a comprehensive doctrine [... A political conception is presented as] expounded apart from, or without reference to, any such wider background. To use a current phrase, the political conception is a module, an essential constituent part, that fits into and can be supported by various reasonable comprehensive doctrines that endure in the society regulated by it (PL, p. 12).

Finally, the content of a political conception 'is expressed in terms of certain fundamental ideas seen as implicit in the public political culture of a democratic society' with its 'tradition of democratic thought' (PL, p. 14). I will refer to these three features as 'the self-imposed limits of a political conception'.

Rawls distinguishes 'the political institutions of a constitutional regime and the public traditions of their interpretation' from 'the background culture' of civil society that is to be found in the practices and traditions of the various voluntary and non-voluntary associations. The background culture includes a diversity of 'comprehensive doctrines', that is, religious, philosophical and moral views that are broad in scope and (potentially) concern the whole of life. In *Political Liberalism* Rawls refers to the background culture as 'the culture of the social, not of the political' (PL, pp. 13-4). However, in later work he clarifies that the background and public political cultures are mediated by what he refers to as 'the non-public political culture' comprising all forms of media.[1] So, the source of the content of a political conception is the *public* dimension of society's political culture.

Thus political liberalism's conception of justice is minimal in three respects: (a) in its scope as applying moral principles to the basic structure; (b) in its presentation as a freestanding view; and (c) in its derivation of the content of its fundamental ideas from the public political culture of a democratic

---

1. John Rawls, *Collected Papers*, Samuel Richard Freeman (ed.), Cambridge, Harvard University Press, 1999, p. 576.

society. A political conception is not general in the scope of the application of its principles; it does not invoke mere strategic principles; it does not appeal to, or rely on, any ethical or particular metaphysical view that could be drawn from the background culture of the society to which its principles are to be applied;[2] and it does not appeal to any ideals as transcendent. There are of course different readings and assessments of Rawls on the question of the degree to which he has abandoned the universalist aspirations of *A Theory of Justice*.[3] On this question, Habermas maintains, correctly in my view, that 'Rawls, *pace* Rorty, has not become a contextualist' in the sense of offering a 'merely hermeneutic clarification of a contingent tradition'.[4] At the same time, however, Habermas is unclear about what more it is that Rawls' theory offers. On my reading, Rawls' contextualized universalism (in the sense explained in 1.1.4) enables him to abstract the *particular content* of ideas drawn from the modern western intellectual tradition in order to combine this abstracted content with the purportedly *universally applicable form* of reasoning that his theory elaborates for the participants in western liberal democracies. (In the next chapter we will see how this form-content differentiation informs the deep structure of Rawls' theory.) As John Gray points out, Rawls contextualizes his theory both by distilling the subject matter of justice as fairness from the civic cultures and political traditions of Western constitutional democracies and by applying it to:

> Western cultural traditions by reference to that moment in the history of our culture, since which we have witnessed the proliferation of incommensurable value-perspectives and worldviews. Indeed one may even say that, abstracted from this moment in the development of our tradition, the central problem of the theory of justice—the liberal problem of establishing fair principles of social cooperation amongst persons having incompatible and incommensurable conceptions of the good—does not exist.[5]

The above observations show that, at the surface level, Rawls' version of political liberalism accords with the features of a minimal political moral-

---

2. In Part III of the book I use the word 'ethical' in the broad sense to refer to values and norms that concern well-being, the nature of the good life or living well as a whole (4.1.2) whereas by 'metaphysical' I mean to refer to Rawls' sense of a '*particular* metaphysical doctrine about the nature of persons, distinctive and opposed to other metaphysical doctrines', Rawls, *Collected Papers*, p. 576.

3. For example, compare Dworkin, 'Foundations of Liberal Equality', pp. 32-4, Rorty, 'The Priority of Democracy to Philosophy'.

4. Jürgen Habermas, 'Reconciliation Through the Public Use of Reason: Remarks on John Rawls's Political Liberalism', *Journal of Philosophy*, vol. 92, no. 3, 1995, pp. 109-31, p. 120.

5. John Gray, 'Contractarian Method, Private Property and the Market Economy', in Chandran Kukathas (ed.), *John Rawls: Critical Assessments of Leading Political Philosophers*, London, Routledge, 2003, pp. 31-66, p. 38.

ity approach to defining liberalism. For, whilst the theory appeals to *moral* reasons as justificatory grounds for its political principles, Rawls' stipulative definition of a political conception restricts the sorts of moral reasons that might be invoked. (Throughout Part III of the book 'a political conception' will refer to the conception just outlined.)

One might nevertheless object to the above claim—that Rawls' theory exemplifies the minimal political morality approach to defining liberalism—given Rawls' own remarks about a political conception. If Rawls *recognizes* the existence of comprehensive liberalisms (PL, pp. 37 & 78), and hence the existence of *both* comprehensive and political liberalisms, why not say instead that his theory exemplifies the limited political thesis approach? Recall from Chapter 4.1.1 that the limited political thesis approach allows for the availability of different understandings of the (need for) justificatory grounds that can be given in support of liberal *political theses*.

Whilst this interpretation of Rawls' theory may be truer to Rawls' own beliefs about what makes his theory liberal, it is not the most satisfactory way of reading the textual implications of *Political Liberalism*. This is because, although Rawls recognizes the existence of comprehensive liberalisms in the *history* of the western democratic tradition, political liberalism's reasonable acceptability implies a reformulation, or, adjustment, to use Rawls' language, of the liberal theories that *historically* have been constituted as comprehensive (PL, p. 160, fn. 25). Yet, such a reformulation would nevertheless be a precondition for supplying *only one* of two stages in the justification of regulatory principles whereas, as we will see below, Rawls' political conception relies on a two-stage model of justification. It follows that Rawls' theory does not recognize comprehensive liberalisms as being on a formal par with other kinds of justification of liberal political theses in the way that the limited political thesis approach to defining liberalism represents different justificatory frameworks. (This, of course, is not to suggest that the limited political thesis approach is committed to some kind of epistemic relativism about different justificatory grounds—it can allow that there are better and worse defences of liberal values. However, in excluding such defences from the internal structure of the idea of liberalism, from the point of view of the complex-structure of this idea they are all equally external justifications.) In Rawls' political conception, then, comprehensive liberalisms are supposedly given their correct proportions *within* a justificatory process created by a framework that already conforms to the restrictions defining a minimal political morality approach.

8.2 The terms of inquiry and the theory's adequacy criterion

From the outset, then, political liberalism's project is not an inquiry into the ethical, epistemological or metaphysical bases of a just socio-political order but is confined to an inquiry into the *minimal moral* grounds for endorsing regulatory principles. The relevant terms of inquiry are that we elaborate a political conception of justice as 'the one most reasonable for us' to accept as distinct from the one that is true. Note here that Rawls explicitly distinguishes the point of view of 'you and me who are elaborating justice as fairness and examining it as a political conception of justice' from the point of view of the ideal citizens who form part of the theory (PL, p. 28). Justice as fairness is thus a political conception that one must assess using one's standard of reasonableness *in one's capacity qua theorist*.

These terms of inquiry are set pursuant to the observation that a 'public justification', in the sense of a justification based on reasons that all citizens could reasonably accept, could not otherwise be found given the modern democratic cultural conditions of 'reasonable pluralism'. Reasonable pluralism holds that, being 'the work of free practical reason within the framework of free institutions' 'a diversity of conflicting and irreconcilable [...] reasonable [...] comprehensive doctrines' is a 'permanent feature' of a democratic culture (PL, pp. 36-7). Accordingly, for Rawls 'many of our most important judgments are made under conditions where it is not to be expected that conscientious persons with full powers of reason, even after full discussion, will all arrive at the same conclusion' (PL, p. 58). Moreover, political liberalism assumes 'the fact of oppression' pursuant to which 'a continuous, shared understanding on one comprehensive religious philosophical or moral doctrine can be maintained only by the oppressive use of state power' (PL, pp. 36-7).

Interestingly, Rawls suggests that the conditions of reasonable pluralism are partly reflected in the prevalence of deep-rooted controversies 'within the tradition of democratic thought itself' (PL, pp. 4-5).

> [P]rofound and long-standing controversies set the stage for the idea of reasonable justification as a practical and not as an epistemological or metaphysical problem [...] We turn to political philosophy when our shared political understandings, as Walzer might say, break down, and equally when we are torn within ourselves [...] The work of abstraction [...] is a way of continuing public discussion when shared understandings of lesser generality have broken down (PL, pp. 44-6).

Notice that in one respect Rawls' insistence that reasonable pluralism is the work of free reason parallels Alasdair MacIntyre's claim that the standards of rationality belonging to different traditions of inquiry are incommensurable, a claim that has been subject to (in my view, mistaken) criticism for supposedly entailing relativism about truth.[6] Both claims attribute *incommensurable* standards to the subjects of reflection that they recognize. However, whereas for MacIntyre the subjects in question are (the members of)

---

6. On the latter see MacIntyre, 'A Partial Response to my Critics', p. 294.

communities of inquiry, for Rawls they are understood to be individual reasoners.[7] In Chapter 11 we will see how Rawls' insistence that reasonable pluralism is the work of free reason implicitly represents incommensurable standards as *the properties of intrinsically private* agents.

So political liberalism proceeds from the claim that no reasonable comprehensive view could possibly serve as the basis of a public justification of regulatory principles given the 'general facts' characterizing the political culture of a democratic society. The search for a reasonable and, hence, publicly justifiable, political conception recognizes from the outset that no reasonable comprehensive doctrine could have any special claims on anyone beyond that person's own view of its merits nor could it reasonably be suppressed through society's corporate coercive power. Recognition of the inevitable existence in modern democratic cultures of equally reasonable irreducibly different comprehensive views shows why a political conception is warranted and, relatedly, why we should limit the role that we ascribe to our comprehensive views in the elaboration of a public justification of regulatory principles (PL, pp. 58-62).

It follows from the account of liberalism elaborated so far that any adequate theory of social justice should meet two conditions. It should (a) remain within the self-imposed limits of a political conception when elaborating the moral grounds of its theorized object, the account of social justice (8.1); and (b) rely only on the theorist's public standard of reasonableness (8.2). To remain within these public-political limits is to meet both aspects of the theory's own criterion of adequacy. For Rawls, justice as fairness has the merit of supplying a morally grounded conception of justice that satisfies both these elements of the theory's own adequacy criterion. Let us see why he thinks this.

8.3 Political constructivism

The kind of inquiry just described and the very idea of a political conception are made possible through the adoption of 'political constructivism'. This is 'a view about the structure and content of a political conception' according to which the theory's structure permits the content in question, the principles of justice, to be represented as the outcome of a constructive procedure that embodies 'the principles of practical reason in union with' appropriate 'conceptions of society and person' (PL, pp. 89-90).

A number of points are worth noting about the reflective process that makes possible a political conception of justice. First, according to Rawls, this process begins by drawing on our 'considered convictions' that we find

---

7. For a feminist discussion of MacIntyre's view of the epistemological subject in comparison with individualist views see Alison Assiter, *Enlightened Women: Modernist Feminism in a Postmodern Age*, London, Routledge, 1996, pp. 77-95.

in 'the shared fund' of 'the public political culture'. The aim is to organize them into a *coherent* conception of citizenship in a 'well-ordered society of justice as fairness' so that this conception satisfies the test of 'reflective equilibrium' pursuant to which 'a political conception of justice, to be acceptable, must accord with our considered convictions, at all levels of generality, on due reflection' (PL, p. 8).[8] The idea of a well-ordered society in turn refers to a society that is effectively regulated due to citizens' recognition of the regulatory principles. That is, the citizens of a well ordered society: (a) accept the same regulatory principles, (b) publicly believe the basic structure to satisfy the principles and (c) generally comply with society's basic institutions (PL, p. 35). Accordingly, citizens' *subjective* recognition that the basic structure is regulated by certain principles that they take to be just is sufficient for well-orderedness. Even though in summing up the second element of this level of public recognition Rawls claims that 'the institutions of the basic structure of society are just (as defined by those [public] principles) and everyone with reason recognizes this' (PL, p. 66), we should not read the conjunction in this sentence as indicating that well-orderedness requires the basic structure to *be* just in addition to merely being *believed to be* just. For, what counts is the citizens' reading of the conformity of the institutions of the basic structure to the regulatory principles they endorse.[9]

So the first thing to note is that when engaging in the reflective process that generates a political conception one must restate enduring controversies at a suitable level of abstraction. To this end, justice as fairness draws from the public political culture of a democratic society the abstractly formulated 'fundamental organizing idea' of 'society as a fair system of cooperation between free and equal persons' (PL, p. 9). This organizing idea brings with it a conception of the person understood as 'someone who can be a citizen, that is, a normal and fully cooperating member of society over a complete life' (PL, p. 18). Note that the capacity for acting cooperatively is a property attributed to the citizen *qua citizen* and cooperation *is defined by* rather than *defines* citizens. Once society is viewed as a fair system of cooperation the question of how to determine a publicly justifiable conception of justice can be understood as a question of how to decide *the terms* of cooperation. Drawing on the social contract tradition, justice as fairness holds that 'fair terms [...] are conceived as agreed to [...] by free and equal citizens' (PL, p. 23).

---

8. For reviews of Rawls' idea of reflective equilibrium see Carlos Santiago Nino, 'Moral Constructivism', *The Ethics of Human Rights*, Oxford, Oxford University Press, 1991, pp. 69-71, T. M. Scanlon, 'Rawls on Justification', in S. Freeman (ed.), *The Cambridge Companion to Rawls*, Cambridge, Cambridge University Press, 2003, pp. 139-67. For an interpretation of the relativistic import of reflective equilibrium methodology as regards the standards of moral justification see ch 4. of Long, *Relativism and the Foundations of Liberalism*.

9. This reading of the meaning of well-orderedness comports both with Rawls' above mentioned definition and with his account of objectivity: Rawls, *Political Liberalism*, pp. 89-125. It is also suggested by Rawls' references to well-orderedness in the Rawls, 'Law of Peoples'.

Second, note that the idea of 'free and equal citizens' defines persons' 'public identity'. Rawls distinguishes a political conception's appeal to persons' public identity from reliance on (a) the metaphysical aspects of personal identity—what makes me one and the same person over time—and (b) persons' 'non-public identity', the 'non-institutional or moral identity' that includes both political and non-political commitments and effectively shapes and guides their social life (PL, pp. 30-1). By invoking this distinction between persons' public and non-public identities Rawls effectively by-passes objections to his conception of the person that focus on different properties as being the essential constitutive features of persons' identities. For example, objecting to Rawls' use of his political/metaphysical distinction Elizabeth Frazer and Nicola Lacey argue:

> the nature of the *political* subject is substantially altered according to our underlying theory of the subject. On a theory of personhood which took sexual difference to be an essential feature (as does much psychoanalytic theory) the idea of what constituted the 'fair terms of social cooperation' might look very different.[10]

In contrast, Rawls takes the view that:

> if metaphysical presuppositions are involved [in the premises of the political conception], perhaps they are so general that they would not distinguish between the metaphysical views [...] with which philosophy has traditionally been concerned (PL, p. 29 fn. 31).

Frazer and Lacey do not show, as a radical critique must do, why the theorist cannot or should not abstract from the differences between theories of subjectivity, including theories of sexual difference, *to a conception of a common political identity of persons* as Rawls proposes. Indeed, their claim merely begs the question against Rawls. After all, he appeals to the idea of a political conception in the light of the very observation of the prevalence of different metaphysical theories.

John Gray, on the other hand, accepts Rawls' methodological distinction between persons' public and non-public identities but proposes a 'Hobbesian construction' of the identity of persons to replace what he sees as the liberal content of Rawls' conception—the idea of persons as free and equal—on the ground that the Hobbesian idea is more suited to the prevalence of a combination of liberal and non-liberal forms of life in contemporary culture.[11] Yet, Gray is not clear on how precisely his preferred conception of the person better captures a public dimension of the political culture perhaps because he overlooks the significance of the work of abstraction involved in Rawls' further specification of the public identity of citizens as free

---

10. Elizabeth Frazer and Nicola Lacey, 'Politics and the Public in Rawls' Political Liberalism', *Political Studies*, vol. 43, no. 2, 1995, pp. 233-47, p. 238.

11. Gray, 'Contractarian Method, Private Property and the Market Economy', pp. 49-50.

and equal. Let us consider what precisely is involved in this specification.

According to Rawls, citizens' public identity refers to 'two moral powers (a capacity for a sense of justice and for a conception of the good) and the powers of reason (of judgment, thought and inference)' (PL, pp. 18-9). Corresponding respectively to citizens' two moral powers are the complementary virtues of 'full' and 'rational autonomy' both of which are distinguished from the broader notion of 'ethical autonomy' (PL, pp. 72-80). Whereas rational and full autonomy are both enabled by, and constitute part of, the political conception of persons as free and equal, ethical autonomy, about which political liberalism purportedly claims nothing, refers to an ideal that applies beyond the political to the whole of life (PL, pp. 77-8). Moreover, rational autonomy defines the character of citizens' reflections when, as a 'single unified agent [...] seeking ends and interests peculiarly its own', each citizen formulates, revises and enters into agreements for the pursuit of his or her conception of the good (PL, p. 50). According to Rawls, the rational applies to how ends and interests are affirmed and given priority as well as to the choice of means, yet the interests with which the self is concerned need not be in the shape of benefits to the self that has the interest in question (PL, pp. 50-1).[12] In contrast to rational autonomy, full autonomy refers to citizens' reflections when, as a plurality of persons, they work out society's regulatory principles pursuant to the exercise of the virtue of reasonableness. In other words, whilst being rational is the virtue of citizens with the capacity to form a conception of the good, being reasonable is the virtue of citizens with a sense of justice. Together these properties constitute the public identity of citizens.

---

12. For the meaning that Rawls gives to the idea that each person has a view of their own good see Rawls, *Political Liberalism*, pp. 30-4. Also, to avoid the objection that Rawls' conception of the person is individualistic, Rawls notes that the idea of a single unified agent need not be embodied in individual selves alone. According to Rawls, a single agent may be 'an individual or association, or a community or government', Rawls, *Political Liberalism*, p. 83. For an argument that responds to Michael Sandel's charge of individualism (*Liberalism and the Limits of Justice*), by pointing out the implications of limiting Rawls' account of citizens' rational autonomy to the idea of their *public* identity see also Doppelt, 'Is Rawls's Kantian Liberalism Coherent and Defensible?'. For a recent defence of Rawls against Sandel see Alan Haworth, 'Liberalism, Abstract Individualism, and the Problem of Particular Obligations', *Res Publica: A Journal of Legal and Social Philosophy*, vol. 11, no. 4, 2005, pp. 371-401. Stephen Mulhall and Adam Swift (Mulhall and Swift, *Liberals and Communitarians*, pp. 210-1.), argue that Rawls' commitment to reasonableness shields his contractarianism from the charge of a-socialism in the substantive sense of failing to recognize society's socializing influence on individuals' understandings of themselves and their relations to others. The theorist's commitment to reasonableness (in Rawls' sense) also explains why Rawls' reliance on contractarianism does not commit him, as Ackerman claims based on his reading of *A Theory of Justice*, to pre-social individualism, that is, to the idea that the appropriate reflective standpoint is that of the 'potential entrant' in the sense of 'somebody who has the choice of entering society or remaining indefinitely in some pre-political state', Ackerman, *Social Justice in the Liberal State*, pp. 327-30.

According to Rawls, as an element of the political conception of persons, reasonableness has two basic aspects: (a) the willingness to propose, discuss and honour fair terms of cooperation that all can reasonably accept and (b) the willingness to recognize 'the burdens of judgment' and the consequent inevitability of reasonable pluralism. Rawls offers an incomplete list of the burdens of judgment that function as sources of reasonable disagreement. It includes the difficulty of assessing or weighing complex and conflicting evidence and the difficulty of assessing different kinds of normative consideration. The important thing to remember about these sources of disagreement, according to Rawls, is that they, unlike factors like prejudice and sectional interests, are compatible with those judging being fully reasonable (see PL, pp. 56-8).

The two aspects of reasonableness conform to the theorist's reliance on a *public* standard of reasonableness (8.2). They define ideal citizens' reasonableness in such broad highly abstract terms in order that their views may consistently count as reasonable unless they can be said to be unreasonable. Moreover, this aspect of persons' public identity supplies the theorist's rationale for identifying the appropriate reflective standpoint from which to formulate regulatory principles. Justice as fairness identifies this as the point of view within the 'original position', the hypothetical situation in which the representatives of the essential interests of free and equal citizens agree upon regulatory principles (PL, pp. 49-54).

The original position imposes limits on the reflective procedure so as to model citizens' public identity, that is, their rational and full autonomy. On the one hand, it is made a case of 'pure procedural justice', that is, 'whatever principles the parties select from the list of alternatives presented to them is accepted as just. [...] This contrasts with perfect procedural justice, where there is an independent and already given criterion of what is just (or fair), and the procedure can be designed to insure an outcome satisfying that criterion' (PL, p. 72). Under conditions of pure procedural justice the contractors must specify the terms of cooperation in the light of what they regard as the rational advantage or good of the citizens they represent. Accordingly, citizens' rational autonomy is modeled by the reflections of the contractors who (a) are not bound by antecedently determined principles of right and (b) are guided by three 'higher-order interests': two correspond to citizens' two moral powers referred to above and the third corresponds to 'having at any given time a determinate conception of the good' (PL, pp. 72-4).

On the other hand, by imposing the 'veil of ignorance' the original position ensures conditions free of the influence of asymmetrical social relations and reasons based on social position, religious or philosophical persuasion or persons' moral identities (PL, pp. 23-5). The veil of ignorance places appropriate limits on the available information so that the parties in the original position do not know:

the social position of those that they represent, or the particular comprehensive doctrine of the person each represents. The same idea is extended to information about people's race and ethnic group, sex and gender, and their various native endowments such as strength and intelligence (PL, pp. 10-11).

Citizens' full autonomy is reflected in these structural aspects of the original position (PL, pp. 78-9). So, both the rational and full autonomy of citizens are respectively represented in the original position as the contractors' mode of (rational) reflection that takes place (reasonably) behind the veil of ignorance. In this way, whilst the idea of citizens' rationality determines the form of reflections to be undertaken by the contractors *within* the original position, that of their reasonableness provides the theorist's rationale for *the set up* of the original position: such is the path open to those who seek *publicly* to justify the terms of their cooperation *in the light of their reasonableness*. Because justified principles are the principles based on reasons that all could reasonably agree upon in the light of the burdens of judgment, these principles must be worked out in fair conditions. As a 'device of representation', the original position formalizes these conditions of fairness (PL, pp. 25-6).[13]

This said, because it is we, the theorists, as distinct from our artificial representatives, the contractors in the original position, who must ultimately be satisfied with the content of the conception of justice (PL, p. 28), namely *all* the ideas and values drawn from the public-political culture (PL, p. 149), political liberalism must also give an account of the relationship of this content to the non-public identities of ideal citizens. This is because the demand for the justification of regulatory principles is faced by the theorist whose inquiry begins and proceeds as it does in the light of a continued awareness that ideal citizens remain profoundly divided due to their reasonable but irreconcilable comprehensive views (8.2). Ideal citizens' continued commitments to such views must, therefore, be brought back into play in the justificatory process in order to establish the continuity of citizens' political and non-political values (PL, p. 10). This brings us to the second proposition making up political liberalism's understanding of the conditions that make possible a just and stable society, the idea of an overlapping consensus of reasonable comprehensive views over the conception of justice.

8.4 The idea of an overlapping consensus

According to political liberalism an overlapping consensus is to be understood as the endorsement of the conception of justice by citizens individual-

---

13. Rawls takes the view that the original position is fair because it represents citizens equally and 'accepting the highly general considered conviction expressed by the precept that equals in all relevant respects are to be represented equally, it follows that it is fair that citizens viewed as free and equal persons when represented equally in the original position, are represented fairly', Rawls, *Political Liberalism*, pp. 79-80.

ly, each from his or her own comprehensive point of view, as 'derived from, or congruent with, or at least not in conflict with, their other values' (PL, pp. 10-1). These other values are the merely social values belonging to the background culture of a democratic society that, as already indicated (8.1), include a variety of the comprehensive views to which citizens are also committed. The satisfaction of this requirement gives the conception of justice a morally binding authoritativeness because in this case, 'citizens are not only appealing to what is publicly seen to be reasonable, but also to what all see as the correct moral reasons from within their own comprehensive view' (PL, p. 127 & also see p. 150).

Given the conditions of reasonable pluralism (8.2), political liberalism holds that the conception of justice must be capable of endorsement by 'widely different and opposing though reasonable comprehensive doctrines' (PL, p. 38). The reasonableness of comprehensive views is given a 'deliberately loose' description. Political liberalism holds that comprehensive views are 'reasonable' when (a) they involve the 'exercise of theoretical reason' covering 'major [...] aspects of human life in a more or less consistent and coherent manner'; (b) they involve the 'exercise of practical reason' in organizing, prioritizing and balancing recognized values so that they can express an intelligible and distinct view of the world; and (c) they normally belong to 'a tradition of thought and doctrine' that 'tends to evolve slowly in the light of what, from its own view, it sees as good and sufficient reasons' (PL, p. 59). This definition enables political liberalism to count as reasonable 'familiar and traditional doctrines [...] even though we could not seriously entertain them for ourselves' (PL, pp. 59-60). Further, political liberalism holds that the morally grounded security of a democratic regime also depends on its being 'willingly and freely supported by at least a substantial majority of its politically active citizens' (PL, p. 38).

In summary, then, 'an overlapping consensus of reasonable comprehensive views over the political conception of justice' refers to (a) the endorsement of the conception of justice (b) individually by a substantial majority of a well-ordered society's politically active citizens (c) from the respective perspectives of their different and opposing reasonable comprehensive doctrines (d) as an essential constituent part of the doctrine affirmed by each one of them. Justice as fairness purports to show that ideal citizens can appropriately endorse the conception of justice (PL, pp. 144-5).

8.5 The idea of a full public justification

The basic ideas of a political conception of justice are developed and defended in the two stage reflective sequence outlined above, the first focusing on the *formulation* of the political values by the contractors in the original position (8.3) and the second on their *endorsement* by ideal citizens participating in an overlapping consensus (8.4). *Together* these stages purport to supply a *full public justification* of the basic structure of a liberal society. Thus Rawls gives an account of the possibility of reasonable pluralism in a well-ordered society by demonstrating, firstly, how the principles of justice can be formulated on the basis of the political conception's public ideas as represented by the original position and, secondly, how citizens can endorse the outcome of this procedure—the principles of justice and other political values—on the basis of their own reasonable comprehensive views.

Political liberalism holds that a society effectively regulated by the principles of justice would be one that meets 'the full publicity condition'. This condition requires that in addition to being well-ordered (8.3), society should satisfy two further levels of publicity: these respectively require the public availability of (a) the beliefs in the light of which the principles can be accepted; and (b) the 'full justification' that includes 'everything that we would say—you and I—when we set up justice as fairness and reflect why we proceed in one way rather than another' (PL, pp. 66-70). Hence, this third level includes the existence of an overlapping consensus of reasonable comprehensive views over the principles of justice.[14]

The first and second levels of publicity are respectively represented in the original position by limiting the contracting parties' choice of principles to publicly recognizable ones and by imposing the veil of ignorance (PL, pp. 66-70). That of the full justification:

> we model by our description of the thought and judgment of fully autonomous citizens in the well ordered society of justice as fairness. For they can do anything we can do, for they are an ideal description of what a democratic society would be like should we fully honor our political conception (PL, p. 70).

So, here Rawls specifies the relationship that should hold between the theorized subject/object (the free and equal citizens of a well-ordered society) and the theorist's ideal society (the society that meets the full publicity condition). What happens when this relationship is realized?

8.6 Liberal citizenship in a society that meets the full publicity condition

When a society meets the full publicity condition (call this 'a fully public society') the political conception of justice gives substance to the 'liberal principle of political legitimacy'. Pursuant to this principle, the power citizens exercise collectively within their society's basic structure is legitimately 'regularly imposed on citizens as individuals and as members of associations' (PL, p. 137).

According to Rawls, the legitimate exercise of citizens' collective coer-

---

14. John Rawls, 'Reply to Habermas' Reconciliation Through the Public Use of Reason', *Journal of Philosophy*, vol. 92, no. 3, 1995, pp. 132-80, pp. 142-3.

cive power defines 'the domain of the political' (PL, p. 38 & also see p. 18). Notice that by identifying the political domain of a fully public society with that of citizens' coercive collective power this 'domain' refers only to the administration of society's constitution and legal system. Two things follow from this. Firstly, Rawls' idea of the political domain cuts across the modern social spheres of household, economic market (civil society) and government/bureaucracy (state). Secondly, it does not include political practice and discourse based on other kinds of power relations and processes. Indeed, in a later paper Rawls explains that, as he uses this term, a 'domain' does not refer to:

> something already given apart from the political conception of justice. A domain is not a kind of space, or place, but rather is simply the result, or upshot, of how the principles of political justice are applied, directly to the basic structure and indirectly to the associations within it.[15]

So, the political domain is, itself, an outcome of the application of the political conception to society. As such, it is determined by, and does not determine, the social application of the principles of justice. Accordingly, Rawls' theory is no exception to the liberal tendency to identify political power with the state's coercive power (PL, p. 136), nevertheless, Rawls' conception of the political domain is at once broader than the traditional liberal representation of the political domain as coextensive with that of the sphere of governmental authority understood in opposition to the sphere of civil society and narrower than the non-juridical conceptions of the political that are effectively coextensive with the social.[16]

A fully public society also imposes on citizens 'the duty of civility' that, in turn, requires them to honour 'the limits of public reason' (PL, p. 217). This ideal of public reason holds that (a) certain matters of 'the public good', namely constitutional essentials and questions of basic justice—questions of (a) the structure of government and the political process and (b) citizens' equal basic rights and liberties though not questions of distributive justice (PL, pp. 227-229)—should be settled by appeal to political values and (b) the political values in question 'normally have sufficient weight to override all other values that may come in conflict with them' (PL, p. 217).[17] This ex-

---

15. Rawls, *Collected Papers*, p. 599.

16. See, for example, J. D. Faubion (ed.), *Michel Foucault: Power, Essential Works of Foucault 1954-1984*, London, Penguin, 1994, Frazer and Lacey, *The Politics of Community*, pp. 32-6, Mouffe, *On the Political*.

17. In 'Political Liberalisms' Ackerman objects that there are no good grounds for excluding matters of distributive justice from the scope of constitutional essentials and basic justice. What Ackerman fails to realize is that Rawls' account of the limits of public reason does not *deny* their application to all questions regarding the coercive power of the state, as Ackerman complains. Rawls notes that the argument of *Political Liberalism* is limited to a consideration of 'the strongest case where the political questions concern the most fundamental matters

ercise of public reason gives priority to political values over values that citizens might draw from their comprehensive views. In his revised account of the idea of public reason Rawls clarifies this relationship of priority by introducing 'the proviso' that 'reasonable comprehensive doctrines [...] may be introduced into public political discussion at any time, provided that in due course proper political reasons [...] are presented'.[18]

There are a number of noteworthy points about the function of Rawls' ideal of public reason. First, the political values that it invokes include, not only the substantive values of a political conception, namely the society's regulatory principles and other political values that are necessary for resolving constitutional essentials and questions of basic justice, but also the procedural guidelines of inquiry that come into play in addressing such issues. Rawls notes that this constitutes the *content* of the idea of public reason[19] that 'has to do with how questions should be decided'.[20] Second, the ideal of public reason does not apply to all discussion about its subject matter but only to discussion within what Rawls refers to as 'the public political forum'. In a revised version of his lecture on the idea of public reason Rawls clarifies that this forum consists of three kinds of discourse, namely those of the judiciary, of government officials and of candidates and campaigners for public office.[21] Third, this delimitation of the scope of the ideal of public reason does not mean that its limits apply only to citizens in an official capacity. Since it is the discourses and not the offices that define the public political forum, the limits of public reason apply to liberal citizens in both their official and *non-official* capacities so long as they engage in public discussion by taking up positions about matters of constitutional essentials or questions of basic justice within any of the three political discourses. This is why Rawls takes the limits of public reason to apply to matters such as how citizens are to vote in public elections (PL, pp. 215-6).[22] The limits of public reason do not apply to discussions beyond the political discourses. Instead such discussions invoke citizens' 'personal deliberations and reflections about political questions or to the reasoning of them by members of associations' (PL, p. 215). Thus the liberal ideal of citizenship positions all the deliberations and reflections that

---

[because] if we should not honour the limits of public reason here, it would seem we need not honour them anywhere' Rawls, *Political Liberalism*, p. 215. So, *Political Liberalism* merely confines its *argument in support* of the limits of public reason to such questions leaving open that of their wider applicability to questions of distributive justice. My reading is supported by Rawls' restatement of this aspect of his ideal of public reason in Rawls, *Collected Papers*, p. 575, esp. fn. 7.

18. Rawls, *Collected Papers*, p. 591.
19. Rawls, *Collected Papers*, pp. 584-5.
20. Rawls, *Collected Papers*, pp. 618-9.
21. Rawls, *Collected Papers*, p. 575.
22. See also Rawls' discussion of 'ordinary citizens' fulfillment of the duty of civility in Rawls, *Collected Papers*, p. 577.

form part of ideal citizens' comprehensive views *alongside* its ideal of public reason in a non-exclusionary relationship.

One aspect of these reflections concerns citizens' 'permissible conceptions of the good'. According to Rawls, this invokes a *political* idea of the good as defined by the political conception. It refers to any view of the good that does not directly oppose the principles of justice. Thus the idea of permissible conceptions of the good allows for at least two classes of conceptions: (1) those belonging to comprehensive liberalisms and (2) those belonging to comprehensive doctrines supported by groups that 'oppose the culture of the modern world' and 'wish to lead their common life apart from its unwanted influences' (PL, pp. 190-200). Here Rawls accommodates the surface level objection concerning adherents of endangered ways of life. As William Galston puts this objection, rather than 'facing a choice [that Rawls offers] between becoming victims [because they must give up their way of life] or oppressors [because they can only sustain their way of life coercively]', adherents of endangered ways of life are more likely to prefer to 'exit from pluralistic societies into communities marked by a greater degree of [...] homogeneity'.[23]

The final point to note about Rawls' account of citizenship within a fully public society is that it constitutes a 'deliberative democracy' in the sense that citizens 'suppose that their political opinions may be revised by discussion with other citizens; and these opinions are not simply a fixed outcome of their existing private and non-political opinions'.[24] Rawls insists that ideal liberal citizens must be willing to listen to others and be prepared to change their views as an outcome of public discussion (PL, p. 253).

It follows from the above observations that the liberal ideal of citizenship plays a dual role. Firstly, it guides liberal citizens' inter-subjective interpretations and realization of constitutional essentials and questions of basic justice; and, secondly, it indirectly determines the very conditions under which they are free to *otherwise* reflect and deliberate upon such matters and to pursue their life plans.

---

23. William A. Galston, 'Pluralism and Social Unity', *Ethics*, vol. 99, no. 4, 1989, pp. 711-26, p. 717.

24. Rawls, *Collected Papers*, pp. 579-80.

9

Publicness and Privateness in the Deep Structure of Political Liberalism

The purpose of this chapter is to expose the deep structure of Rawls' account of political liberalism. I aim to demonstrate that political liberalism embodies a model of the public-private dichotomy that attributes an alternate defining role to each of the basic categories as regards *both* the form and content of the ideas it relies on. Let us call this model 'MBC4'. In the process of revealing the distinguishing features of MBC4 as these are to be found in political liberalism, I will also be drawing the reader's attention to the kinds of misunderstandings of the theory that might arise in the absence of an appreciation of this structure. The point of this aspect of my discussion is not to offer a comprehensive review of where Rawls stands in relation to his critics but to highlight the benefits of pursing the kind of critical reconstruction that I am advocating for the radical critic.

9.1 The publicness of the theory's reflective starting point

Like the accounts of liberalism discussed in Part II, the focus of Rawls' theory is on distinctively public reasoning in so far as it is aimed at supplying a *public* justification of political principles. So, once again we encounter liberal theory's presumption in favour of public access to reasons.[1] Even so, whereas Rawls' view of the publicness of a justification and those of the theories already examined all function as complex-structured concepts, the degree of their complexity differs significantly. In the case of Rawls' theory more and different relationships obtain between different senses of publicness. To be-

---

1. Recall (3.3.2) that, as Benn and Gaus have observed, in the dimension of access liberal theory typically treats the category of publicness as a residual category.

gin with, Rawls' idea of a public justification determines the *standard* of reasoning that the theorist explicitly recognizes and not just his understanding of the theorized object, the conception of justice. By specifying the terms of the inquiry as a matter of working out what is reasonable, using a deliberately low standard of reasonableness, and not what is true (8.2), the theorist invokes a publicly accessible standard.

Similarly, from the outset, the public character of the theorized object, the conception of justice, is abstractly defined in terms of the special limiting features of a political conception (8.1). A political conception is public in the sense that it applies persons' common practical reason to ideas whose source is limited to the *public* political culture, that is to shared cultural and intellectual practices including those defining persons' public identity (theorized subject), and it restricts its inquiry to the question of the integration of the basic institutional structure of society, that is to the way in which the shared institutions form a unity (theorized object).

A failure to appreciate the significance of abstracting *the publicness* of the theorized object from its complex relationship to the non-public aspects of society lead early commentators on *Political Liberalism* to question his claim to have drawn the idea of society as a fair system of co-operation out of the public political culture of a democratic society. Russell Hittinger is a case in point. He argues that Rawls' appeal to a political conception leaves unjustified (a) its reliance on contingent conditions that the theory treats as morally significant and (b) its exclusion of perfectionist ideals.[2] Yet within an intellectual practice that treats the idea of justification in terms of the basic category of publicness, it is the very non-publicness of perfectionist ideals and, conversely, the publicness of the ideas that the theory invokes that are supposed to justify their respective exclusion and inclusion. Hittinger fails to offer any reason for thinking that such a theory need offer any further *justification* for treating as morally significant ideas that are specified in terms of their publicness.

By abstracting its shared aspects—the social properties that are common to its citizens—from the idea of society, political liberalism treats the remainder of society as the *merely* social, background culture of civil society. Does Rawls' account accord with Kymlicka's claim (2.2.3) that liberalism is committed to a public-private distinction that renders political and social institutions as separate domains governed by different principles? Despite appearances, this is not quite the point of the distinction. Its significance is in specifying a relation of exclusion of the background culture as *a potential source of the content of ideas* from which to construct the principles regulating the basic structure.[3]

---

2. Russell Hittinger, 'John Rawls, Political Liberalism', *Review of Metaphysics*, vol. 47, no. 3, 1994, pp. 585-602.

3. See also Rawls' later clarification that political liberalism does not regard the polit-

Significantly, the different forms of reasoning that are internal to the cultural and intellectual practices and institutions of the background culture—the various comprehensive views—are thus rendered as private. To be sure, Rawls explicitly denies the existence of 'private reason' preferring to talk instead in terms of 'non-public' reasoning—such as the 'social reasons' of associations and the 'domestic reason' of families in the background culture of society in which citizens participate (PL, p. 220 fn. 7). Nevertheless, it is clear from his remarks that in distancing his public/non-public distinction from the public-private dichotomy what he has in mind in the latter case is the surface level social differentiation to which, feminists amongst others, have been opposed (2.2.2) and which I have distinguished from the public-private dichotomy operative at the deep structural level of liberal theories (4.3). With this qualification in mind, we can continue to talk in terms of 'private' (non-public) reason without imputing to Rawls any commitment to an a-social or decontextualized view of the different forms of reason employed in liberal society's non-public spaces. This said, for our purposes the important point to note is that the above mentioned initial abstraction of the public-political from the social that is, in turn, rendered private, attributes a defining role to the category of publicness in the theory's reflective starting point.

9.2 The differentiation of the form and content of ideas

The second noteworthy point about political liberalism's reflective starting point is that, unlike the other theories discussed so far, in addressing the public and private dimensions of the ideas it employs, political liberalism explicitly differentiates between the public or private *form* of those ideas and their public or private *content*. Thus, the defining role that is initially attributed to the category of publicness explicitly extends to both the content and the form of the ideas used to formulate political principles. Recall that in constructing political principles a political conception not only must draw the content of its ideas from the public-political culture, it must also *present* them as freestanding, that is, as having a form other than the one(s) they have within comprehensive views. Accordingly, the theory attributes a defining role to the category of publicness when laying out the procedure of construction, the particular features of the original position (8.3). Moreover, in rejecting the idea that the theorist constructs the correct procedure of construction—as he does the political conception's content—Rawls claims that the procedure of construction is, instead, *to be found* in the sense of being 'simply laid out using as starting points the basic conceptions of society and

---

ical and non-political domains 'as separate, disconnected spaces', John Rawls, 'The Idea of Public Reason Revisited', in Samuel Richard Freeman (ed.), *Collected Papers*, Cambridge, Harvard University Press, 1999, pp. 573-615, p. 598.

person, the principles of practical reason, and the public role of a political conception of justice' (PL, pp. 96-7 & 103-4). Discovering the correct procedure of construction—the form of thought—is, therefore, thoroughly to be guided by public ideas and ends to the exclusion of private ones.

The explicit differentiation of the public or private *form* from the public or private *content* of ideas characterizes the intellectual practice of the theory throughout. Due to this greater sophistication, at the surface level the theory is able to recognize the inter-relationship of ideas whose content is rendered private and a public form of reasoning, as well as the reverse. For example, because Rawls claims that the principles of justice are formulated using only public ideas a political conception supposedly appeals only to citizens' *public* identity. Even so, he claims, on the one hand, that this identity is constituted by the reasonable and the rational (8.3) and, on the other, 'the reasonable is public in a way that the rational is not' (PL, p. 53). This sort of tension is only apparent once we have regard to the complex interplay of a public *form* of reasoning with ideas whose *content* is rendered private. As I will show at 9.3.2(a) below, the deep structure of Rawls' theory allows that whilst citizens' rationality constitutes an aspect of the *public form* that their reason takes, it is, nevertheless, exercised in relation to their private conceptions of the good, that is, to ideas whose *content* is taken to be *private*. Similarly, in the reflective procedure that the idea of an overlapping consensus defines, a range of *private forms* of reason are supposed to be exercised in relation to the principles of justice, principles whose content is rendered *public*. This claim will be developed at 9.3.2(b) below. Presently, the point I want to make is that, unlike the theories discussed so far, Rawls' theory relies explicitly on a certain form-content differentiation when addressing public and private ideas.

Significantly, it is this form-content differentiation of public and private ideas that enables the theory consistently to incorporate ideas of the good whose content is not, or cannot be said to be, drawn from the culture of a so-called liberal democracy. This is the case with the political idea of a permissible conception of the good. Notice that the theory's surface level recognition of the existence within a well-ordered society of communities that, nevertheless, 'oppose the culture of the modern world' (8.6) presupposes that they do not thereby also oppose the political conception. In their case non-opposition to the political conception must derive from the groups' members willingness not to participate in the public political forum. This, in turn, implies that the pursuit of the lifestyles in question does not require the realization of *public* politically active citizenship. Such lifestyles must involve conceptions of the good that have *no all-inclusive public political dimension* of their own in order not to face any *internal* obstacle to endorsing the political conception. They will not characterize the publicness of the political domain in competing terms as long as the content of their (primary) values can be expressed with indifference to the nature of the public form of (the values of) political life as defined by Rawls' fully public well-ordered society. It follows that all permissible conceptions of the good belong to comprehensive views that satisfy what we can refer to as a condition of non-publicness that is a necessary feature of *the content* of their values. This is the effect of Rawls' interpretation and endorsement of the idea of the priority of the right over the good.

9.3 The sequential differentiation of three forms of reasoning

Unlike the theories already examined, Rawls' theory treats differently the construction, endorsement and application of the regulatory principles. The contractors behind the veil of ignorance explicitly differentiate the procedure of *construction* of the principles from that of their *endorsement* by citizens participating in an overlapping consensus (8.4) as well as from the way in which citizens are supposed to exercise their reason when interpreting and *applying* the conception of justice to a fully public well-ordered society (8.6). Even though Rawls talks largely in terms of the differences between *two* types of reasoning—as in his claim that 'there are many non-public reasons and but one public reason' (PL, p. 220)—what we have here is the differentiation of *three* forms of reasoning corresponding to three steps in political liberalism's reflective process. These forms of reasoning, I will argue, differ both as regards their respective purposes and as regards the roles that they respectively attribute to the basic categories. Before proceeding to elaborate these I should distinguish my interpretation from that of Tim Scanlon who also suggests that there are three ideas of justification operating in Rawls' account. Scanlon does not include the idea of an overlapping consensus as one of them but focuses instead on the notions of the original position, public reason and reflective equilibrium.[4] However, we shall see from the analysis that follows that it becomes possible to blur the different forms of reasoning operating in Rawls' account only in the absence of an appreciation of their respective deep structural commitments. Indeed, discussions like Scanlon's serve to illustrate the ways in which this blurring proceeds.[5]

9.3.1 Different purposes for the different forms of reasoning

The two stages constituting the full public justification are concerned with two different ways of elaborating morally grounded political values. The contractors' reflections are directed to the *objective formulation* of the principles of justice whilst ideal citizens' reflections are directed to the *subjective endorsement* of the already formulated principles. At the first stage the aim is

---

4. See Scanlon, 'Rawls on Justification'.
5. See also James W. Boettcher, 'What Is Reasonableness?', *Philosophy and Social Criticism*, vol. 30, no. 5-6, 2004, pp. 597-621.

to formulate principles that are objectively universal in the sense of being constructed in such a way as to be a potential object of choice for any subject and not just for some specific subject (8.3). At the second stage the aim is for citizens individually, as distinct from inter-subjectively, to endorse the conception of justice as their own in the light of their private identities (8.4). These two aspects of the model of justification respectively address the distinct problems of system and social integration.[6]

In contrast to the first two merely justificatory steps in the reflective process (8.5), the third step deals only with reflections that concern the justified collective *realization* of the conception of justice. At this point the citizens of a fully public society—those to whom a full public justification of the conception of justice is already available (8.6)—focus on the inter-subjective interpretation and institutional embodiment of the already objectively formulated and subjectively endorsed principles.

Note also that the different purposes that define the three steps in the theory's reflective process render this process sequential. Since the pursuit of the second and third steps depends on the results of the immediately prior one the reflective process is supposed to be uni-directional. To avoid confusion, it is worth noting here that Rawls identifies a four stage sequence that belongs to his 'framework of thought': (1) the two part justification of the principles of justice in the original position; (2) a Constitutional convention where the citizens who accept the principles of justice draw up the Constitution in the light of them; (3) the enactment of laws in accordance with the Constitution; and (4) the interpretation of the Constitution and laws.[7] Although the specific objectives of Rawls' stages (2) - (4) differ, they are no less aspects of what political liberalism refers to as public discussion of constitutional essentials and questions of basic justice on the basis of the political conception (8.6). So, we should understand my reference to a *third* step in the theorist's reflective process, that consisting of the inter-subjective interpretation and institutional embodiment of the conception of justice, as applying to stages (2) - (4) of Rawls' framework of thought. Without ignoring the distinctions he draws between these stages, they nevertheless take the same deep structural form. At the same time, because, as I will argue, the deep structural commitments of the two part justification of the principles of justice in the original position (Rawls' stage 1) differ in highly significant ways, I will insist on distinguishing them as two different *steps* in the theorist's reflective process.

9.3.2 Different roles for the basic categories

The three forms of reasoning that constitute the reflective process as a whole

---

6. On this see Claus Offe cited in Seyla Benhabib, *Critique, Norm, and Utopia: A Study of the Foundations of Critical Theory*, New York, Columbia University Press, 1986, p. 127.

7. See Rawls, 'Reply to Habermas', pp. 151-2.

also attribute different roles to the categories of publicness and privateness. Consider each form of reasoning in turn.

9.3.2(a) Reasoning behind the veil of ignorance

The contractors' reasoning behind the veil of ignorance constitutes a *public* form of reasoning. Recall that the contractors' reflections model ideal citizens' rational autonomy whilst the conditions under which they deliberate model citizens' full autonomy. These are both features of ideal citizens' public identity whereas their private identities, and especially their ethical autonomy, is denied any role in the formulation of regulatory principles (8.3).

Indeed, all private forms of reasoning are completely inaccessible to the contractors' reflective standpoints in order to meet the first and second levels of publicity (8.5). Notice also that whilst this form of public reasoning is defined through an exclusion of all reasoning that takes a private form, this exclusion is explicitly the work of the theorist who determines the nature of, and conditions under which, the contractors' public form of reasoning is to function. The contractors themselves are simply blind to a range of facts about the social position and reasoning of the citizens they represent. They are not presented as setting aside any facts or determining the range of facts to be set aside. Nor do they themselves model the full autonomy of the citizens they represent (8.5). Since the imposition of the veil of ignorance and the discovery of its precise features are worked out from the theorist's reflective standpoint and not from that of the contractors, from this latter standpoint private forms of reasoning are effectively non-existent; to reason is to reason in the form provided by the contractors' public reasoning. It is in this sense that the category of publicness plays the defining role in the contractors' reflections.

The contractors' exclusive public reasoning—the use of a public form of reasoning and exclusion of all private forms of reasoning in the way just outlined—does not also extend to the *content* of their ideas. To be sure, the role of the contractors is to formulate the theorized object, the regulatory principles whose content is *public*. Even so, recall that one of the three higher-order interests that guide their reflections is a determinate conception of the good. The content of this idea is rendered private by making the original position a case of pure procedural justice (8.3). This is because the latter ensures that, when represented in the original position all conceptions of the good appear in abstraction from any relationship that they might otherwise bear (within comprehensive views) to what are taken to be antecedently determined principles of right. Accordingly, the contents of conceptions of the good appear in the original position as *private* in the sense of being differentiating properties of the represented citizens and they appear in abstraction from the (private) forms of reasoning on the basis of which citizens might actually endorse them. Note that this aspect of the reconstruction reveals the precise sense in which Rawls' theory need not exclude 'knowledge of differing conceptions of the good from the original position', as critics like William Galston have suggested.[8]

So, in modeling citizens' rational autonomy, that side of theorized subjects' identity that the contractors represent is constituted by the combination of a *public form* of reasoning and a *private content*. This explains how it is that in his account of the original position Rawls can consistently refer to the contracting *parties* in the plural and insist that the standpoint of one randomly selected party supplies the parties' choice of regulatory principles.[9] What we have here is the combination of a differentiated content (the plurality of private contents) and a common form (a singe public form of reason) so that the assessment of options in the light of their impact on the availability of 'primary goods' can be flexible enough to accommodate various readings of the psycho-social reality without this resulting in a failure to reach a 'unanimous' choice of regulatory principles.

To sum up, then, the contractors must (a) construct principles with a public content by relying (b) on their public form of reasoning and (c) on ideas with a private content while (d) being blind to private forms of reasoning. The category of publicness, on the one hand, subordinates ideas with a private content to those with a public content and, on the other, excludes altogether private forms of reasoning.

9.3.2(b) Reasoning as participants in an overlapping consensus

Despite the nature of the contractors' reflections, private forms of reasoning do not fall entirely beyond the scope of a full public justification. They are operationalized with the introduction of the idea of an overlapping consensus into the model of a full public justification. Now for the purposes of a deep structural analysis, we can focus here on the form of reasoning belonging to each citizen who *ideally* participates in an overlapping consensus over the principles of justice, leaving aside a feasibility question concerning the process of social transformation that might produce an overlapping consensus, say, via a 'constitutional consensus'.[10] Notice that the reasoning of citizens qua participants in an overlapping consensus constitutes a *private form* of reasoning. Recall that in their individual reflections citizens should endorse the conception of justice as an essential part of their respective reasonable comprehensive views and that since these views belong to the background culture of civil society (8.4) they are to be understood as private. Citizens participating in an overlapping consensus are not supposed to decide

---

8. Galston, 'Pluralism and Social Unity', p. 74.

9. Rawls, *A Theory of Justice*, pp. 139-40. See also Kukathas and Pettit, *Rawls: A Theory of Justice and its Critics*, pp. 20-1 & 33-4.

10. For Rawls' theory of social transformation see Rawls, *Political Liberalism*, pp. 158-68. See also Baier, 'Justice and the Aims of Political Philosophy'.

whether they can find any satisfactory reasons for endorsing the conception of justice, whether public or private. They are supposed to rely on criteria of validity or truth that are generally available to them in the background culture of civil society and, in any particular case, an individual is supposed to rely on *whatever criteria of correctness belong to the comprehensive doctrine that she happens to endorse*. Because each citizen is supposed to find reasons to view the conception of justice as part of her own private comprehensive view the reflection in question takes the form of private reasoning in the sense of reasoning in abstraction from, and other than, that characterizing citizens' public identity.

Indeed, the private reasoning of citizens qua participants in an overlapping consensus is supposed to exclude the form of public reasoning from which the conception of justice is itself formulated. Whilst citizens qua participants in an overlapping consensus are supposed to deliberate upon every aspect of the content of the conception of justice (8.4), they are not supposed to do the same for its procedure of construction for this would be to defeat the purpose of introducing the idea of an overlapping consensus in the first place. Precisely because the latter idea is meant to show how people can affirm the same political values even though their reasoning about them differs, the public form of reasoning that gives rise to the conception of justice is not supposed to concern citizens from the reflective standpoint of their comprehensive views.[11]

Notice also that this exclusion of the public form of reasoning from the participants' reflective standpoints is the work of the theorist and not of the citizen qua participant in an overlapping consensus. From within the latter standpoint the requirements of any public form of reasoning are not at issue; to reason is to reason in accordance with the requirements and criteria supplied by one's private comprehensive view. So, just as the first step in the reflective process attributes a defining role to the category of publicness, the second step attributes this role to the category of privateness. With this deep structural clarification in mind we can see why John Gray attributes too much conceptual work to this reflective process when he complains: 'it seems highly questionable to suppose that any overlapping consensus can be discerned in the welter of forms of life among which we move'.[12] Gray does not take into account the work of abstraction in which the participants in an overlapping consensus engage.

Moreover, the exclusive private reasoning characterizing the reflective standpoint of citizens participating in an overlapping consensus is not re-

---

11. Samuel Scheffler also makes this point in Scheffler, 'The Appeal of Political Liberalism', pp. 13-4. However, he argues that Rawls' account of an overlapping consensus is ambiguous in a way that renders it implausible. Shortly (8.2.3(iii)(b)) I will explain why Scheffler misunderstands Rawls' theory.

12. Gray, 'Contractarian Method, Private Property and the Market Economy', p. 49.

stricted to the form but extends to the content of whatever ideas they use to assess the conception of justice. One must suppose the privateness of the content of all the ideas belonging to a comprehensive view in order to ensure that such ideas do not inevitably conflict with the public ideas of the conception of justice. For example, Rawls' claim that one could endorse the conception of justice from the standpoint of utilitarianism (PL, p. 170), a particular comprehensive view, presupposes a commitment to the view that the principle of utility lacks a public dimension. Samuel Scheffler doubts Rawls' claim that utilitarianism could be included in an overlapping consensus because he fails to appreciate this point.[13] He does not take into account that Rawls can consistently criticize the utilitarian's attempt to justify the utility principle as a *public* principle whilst also recognizing that a utilitarian who accepts that the principle of utility lacks a public dimension may endorse the conception of justice from this modified standpoint. Even though Rawls appears to require only that the comprehensive views participating in an overlapping consensus be reasonable in the deliberately loose sense already mentioned (8.4) and this might lead one to think that revisions should not have to be made to them in order to render them capable of endorsing a political conception, it is worth noting Rawls' claim that, in endorsing the political conception, a comprehensive view may well involve 'adjusting its requirements'. He thinks that this does not constitute a 'political compromise' because it is an adjustment to the conditions of reasonable pluralism made by those *committed to seeking a public justification* (PL, p. 171).[14] My analysis of the theory's deep structure suggests that the sort of adjustment that one must be willing to make need not concern the content of comprehensive ideas per se, but only the view one takes as to their publicness or privateness. This is why it is misleading simply to suggest, as Tim Hurley has, that in *Political Liberalism* Rawls puts forward an argument 'that is supposed to convince all reasonable persons and the conclusion of which is that an acceptable theory of justice must be neutral between comprehensive doctrines'.[15]

So far I have suggested that at this second stage of reflection the identity of the theorized subject, the citizen qua participant in an overlapping consensus, is constituted as the combination of a private form of reasoning and ideas whose content is also private. It is on the basis of this private identity that the theorized subject reflects upon the theorized object, the already formulated principles of justice and other political values. As already indicated,

---

13. Scheffler, 'The Appeal of Political Liberalism', pp. 9-10.

14. See also Rawls' comments to the effect that any reasonable comprehensive doctrine will not override the political values of a reasonable political conception in Rawls, 'The Idea of Public Reason Revisited', p. 609.

15. T. Hurley, 'John Rawls and Liberal Neutrality', in Chandran Kukathas (ed.), *John Rawls: Critical Assessmments of Leading Political Philosophers*, London, Routledge, 2003, pp. 30-54, p. 43.

the content of this conception is constituted as public (9.3.2(a)). It is worth noting, however, that since the consensus over the conception of justice is produced indirectly out of the coincidence of a majority of the citizens' like private endorsements of it, from within the reflective standpoint of the participant in an overlapping consensus the content of the conception of justice is only *potentially* public. That is, one does not reflect upon the publicness or otherwise of regulatory principles from this reflective standpoint.

To sum up, each citizen qua participant in an overlapping consensus must individually endorse the conception of justice by (a) affirming its potentially public content (though not the potential of the content to be public); (b) relying on his or her private form of reasoning; and (c) relying on ideas whose content is private; but (d) being blind to any public form of reasoning. The public content of a conception of justice is confirmed as a by-product of its like private endorsement by a majority of citizens.

9.3.2(c) Reasoning as ideal liberal citizens

In the first two steps of the reflective process the public or private form of reasoning constituting the respective theorized subjects' identities defines the limits of their reflections. Even so, the limits in question—the exclusion of their respective opposite form of reasoning—are not determined by, nor are they matters of interest from, these reflective standpoints. Instead they constitute the pre-given frameworks within which to conduct the respective reasoning attributed to the theorized subjects. In contrast to contractors behind the veil of ignorance and ideal citizens qua participants in an overlapping consensus, at the third step in the theory's reflective process the theorized subjects are constituted as the ideal citizens *of a fully public well-ordered society* (8.5). The citizens who embody the liberal ideal of citizenship (hereafter 'liberal citizens') engage in inter-subjective processes of deliberation concerning constitutional essentials and questions of basic justice (8.6). So, liberal citizens employ the third form of reasoning in their capacity as social participants.

Now, there are two aspects to the identity of liberal citizens. First, in their capacity as social participants they deliberate using *both* their public and private reasoning. Recall that because their identities are constituted by their commitment to the political conception of justice and the related duty of civility, on the one hand, liberal citizens are supposed to recognize the limits of public reason in public political discussion. On the other, outside the public political forum they are free to give priority to their private reasoning when participating in non-public political discussion and in connection with their permissible conceptions of the good life (8.6). Whereas the former type of reasoning is defined by giving priority to ideas whose form and content are public, the latter is defined by giving priority to ideas whose form and content are private. Accordingly, this third form of reasoning is constituted by a differentiation of the form and content of ideas that gives priority to the basic categories of publicness and privateness, each within its own domain.

The priority in question allows liberal citizens to invoke their public or private reasoning in their respective domains *exclusively* but it does not require them to do so. All that is required is that, even within their own domain, appeals to private reason should be restricted to those that do not conflict with the values of public reason. Whilst the deep structure of the ideal of liberal citizenship relates the basic categories in a way that permits each to play a defining role within its designated domain, the co-presence of both public and private reasoning in the theorized subject's awareness is supposed to ensure that private views do not oppose the public content. Recall that, irrespective of how they are supported, Rawls' theory excludes from the social domain of a fully public society all conceptions of the good that oppose the principles of justice (8.6). The recognition by liberal citizens of the limits of their public reason, therefore, constitutes the social embodiment of the theorist's recognition of the self-imposed limits of a political conception (8.1).

The second aspect of the identity of liberal citizens concerns their capacity to take up the standpoint of the liberal theorist. Recall that liberal citizens have available to them a full public justification of their conception of justice that includes everything that the theorist would say in the elaboration of political liberalism. Qua *potential theorist* the liberal citizen is also supposed potentially to embody the full awareness belonging to the theorizing subject (8.5). The liberal citizen does not just embody the third form of reasoning outlined above. Instead, he or she is also potentially aware of the theory's first two forms of reasoning in which each of the basic categories exclusively define the forms of reason that are used, in turn, respectively to address ideas differentiated in virtue of their public or private contents (9.3.2(a) and 9.3.2(b)). It follows from this that liberal citizens *combine* awareness of the public form and content of the reasoning belonging to their political conception of justice and the private form and content of that belonging to their comprehensive views. In this way the deep structure of the idea of liberal citizenship supposes that both the basic categories, publicness and privateness, exclusively define the forms of reason that are, in turn, used respectively to address ideas differentiated in virtue of their public or private contents. Accordingly, MBC4 gives primacy to each of the public and private forms of reasoning within their respective domains.

9.3.3 Assessing the overall adequacy of Rawls' theory

The above discussion of what I will refer to as 'the theory's sequential form differentiation of reasoning' shows how each category is supposed to play a defining role with respect to the form, rather than merely with respect to the content, of ideas. MBC4 thus accords with the requirement that an adequate interpretation of MBC should acknowledge the respective public and private roles of different forms of reasoning (7.4). An understanding of the theory's sequential form differentiation of reasoning is a crucial prerequisite to any assessment of the overall adequacy of Rawls' theory. I want to lend some indirect support to this position by showing how in its absence even Rawls' most astute commentators have been unable to make sense of some of the most important claims in *Political Liberalism*. I will take as my examples three types of objection that have been addressed to key aspects of the theory. The first of these concerns the question of whether or not the two-stage justification of the principles of justice is necessary and sufficient. The second concerns the political nature of institutions under Rawls' conception of justice and the third addresses the question of who is supposed to be aware of the political conception's self-imposed limits. Let us take these in turn.

9.3.3(a) The two-stage justification of the principles of justice

I argued above (9.2.3(a) and 9.2.3(b)) that the categories of publicness and privateness respectively play the defining role in the two-stage justification of the principles of justice and that they do so by defining their respective theorized subjects'—the contractors and the participants in an overlapping consensus—*form* of reasoning. The deep structural differences between these two reflective standpoints form the basis of an explanation of the need for both stages of Rawls' model of justification (8.5). For they suggest that in a full public justification of regulatory principles both the public and private aspects of the theorists reasoning need to be satisfied, albeit in different ways. This is what revisionist critics of Rawls, such as Bruce Ackerman and Brian Barry, who have called for the abandonment of either the imposition of the veil of ignorance or the overlapping consensus requirements, fail to appreciate.[16]

On the other hand, Jon Mahoney argues against the sufficiency of Rawls' justificatory model maintaining that, in the absence of relying on a comprehensive view in Rawls' sense of this phrase, liberalism's moral foundation becomes indistinguishable from a modus vivendi or else it amounts to a dogmatic presupposition.[17] Yet the possible defences of liberalism's moral foun-

---

16. Ackerman, 'Political Liberalisms', Barry, 'John Rawls and the Search for Stability'. Similarly, because he does not appreciate the defining role that the category of privateness plays in Rawls' idea of an overlapping consensus, Harte misconstrues this idea and suggests that it is either incoherent or superfluous: Liam Harte, 'Overlapping Consensus: Incoherent or Superfluous', *Review Journal of Political Philosophy*, vol. 1, no. 1-2, 2003, pp. 249-80.

17. Jon Mahoney, 'Public Reason and the Moral Foundation of Liberalism', in T. Brooks and F. Freyenhagen (eds.), *The Legacy of John Rawls*, New York, Continuum, 2005, pp. 85-106. Similarly, Peter de Marneffe's argument against Rawls' appeals to public reason and to acceptable reasons on the ground that they cannot sufficiently distinguish between neutral and non-neutral reasons rests on a failure to appreciate the work of the sequential form differen-

dations that Mahoney critiques all rest on a failure to differentiate between the subtleties characterizing the sequential form differentiation of reasoning that I have attributed above to Rawls' account. Once we adopt this interpretive standpoint we can see how Mahoney's claim that Rawls relies on a dogmatic presupposition itself conflates the exclusionary publicness characterizing reflection in the original position and the prioritizing publicness distinctive of the exercise of public reason. We also find support for Tom Nagel's impression that political liberalism does indeed succeed in going beyond a modus vivendi.[18] Within Rawls' scheme, it becomes clearly inappropriate to read any strategic element into the various private reflections that an overlapping consensus operationalizes since the (potential) publicness of regulatory principles falls beyond the scope of this reflective standpoint.

9.3.3(b) The political nature of institutions

By drawing together Rawls' scattered references to the family, Susan Moller Okin identifies what she takes to be a 'confusion' in the theory about whether or not political liberalism views the family as a *political* institution and, so, as an institution to which the standards of justice apply.[19] The confusion arises, according to her, because, on the one hand, Rawls claims that the family forms part of the basic structure of society and, so, correctly indicates that it should be regulated by standards of justice. On the other hand, drawing attention to Rawls' claim that the family is 'non-political' because 'affectional', Okin adds:

> because they are based in affection [families] do not need to be regulated by the principles of justice. [...] There seems to be a clear inconsistency here. How can families be both part of the basic structure and not political?[20]

It is worth noting that the opposition between ties of affection and their regulation by the principles of justice is Okin's gloss on Rawls' reference to the family as an 'affectional', 'non-political' institution. Here Okin conflates the question of the application of the principles of justice and that of the application of the term 'political'. How and why can this occur in the absence of an understanding of the sequential form differentiation of the reasoning to

---

tiation of reasoning operating at the deep structural level of Rawls' account: de Marneffe, 'The Slipperiness of Neutrality', pp. 28-33.

18. Nagel, 'Rawls and Liberalism', p. 78.

19. Susan Moller Okin, 'Political Liberalism, Justice, and Gender', *Ethics*, vol. 105, no. 1, 1994, pp. 23-43. See also Susan Moller Okin, '"Forty Acres and a Mule" for Women: Rawls and Feminism', *Politics, Philosophy and Economics*, vol. 4, no. 2, 2005, pp. 233-48, pp. 241-3.

20. Okin, 'Political Liberalism, Justice, and Gender', pp. 25-7. Okin then argues that this confusion creates further problems internal to the theory. Okin, 'Political Liberalism, Justice, and Gender', pp. 37-8 & esp. 28-35. However, I will not examine the specifics of her claims since I will show, shortly, that it is she who brings to the text the confusion she identifies.

which the theory's deep structure is committed?

First, as part of Rawls' idea of the basic structure of society, the idea of the family constitutes part of the subject matter for which a political conception of justice elaborates regulatory principles. For this reason, the principles of justice apply both to activities of individuals that are directed to their family members and to families, as social units that are related to other social units (PL, pp. 258 & 21 fn. 8).[21] Rawls' idea of the political does play the role of differentiating aspects of social life to which the liberal state and liberal citizens should *apply* the principles of justice. Okin's failure to see how Rawls can allow for the fact that not every aspect of the life of a family is supposed to be regulated by the principles of justice reflects the limitations of feminist critiques of the liberal public-private dichotomy that remain at a surface level (2.2.2) (see PL, p. 27). This said, recall that, as well as using it to refer to the political domain of society, Rawls gives the term 'political' a stipulative definition for the purposes of the theorist's inquiry (8.1 and 8.6). That is, in addition to delimiting (the reasoning appropriate to questions relating to) the application of the principles of justice to the political aspect of society, that comes into play in the third reflective step of the theory, the concept of the political also plays the role of imposing limits on the sorts of ideas that can be invoked in the elaboration of the first two justificatory stages of the reflective process. (Recall the self-imposed limits of a political conception outlined in 8.1.)

On this reading, when Rawls refers to the family as a non-political institution in the process of elaborating the idea of an overlapping consensus—the second step in the reflective process that deals with the subjective endorsement of the principles of justice—the point of his remark is to explain, by way of contrast, the idea of a 'political relationship' that is used in a conception of justice remaining within the self-imposed limits of a political conception. These are, of course, limits that already include the idea of the family as part of the theorized object. The idea of the family is non-political in the sense that its members' relationships are (ideally) mediated by mutual affection in contrast to state-citizen and citizen-citizen relationships that are mediated by the state's coercive power.[22] Thus whereas the essence of the idea of the family is non-political, families, the social units and individuals within them, embody political relationships as well as essentially famil-

---

21. This reading accords with Rawls' later discussion of the family in Rawls, 'The Idea of Public Reason Revisited', pp. 595-601.

22. In *Justice, Gender and the Family* Okin is also very critical of Rawls' narrow conception of power. However, as radical critics have successfully argued, simply to reject it whilst remaining within a liberal framework, as Okin does, collapses the modern society-political state distinction thereby implying that no area of social life should be free of state intervention. For examples of this argument see, Cornelius Castoriadis, 'Power, Politics, Autonomy', *Philosophy, Politics, Autonomy: Essays in Political Philosophy*, Oxford, Oxford University Press, 1991, pp. 143-74, Frazer and Lacey, 'Politics and the Public in Rawls' Political Liberalism', pp. 72-6.

ial ties. Only in the absence of some understanding of the sequential form differentiation of reasoning that characterizes Rawls' theory can Okin simply juxtapose and, consequently, confuse the significance of Rawls' various statements about the political and the family.

9.3.3(c) The subject of awareness in an overlapping consensus

As part of an argument that Rawls' account of an overlapping consensus involves an ambiguity affecting the plausibility of his position, Samuel Scheffler identifies what he takes to be a damaging 'puzzle' in the text.[23] This 'concerns the attitude that participants in the overlapping consensus are supposed to have toward the political conception of justice on which they converge'.[24] Scheffler observes correctly that given the degree of meta-ethical uniformity that would be warranted,

> any requirement that the participants in an overlapping consensus must view the conception of justice as political would appear to be incongruous with the motivation for introducing the idea of such a consensus in the first place.[25]

He then cites Rawls on the question of how the citizens of a well-ordered society should conduct public discussion and maintains that 'Rawls does at times appear to require that the participants in an overlapping consensus regard the conception of justice as political'.[26] On the basis of the ambiguity that Scheffler identifies he argues for the abandonment of any requirement that the participants in an overlapping consensus should view Rawls' conception of justice as political. His reasons are that as well as conflicting with the motivation for introducing the idea of an overlapping consensus and 'mak[ing] an overlapping consensus more difficult to achieve', such a requirement 'would add little that is plausible to an adequate account of public reason'.[27]

Rawls' theory faces none of these problems, nor does there appear to be any 'damaging ambiguity' in the text when the theorist has regard to the theory's sequential form differentiation of reasoning that I have identified above. To begin with, if we take Rawls' elaboration of the idea of an overlapping consensus as constituting the second of a three step reflective sequence directed to the endorsement of regulatory principles we can distinguish this from the reflection of the ideal liberal citizen in the capacity of social participant that is elaborated as the third step in the theorist's reflective process. Then, if we acknowledge the defining role that is played by private forms

---

23. Scheffler, 'The Appeal of Political Liberalism'.
24. Scheffler, 'The Appeal of Political Liberalism', p. 13.
25. Scheffler, 'The Appeal of Political Liberalism', p. 14.
26. Scheffler, 'The Appeal of Political Liberalism', p. 14.
27. Scheffler, 'The Appeal of Political Liberalism', p. 19.

of reasoning in the reflection characterizing the idea of an overlapping consensus, as I have argued above (9.3.2(b)), it is clear that the theory requires ideal citizens qua participants in an overlapping consensus to reflect upon the *content* of the political conception—the abstract ideas used to formulate the regulatory principles as well as the formulated principles and political values—*in abstraction from the public procedure of its construction*. Accordingly, an awareness of the limits imposed by the political conception should not enter into the reflective standpoint of citizens qua participants in an overlapping consensus. This accords with what Rawls says about the motivation for introducing the idea of an overlapping consensus as well as about how an overlapping consensus is to be achieved.

Finally, we can consistently attribute the awareness of the political nature of the conception of justice to the differently structured reasoning characterizing the third step in the theory's reflective process. Since it is at this point in the theory that Rawls offers an account of the public reason belonging to the citizens of a fully public well-ordered society, it is consistent that citizens qua social participants *should view* their conception of justice as part of a political conception. This is because the full justification of the conception of justice is supposed to be *available* to the participants in such a society. However, none of this requires that they view the conception of justice as political *qua participants in an overlapping consensus* especially since a consensus logically precedes the existence of a fully public well-ordered society (8.6). When Rawls' ideal of public reason refers to the reflection that is supposed to take place in public discussion amongst the citizens of a fully public well-ordered society, this ideal refers to the reflections of citizens to whom a full justification is already available. Precisely because such a justification includes the awareness of the political nature of the conception of justice (stage one) as well as the achievement of an overlapping consensus (stage two), in this capacity citizens are taken to have access to the awareness in question.

9.4 The theorist's role in maintaining the unity of the theory

9.4.1 The theorizing subject's external reflective standpoint

Unlike the theories discussed in Part II, MBC4 also explicitly recognizes a standpoint of reflection that is not reducible to the exclusive standpoint of either of the basic categories. Recall that at the surface level the theory recognizes the point of view of the theorist who seeks to supply a full public justification that is the most reasonable for us to accept and that this point of view is distinguished from both that of the contractors in the original position and that of ideal citizens (8.3). Also, my analysis of the role attributed to the basic categories (9.3.2) shows that the determination of the conditions under which the theorized subjects are supposed to reflect is a matter for the theorizing subject whose reflective standpoint, unlike that of the theorized subjects, is not *exclusively* identified with one of the basic categories.

Indeed, the different steps in the reflective process and their associated forms of reasoning are made possible by the theorizing subject's initial *abstraction* of the basic categories from their concrete inter-relationship in (ideal) citizens' (public and private) identities (8.1). The theorizing subject makes the categories play an exclusive defining role by defining the form of reasoning, first, in abstraction from citizens' private identities (9.3.2(a)) and, then, in abstraction from their public identity (9.3.2(b)). Accordingly, the theorizing subject's awareness, that each of the categories exclusively defines a form of reasoning, belongs to a standpoint of reflection that must be external to those defined by the basic categories. It follows that the recognized presence of what we might call 'the theorist's external reflective standpoint' gives the theory its unity and motivates the transition from one step of the reflective process to the next.

Of course, in attributing a defining role to the category of publicness in the theory's reflective starting point, a certain priority is given to the theorizing subject's public identity in so far as he or she must rely on a public standard of reasonableness when determining and applying society's regulatory principles (9.1). Even so, this aspect of the theorizing subject's identity places constraints on the use of private reasoning; it is not exclusive in the sense of rendering the theorizing subject blind to private reasoning. (For, this would be to eliminate the motivational basis for moving to the theory's second justificatory stage.) So, the theorizing subject's identity is supposed to be constituted by both a public aspect that restricts the use of private reasoning and an external reflective standpoint that plays the role of bringing the theory into a unity.

Notice, finally, that the theorizing subject's external reflective standpoint is ideally supposed to be socially embodied by the liberal citizen. This follows from the fact that qua *potential theorist* the liberal citizen is supposed potentially to embody the full awareness belonging to the theorizing subject (8.5). In this sense, the liberal citizen is supposed potentially to embody full transparency.

In summary, the three steps constituting the reflective process as a whole are viewed as a totality from the external reflective standpoint of the theorizing subject whose awareness is potentially embodied in that of the liberal citizen. This, then, is the reflective standpoint from which the full inter-relationship of the categories of publicness and privateness is supposed to be viewed within MBC4.

9.4.2 Habermas on Rawls' model of justification

The political conception's *model of justification* depends upon an appreciation of the above understanding of the theorist's presence in terms of the theorizing subject's external reflective standpoint (9.4.1)) along with the theory's sequential form differentiated reasoning (9.3). I want to illustrate this point by showing how, without the aid of this understanding, Jürgen Habermas' review of *Political Liberalism* misconstrues Rawls' model of justification. Habermas examines Rawls' employment of the idea of an overlapping consensus and his account of stability in order to assess their general significance for Rawls' account of the *justifiedness* of justice as fairness.[28] He notes: 'it needs to be shown that this conception [justice as fairness] is neutral toward conflicting world views and remains uncontroversial after the veil of ignorance has been lifted'. Habermas thinks that Rawls' distinction between metaphysical and political ideas 'indicates a certain unclarity about the precise character of what is in need of justification; from this, in turn, there results an indecisiveness as to how the validity claim of the theory itself should be understood'.[29] So, the question Habermas poses is:

> whether the overlapping consensus on which the theory depends, plays a cognitive or merely instrumental role: whether it primarily contributes to the further justification of the theory or whether it serves, in the light of the prior justification of the theory, to explicate a necessary condition of social stability.[30]

As my outline of Rawls' position suggests (8.5), I think that Rawls wants the idea of an overlapping consensus to 'contribute to the further justification of the theory' *as well as* to define the conditions of social stability. Habermas, however, presents these possibilities disjunctively because he thinks that Rawls' account cannot do both. He claims that Rawls has failed to appreciate the difference between two kinds of test. On the one hand, there is a 'test of acceptability' of the political conception's central ideas from 'the interpretive perspectives of different world views' (whose satisfaction would demonstrate the neutrality of the political conception toward conflicting world views). On the other hand, there is 'the test of consistency he [Rawls] previously undertook [in *A Theory of Justice*] with reference to the well-ordered society's potential for self-stabilization' (for example, by generating the 'functionally necessary motivations from its own resources through the requisite political socialization of its citizens').[31] Habermas argues that Rawls' assumption that the test of acceptability is of the same kind as the test of consistency as a 'methodological parallel is problematic' because whereas the latter test can be undertaken as 'a move within the theory', the test of acceptability, that brings the fact of pluralism into play, is applied by 'real citizens of flesh and blood' rather than by 'the fictional citizens of a just so-

---

28. Habermas, 'Reconciliation Through the Public Use of Reason', pp. 119-22.
29. Habermas, 'Reconciliation Through the Public Use of Reason', p. 119.
30. Habermas, 'Reconciliation Through the Public Use of Reason', p. 119.
31. Habermas, 'Reconciliation Through the Public Use of Reason', p. 120.

ciety about whom statements are made within the theory'. Habermas suggests further that:

> the philosopher can at most attempt to anticipate in reflection the direction of real discourses as they would probably unfold under the conditions of a pluralistic society. But such a more or less realistic simulation of real discourses cannot be incorporated into the theory in the same way as the derivation of possibilities of self-stabilization from the underlying premises of a just society.[32]

Now, the problem, according to Habermas, is that 'this misleading parallel' casts the overlapping consensus in the wrong light:

> the overlapping consensus merely expresses the functional contribution that the theory of justice can make to the peaceful institutionalization of social cooperation; but in this the intrinsic value of a *justified* theory must already be presupposed. From the functionalist perspective, the question of whether the theory can meet with public agreement [...] would lose an epistemic meaning essential to the theory itself. The overlapping consensus would then be merely an index of the utility, and no longer a confirmation of the correctness of the theory; it would no longer be of interest from the point of view of acceptability, and hence of validity, but only from that of acceptance, that is, of securing social stability.[33]

Habermas suggests that Rawls wants to collapse the distinction between the theory's 'acceptability' and its 'actual acceptance' whereas he ought to have insisted on it and focused on acceptability in order that the idea of an overlapping consensus do more than provide 'a purely instrumental understanding of the theory'. He points out, quite correctly, that the latter kind of understanding 'is already invalidated by the fact that the citizens must first be *convinced* by the proposed conception of justice before such a consensus can come about'.[34] He concludes,

> if Rawls rules out a functionalist interpretation of justice as fairness, he must allow some *epistemic* relation between the validity of his theory and the prospect of its neutrality toward competing world views being confirmed in public discourses. The stabilizing effect of public discourses would then be explained in cognitive terms, that is, in terms of the confirmation of the assumption that justice as fairness is neutral toward 'comprehensive doctrines'. I do not mean to say that Rawls accepts premises that would prevent him from drawing this consequence; I mean only that he hesitates to assert it because he associates with the characterization 'political' the proviso that the theory of justice should not be burdened with an epistemic claim and that its anticipated practical

---

32. Habermas, 'Reconciliation Through the Public Use of Reason', p. 121.
33. Habermas, 'Reconciliation Through the Public Use of Reason', pp. 121-2.
34. Habermas, 'Reconciliation Through the Public Use of Reason', p. 122.

Publicness and Privateness in the Deep Structure of Political Liberalism 215

effect should not be made contingent on the rational acceptability of its assertions.[35]

My reconstruction of the deep structure of Rawls' theory can show why Habermas' objection introduces into his interpretation of political liberalism two ideas that are inappropriate and unnecessary in the second justificatory stage of the theory (the stage that invokes the idea of an overlapping consensus). The first of these is a notion of fully concrete beings—Habermas refers to 'real discourses' amongst 'real citizens of flesh and blood'—and the second is a notion of 'rational acceptability' whose meaning remains implicit in Habermas' comments on Rawls but, I suggest, must refer to something like the *universalist* cognitive norm validation procedure that Habermas develops in his own theory of discourse ethics.[36] That Habermas is alluding to a cognitivist norm validation procedure is evident from points of comparison that he draws between Rawls' theory and his own account of the moral point of view.[37]

To begin with, my deep structural reconstruction of the theory clarifies why the notion of fully concrete beings does not come into play in the second stage of Rawls' model of justification. Fully concrete beings enter into the theory in two ways. On the one hand, having recognized the theorizing subject's presence as distinct from that of ideal citizens, fully concrete beings play the role attributed to the theorist (8.2). When doing so they/we are supposed to employ the external reflective standpoint that is constitutive of the theorizing subject. On the other hand, fully concrete beings enter into the theory qua liberal citizens when their/our reflective standpoint combines their/our public and private reasoning. However, as already noted, in this case the purpose of public discussion is to *apply* the already justified principles of justice (9.3.2(c)). To insist on this distinction is not to deny that the two reflective standpoints combine when we as citizens of a reasonably well-ordered society accept justice as fairness and apply its principles.[38] Rather, my analysis of the sequential form differentiated reasoning shows that this combined reflective standpoint also differs from those respectively attributed to the ideal citizen in the first and second steps of the theory's reflective process (9.3.2(a) and 9.3.2(b)). According to the deep structural analysis, in so far as ideal citizens are supposed to employ their *exclusively private* form of reasoning at the second stage of the justificatory project that invokes the idea of an overlapping consensus, their identity is constituted as

---

35. Habermas, 'Reconciliation Through the Public Use of Reason', p. 122. In his 'Reply to Habermas' Rawls repeats his understanding of a public justification but does not address Habermas' objection directly.

36. See Jürgen Habermas, *Justification and Application*, Cambridge, Polity, 1993.

37. See Habermas, 'Reconciliation Through the Public Use of Reason', p. 127.

38. That the two standpoints merge in this case is also implied in a clarificatory point that Rawls makes in connection with a different point in Rawls, 'Reply to Habermas', p. 151.

an *abstraction* from that of fully concrete beings. It follows that Habermas' view that the idea of an overlapping consensus calls for the endorsement of the principles of justice and of their neutral derivation *from the reflective standpoint of fully concrete beings* cannot be justified by appeal to the demands that the theory places on either the liberal theorist or the ideal of liberal citizenship. Habermas offers no immanent reasons for thinking that the differentiated reflective standpoints of ideal citizens should or must be otherwise understood.

Furthermore, there is no obvious reason for thinking that ideal citizens' exclusively public and exclusively private forms of reasoning cannot both be understood as cognitive processes involving a universalistic element. Nor is there any reason for thinking that reflections from the theorist's external standpoint cannot involve 'epistemic' claims in the sense of seeking to establish a kind of 'cognitive' relationship between 'the validity of the theory' and 'the confirmation of the assumption that justice as fairness is neutral toward 'comprehensive doctrines'. Habermas cites Rawls' claim that the aim of a political conception is 'practical and not metaphysical or epistemological' to substantiate his impression that Rawls collapses the distinction between rational acceptability and acceptance because he wants to avoid making epistemic claims.[39] However, my earlier discussion of Rawls' idea of reasonableness (8.3) shows, that this does not mean, *pace* Habermas, that Rawls gives up the aim of supplying some kind of cognitive validation of the substance of the theory of justice in favour of merely advocating a reflective attitude of toleration. One need only bear in mind the various constraints imposed on the reflective standpoints of theorizing and theorized subjects as well as the theorized subject's form differentiated reasoning. Where the latter is concerned, political liberalism *fully determines* only the procedure and content of ideal citizens' public reason even though the operation of both the exclusively public and exclusively private aspects of citizens' reflection are involved in the provision of a fully public justification of the political conception.

If my interpretation is correct it is also inappropriate to suggest that Rawls wants to avoid making the demonstration of stability contingent upon the 'rational acceptability' of the theory's claims. Habermas cannot justifiably rely on his conception of a universalist cognitive validation procedure to support this suggestion since it does not permit sufficient discrimination between the exclusively public and exclusively private aspects of citizens' reflection nor any consideration of the mode of their inter-relationship.

So, Habermas' critique of Rawls' theory serves as an example of the kind of *external* critique of liberal theory from which I distinguish my own

---

39. Habermas, 'Reconciliation Through the Public Use of Reason', p. 122.

approach in 2.1.2. His claims against Rawls are reflective of a characteristic weakness of such critique, namely a tendency to be at cross-purposes due to the critic's reliance on concepts that are not shared by the liberal theorist.

10

The Relative Superiority of Political Liberalism

The potential power of a radical critique of MBC4, the model of the public-private dichotomy that I attribute to political liberalism, rests in part on the claim that this conception is indeed superior to the alternative versions of MBC. In this chapter I will defend the view that, on both the surface and deep structural levels, Rawls' political liberalism is superior to alternative versions of the minimal political morality approach to defining liberalism. I will try to show why this holds even in relation to accounts of liberalism, like those examined in Part II of the book, despite their having been developed partly in response to perceived weaknesses in Rawls' own theory. Without exception, Kymlicka, Waldron and Larmore claim to be offering more defensible accounts of some idea that they extract from Rawls' work.[1] One of the conclusions that this chapter will draw by way of a critical comparison of Rawls' theory with their accounts of liberalism is that because the deep structure of the former incorporates the strengths of each of the latter, without being subject to their respective limitations, its similar surface level positions face none of their limitations.

My claim is that the strengths of MBC4, the model of the public-private dichotomy to which the deep structure of Rawls' theory is committed, are to be found in its relative complexity. This complexity, as we saw in the previous chapter, derives from the theory's reliance on the sequential form differentiation of reasoning and its related form-content differentiation as well as on its recognition of the unifying role that is played by the theorizing subject's external reflective standpoint. I will argue that, for these reasons, MBC4 offers the most complete interpretation of the basic claim that one

---

[1]. See Kymlicka, *Liberalism, Community, and Culture*, Larmore, 'Political Liberalism', Waldron, 'Theoretical Foundations of Liberalism'.

category plays the defining role in the public-private dichotomy. This argument will establish that the minimal political morality approach to defining liberalism stands or falls with a theory whose deep structure conforms to MBC4.

10.1 The relative superiority of MBC4

The previous chapter demonstrated that, due to its sequential form differentiation of reasoning (9.3) MBC4 gives equal expression to the claims that publicness plays an exclusive defining role; that privateness plays an exclusive defining role; and that the basic categories alternate this role as regards both the content and the form of ideas. MBC4 thus incorporates each of the principles embodied by the three models of the dichotomy that were assessed in Part II. The patterns of inter-relating the basic categories *within* each of the three forms of reasoning examined in Chapter 9.3.2 respectively correspond to those characterizing MBC1 to MBC3. That is, the deep structural commitments of the form of reflections undertaken by the contractors in the original position (9.3.2(a)) follow the same pattern as those that define MBC1 (see 5.2). Similarly, the deep structural commitments of the form of reflections undertaken by ideal citizens participating in an overlapping consensus (see 9.3.2(b)) follow the same pattern as those that define MBC2 (see 6.2). Those characterizing the form of reflections undertaken by the liberal citizens of a fully public well-ordered society (9.3.2(c)) follow the same pattern as those that define MBC3 (see 7.2).

In addition to the ways in which public and private categories are related at each step of the reflective process, we have also seen that unlike MBC1 to MBC3, MBC4 explicitly differentiates public and private forms of reasoning and makes room for both within its model of justification. The relatively complex combination of the basic categories that characterizes MBC4 results both from the sequential form differentiation of the theory's reasoning (9.3) and from the recognized presence of the theorist's external reflective standpoint (9.4). Whereas the former permits the basic categories to play different roles at each step of the inquiry, the latter views these different forms of reasoning as belonging to one and the same process of inquiry. By incorporating the variety of interpretations to which MBC is open in the way just outlined, MBC4 constitutes the most complete interpretation of MBC.

Despite the similarities with the earlier models of the public-private dichotomy, MBC4's incorporation of the variety of interpretations to which MBC is open does not expose MBC4 to the limitations of the earlier models of the dichotomy. This is because, unlike them, it does not take any one of the isolated interpretations to define the model of the dichotomy *in its totality*. Let me illustrate this claim with two examples. Firstly, whereas in MBC1 and MBC2 the respective failure of the models to recognize the reciprocal defining roles of the basic categories had the effect of exposing their respective limitations, MBC4 allows each of the basic categories to play a role in which they do not recognize the categories' reciprocity (in the first and second steps of the reflective process) yet it also recognizes basic categorial reciprocity (from the theorist's external reflective standpoint). Secondly, whereas the limitations of MBC3 were exposed through an analysis of this model's unacknowledged restriction of the categories' alternate defining roles to the content of their ideas, MBC4 repeats this understanding of the basic categories' inter-relationship (in step three of the reflective process) without, however, limiting itself to this understanding. That MBC1 to MBC3 represent incomplete abstractions of MBC is thus rendered visible in the light of MBC4.

I have been arguing that the deep structural model of the public-private dichotomy that Rawls' theory embodies offers the most complete interpretation of the basic claim that one category plays the defining role in the public-private dichotomy. Its relative superiority stems from its recognition of the theorist's external reflective standpoint because this is what enables the basic categories alternately to define the different forms of reasoning involved in the reflective process. The model is thus able to acknowledge that each of the basic categories plays a defining role that is, nevertheless, exclusive in relation to both the form and content of ideas. This is something that cannot be acknowledged within the respective frameworks of the inter-relationships that constitute each step of the reflective process taken in abstraction from the rest. What is the significance of these reconstructive claims? We will answer this question by seeing how the relative deep structural superiority of Rawls' theory is also mirrored at the theory's surface level in comparison with the theories already examined.

10.2 The relative strengths of political liberalism

If the previous chapter's reconstruction of the deep structure of Rawls' theory is correct, a surface level comparison of the theory with the other exemplary versions of the minimal political morality approach to defining liberalism should show that it overcomes their limitations at the surface level as well. Consider first the relative strengths of Rawls' theory as compared to Kymlicka's account of liberalism.

10.2.1 Rawls and Kymlicka

As already suggested above (10.1), the model of the dichotomy that Kymlicka's theory embodies, MBC1, and the reflections of the contractors in Rawls' original position follow the same pattern of basic categorial inter-relations. The discussion in Chapter 5.3 showed that, at the surface level,

Kymlicka's theory is unable to satisfy its adequacy criterion of effectively distinguishing between an objectively good life and a life that is merely subjectively good even though the theory's foundational idea relies on the former *to the exclusion of* the latter. By taking the abstract idea of persons' essential interest in leading an objectively good life to be the moral foundation of liberalism Kymlicka's theory commits liberal political morality to a problematic way of viewing its relationship to ethics. Recall also that the source of this problem was traced to a fundamental flaw in MBC1 that attributes a defining role to the category of publicness in a way that enables the category of privateness to undermine the primacy of the public. We have also seen that, like Kymlicka, Rawls appeals to the idea of persons as having an essential interest in leading a good life and his theory recognizes the role of subjectivity in the determination of conceptions of the good. However, this is part of his account of the public political conception of persons as free and equal and this, in turn, forms part of the fundamental organizing idea of society as a fair system of cooperation that is drawn from the public political culture of a democratic society (8.3). Now, Simon Caney objects that in ascribing to persons a higher order interest in terms of the capacity to form a conception of the good Rawls overlooks the arguments of authors like Kymlicka and communitarians that:

> citizens have other important interests including an interest in pursuing and adhering to valuable conceptions of the good. We would like to live valuable lives and wish to avoid shabby, boring and worthless conceptions of the good. [... C]itizens also have an interest in well-being'.[2]

It is unclear from Caney's remarks whether he means to challenge Rawls' for insisting on a subjectivist formulation of persons' higher order interests regarding conceptions of the good or whether he means to challenge Rawls' use of the distinction between ethical autonomy, on the one hand, and rational and full autonomy, on the other (8.3). Still, in the light of our deep structural reading we can make two points in Rawls' defence. First, Rawls' conception of persons' public identity does not assume the correctness of subjectivist views of the good but merely does not presuppose the correctness of objectivist views in the way that Kymlicka's account does. Second, although Rawls excludes from his account of the public dimensions of personality references to persons' ethical autonomy and, hence, to (aspects of) their well-being conceived as extending to the whole of life, he does not deny the existence or significance of such interests but limits their determining power so that they enter into Rawls' justificatory scheme in their determinate form only when the question of the endorsement of already formulated principles arises. Caney's objection, based on the observation that we have

---

2. Simon Caney, 'Anti-Perfectionism and Rawlsian Liberalism', *Political Studies*, vol. 43, no. 2, 1995, pp. 248-64, pp. 260-1.

an interest in flourishing, does nothing to show why the imposition of such limits should be rejected.

Indeed, Rawls' scheme affirms this interest by including each person's higher-order interest in some determinate—though, because of the operation of the veil of ignorance, unspecified—conception of the good as one of the factors that guides the reflections of the contractors in the original position, the representatives of the interests of citizens who have such determinate conceptions. The upshot of this more elaborate account is that it purports to justify reliance on this interest by placing it in the framework of the constructivist procedure. In doing so, the idea of our having at any given time formed a revisable determinate conception of the good remains an equally abstract idea since subjectively endorsed conceptions of the good enter into the contractors' reflections as universal objects (in the sense of being potential objects of choice for any subject) as they do in Kymlicka's theory as well.

At the same time, however, in Rawls' theory the concrete meanings given to this idea are no longer arbitrarily—*merely* subjectively—determined for the purposes of the contractors' reflections. This is because MBC4's form-content differentiation (9.2) enables the sum total conceptions of the good (including those sought to be captured by Kymlicka's idea of an objectively good life) to be listed as the range of private conceptions that should be taken into account by the contractors when formulating regulatory principles in the original position. This inclusion of *private* conceptions of the good in a reasoning process that gives primacy to the category of *publicness* does not—as it does in Kymlicka's theory—generate any contradiction since in the first step of MBC4's reflective process (a) privateness refers only to the *content* of this idea whereas publicness refers to its *form*; and (b) the primacy of the category of publicness does not depend on an exclusion of the private content of conceptions of the good. (Recall from 9.3.2(a) that in the first step of the reflective process, the defining role attributed to the category of publicness is specified through the exclusionary relationship of the *form* of the contractors' public reasoning to all private *forms* of reasoning that may be involved in the construction of conceptions of the good and the *subordination* of private to public content.)

10.2.2 Rawls and Waldron

In Chapter 6 I argued that Waldron's attempt to locate the moral foundation of liberalism in the idea of hypothetical consent ultimately fails given its view of public justification and its inability to specify a suitable method for bridging the gap that it creates between a rational hypothetical agreement and the observation that ordinary people are not necessarily reasonable. The theory's failure to meet its adequacy criterion was traced to the limitations of MBC2, the model of the dichotomy in which the primacy of the category of privateness is undermined by the unacknowledged role played by the category of publicness.

As suggested above (10.2.1), MBC2 and the reflections of the participants in Rawls' overlapping consensus follow the same pattern of basic categorial inter-relations. At the surface level, too, Rawls, like Waldron, acknowledges the relevance of the idea of consent as is indicated in the ways in which he, too, draws on the social contract tradition. We have already seen evidence of this in his presentation and use of the original position and his account of rational autonomy as including the ability to form (self-interested) agreements.

However, in the case of Rawls' theory political legitimation does not depend on rational, hypothetical consent alone. On the one hand, both his conception of rational autonomy and the way in which the original position is set up are explicitly made dependent upon the virtue of reasonableness that characterizes the theorist as well as his ideal of citizenship (8.2 and 8.3). On the other, political legitimacy also depends on the satisfaction of the conditions of morally grounded stability that are produced by the existence of an overlapping consensus. Only when met do such conditions produce the *full public justification* of the principles governing the basic structure of society (8.5). We can trace these two surface level differences in Rawls' theory back to the relative complexity of MBC4 that, in turn, explains why Rawls' theory does not face the limitations of MBC2, despite having incorporated its principle of basic categorial inter-relations as the second step in its sequential form differentiated reasoning.

Recall that each citizen qua participant in an overlapping consensus must individually endorse the conception of justice by (a) affirming its potentially public content; (b) relying on one's private form of reasoning; and (c) relying on ideas whose content is private; but (d) being blind to any public form of reasoning (9.3.2(b)). Here, the potentially public content of the principles of justice cannot undermine the primacy of citizens' private reasoning. This is because the theory's form-content differentiation enables the form of private reasoning to be defined through the exclusion of public *forms* of reasoning. Yet this does not mean—as it must do in MBC2—that the form of citizens' private reasoning that is directed to the assessment of regulatory principles may also be defined through the exclusion of those principles' public *content*. On the contrary, the former is partly defined through its positive relationship to this content. (Recall that in an overlapping consensus the (public) content of the principles of justice constitutes an essential constituent part of citizens' (private) comprehensive views (8.3).) This is why at the surface level Rawls' two-stage model of justification does not face the same problems as Waldron's theory regarding the effect of citizens' subjective reflections upon regulatory principles, even though both theories draw upon the social contract tradition's idea of rational, hypothetical consent.

Notice also that this comparative strength of Rawls' theory depends not only upon differentiating but also upon *bringing together* the outcome of reflections in the two stages of the justificatory process. As already suggested, this reflective activity is made possible by the recognition of the theorist's external reflective standpoint. (Recall from 9.4 that this standpoint is external to the basic categories in that it is not exclusively identified with either one of them.) For this reason, Waldron's problem—the realization that a liberal contractarian view of political legitimacy must assume that everyone is reasonable when *in fact* they are not—cannot even arise in Rawls' model of justification. In Rawls' theory every *relevant* person must be able *to think of herself* as reasonable (in the sense outlined in 8.3) and this ideal of reasonableness is not a problematic assumption about the nature of human beings—it does not falsely universalize—since it is not assumed that human beings *are* all reasonable. Whilst the theorist's recognition of the ideal of reasonableness as a political virtue is presupposed, reasonableness is not assumed to define the reflective standpoint of every actual person.

A number of points should be clarified here. First, notice that in the absence of the operation of the ideal of reasonableness political liberalism's justificatory project could not even get off the ground. By appealing to a conception of justice that remains within the self-imposed limits of the political, political liberalism distinguishes between claims about *what we are* and claims about *how we can think of our public identity* and it focuses exclusively on the latter. Recall that by thinking of our public identity in terms of participation in society understood as a system of fair cooperation between free and equal citizens the demand for a *public* justification of regulatory principles is necessarily understood as the concern of *reasonable* people. That is, the set of persons who are reasonable (in Rawls' sense of thinking of themselves as willing to find terms of cooperation all can reasonably accept and as recognizing the burdens of judgment) is equivalent to that of those who take up the theorist's reflective standpoint in order to elaborate and assess justice as fairness or a similar political conception of justice (the theorizing subject).

Next recall that we who elaborate justice as fairness lay out the original position in the light of our reflection upon the meaning of fair terms of cooperation between free and equal citizens as fully autonomous citizenship of a well-ordered society. Our use of the device of the original position to work up our ideal of fully autonomous citizenship (the theorized subject) and hence of a fully public well-ordered society (the theorized object) is enabled by our conception of the virtue of reasonableness. The fairness characterizing the original position and its outcome is that which is made possible by our ideal of a well-ordered society that meets the full publicity condition. If we adopt the original position as our device of representation *we/the theorists* are bound by the principles that would be agreed to in it (provided they satisfy the test of reflective equilibrium).

At the same time, this construction of the principles of justice makes possible our *existence* as citizens of a fully public well-ordered society. This is a society in which the justification of the principles can be found in the public political culture and its intellectual tradition (8.3). As already indicated, Rawls maintains that a well-ordered society must be fully public in order for citizens to realize their full autonomy because full publicity is a condition of citizens' ability fully to justify the principles of justice—to lay out, and pursue reflection in, the original position should we wish to. It is, therefore, not only the case that the ideal of a fully public well-ordered society is presupposed for the construction of the principles in the original position. It is also the case that in laying out the original position and constructing the principles of justice we give appropriate shape to the initially abstract ideas of the public political culture and thereby render a well-ordered society *fully public*. Recall that this is a society in which the full justification is *available* to all citizens as distinct from one in which it is known to everyone (8.5). It follows that Rawls' account does not, and need not, envisage a difference between the citizens to whom the principles *ought* to be justified and those to whom the justification *is* indeed available. If they are at all justified, the regulatory principles are justified to *all* the citizens of a fully public well-ordered society.

Having said the above, notice that the supposed identity between the class of persons to whom the justification ought to be available and that to whom one is available need not deny that there exist unreasonable people in a well-ordered society. In Rawls' theory observations such as those made by Waldron about ordinary people being unreasonable are not irrelevant but they are reduced to being one of the factors that the contractors behind the veil of ignorance must take into account. More precisely, according to Rawls, since the subjective circumstances of justice inevitably include 'pluralism as such', as well as reasonable pluralism, the parties in the original position examine the principles of justice in the light of both kinds of circumstance and come up with the same principles of justice in both cases, though for different reasons. When supposing that pluralism as such obtains they select the principles of justice in order to protect citizens' interests from those who would act unreasonably.[3]

---

3. Even though there can be no question of the *application* of the principles to unreasonable people (since, as already indicated, the principles apply only to the basic institutional structure and not to people, whether reasonable or unreasonable) and unreasonable people's lives are also affected by the regulation of the basic structure in accordance with the principles of justice, the question of unreasonableness only arises as a matter of how to deal with unreasonable views within a society that is already well-ordered. Within the framework of Rawls' theory, from the point of view of those of us who seek a public justification in the shape of a political conception, there can be no question of seeking to justify the principles of justice to the unreasonable for this would be mistakenly to accept that the content of the principles should be somehow influenced by 'the existence of unreason', to use Rawls' expres-

The final point to note is that Rawls' account does not dogmatically presuppose that there is an identity between those of us who seek a public justification and the citizens of a fully public well-ordered society. This position is worked out, albeit through the employment of circular reasoning. As suggested above, Rawls' understanding of the demand for a public justification as the concern of *reasonable* people shapes the whole justificatory project in its first stage, as one that is taken up by a certain kind of theorizing subject. From this reflective standpoint, the theorized subjects' public identity—their rationality and reasonableness—and their circumstances are initially specified wholly abstractly—in the idea of society as a fair system of cooperation amongst free and equal citizens—and they are progressively filled out in the terms of liberal citizenship in a fully public well-ordered society.

10.2.3 Rawls and Larmore

Like Larmore, Rawls wants to carve out a conceptual space for political liberalism that permits the latter to by-pass long-standing philosophical controversies in order to arrive at a vision of the liberal order that all citizens can reasonably endorse. On a surface level, this space is created by taking into account the fact of reasonable pluralism and the burdens of judgment (Rawls) or, using Larmore's terms, the fact of reasonable disagreement. Recall from Chapter 7, Larmore's claim that two norms of reason, the norms of rational dialogue and equal respect, define liberalism as a discursive procedure that generates moral political principles whilst taking reasonable disagreement seriously. They require that the discussion of political principles should appeal to the participants' shared beliefs and that compliance with political principles should be based on grounds that are justifiable to those affected by them. Both these norms operate in Rawls' account as well. The norm of rational dialogue is effectively the same as that which constitutes the substance of Rawls' justificatory model's second publicity condition for a well-ordered society (8.5), a condition that Rawls takes to be socially realized when liberal citizens adhere to the limits of public reason (8.6). Similarly, the norm of equal respect forms part of the rationale for Rawls' introduction of the idea of an overlapping consensus into his model of justification (8.4) and it is socially realized when a well ordered society meets the third publicity condition, the further requirement that its full justification be available to all citizens (8.5). This why Larmore is correct in his impression that Rawls' account relies upon a principle of equal respect whose moral authority functions independently of agreement. (Larmore takes the view that this principle is nevertheless underdeveloped in Rawls, perhaps because Larmore does not appreciate the implications of the rela-

---

sion (Rawls, *Political Liberalism*, pp. 64-5.). See also Gaut, 'Rawls and the Claims of Liberal Legitimacy', p. 18.

tive complexity of Rawls' position.) [4]

So, in Rawls' version of political liberalism, just as in Larmore's, citizens' *shared* beliefs and form of reasoning function as the legitimate basis for public discussion of political principles. Yet, unlike Larmore, Rawls does not conflate the reflective and discursive procedures respectively involved in the justification and interpretation of society's regulatory principles (9.3.2). This, as we have seen, is made possible by the theory's deep structural endorsement of a sequential form differentiation of reasoning that distinguishes between public-political reasoning for different purposes (9.3.1).

Due to this deep structural complexity, the third step in the reflective process that defines Rawls' theory can incorporate the same pattern of basic categorial inter-relations as that defining Larmore's theory without also suffering from its limitations. Recall from the analysis of the deep structure of Larmore's theory in Chapter 7 that it conforms to MBC3, a model of the public-private dichotomy that attributes an alternate defining role to the basic categories in such a way as to privilege an intrinsically private form of reasoning without acknowledging this. This, I argued, is the effect of rendering private ideas whose content citizens do not share, whilst also failing to distinguish between the public or private form and the public or private content of ideas. On the surface level, MBC3 was shown to be the conceptual source of the inability of Larmore's theory to satisfy its adequacy criterion of supplying a neutral and moral justification for its ideal of liberal citizens' public-political discursive procedure. Larmore's model of discourse is not neutral since, by treating them as private, it unjustifiably excludes all other forms of reasoning from the justificatory process. The principles generated by this discursive procedure also lack the special authority of moral principles since they unjustifiably invoke intrinsically private reasoning in the public domain.

On the surface level of Rawls' theory, these problems do not arise despite the facts that (a) its view of liberal citizens' ideal of public reason also denies to private forms of reasoning any priority in public discussion (8.6); and (b) the second stage of its model of justification invokes intrinsically private forms of reasoning (8.4). The theory's sequential form differentiation of reasoning enables both these moves. It allows liberal citizens engaged in public discussion to invoke the limits of public reason *in the light of* the already available full public justification of a well-ordered society's principles of justice. Rawls' liberal citizens do not—as they must in a theory embodying MBC3—thereby commit themselves to a justificatory model of political principles that purports to deny some place to their private forms of reasoning since they may *also* take up the different reflective standpoint of the theorist qua participant in an overlapping consensus. Thus, working from

---

4. Larmore, 'The Moral Basis of Political Liberalism'.

essentially the same elements in his view of citizens' reasonableness, Rawls' theory escapes the problems we found in Larmore's account due to MBC4's relatively complex deep structure. Because she fails to appreciate these deep structural differences in Rawls' and Larmore's models of justification, Chantal Mouffe mistakenly attributes the same surface level weakness to the two models of public discussion. Mouffe argues that both Rawls' and Larmore's versions of political liberalism are unable to conceptualize the properly political, namely power and antagonism, in so far as they justify their exclusions on the grounds of free agreement.[5] However, her critique makes no allowance for the relative complexity of Rawls' position.

This completes the argument of the present chapter that the minimal political morality approach to defining liberalism stands or falls with an assessment of Rawls' political liberalism. We are now in a position to undertake a radical critique of this approach.

---

5. Mouffe, 'Political Liberalism: Neutrality and the Political', pp. 318-20. See also Brian Barry, 'In Defense of Political Liberalism', *Ratio Juris: An International Journal of Jurisprudence and Philosophy of Law*, vol. 7, no. 3, 1994, pp. 325-50, Mouffe, *The Return of the Political*, pp. 136-47.

11

The Radical Critique of the Minimal Political Morality Approach

So far, I have argued that Rawls' political liberalism is superior to alternative versions of the minimal political morality approach to defining liberalism. At the deep structural level the model of the public-private dichotomy it exemplifies constitutes the most complete interpretation of the basic claim that one category plays the defining role. This relative complexity enables it to stay clear of the kinds of surface level objections that can be mounted against the less sophisticated models. As we saw in the previous chapter, the theory's complexity derives from its explicit differentiation between the form and the content of the ideas it invokes, the consequent differentiation and use of three forms of reasoning in its model of justification and an explicit recognition of the unifying role played by the reflective standpoint of the theorizing subject that remains external to the basic categories.

The superiority of Rawls' account of political liberalism is what makes it the appropriate object of critique with radical aspirations. In the Introduction to Part III I indicated that this object should be understood to be the very nature of a political conception, as distinct from the substantive claims of such a conception. Rawls himself has insisted that the important thing about political liberalism is that it advocates a *political* conception, though there may be continuing discussions about the substantive principles and procedure of construction that such a conception advances (PL, pp. 226-7 & 266-7).[1]

I have also already suggested that the success of radical critique depends on an appreciation of the dynamics of a political conception *taken as a whole*.

---

1. See also Rawls, *Collected Papers*, pp. 585, esp. fn. 35.

This gives rise to the question of precisely how the radical critique of Rawls' political conception should proceed. In other words, just how might one expose any fundamental flaw at the level of the theory's deep structural commitments? From the reconstruction of the theory, in Chapter 9, we can see that since its overall unity is due to the recognized presence of the theorist, the focus of radical critique needs to be the adequacy of the *theorizing subject's* reflective standpoint (9.4) as distinct from any of the theorizing subject's isolated claims about the theorized object's model of justification.

Indeed, isolated objections raised against particular features of political liberalism, like its reliance on the reflective standpoint of contractors behind the veil of ignorance or on that of participants in an overlapping consensus can at best show the need for revisionist modifications to the theory. Given that they do not address the external reflective standpoint of the theorizing subject, attacks on the internal workings of these forms of reasoning do not challenge the adequacy of Rawls' idea of a political conception. Let me give an example. When David Archard objects (correctly, in my view) that 'Rawls makes it too easy for himself' when he confines disagreements amongst the participants in an overlapping consensus to 'reasonable liberalisms', Archard nonetheless leaves open the possibility of a revision of Rawls' defence of the idea of an overlapping consensus to demonstrate the possibility of an even wider consensus that still remains within the self-imposed limits of a political conception.[2] If my observation is correct, then for the purposes of a critique with radical aspirations there is no need to further examine the *separate internal workings* of the two justificatory stages that define the first two steps of the reflective process.

The situation is quite different in the case of the third step of the theorist's reflective process, the form of reasoning available to ideal liberal citizens. Recall that MBC_4 attributes the potential for full transparency to ideal liberal citizens and that this awareness extends to the external reflective standpoint of the theorizing subject (9.4.1). Recall also that this is the reflective standpoint from which to view the full inter-relationship of the categories of publicness and privateness within MBC_4. It follows that a radical critique needs to focus on the character of the reflection defining the identity of the ideal liberal citizen. This is where we should expect to find any evidence of MBC_4's deep structural flaw. This calls for an examination of the deep structural commitments underlying the idea of the ideal liberal citizen in his or her dual capacity as a theorist seeking a public justification for a political conception of justice and as a social participant who seeks to honour the limits of public reason.

The argument of this chapter will proceed in four sections. In the first section I will argue that because MBC_4's supposition of categorial prima-

---

2. D. Archard, 'Fair Enough?: John Rawls' Political Liberalism', *Radical Philosophy*, vol. 66, 1994, pp. 47-9 p. 48.

The Radical Critique of the Minimal Political Morality Approach   233

cy is contradicted in two crucial ways this model collapses. The collapse is due to the theorizing subject's unacknowledged reliance, firstly, on the identity of intrinsically private agency and, secondly, on an ineffective principle of basic categorial complementarity. Whereas the first of these unacknowledged presuppositions contradicts MBC4's attribution of priority to the theorizing subject's commitment to a public reflective starting point, the second contradicts the principle of basic categorial primacy. To make out these claims I will focus attention, firstly, on the deep structural commitments underlying the theorizing subject's reflective starting point and then on those underlying his or her external reflective standpoint. In the next two sections I will proceed to show how the collapse of MBC4 at the deep structural level offers an explanation for why Rawls' theory fails at the surface level to satisfy the two aspects of its adequacy criterion. The second section will focus on problems in connection with political liberalism's requirement that the liberal theorist should employ a public standard of reasonableness whereas the third section will address the limitations of the requirement that the theory should be elaborated within the self-imposed limits of a political conception. Having completed the surface level critique of Rawls' theory, in the fourth section I will take up some commentaries on Rawls' ideal of liberal citizenship in order to illustrate further the importance of a deep structural analysis for critique with radical aspirations. For reasons explained in the previous chapter, the success of this critique should be taken to demonstrate the collapse, not only of MBC4, but more generally of MBC.

11.1 *The collapse of MBC(4)*

11.1.1 The theorizing subject's intrinsically private agency

Recall the theory's deep structural supposition that the theorizing subject's reflective starting point is constituted as public (9.1). The attribution of priority to the category of publicness at this initiating point in the theory's process of elaboration is meant to ensure that the outcome of the reflective process is widely endorsable. Yet, contrary to this initial supposition, what remains unacknowledged is that the theorizing subject's identity is also constituted as intrinsically private. Recall that intrinsically private agents can, in principle, define their ideals as singular agents regardless of whether or not they (choose or need to) pursue them in groups. I want to show, firstly, that this intrinsically private identity is evident in the monological nature of the reflection that the theorizing subject undertakes and then I will go on to indicate why this identity must remain unacknowledged at the deep structural level.

What is meant by 'the monological nature of the theorizing subject's reflection'? The nature of monological reflection is best illustrated by way of a broad comparison with a dialogical model of discourse. Drawing on Seyla

Benhabib's revision of Habermas' discourse model of ethical reasoning,[3] notice, firstly, that even though the justification of political arrangements is a matter for practical agents in both models, their respective understandings of the situatedness of such agents differ in at least one important respect. On a dialogical model justification is a matter of actual or pragmatic discourse *between* fully concrete social beings whereas on a monological model it is given via a thought experiment that the theorizing subject—an individual self or a collectivity—undertakes in his or her singularity. This latter case accurately describes the reflective standpoint of Rawls' theorizing subject.

In contrast to it, pragmatic discourse, which is a procedure for testing the validity of norms at the theoretical level, cannot be undertaken as a private thought experiment. Instead, fully concrete practical agents must engage *with others*. Accordingly, whilst both models leave no room for reflection from a standpoint that is not reducible to that of practical agents, still their understandings of *the situation* of practical agents render their respective reflective standpoints intrinsically public and intrinsically private. The reflective standpoint of a dialogical model is intrinsically public when it takes the inherent logic of a justified socio-political order to be, in principle, detectable from the reflective standpoint of the social participant who is *in the process of being discursively engaged with others*. The reflective standpoint of Rawls' theorizing subject is intrinsically private because its logic can be detected from the standpoint of the social participant only after the social participant has abstracted from the inter-subjective domain of public discussion in order to draw upon relevant capacities for imaginative reflection. Thus the theorizing subject's reflective starting point is not subject to the mediation of others' reflection.

So, there is, after all, more to the theorizing subject's identity than the publicness of the reflective starting point that Rawls account acknowledges. Given that the conception of justice is elaborated monologically the theorizing subject's identity is also constituted as that of an intrinsically private agent. Next I want to argue that the structure of MBC4 precludes the theorizing subject from acknowledging any *complementary* relationship between the public and private aspects of his or her reflective standpoint. To do this we need to turn to an examination of the theorizing subject's external reflective standpoint.

---

3. Benhabib, 'Models of Public Space'. See also Mouffe, *The Return of the Political*, pp. 150-3. This interpretation of a dialogical model is more useful for my purposes since Habermas' discussion of the differences between a discourse model that is employed as a norm *validation* procedure and one that is used in the *application* of valid norms in *Justification and Application* (Habermas, *Justification and Application*, pp. 153-4.) gives rise to questions about the genuineness of the dialogical nature of the former that I do not need to go into here.

The Radical Critique of the Minimal Political Morality Approach   235

11.1.2 The theorizing subject's external reflective standpoint

As we saw in the deep structural reconstruction of Rawls' theory, what I termed 'the theorizing subject's external reflective standpoint'—the reflective standpoint that is not exclusively identifiable with either one of the basic categories—emerges as the standpoint from which to view the three step reflective process as a whole (9.4.1). In other words, it is supposed to be the reflective standpoint from which to meet the demands of the theory's self-construction, whatever these might be. Now I want to argue that one such demand arises out of the operation of the reflective standpoint of ideal liberal citizens in their capacity as social participants. However, it is the sort of demand that cannot successfully be met within, MBC_4, the theory's deep structural framework. More specifically, in this section I will develop the abstract claim (a) that the combined presence of the basic categories in the third step of the reflective process attributed to ideal liberal citizens (9.3.2(c)) gives rise to the need for the introduction of a principle of *basic categorial complementarity* into the theorizing subject's external reflective standpoint; and that (b) basic categorial complementarity cannot be acknowledged within MBC_4 and, hence, within MBC.

Recall that in his or her capacity as a social participant Rawls' ideal liberal citizen is supposed to view her public and private forms of reasoning as each taking priority within its own domain. What this means is that, depending on the action domain, the liberal citizen should employ the appropriate form of reasoning and, in the case of the political domain as understood by Rawls (8.6), refrain from relying exclusively or as a matter of priority on (the values of) her private reasoning. Recall also that the *co-presence* of these public and private forms of reasoning is a distinguishing feature of the liberal citizen's reflective standpoint and that the copresence of the basic categories renders them mutually exclusive in the sense of being defined in opposition to one another (9.3.2(c)). However, unlike the exclusive standpoints of the contractors in the original position and the citizens qua participants in an overlapping consensus who are blind to the form of reasoning defined by their opposite basic category (9.3.2(a) and 9.3.2(b)), as the ideal social embodiment of the theorist's reflective standpoint, the liberal citizen embodies the *combined* outcome of the reflective standpoints characterizing the first two steps of the theorizing subject's reflection. For this reason the idea of different domains of application for her different forms of reasoning invokes a view of the supposed primacy of the respective basic categories as *contained within*, or *framed by*, a different kind of relationship. The co-present mutually exclusive basic categories must be contained within a relationship that takes them to be *complementary*.

Now, to view the basic categories as complementary is to view them in a relationship of *difference*, as distinct from primacy. This relationship cannot be recognized within the dichotomous thought that defines MBC4. Consider first why MBC4, as reconstructed from the surface level claims of Rawls' theory, does not recognize the idea of basic categorial difference as complementarity. To begin with, recall that the respective reflective standpoints of the categories of public and private forms of reasoning are constituted as standpoints of categorial *primacy;* public and private reasoning are not only mutually exclusive and mutually exhaustive but also hierarchically related giving respective primacy to each category. For this reason, were the complementarity of the basic categories to be recognized, this would need to be done from a reflective standpoint that is not reducible to either of the basic categories. Since the reconstruction has shown that MBC4 attributes this external reflective standpoint to the theorizing subject, the basic categories' complementary relationship would need to be recognized from the theorizing subject's external reflective standpoint.

As already argued, the theorizing subject's external reflective standpoint is supposed to be embodied in ideal liberal citizens in such a way as to enable them to take up the justificatory inquiry following their removal from public discussion regarding the interpretation and institutional embodiment of their society's regulatory principles. That is, MBC4 does not acknowledge an external reflective standpoint as belonging to the ideal liberal citizen *qua social participant* but only to the liberal citizen qua (potential) theorist. From this latter standpoint, the two-stage justificatory process recognizes *only* the alternate primacy of the basic categories or, what is the same thing, defines them only in terms of respective primacy in order to then arrive at an ideal of liberal citizenship that gives primacy to each of the categories *within their own domains.* It follows that the relationship of difference that is implied by the idea that liberal citizens' public and private forms of reasoning are each to be given priority within their different domains remains external to, and unacknowledged within, each of the three available reflective standpoints. If this argument is correct, then Rawls' ideal liberal citizens lack the potential for full transparency that MBC4 attributes to them.

Furthermore, in so far as he or she must rely on the external basic categorial inter-relationship of difference as complementarity, the ideal liberal citizen relies on a reflective standpoint that is not merely unacknowledged. Significantly, it *cannot be acknowledged* within any model of the public-private dichotomy that conforms to an interpretation of MBC precisely because, while the former refers to a standpoint that is not reducible to that of *one* of the basic categories, the latter is defined in terms of basic categorial primacy.

Notice that this limitation cannot be overcome simply by stipulating that in their combined relationship the basic categories can, indeed, be mutually informing in some ways or to some degree. We are dealing with basic categories whose form is given by relationships that (a) attribute priority to one basic category over another and (b) define the category that is attributed priority through its opposition to that subordinated. It follows from this that any element of mutual informing must itself be subordinated to this structure of relations. Any attempt to include the other basic category within the respective domains of operation of the combined basic categories (the categories as they are supposed to operate in the third step of the theory's reflective process) would, therefore, need to be restricted to the ways in which their *content* might be inter-related.

This, then, is the fundamental flaw of MBC4. Being based on relations of categorial primacy, MBC4 cannot consistently invoke an overriding principle of basic categorial complementarity. Yet this deep structural framework relies on basic categorial complementarity to complete its account of (a) the supposed operation of the theorizing subject's external reflective standpoint; and (b) the theorizing subject's reliance on essentially private agency despite the commitment to a public reflective starting point. These two limitations explain why MBC4 collapses. Since, as I argued in Chapter 10, MBC4 provides the conceptual conditions under which to test MBC itself, and not just one of its formulations as was the case with the three models assessed in Part II of the book, we can conclude that MBC collapses for the same reasons. In order to develop the argument for the collapse of MBC further I turn next to an analysis of the surface level implications of the above deep structural critique.

11.2 *Failure to rely on a public standard of reasonableness*

In the previous section I argued that contrary to the deep structural supposition that the theorizing subject's reflective starting point gives priority to the category of publicness, it invokes the unacknowledged identity of intrinsically private agency. Recall that the theory's deep structural supposition regarding the publicness of the theorizing subject's reflective starting point is embodied in the theory's surface level adequacy criterion that the theorist should employ a low standard of reasonableness in the elaboration of the conception of justice (9.1).[4] Here, I want to show why this criterion cannot be satisfied within a conceptual framework that relies on the intrinsically private identity of the theorist.

Recall that in his elaboration of justice as fairness Rawls presents as reasonable the theorist's initial act of abstracting the idea of society as a fair system of co-operation from the public political culture of a democratic society (8.3). This kind of initiation of the inquiry into the formulation of principles of justice requires the theorist to abstract some public content from both the content's own form and from its relationship to other private contents in or-

---

4. For a discussion of Rawls' 'low standard' of reasonableness see Gaut, 'Rawls and the Claims of Liberal Legitimacy'.

der for this abstracted content to play the role of the theory's fundamental organizing idea (9.2). Indeed, as the reconstruction has shown, it is this kind of abstraction of the basic categories from their inter-relationship in ideas drawn from a democratic culture that makes possible the categorial primacy that defines Rawls' two-stage justificatory model (9.3.2 (a) and 9.3.2 (b)). Significantly, however, the theorist's selection of ideas is also not subject to the mediation of others' reflection as a pre-requisite for it to be taken as a suitable starting point for the theory. Nor could it be. To do so would be to admit potentially serious obstacles to the elaboration of a political conception of justice. Such obstacles could emerge if the possibility of reasonable disagreement amongst theorists about which ideas should constitute the theory's starting point were taken as giving rise to the need for some mechanism for dealing with such reasonable disagreements. Let me explain.

My point is not that Rawls denies the possibility of reasonable disagreement amongst theorists about the best reflective starting point unless they remain within a liberal framework.[5] For Rawls, the liberal theorist might reasonably begin the elaboration of a political conception proposing a different organizing idea as the public content, or even a different mechanism, other than the original position, for representing the regulatory principles. What is never questioned, however, is the view that when reflecting in one's capacity as a liberal theorist, irrespective of the content one draws from one's culture, that content should be viewed, firstly, as *public* content and, secondly, as abstracted (a) from its relationship to the rest of the cultural content and (b) from its own form. After all, it is this type of intellectual activity, this structure of thought—and not so much the specifics of justice as fairness—that generates the categorial primacy characterizing the form of thought of political liberalism's model of justification.

Although the possibility of reasonable disagreement amongst theorists about the best reflective starting point is not denied, it can only be treated as incapable of presenting serious obstacles to the elaboration of a political conception of justice—obstacles that would not permit this sort of inquiry to get off the ground—when this process of elaboration is taken to be a monological and, hence, an intrinsically private exercise. To see how this observation connects with radical critique that targets Rawls' use of the concept of reasonableness to frame his theoretical starting point, let us take as an example the position of Chantal Mouffe. In a series of works she argues that Rawls' use of the concept of reasonableness amounts to a disingenuous way of denying genuine diversity in that it excludes antagonism and conflict and defines as reasonable only persons who already accept the principles of political liberalism.[6] Rather than aspiring unrealistically to 'a consensus that would not

---

5. On this see Chantal Mouffe, 'The Limits of John Rawls' Pluralism', *Politics, Philosophy and Economics*, vol. 4, no. 2, 2005, pp. 221-31.

6. Mouffe, *The Return of the Political*, Mouffe, 'The Limits of John Rawls' Pluralism'.

be based on any form of exclusion', Mouffe advocates the need to recognize a 'conflictual consensus':

> What I mean is that, while there should be consensus on what I call the 'ethico-political' principles of the liberal democratic regime, that is, liberty and equality for all, there should always exist the possibility of serious dissent about their interpretation, a dissent that can never be overcome thanks to rational procedures.[7]

My deep structural analysis suggests that the critical force of a position like Mouffe's lies not in asserting that a certain form of disagreement (dissent) or even a certain political content (antagonism and conflict) are excluded from Rawls' conceptual framework but rather that this framework unjustifiably precludes *engagement with the other as such*. In other words, the radical critic should not represent the fundamental flaw in Rawls' theory in terms of what it *excludes* from its reflective starting point, especially when, like Mouffe, one does not wish to assert the normative significance of so-called simple pluralism, since it becomes possible to counter such arguments against Rawls by drawing attention to the suitability of his approach under conditions of democratic pluralism. As Sebastiano Maffetone puts it, Rawls' concept of reasonableness is indeed emptied of normative significance unless one grants the normative value of liberal democracy, something that Rawls' critics also assume.[8]

Focusing instead on what Rawls' theory *includes* we note that in addition to the requirement that the theorist apply a certain standard of reasonableness that is meant to ensure the publicness of the theory's reflective starting point, the theory also requires this starting point to be determined by a theorist who treats his or her identity as intrinsically private. Yet, the role played by the theorizing subject's private identity (in restricting the form of the theorizing subject's reflections to monological reasoning) cannot, itself, be justified within the operative framework of thought. This is due to the very way in which the design of the theory's model of justification is undertaken. To begin with, notice that the monological character of the theorist's own reflection cannot be justified by a direct appeal to the conditions that warrant the theorist's introduction of the non-interactive form of reflection defining the original position namely, conditions of fairness. This is because the theorist's reflective standpoint makes possible and, hence, cannot be identified with that of the contractors behind the veil of ignorance (9.3.2(a) and 9.4). Recall that the theorist is supposed to remain within the limits of the terms of the inquiry, namely the publicly accessible, whilst in the very process of designing the theory's two-stage model of justification (9.1). Accord-

---

7. Mouffe, 'The Limits of John Rawls' Pluralism', p. 228.

8. Sebastiano Maffettone, 'Political Liberalism: Reasonableness and Democratic Practice', *Philosophy and Social Criticism*, vol. 30, no. 5-6, 2004, pp. 541-77, p. 569.

ingly, *these terms* determine the specifics of the justificatory model's features and not the reverse. Given that the theorist's private identity effectively functions as a necessary aspect of the terms of the inquiry, any attempt to apply the theory's model of justification to the theorist's private identity would amount to an inappropriate reversal of this order of explanation.

What the above analysis shows is that the role that the theorist's intrinsically private identity plays itself *lacks justification*. At the theory's surface level, there is no way to justify the theorist's application of the standard of reasonableness *in the light of* his or her monological reflection. This renders the liberal theorist's reflective standpoint as partial. Accordingly, the non-liberal theorist can accept Rawls' claim about the need to apply a publicly accessible standard of reasonableness and still be justified in rejecting Rawls' apparently partial use of this standard. Berys Gaut seems to capture this insight when he claims that political liberalism's key features are all subject to reasonable disagreement in the sense that it is not *unreasonable* to reject them.[9] The *reasonable* non-liberal theorist does not appear to have good grounds for adopting the limited terms of inquiry that Rawls advocates because Rawls' standard of reasonableness fails to satisfy its own adequacy criterion of constituting a (potentially) shared standard. The problem is not that the intrinsically private reasoning he relies on is unreasonable, but that within this conceptual framework it is unreasonable to insist on his standard of reasonableness *on the grounds of its publicness*.

11.3 *Failure to remain within the self-imposed limits of a political conception*

The argument of the previous section has shown that Rawls' theory cannot consistently insist on remaining within the limited terms of its inquiry. Now I turn to a consideration of the surface level requirement that the theory remain with the self-imposed limits of a political conception (8.2). The aim is to demonstrate that the deep structural limitations of MBC_4 explain why the theory cannot satisfy this second aspect of its surface level adequacy criterion.

In section 11.1.2 I argued that Rawls' ideal liberal citizens lack the potential for full transparency that MBC_4 attributes to them because in their capacity as social participants liberal citizens' reflections rely on a relationship

---

9. Gaut, 'Rawls and the Claims of Liberal Legitimacy', p. 16. Gaut argues for a standard of 'maximal reasonableness' which holds a person's views to be reasonable 'when she has taken into consideration all the reasons relevant to affirming or denying it, and all [...] or [...] the balance of reasons that support the view', p. 16. Note that this high standard of reasonableness cuts across the division between true and reasonable grounds that Rawls relies upon so that issues of truth and, indeed, comprehensive views generally would be admitted back into the range of legitimate grounds for the elaboration of a conception of justice. In the case of a substitution of a higher standard of reasonableness Rawls' idea of a political conception would, therefore, have to be abandoned.

The Radical Critique of the Minimal Political Morality Approach 241

of basic categorial difference that remains unacknowledged within, each of the three reflective standpoints that are available to them. This deep structural flaw is reflected at the surface level in the supposed operation of the idea that liberal citizens' combined public and private forms of reasoning are each to be given priority within their different domains (9.3.2(c)). Consider the specifics of this aspect of the theory.

At any given moment in their capacity as social participants liberal citizens, who are supposed to attribute priority to their public or private reason depending on the action domain, face the problem of having to invoke the appropriate form of reasoning. That is, the choice between the use of their public or private reason must itself become an object of their reflections. This introduces into their reflection a further step over and above that which supposedly combines the abstracted reflective standpoints of the contractors in the original position and the participants in an overlapping consensus. For, whereas the combined standpoint is defined in terms of two forms of reasoning, the liberal citizen's practice of the duty of civility to others (8.6) requires something more than this. To do one's duty qua social participant is, first and foremost, to determine which form of reason takes priority in a particular discussion. So, the identity of the liberal citizen is also constituted by a reflective standpoint that is not reducible to that of her combined public-private forms of reason. This constitutes an external reflective standpoint of the kind that belongs to liberal citizens in their capacity as theorists (9.4.1), the only difference being that it is a reflective standpoint from which to define the *practical scope* of each form of reasoning.

The problem, however, is that citizens' external reflective standpoint is empty; it does not supply liberal citizens with any criterion on the basis of which to make the necessary discriminations for the proper use of the different forms of reason in concrete situations. This is because the external reflective standpoint that they can take up in their capacity as liberal theorists unifies the different steps in the theory's reflective process simply by supplying the theorist with the awareness that is presupposed for motivating the movement from one reflective step to the next (9.4.1). Of itself, this kind of awareness provides no further criteria that could be used to resolve questions regarding the choice of whether to employ public or private reason or, more precisely, when exactly to revert to public reason since, as Charles Larmore explains:

> Rightly conceived, it [Rawls' ideal of public reason] does not thwart the uninhibited political discussions which are the mark of a vigorous democracy. We can argue with one another about political issues in the name of our different visions of the human good while also recognizing that, when the moment comes for a legally binding decision, we must

take our bearings from a common point of view.[10]

Now on Larmore's reading the line between the 'open discussion' he describes here and the moment of making a legally binding decision would be quite clear but for Rawls' misguided revision of his ideal of public reason in favour of the so-called 'wide' conception:

> Rawls' 'wide' conception seems motivated by the wish to make room for the freewheeling arguments about political issues that belong to the public life of an energetic democracy. [...] To permit them in the 'public political culture' as Rawls now proposes (subject to the proviso) is to be misled by what the term suggests as opposed to the way that he himself defined it. In the forum where citizens officially decide the basic principles of their political association and where the canons of public reason therefore apply, appeals to comprehensive doctrines cannot but be out of place—at least in a well-ordered society. The earlier 'inclusive' conception, which allows departures from public reason only when its most elementary ingredients are in wide dispute, appears to be the better view.[11]

Notice, however, that this objection—that the less strict view of the use of private reasoning in public political discussions is incompatible with Rawls' own account of public reason—merely presupposes the division between the *decision making* and the *debating* moments of public political forums but does nothing to explain how this abstract division translates into public political practice in Rawlsian terms. The *practical* problem of determining when to make the shift from private to public reasons remains regardless of whether one adopts Rawls' narrow or wide conception of the place of private reasons in public political forums.

The following example illustrates how the practical problem arises. As a member of a feminist group interested in advancing women's social equality, I belong to what Rawls views as a non-public association. This means that along with other members I am free to develop my view and policies about the best ways to achieve women's equality using what Rawls refers to as 'non-public', 'social reasons' that, as we have seen, the theory's deep structure attributes to private form(s) of reasoning (9.1). Of course, many of the group's policies will address the subject matter of constitutional essentials and questions of basic justice (8.6). This does not preclude me from relying exclusively on my private reasoning in discussions, for example, for the purposes of consciousness-raising activities, since these fall outside Rawls' definition of the public political forum that gives priority to the use of public reason. Recall that this forum is defined in terms of the discourses of the judiciary, of government officials and candidates and campaigners

---

10. Larmore, 'Public Reason', p. 383.
11. Larmore, 'Public Reason', p. 387.

The Radical Critique of the Minimal Political Morality Approach 243

for public office (8.6).

Yet, since issues concerning the advocacy of constitutional interpretation and legal reform will inevitably arise, in order to fulfill my duty of civility to others as an ideal liberal citizen I should at some point, as should every other member of this group, switch to the use of public reason. This follows from the fact that the advocacy of women's social equality inevitably bears upon the domain of the political understood as the coercive power of citizens as a collective body. Indeed, the feminist group's terms of association may well include lobbying for legal reforms in which case the duty of civility would require the ultimate use of public reason since this would be a case of contributing to the political discourses of government officials and the judiciary.

Notice, however, that the supposedly non-public activity of consciousness-raising may also have the effect of impacting upon the discourses constituting the public political forum. The writing and cultural, social and legal impact of Betty Friedan's *The Feminist Mystique* is an excellent case in point. In so far as it produced a mind-shift it *generated* content that was eventually rendered as public. Still, the writing and publication of the text amounted to a consciousness-raising exercise conducted on a broad impersonal scale that *simultaneously* advanced the cause of feminist legal reform in the USA. As an example of the former type of activity it does not conform to Rawls' definition of activity in the political public political forum and so falls outside the scope of public reason but as an example of the latter type of activity it is a case in which liberal citizens' duty of civility is meant to apply.

How does one decide where to draw the line between the attribution of priority to public or private reason? Nothing in the elaboration of the idea of a fully public society (8.6) can be used to assist the liberal citizen to answer this question in a principled way. To begin with, he or she cannot invoke Rawls' idea of the political domain for this purpose. This is because, as we saw in Chapter 8, not only does it cut across the modern social spheres of household, economic, governmental and bureaucratic activity, but, since it is defined as an outcome of the application of the political conception of justice to society, it cannot be used to determine the social application of the political conception.

Secondly, nothing in the specification of the content of the idea of public reason (8.6) provides the liberal citizen with a suitable criterion for deciding when a particular situation requires one to attribute priority to public reason over his or her private reason. That is, nothing in its specification determines its practical limits in a principled way. The guidelines of public inquiry that Rawls views as part of the content of the conception of justice are supposed to assist in the exercise of public reason within a forum that is already delimited. So, whilst this content determines the question of *how* issues that fall within its scope are to be decided, it does not determine *what* falls within its scope.

At the same time, whilst the limits of public reason forbid the overriding use of private reason in the public political forum, as we have seen (8.6), this restriction only serves to exclude the operation of private forms of reason that deny the limits of public reason and would oppose the principles of justice. It does not address the liberal citizen's on-going problem qua social participant of how to decide when precisely to refrain from relying exclusively or as a matter of priority on the private form of reasoning belonging to one's *admittedly* reasonable comprehensive view.

A few clarifications are in order here. Firstly, the problem I have identified above is neither generated nor overcome by Rawls' revision of the idea of public reason that introduces the proviso that liberal citizens may legitimately introduce private reasons into discussion within the public political domain so long as they invoke public reason at the appropriate time. This is because the proviso reaffirms the content of the idea of public reason, that is, the overriding value of the political principles and guidelines of inquiry that define public reason. It does not deal with the delimitation of the public political forum itself.

Secondly, liberal citizens cannot draw upon the resources of either of the two forms of reflection that are respectively employed by the contractors behind the veil of ignorance and the participants in an overlapping consensus in order to address the problem of determining the boundaries of the practical operation of their combined public and private reasoning. As the reconstruction has shown, whilst each of these takes priority within its domain, the boundaries of this domain are not, themselves, defined from within the exclusive standpoint of the respective forms of reasoning (9.3.2). At the surface level, this means that, on the one hand, private forms of reasoning are not self-limiting. Recall that, by definition, comprehensive views may cover the whole of life. On the other hand, the reflection of contractors in the original position cannot be called upon to represent a substantive criterion of the kind that is needed to determine the occasions for reverting to public reason because such a task would require awareness of the different private forms of reasoning. As the reconstruction has shown, the strength of the original position lies in the fact that it is defined by reference to the exclusion of awareness of private forms of reason.

Finally, it is worth noting how my objection differs from one that Micah Lott has raised and that is similarly focused on problems associated with the exercise of Rawlsian public reason. Lott argues that where there is a higher order interest at stake, such as the duty to protect innocent life, Rawls' liberal citizen may be justified in invoking private reasons despite the requirements of the duty of civility.[12] Notice that such an objection simply counter-asserts

---

12. Micah Lott, 'Restraint on Reasons and Reasons for Restraint: A Problem for Rawls' Ideal of Public Reason', *Pacific Philosophical Quarterly*, vol. 87, no. 1, 2006, pp. 75-95.

The Radical Critique of the Minimal Political Morality Approach   245

the deep structural priority of privateness over publicness. By contrast, my critique remains immanent in that it follows through the full implications of the already identified deep structural commitments of the theory.

It follows from the above discussion that at the surface level, Rawls' ideal liberal citizen is left with no principled way of discerning the appropriate occasions for the proper uses of public and private reasoning and, hence, with no successful way of relating her two forms of reasoning. Accordingly, the theory fails to demonstrate how it is possible for liberal citizens to function effectively within the self-imposed limits of a political conception. This weakness is due to the deep structural limitations of the theory, as evidenced in the analysis of MBC4. As the deep structural reconstruction has shown (11.1.2), in the capacity of social participant the liberal citizen's reflective standpoint is defined in terms of his or her combined awareness of his or her public and private forms of reason and these are, in turn, defined by their respective primacy rather than a reflective standpoint that is external to the basic categories and provides some criterion to account for their mutually informing relationship. Such a criterion cannot be forthcoming given that, as the deep structural analysis has shown, the basic categories' different but complementary roles must remain unacknowledged within MBC4. Accordingly, there is no conceptual space within which to account for this sort of relationship.

11.4 The importance of deep structural analysis to radical critique

What I have been arguing above is not intended as a selective or isolated rejection of Rawls' account of the limits of public reason. If correct, my criticism has much wider implications for liberal theory and the minimal political morality approach to defining liberalism. This is because it locates the primary source of the theory's surface level problem in the theory's deep structural commitments. In doing so, it suggests that we should expect to find any theory whose deep structure is similarly constituted similarly to face intractable surface level problems. It also facilitates the radical critic's anticipation of the ineffectiveness of proposed surface level revisions to the theory.

Consider the merits of my approach by way of comparison with other critical approaches. As already noted, critics of Rawls have argued against his ideal liberal citizenship and its view of public reason. Note, however, that they have mainly appealed to their contrary moral intuitions and to the obvious lack of fit between the normative restrictions required by the limits of public reason that Rawls advocates and the psycho-social reality of modern democratic public discourse. For example, Samuel Scheffler challenges the plausibility of Rawls' idea of the limits of public reason by listing examples of 'instances in [his] own society in which people have appealed to comprehensive moral doctrines in ways that many would regard as appropriate'. Noting Rawls' exception that appeals to comprehensive views should be allowed when necessary to strengthen the ideal of public reason itself, Scheffler concludes that 'the idea that in all such examples the reliance on a comprehensive moral or religious doctrine must either be necessary to strengthen the ideal of public reason or else be unjustified seems highly questionable'.[13] Similarly for Thomas McCarthy 'the conceptual, psychological, cultural and institutional problems this [Rawls'] avoidance strategy raises are formidable'. McCarthy takes Rawls' ideal of liberal citizenship unrealistically to burden individuals with what he refers to as 'the weight of the art of separation' between their public and private uses of reason. So, the surface level problem he identifies is similar to that to which I have drawn attention.[14] He goes on to suggest that because Rawls' prescriptions about the limits of public reason 'clash with our considered convictions about the openness of debate in the democratic public sphere [...] there will likely have to be made adjustments elsewhere in the theory'.[15] More recently, Jocelyn Maclure has argued that Rawls' has 'yet to explain how we are to judge in specific cases whether a reason is of general or particular nature', or to use the terminology of the present discussion, whether it is public or private. She thinks that the solution is to revise the language of public reason in order to include a wider variety of reasons in its purview and introduces a mechanism for determining the publicness of a reason.[16]

If I am right about the deep structural source of the problem with Rawls' ideal of liberal citizenship, then 'adjustments elsewhere in the theory' will not produce a more adequate ideal of liberal citizenship. As long as the theory's deep structure embodies either MBC4, or one of the models discussed in Part II, the surface level elaboration of the theory should inevitably suffer the limitations of being so committed. Let me illustrate this point by engaging briefly with McCarthy's own analysis of the source of the problem he identifies in Rawls' theory. McCarthy observes that the restrictions that Rawls places on public discourse derive from his effort to address the question of social stability in his model of public justification. He suggests that for this reason Rawls does not give enough weight to the perspective of social participants, which McCarthy describes as belonging to those of us who— much like one of the two aspects of Rawls' account of ideal citizens' reasonableness—want to justify our actions to others on grounds that all could ra-

---

13. Scheffler, 'The Appeal of Political Liberalism', pp. 16-7.
14. Thomas A. McCarthy, 'Kantian Constructivism and Reconstructivism: Rawls and Habermas in Dialogue', *Ethics*, vol. 105, no. 1, 1994, pp. 44-63, p. 52.
15. McCarthy, 'Kantian Constructivism and Reconstructivism', p. 53.
16. Jocelyn Maclure, 'On the Public Use of Practical Reason: Loosening the Grip of Neo-Kantianism', *Philosophy and Social Criticism*, vol. 32, no. 1, 2006, pp. 37-63.

tionally [Rawls would say, reasonably] accept'.[17] Instead,

> Rawls in effect cedes a certain primacy to the observer's perspective [that which recognizes the burdens of judgment]: the concern with stability in the light of the fact of reasonable pluralism limits the scope of what may count as good reasons in matters of public discussion.[18]

Motivated by the concern that Rawls' ideal of citizenship effectively blocks critical political debate aimed at radical social transformation,[19] McCarthy notes that Rawls' proposal that certain questions, namely those concerning constitutional essentials and basic justice (8.6), be removed from the political agenda 'once and for all' distorts the character of 'ongoing processes of public political communication' in which the political agenda is itself contested.[20]

> When awareness of the burdens of judgment is incorporated into the participant's perspective, there is an obvious alternative to Rawls' opposition between unreasonable insistence on the truth of one's beliefs and reasonable avoidance to claims to truth—namely, reasonable discussion of truth or validity claims.[21]

Thus McCarthy advocates a revision of Rawls' ideal of citizenship and concludes that 'there is no reason [...] why the similarly situated members of a well-ordered society should settle for anything less than a deliberative democracy with unrestricted public reasoning'.[22] Chantal Mouffe and James Bohman have raised similar complaints.[23] This counter-proposal would, of course, appeal to feminists, democratic socialists and 'most other social movements agitating for basic change' whose comprehensive arguments McCarthy correctly points out would have no place in the public discussion of Rawls' fully public well-ordered society.[24]

Without overlooking McCarthy's motivation for putting forward this counter-proposal about the conduct of public discussion, his surface level explanation of the source of Rawls' problematic view of public reason misconstrues Rawls' theory whilst the counter-proposal under-estimates its relative strengths. As my reconstruction has shown, differences in the various reflec-

---

17. McCarthy, 'Kantian Constructivism and Reconstructivism', p. 58.
18. McCarthy, 'Kantian Constructivism and Reconstructivism', p. 60.
19. On this see McCarthy, 'Kantian Constructivism and Reconstructivism', p. 51 and the examples of excluded arguments he lists on p. 53.
20. McCarthy, 'Kantian Constructivism and Reconstructivism', p. 61.
21. McCarthy, 'Kantian Constructivism and Reconstructivism', p. 62.
22. McCarthy, 'Kantian Constructivism and Reconstructivism', p. 63.
23. James F. Bohman, 'Public Reason and Cultural Pluralism: Political Liberalism and the Problem of Moral Conflict', *Political Theory: An International Journal of Political Philosophy*, vol. 23, no. 2, 1995, pp. 253-79, Mouffe, 'Political Liberalism: Neutrality and the Political', Mouffe, 'The Limits of John Rawls' Pluralism'.
24. McCarthy, 'Kantian Constructivism and Reconstructivism', p. 53.

tive standpoints that the theory relies on are, indeed, crucial to an adequate understanding of how the theory works as a totality. However, McCarthy's suggested way of differentiating between them does not accord with Rawls' theory. There is no good reason to think that Rawls' liberal citizen or, using McCarthy's terminology, the participant perspective is defined by a concern with justifying one's actions on grounds that all could reasonably accept *and not* with recognizing the burdens of judgment. As we have seen, Rawls takes both these aspects of the virtue of reasonableness to belong (ideally) to liberal citizens' identities given that in different ways they inform the two-stage model of justification that is supposed to be available to liberal citizens who adopt the standpoint of the liberal theorist (PL, p. 224).

Furthermore, Rawls' position does not imply otherwise. We can grant that the theory does incorporate into the participant's perspective, awareness of the burdens of judgment when justifying *one's actions* to others, whilst also making available to the liberal citizen qua *potentially theorizing* subject— an observer perspective—a model of justification that is devised specifically for justifying the basic institutional structure of *one's society* (as distinct from one's actions). Once this complexity in Rawls' thought is admitted, McCarthy's counter-proposal can be seen effectively to advocate the collapse of the theory's sequential form differentiation of reasoning (9.3.2) into a single *form* of reasoning. Accordingly, to introduce the idea of unrestricted public discussion into Rawls' scheme would be to revise it in such a way as to regress to a less sophisticated model of public justification since its deep structure would conform to that of MBC_3 taking Larmore's account as our example. We have already seen that a theory whose deep structure embodies MBC_3 is relatively inferior to MBC_4 at both the deep structural and surface levels. Advocates of an ideal of unrestricted public discussion develop two types of procedural model. One, most clearly associated with the work of Jürgen Habermas, endorses the idea of a *uniform* model of public reasoning, whilst the other supports some kind of pluralistic model.[25] In the light of McCarthy's criticism of Habermas' theory, he too seems to prefer this second type of procedural model. An argument along the lines of the one developed above against McCarthy's views can also be used to defend Rawls against Bowman's critique of his ideal of public reason. Bohman argues that 'deep conflicts' that challenge a society's very principles of adjudication cannot be resolved and, indeed, are denied existence by Rawls' ideal of public reason. He advocates a revision of this ideal making it 'pluralistic' and 'dynamic' in the sense that it should recognize the possibility of public agreement on the basis of *different* reasons.[26] However, with this proposed revision the deep structure of Rawls' theory would revert to that of MBC_3.

---

25. See, for example, Bohman, 'Public Reason and Cultural Pluralism'.
26. Bohman, 'Public Reason and Cultural Pluralism', pp. 260-7.

Rawls indicates why his model of public justification should not, as Larmore's account does, leave all aspects of reflection and decision about setting the political agenda to liberal citizens qua political participants engaged in public discussion. Bearing in mind that to remove certain issues from the political agenda is to treat them as 'settled once and for all' because they are 'not appropriate subjects for political decision *by majority or other plurality voting*' (PL, pp. 151, fn. 16, my emphasis), Rawls points out that his conception of justice does not advocate the removal of questions 'solely because they are a source of conflict' (PL, p. 151). To do so would be to follow Larmore in advocating the removal of (reasonably) controversial issues from the common ground of public discourse. Instead, Rawls advocates the removal from public discussion only of those issues that should reasonably be worked out by liberal citizens *in their capacity as theorists* (rather than as active political participants). He insists that only those matters that are settled in the original position, the specification of the principles of justice and political virtues, should be removed from public discussion. At the same time, controversial questions relating to the concrete interpretation and institutional embodiment of these political values remain open for inclusion on the collective decision-making political agenda. So, for example, from the standpoint of liberal citizens active in public discussion—the political domain of a fully public well-ordered society—we are precluded from debating the justifiedness of slavery for the purposes of deciding whether to recognize this form of social relationship but not what it means for citizens' equal liberties to be socially recognized (PL, pp. 151-2). Of course, many of the arguments of feminists and social democrats to which McCarthy alludes in order to lend support to the ideal of unrestricted public discussion address this second question. Thus McCarthy's appeals to unrestricted debate in the name of democratic processes do not show why Rawls' proposed restrictions on public discussion are not, as they claim to be, genuine mechanisms for safeguarding the social conditions that make democratic debate possible.[27]

Because McCarthy's argument does not pose a direct challenge to the deep structure of Rawls' theory and, in particular to that structure's model of the public-private dichotomy, both his explanation of the source of the problem he identifies on the surface level and his counter-proposal appear unconvincing. This said he correctly draws attention to the *consequences* of Rawls' theory for the theorist-social critic who would engage in public criti-

---

27. Bohman objects *on practical grounds* that devices to effect the removal of issues from the political agenda, such as gag rules, do not always work democratically. He thinks that such mechanisms change the nature of public debate about the issues, Bohman, 'Public Reason and Cultural Pluralism', p. 255. However, his argument does not distinguish appropriately between practical devices for the removal of issues from the legal forum's agenda that are inadequate due to their imperfect execution and those that are inadequate even when flawlessly executed.

cism with a view to justifiably pressing for radical social transformation. There is no doubt that the theory denies the radical social critic's power discursively to transform (understandings of) the basic structure of a fully public well-ordered society. The limits of public reason do not just apply to the conduct of individual citizens' public discussion concerning their collective coercive power that is embodied in the political state. They also apply to the potential transformative power of social movements informed by radical theoretical criticism of the modern liberal social order. Nevertheless, for Rawls, the existence of such social movements in a particular society could be interpreted as evidence to suggest that the society in question is *not yet* sufficiently well-ordered. So, it is not enough for Rawls' radical critic simply to make these observations by way of a complaint about the *consequences* of the theory. Such concerns about the consequences of the theory for the place of a radical theorist's social criticism should, instead, lead to a questioning of Rawls' view of the theorist's *terms of inquiry* and, relatedly, to the deep structure underlying this view. The previous sections have established that this deep structure, MBC_4, collapses, like the interpretations of MBC before it. Moreover, recognition of the collapse of MBC_4 and, hence, of MBC, in turn, generates what would be an epistemological crisis (in the sense explained in 3.2) within the minimal political morality approach to the problem of liberalism's definition were liberalism to view itself as a tradition of inquiry. This leads us to a consideration of the specifics of this crisis for the deep structure of liberal theory.

11.5 *The minimal political morality approach and MBC in epistemological crisis*

Like the interpretations of MBC before it, MBC_4 collapses. The argument of Part III shows that MBC's claim, that one of the basic categories plays the defining role in their inter-relationship, is only partially correct. Even though it gives expression to the reliance of liberal inquiring practice on the dichotomous inter-relationship of the basic categories of publicness and privateness, MBC cannot acknowledge the reliance of liberal discourse on the basic categories' *complementary relationship*, their relationship of difference as distinct from primacy. The analysis has also shown that the basic categories' complementarity is as much constitutive of the liberal theorizing subject's identity as it is of the theorized object. Yet here too MBC lacks the conceptual resources to recognize the complementary role played by the basic categories. Because it recognizes the theorizing subject's distinct presence as an *exclusively public* identity, MBC cannot justify its co-reliance on the liberal theorizing subject's *intrinsically private* identity. MBC's incoherence provides an explanation for the surface level failure of liberalism's minimal political morality approach to propose a view of justification that satisfies its own adequacy criteria. Even in its most complete version, the liberal theorist's model of justification invokes, but cannot consistently supply an account of, the complementary relationship of liberal citizens' public and private forms of reason. Nor can it be used to justify the liberal theorist's reliance on monological reasoning.

The radical critique of the minimal political morality approach to defining liberalism does not merely show that due to its deep structure this kind of approach gives rise to theories that fail to satisfy their own adequacy criteria. More importantly, the collapse of MBC generates an *epistemological crisis* of the kind that was sketched in Chapter 3.2. Recall that this refers to the state of affairs characterized, firstly, by the dissolution of what would be a historically founded certitude of the minimal political morality approach to defining liberalism were the liberal intellectual tradition fully self-aware and, secondly, by the inability of adherents of this approach to make rational progress with their available methods of inquiry. The 'certitude' at issue here is, of course, the principle expressed by MBC whereas the 'methods of inquiry' are those employed by a *sequential* form differentiated reasoning whose unity is supposed to depend only on the theorizing subject's' *exclusively public* identity. Recall further the suggestion that the successful resolution of an epistemological crisis calls for the framing of new theory and the discovery or invention of concepts that are new to the tradition in crisis. Because the source of the surface level inadequacies of the minimal political morality approach to defining liberalism has been shown to be the deep structural idea of basic categorial primacy, the incoherence of this mode of liberal dichotomous thought cannot be overcome through any reinterpretation of MBC. What is required instead is the substitution of a different formulation of BC itself. The introduction of concepts not previously employed in MBC would constitute the framing of a 'new theory' even though BC continues to focus on the inter-relationship of the basic categories.

We already have a rough idea of the required 'new concepts' in so far as the reason for the collapse of MBC also gives rise to two desiderata for a superior formulation of BC. These are, firstly, that in recognizing the appearance of categorial primacy, the theorizing subject should be in a position to *account for the complementarity* of public and private forms of reasoning. Secondly, the theorizing subject's own use of an intrinsically private form of reasoning should also constitute that which is (to be) justified by the theory. This means that the theory's model of justification should be capable of being applied to *the theorizing subject's intrinsically private identity*. I test the merits of an account of liberalism that meets these desiderata in the second volume of *In Memory of a Vision*.

conclusion

Conclusion

Liberal Theory in Epistemological Crisis

I have been arguing that a critical understanding of liberal theory rests on an appreciation of the nature of contemporary liberal inquiring practice. This practice operates on two distinct yet inter-related levels of discourse, the surface and deep structural levels. Even though liberal political theorists (and their critics) engage in debates on the familiar issues at a surface level, it is liberal theory's *deep structural discourse* that warrants the special attention of the radical critic. In determining that the incoherence of the minimal political morality approach to defining liberalism stems from its deep structural commitment to a certain form of the public-private dichotomy, the argument of this book offers some support for the claim that the deep structure of liberal discourse consists in various ways of dichotomously inter-relating the abstract categories of publicness and privateness and that these in turn play the decisive role in determining the conceptual parameters of liberal modes of inquiry.

However, the full defence of this claim depends on the further argument I develop in the second volume of *In Memory of a Vision*. There I argue that a liberal theory whose deep structure conforms to CBC—the form of the public-private dichotomy whose principle holds that whereas the basic categories appear dichotomously related, they are in fact mutually defining —has the conceptual resources to meet the desiderata that we identified with the collapse of MBC. I argue for the rational superiority of CBC over MBC by showing that CBC's 'new concepts'—the concepts of basic categorial complementarity and justifiable intrinsically private agency—meet the three conditions for the successful resolution of an epistemological crisis. As we saw in Chapter 3.2, in order successfully to resolve an epistemological crisis, an intellectual tradition's new concepts must (1) provide a solution to the problems previously proved intractable, (2) account for the previous sterility and/or incoherence of the tradition and (3) ensure fundamental continuity between the old and the new conceptual structures. This part of the argument aims to show why CBC and its related surface level approach to defining liberalism, the comprehensive approach, are the proper objects of the radical critic's investigation.

There are a number of advantages in identifying the precise function of different formulations of the public-private dichotomy at the deep structural level of liberal inquiring practice. One is that it gives rise to the possibility of viewing in a non-reductive yet systemic way the surface level variety of specific and concrete issues that are usually associated with liberalism. Without attention to the deep structure, the characteristic features of liberal theory can only be ordered on the surface level in accordance with whatever happens to be the theorist's focus of the moment. Through my extensive discussion of the ways in which the surface and deep structural levels of liberal discourse inter-relate, I hope to have demonstrated that the deep structure of liberal theory can be used to justify a certain ranking of different modes of liberal inquiring practice. A systemic reconstruction can show why the currently popular minimal political morality approach to defining liberalism, that John Rawls' political liberalism exemplifies, ultimately lacks the abstract conceptual resources to offer a more defensible liberal theory than the comprehensive liberalism that Ronald Dworkin's later work on liberalism exemplifies.

The deep structural analysis of particular liberal theories enables their positioning in a logical progression from less to more advanced formulations because liberal theory's deep structure frames its surface level discourse by supplying the theory's organizing principle. My analysis also offers an explanation for why those liberals who have attempted to specify liberalism's organizing principle have not been very successful. Even though liberal theory's deep structure supplies the theory's organizing principle, the liberal theorist cannot acknowledge this precisely because the deep structure of liberal theory enables the articulation of liberal discourse but is not itself articulated by it.

The systemic reconstruction of particular liberal theories in a rational progression from less to more advanced accounts of liberalism also enables the radical critic to put to the test the most advanced mode of liberal inquiring practice. In this way radical critique goes further than at best explaining why particular liberal theories systematically fail to meet their adequacy criteria. It can also justifiably claim to be thorough in supplying sufficient grounds for rejecting liberalism *as such*. When the radical critic restricts his or her critique to liberalism's surface level claims the possibility of a seemingly coherent reformulation of liberalism always remains open. This is because a critique that remains focused on the surface level of liberal discourse, will not adequately locate the conceptual *source* of the problems it identified, no matter how radical its aspirations. Because all aspects of the surface level of liberal discourse are open to endless reformulation and revision, a complete assessment seems an impossible task unless, and until, its fundamental abstract conceptual continuities are brought to the surface, in order to give a full picture of the modes and limits of liberal inquiring practice. I have tried to show that liberal theories' conceptual continuities are located in its deep structure and that it is the *co-presence* of the two levels of liberal discourse that exposes its ultimate incoherence. With Volume 2 of *In Memory of a Vision* I complete the argument that the most advanced mode of liberal inquiring practice overcomes the limitations of less adequate alternatives but it does so at the cost of facing an irresolvable epistemological crisis. If the argument succeeds then it shows why liberal theory fails to supply a coherent account of its own conceptual conditions of possibility.

So much for the *form* of liberal inquiring practice. What of its substance? I have tried to show, firstly, that, irrespective of the particular form of their inquiring practices, a *constitutive* feature of the liberal theorists' inquiring identity is their inability to recognize (a) the deep structure of their discourse and (b) the organizing role that such a deep structure plays in their theory construction. Secondly, I have shown that liberal theorists' intrinsically private identity ultimately grounds the public-private dichotomy that defines the deep structure of their theory. The second volume of *In Memory of a Vision* will complete this argument by showing that liberal theory cannot consistently rely upon this idea. Liberalism's unavoidable incoherence is rendered visible when, as its most advanced articulations reveal, the commitment to intrinsically private agency forms an explicit part of the articulation of liberal theory. From this it follows that the liberal inquiring practice of *unjustifiably privileging intrinsically private agency* is what makes liberal theory liberal and, relatedly, what makes the liberal theorist, liberal.

bibliography

Bibliography

Ackerman, Bruce A., *Social Justice in the Liberal State*, New Haven, Yale University Press, 1980.
Ackerman, Bruce A., 'Political Liberalisms', *Journal of Philosophy*, vol. 91, no. 7, 1994, pp. 364-86.
Anderson, K. et. al., 'Roundtable on Communitariansim', *Telos*, vol. 76, 1988, pp. 2-32.
Archard, D., 'Fair Enough?: John Rawls' Political Liberalism', *Radical Philosophy*, vol. 66, 1994, pp. 47-9
Arendt, Hannah, 'Philosophy and Politics', *Social Research*, vol. 57, no. 1, 1990, pp. 73-103.
Arneson, Richard J., 'Neutrality and Utility (Religious and Other Forms of Tolerance by the State)', *Canadian Journal of Philosophy*, vol. 20, no. 2, 1990, pp. 215-40.
Assiter, Alison, *Enlightened Women: Modernist Feminism in a Postmodern Age*, London, Routledge, 1996.
Avineri, Shlomo and Avner De-Shalit (eds.), *Communitarianism and Individualism*, Oxford, Oxford University Press, 1992.
Badiou, Alain, *The Century*, trans. Alberto Toscano, London, Polity, 2007.
Baier, Kurt, 'Justice and the Aims of Political Philosophy', *Ethics*, vol. 99, no. 4, 1989, pp. 771-90.
Barber, Benjamin, 'Justifying Justice: Problems of Psychology, Politics and Measurement in Rawls', in Norman Daniels (ed.), *Reading Rawls: Critical Studies on Rawls' A Theory of Justice*, Oxford, Blackwell, 1975, pp. 292-318.
Barber, Benjamin, 'Liberal Democracy and the Costs of Consent', in N. L. Rosenblum (ed.), *Liberalism and Moral Life*, London, Harvard University Press, 1989.
Barry, Brian, 'How Not to Defend Liberal Institutions', *British Journal of Political Science*, vol. 20, no. 1, 1990, pp. 1-14.
Barry, Brian, 'In Defense of Political Liberalism', *Ratio Juris: An International Journal of Jurisprudence and Philosophy of Law*, vol. 7, no. 3, 1994, pp. 325-

50.
Barry, Brian, 'John Rawls and the Search for Stability', *Ethics*, vol. 105, 1995, pp. 874-915.
Baynes, Kenneth, James Bohman and Thomas McCarthy (eds.), *After Philosophy: End or Transformation?*, Cambridge, MIT Press, 1987.
Beiner, Ronald, *What's the Matter with Liberalism?*, Berkeley, University of California Press, 1995.
Benhabib, Seyla, *Critique, Norm, and Utopia: A Study of the Foundations of Critical Theory*, New York, Columbia University Press, 1986.
Benhabib, Seyla, 'Models of Public Space', in *Situating the Self: Gender, Community and Postmodernism in Contemporary Ethics*, Cambridge, Polity Press, 1992, pp. 89-120.
Benhabib, Seyla, *Situating the Self: Gender, Community and Postmodernism in Contemporary Ethics*, Cambridge, Polity Press, 1992.
Benhabib, Seyla, *Feminist Contentions: A Philosophical Exchange*, New York, Routledge, 1995.
Benn, Stanley I., 'Community as a Social Ideal', in Eugene Kamenka (ed.), *Community as a Social Ideal*, London, Edward Arnold, 1982, pp. 43-62.
Benn, Stanley I. and Gerald F. Gaus, 'The Liberal Conception of the Public and Private', in Stanley I. Benn and Gerald F. Gaus (eds.), *Public and Private in Social Life*, London, Croom Helm, 1983, pp. 31-65.
Benn, Stanley I. and Gerald F. Gaus, 'The Public and the Private: Concepts and Action', in Stanley I. Benn and Gerald F. Gaus (eds.), *Public and Private in Social Life*, London, Croom Helm, 1983, pp. 3-27.
Bernstein, Richard J., *Beyond Objectivism and Relativism: Science, Hermeneutics and Praxis*, Oxford, Longman Cheshire, 1983.
Bernstein, Richard J., *The New Constellation: The Ethical-Political Horizons of Modernity/Postmodernity*, Cambridge, MIT Press, 1991.
Boettcher, James W., 'What Is Reasonableness?', *Philosophy and Social Criticism*, vol. 30, no. 5-6, 2004, pp. 597-621.
Bohman, James F., 'Public Reason and Cultural Pluralism: Political Liberalism and the Problem of Moral Conflict', *Political Theory: An International Journal of Political Philosophy*, vol. 23, no. 2, 1995, pp. 253-79.
Brake, E., 'Rawls and Feminism: What Should Feminists Make of Liberal Neutrality?', in T. Brook and F. Freyenhagen (eds.), *The Legacy of John Rawls*, New York, Continuum, 2005, pp. 67-84.
Buchanan, Allen E., 'Assessing the Communitarian Critique of Liberalism', *Ethics*, vol. 99, no. 4, 1989, pp. 852-82.
Butler, Judith and Gayatri Chatravorty Spivak, *Who Sings the Nation-State?: Langauge Politics Belonging*, Calcutta, Seagull Books, 2007.
Caney, Simon, 'Liberalism and Communitarianism: a Misconceived Debate', *Political Studies*, vol. 40, no. 2, 1992, pp. 273-89.
Caney, Simon, 'Anti-Perfectionism and Rawlsian Liberalism', *Political Stud-*

ies, vol. 43, no. 2, 1995, pp. 248-64.

Caney, Simon, 'Cosmopolitanism and the Law of Peoples', *Journal of Political Philosophy*, vol. 10, no. 1, 2002, pp. 95-123.

Castoriadis, Cornelius, 'Power, Politics, Autonomy', in *Philosophy, Politics, Autonomy: Essays in Political Philosophy*, Oxford, Oxford University Press, 1991, pp. 143-74.

Ceva, Emanuela, 'Liberal Pluralism and Pluralist Liberalism', *Res Publica: A Journal of Legal and Social Philosophy*, vol. 11, no. 2, 2005, pp. 201-11.

Chanter, Tina, *Gender: Key Concepts in Philosophy*, London, Continuum, 2006.

Choudhry, Sujit, 'National Minorities and Ethnic Immigrants: Liberalism's Political Sociology', *Journal of Political Philosophy*, vol. 10, no. 1, 2002, pp. 54-78.

Cochran, Clarke E., 'The Thin Theory of Community: The Communitarians and Their Critics', *Political Studies*, vol. 37, no. 3, 1989, pp. 422-35.

Code, Lorraine, *What Can She Know? Feminist Theory and the Construction of Knowledge*, Ithaca, Cornell University Press, 1991.

Collier, Andrew, *Socialist Reasoning: An Inquiry Into the Political Philosophy of Scientific Socialism*, London, Pluto Press, 1989.

Cornell, Drucilla, 'The Post-structuralist Challenge to the Ideal of Community', *Cardozo Law Review*, vol. 8, 1987, pp. 989-1022.

Cornell, Drucilla, *The Philosophy of the Limit*, London, Routledge, 1992.

de Marneffe, Peter, 'Liberalism, Liberty, and Neutrality', *Philosophy and Public Affairs*, vol. 19, no. 3, 1990, pp. 253-74.

de Marneffe, Peter, 'The Slipperiness of Neutrality', *Social Theory and Practice: An International and Interdisciplinary Journal of Social Philosophy*, vol. 32, no. 1, 2006, pp. 17-34.

Derrida, Jacques, *Of Grammatology*, Baltimore, Johns Hopkis University Press, 1976.

Doppelt, Gerald, 'Is Rawls's Kantian Liberalism Coherent and Defensible?', *Ethics: An International Journal of Social, Political, and Legal Philosophy*, vol. 99, no. 4, 1989, pp. 815-51.

Downing, Lyle A. and Robert B. Thigpen, 'Beyond Shared Understandings', *Political Theory*, vol. 14, no. 3, 1986, pp. 451-72.

Dunn, John, *Western Political Theory in the Face of the Future*, Cambridge, Cambridge University Press, 1993.

Dussel, Enrique D., *The Invention of the Americas: Eclipse of the 'Other' and the Myth of Modernity*, trans. Michael D. Barber, New York, Continuum, 1995.

Dworkin, Ronald, *A Matter of Principle*, Oxford, Oxford University Press, 1986.

Dworkin, Ronald, 'Liberalism', in *A Matter of Principle*, Oxford, Oxford University Press, 1986.

Dworkin, Ronald, 'Liberal Community', *California Law Review*, vol. 77, no.

3, 1989, pp. 479-504.
Dworkin, Ronald, 'Foundations of Liberal Equality', in Grethe B. Peterson (ed.), *The Tanner Lectures on Human Values*, vol. 11, Salt Lake City, University of Utah Press, 1990, pp. 1-119.
Eisenberg, Avigail I. and Jeff Spinner-Halev (eds.), *Minorities Within Minorities: Equality, Rights, and Diversity*, Cambridge, Cambridge University Press, 2005.
Ellis, Ralph D., 'Toward a Coherent Definition of Liberalism', *Southwest Philosophical Review*, vol. 7, no. 2, 1991, pp. 31-46.
Ellis, Ralph D., 'Toward a Reconciliation of Liberalism and Communitarianism', *Journal of Value Inquiry*, vol. 25, no. 1, 1991, pp. 55-64.
Elshtain, Jean Bethke, *Public Man Private Woman: Women in Social and Political Thought*, Princeton, Princeton University Press, 1981.
Estlund, David M., 'Jeremy Waldron on Law and Disagreement', *Philosophical Studies: An International Journal for Philosophy in the Analytic Tradition*, vol. 99, no. 1, 2000, pp. 111-28.
Ewin, R. E., 'The Presumption of Non-Interference', in *Liberty, Community and Justice*, New York, Rowman and Littlefield, 1987.
Faubion, J. D. (ed.), *Michel Foucault: Power, Essential Works of Foucault 1954-1984*, London, Penguin, 1994.
Ferrara, Alessandro, 'Universalisms: Procedural, Contextualist and Prudential', in David M. Rasmussen (ed.), *Universalism vs. Communitarianism: Contemporary Debates in Ethics*, 1st MIT Press ed., Cambridge, MIT Press, 1990, pp. 11-38.
Fisher, David, 'Crisis Moral Communities: An Essay in Moral Philosophy', *Journal of Value Inquiry*, vol. 24, no. 1, 1990, pp. 17-30.
Fishkin, James S., 'Liberal Theory: Strategies of Reconstruction', in A. J. Damico (ed.), *Liberals on Liberalism*, New Jersey, Rowman and Littlefield, 1986, pp. 54-66.
Fisk, Milton, *The State and Justice: An Essay in Political Theory*, Cambridge, Cambridge University Press, 1989.
Fraser, Nacey, 'Mapping the Feminist Imagination: From Redistribution to Recognition to Representation', *Constellations*, no. 12, 2005, pp. 295-307.
Fraser, Nancy, *Unruly Practices: Power, Discourse and Gender in Contemporary Social Theory*, Cambridge, Polity Press, 1989.
Fraser, Nancy, 'Rethinking Recognition', *New Left Review*, no. 3, 2000, pp. 107-20.
Fraser, Nancy and Axel Honneth, *Redistribution or Recognition?: A Political-Philosophical Exchange*, London, Verso, 2003.
Frazer, Elizabeth, 'Politics, Culture and the Public Sphere: Toward a Postmodern Conception', in Steven Seidman and Linda J. Nicholson (eds.), *Social Postmodernism: Beyond Identity Politics*, Cambridge, Cambridge

University Press, 1995, pp. 287-312.
Frazer, Elizabeth and Nicola Lacey, *The Politics of Community: A Feminist Critique of the Liberal-Communitarian Debate*, New York, Harvester Wheatsheaf, 1993.
Frazer, Elizabeth and Nicola Lacey, 'Politics and the Public in Rawls' Political Liberalism', *Political Studies*, vol. 43, no. 2, 1995, pp. 233-47.
Freeden, Michael, *Rights*, Milton Keynes, Open University Press, 1990.
Fukuyama, Francis, *The End of History and the Last Man*, New York, Penguin, 1992.
Galston, William A., 'Pluralism and Social Unity', *Ethics*, vol. 99, no. 4, 1989, pp. 711-26.
Galston, William A., *Liberal Purposes: Goods, Virtues, and Diversity in the Liberal State*, Cambridge, Cambridge University Press, 1991.
Galston, William A., *Liberal Pluralism: The Implications of Value Pluralism for Political Theory and Practice*, Cambridge, Cambridge University Press, 2002.
Gatens, Moira, *Feminism and Philosophy: Perspectives on Difference and Equality*, Cambridge, Polity, 1991.
Gaus, Gerald F., *Value and Justification: The Foundations of Liberal Theory*, Cambridge, Cambridge University Press, 1990.
Gaut, Berys, 'Rawls and the Claims of Liberal Legitimacy', *Philosophical Papers*, vol. 24, no. 1, 1995, pp. 1-22.
Geise, J. P., 'Liberal Goods', *International Journal of Moral and Social Studies*, vol. 5, no. 2, 1990, pp. 95-115.
Goodin, Robert E. and Andrew Reeve, *Liberal Neutrality*, London, Routledge, 1989.
Gorz, André, *Critique of Economic Reason*, London, Verso, 1989.
Gray, John, 'Contractarian Method, Private Property and the Market Economy', in Chandran Kukathas (ed.), *John Rawls: Critical Assessments of Leading Political Philosophers*, London, Routledge, 2003, pp. 31-66.
Gray, John, *Liberalisms: Essays in Political Philosophy*, London, Routledge, 1991.
Gray, John, 'Postscript: After Liberalism', in *Liberalisms: Essays in Political Philosophy*, London, Routledge, 1991, pp. 239-66.
Greschner, Donna, 'Feminist Concerns with the New Communitarianism', in Allan C. Hutchinson and Leslie J. M. Green (eds.), *Law and the Community: The End of Individualism?*, Toronto, Carswell, 1989, pp. 119-50.
Groz, Elizabeth, 'A Note on Essentialism and Difference', in Sneja Marina Gunew (ed.), *Feminist Knowledge: Critique and Construct*, London, Routledge, 1990, pp. 332-44.
Gutmann, Amy, 'Communitarian Critics of Liberalism', in Shlomo Avineri and Avner De-Shalit (eds.), *Communitarianism and Individualism*, Oxford, Oxford University Press, 1992, pp. 120-36.

Gutmann, Amy, 'Review: Communitarian Critics of Liberalism', *Philosophy and Public Affairs*, vol. 14, no. 3, 1985, pp. 308-22.
Habermas, Jürgen, 'Life-Forms, Morality and the Task of the Philosopher', in Peter Dews (ed.), *Autonomy and Solidarity: Interviews with Jürgen Habermas*, London, Verso, 1986, pp. 187-211.
Habermas, Jürgen, 'Philosophy as Stand-in and Interpreter', in Kenneth Baynes, James Bohman, and Thomas McCarthy (eds.), *After Philosophy: End or Transformation?*, Cambridge, MIT Press, 1987, pp. 296-318.
Habermas, Jürgen, *The Structural Transformation of the Public Sphere: An Inquiry into a Category of Bourgeois Society*, Cambridge, MIT Press, 1989.
Habermas, Jürgen, *The Philosophical Discourse of Modernity: Twelve Lectures*, trans. Frederick G. Lawrence, Cambridge, MIT Press, 1992.
Habermas, Jürgen, *Justification and Application*, Cambridge, Polity, 1993.
Habermas, Jürgen, 'Reconciliation Through the Public Use of Reason: Remarks on John Rawls's Political Liberalism', *Journal of Philosophy*, vol. 92, no. 3, 1995, pp. 109-31.
Hampton, Jean, 'Should Political Philosophy be Done Without Metaphysics?', *Ethics*, vol. 99, no. 4, 1989, pp. 791-814.
Hardimon, Michael O., *Hegel's Social Philosophy: The Project of Reconciliation*, Cambridge, Cambridge University Press, 1994.
Harte, Liam, 'Overlapping Consensus: Incoherent or Superfluous', *Review Journal of Political Philosophy*, vol. 1, no. 1-2, 2003, pp. 249-80.
Haworth, Alan, 'Liberalism, Abstract Individualism, and the Problem of Particular Obligations', *Res Publica: A Journal of Legal and Social Philosophy*, vol. 11, no. 4, 2005, pp. 371-401.
Hegel, G. W. F., *The Philosophy of Right*, trans. T. M. Knox, Oxford, Oxford, 1976.
Hegel, G. W. F., *Science of Logic*, trans. A.V. Miller, New Jersey, Humanities Press, 1997.
Held, Virginia, 'Non-Contractual Society: The Post-Patriarchal Family as Model', in *Feminist Morality: Transforming Culture, Society, and Politics*, Chicago, University of Chicago Press, 1993, pp. 192-214.
Hirsch, H. N., 'The Threnody of Liberalism: Constitutional Liberty and the Renewal of Community', *Political Theory*, vol. 14, no. 3, 1986, pp. 423-49.
Hirschmann, Nancy J., *Rethinking Obligation: A Feminist Method for Political Theory*, Ithaca, Cornell University Press, 1992.
Hittinger, Russell, 'John Rawls, Political Liberalism', *Review of Metaphysics*, vol. 47, no. 3, 1994, pp. 585-602.
Hobsbawm, Eric J., *Age of Extremes: The Short Twentieth Century, 1914-1991*, London, Abacus, 1995.
Honneth, Axel, *Critique of Power: Reflective Stages in a Critical Social Theory*, Cambridge, M.I.T. Press, 1991.

Horton, John and Susan Mendus, 'After MacIntyre: After Virtue and After', in John Horton and Susan Mendus (eds.), *After MacIntyre: Critical Perspectives on the Work of Alasdair MacIntyre*, Cambridge, Polity, 1994, pp. 1-15.

Hurley, T., 'John Rawls and Liberal Neutrality', in Chandran Kukathas (ed.), *John Rawls: Critical Assessmments of Leading Political Philosophers*, London, Routledge, 2003, pp. 30-54.

Hutchinson, Allan C. and Leslie J. M. Green (eds.), *Law and the Community: The End of Individualism?*, Toronto, Carswell, 1989.

Irigaray, Luce, *Speculum of the Other Woman*, Ithaca, Cornell University Press, 1989.

Ivison, Duncan, *Postcolonial Liberalism*, Cambridge, Cambridge University Press, 2002.

Ivison, Duncan, Paul Patton and Will Sanders (eds.), *Political Theory and the Rights of Indigenous People*, New York, Cambridge University Press, 2000.

Jaggar, Alison M., *Feminist Politics and Human Nature*, Brighton, Rowman & Littlefield, 1983.

Jagger, Alison M., 'Taking Consent Seriously: Feminist practical Ethics and Actual Moral Dialogue', in E. R. Winkler and J. R. Coombs (eds.), *Applied Ethics: A Reader*, Oxford, Blackwell, 1993, pp. 69-86

Julia, Annas, 'Review: MacIntyre on Traditions', *Philosophy and Public Affairs*, vol. 18, no. 4, 1989, pp. 388-404.

Kateb, George, 'Individualism, Communitarianism, and Docility', *Social Research*, vol. 56, no. 4, 1989, pp. 921-42.

Kelly, Michael, 'MacIntyre, Habermas and Philosophical Ethics', *Philosophical Forum*, vol. 21, 1990, pp. 70-93.

Kristeva, Julia, *In the Beginning Was Love: Psychoanalysis and Faith*, New York, Columbia University Press, 1987.

Kukathas, Chandran and Philip Pettit, *Rawls: A Theory of Justice and its Critics*, Cambridge, Polity Press, 1992.

Kymlicka, Will, 'Liberalism and Communitarianism', *Canadian Journal of Philosophy*, vol. 18, no. 2, 1988, pp. 181-204.

Kymlicka, Will, *Contemporary Political Philosophy: An Introduction*, Oxford, Oxford University Press, 1989.

Kymlicka, Will, *Liberalism, Community, and Culture*, Oxford, Oxford University Press, 1989.

Kymlicka, Will, 'Liberalism, Individualism and Liberal Neutrality', *Ethics*, vol. 99, no. 4, 1989, pp. 883-905.

Kymlicka, Will, *Multicultural Citizenship: A Liberal Theory of Minority Rights*, Oxford, Oxford University Press, 1995.

Kymlicka, Will (ed.), *The Rights of Minority Cultures*, Oxford, Oxford University Press, 1995.

Kymlicka, Will, *Politics in the Vernacular: Nationalism, Multiculturalism and Citizenship*, Oxford, Oxford University Press, 2001.
Kymlicka, Will, Bruce Berman and Dickson Eyoh (eds.), *Ethnicity and Democracy in Africa*, Athens, Ohio University Press, 2004.
Kymlicka, Will and Baogang He, *Multiculturalism in Asia*, Oxford, Oxford University Press, 2005.
Kymlicka, Will and Wayne Norman (eds.), *Citizenship in Diverse Societies*, Oxford, Oxford University Press, 2000.
Kymlicka, Will and Magdalena Opalski (eds.), *Can Liberal Pluralism be Exported?: Western Political Theory and Ethnic Relations in Eastern Europe*, New York, Oxford University Press, 2001.
Laclau, Ernesto, 'Introduction', in Ernesto Laclau (ed.), *The Making of Political Identities*, London, Verso, 1994, pp. 1-10.
Laclau, Ernesto and Chantal Mouffe, *Hegemony and Socialist Strategy: Towards and Radical Democratic Politics*, London, Verso, 1985.
Larmore, Charles, 'Review of Michael Sandel's Liberalism and the Limits of Justice', *The Journal Of Philosophy*, vol. 81, no. 6, 1984, pp. 336-43.
Larmore, Charles, *Patterns of Moral Complexity*, Cambridge, Cambridge University Press, 1987.
Larmore, Charles, 'Political Liberalism', *Political Theory*, vol. 18, no. 3, 1990, pp. 339-60.
Larmore, Charles, *The Morality of Modernity*, Cambridge, Cambridge University Press, 1996.
Larmore, Charles, 'The Moral Basis of Political Liberalism', *Journal of Philosophy*, vol. 96, no. 12, 1999, pp. 599-625.
Larmore, Charles, 'Public Reason', in S. Freeman (ed.), *The Cambridge Companion to Rawls*, Cambridge, Cambridge University Press, 2003, pp. 368-93.
Lilla, Mark, *New French Thought: Political Philosophy*, Princeton, Princeton University Press, 1994.
Livadites, Tasos, *Small Book for Large Dreams (Greek)*, Athens, Kethros, 1987.
Lloyd, Genevieve, *The Man of Reason: 'Male' and 'Female' in Western Philosophy*, London, Methuen, 1984.
Long, Graham M., *Relativism and the Foundations of Liberalism*, Exeter, Imprint Academic, 2004.
Lott, Micah, 'Restraint on Reasons and Reasons for Restraint: A Problem for Rawls' Ideal of Public Reason', *Pacific Philosophical Quarterly*, vol. 87, no. 1, 2006, pp. 75-95.
Lyshaug, Brenda, 'Authenticity and the Politics of Identity: A Critique of Charles Taylor's Politics of Recognition', *Contemporary Political Theory*, vol. 3, no. 3, 2004, pp. 300-20.
MacIntyre, Alasdair C., *After Virtue: A Study in Moral Theory*, 2nd ed., London, Duckworth, 1985.

MacIntyre, Alasdair C., *Whose Justice? Which Rationality?*, Notre Dame, University of Notre Dame Press, 1988.
MacIntyre, Alasdair C., 'A Partial Response to my Critics', in John Horton and Susan Mendus (eds.), *After MacIntyre: Critical Perspectives on the Work of Alasdair MacIntyre*, Cambridge, Polity, 1994, pp. 283-304.
MacIntyre, Alasdair C., 'The Spectre of Communitariansim', *Radical Philosophy*, no. 70, 1995, pp. 34-5.
MacLean, Douglas and Claudia Mills, 'Introduction', in Douglas MacLean and Claudia Mills (eds.), *Liberalism Reconsidered*, Totowa, Rowman & Allanheld, 1983.
MacLean, Douglas and Claudia Mills (eds.), *Liberalism Reconsidered*, Totowa, Rowman & Allanheld, 1983.
Maclure, Jocelyn, 'On the Public Use of Practical Reason: Loosening the Grip of Neo-Kantianism', *Philosophy and Social Criticism*, vol. 32, no. 1, 2006, pp. 37-63.
Maffettone, Sebastiano, 'Political Liberalism: Reasonableness and Democratic Practice', *Philosophy and Social Criticism*, vol. 30, no. 5-6, 2004, pp. 541-77.
Mahoney, Jon, 'Public Reason and the Moral Foundation of Liberalism', in T. Brooks and F. Freyenhagen (eds.), *The Legacy of John Rawls*, New York, Continuum, 2005, pp. 85-106.
McCarthy, Thomas A., 'Kantian Constructivism and Reconstructivism: Rawls and Habermas in Dialogue', *Ethics*, vol. 105, no. 1, 1994, pp. 44-63.
McKeen, C., 'Gender, Choice and Partiality: A Defence of Rawls on the Family', *Essays in Philosophy*, vol. 7, no. 1, 2005, pp. 1-15.
Mendus, Susan, *Toleration and The Limits of Liberalism*, Basingstoke, Macmillan, 1989.
Mill, Harriet Taylor, 'Enfranchisement of Women', in Alice S. Rossi (ed.), *Essays on Sex Equality*, Chicago, University of Chicago Press, 1970, pp. 89-121.
Mill, John Stuart, *The Subjection of Women*, London, Dent, 1985.
Miller, David, 'In What Sense Must Socialism Be Communitarian?', *Social Philosophy and Policy*, vol. 6, 1989, pp. 51-73.
Modood, Tariq, *Multiculturalism: A Civic Idea*, Cambridge, Polty Press, 2007.
Modood, Tariq, Judith Squires and Stephen May (eds.), *Ethnicity Nationalism and Minority Rights*, Cambridge, Cambridge University Press, 2004.
Monohan, Michael, 'Private Property and Public Interest', *Philosophy in the Contemporary World*, vol. 12, no. 2, 2005, pp. 17-21.
Moore, Margaret, *Foundations of Liberalism*, Oxford, Oxford University Press, 1993.
Mouffe, Chantal, *The Return of the Political*, London, Verso, 1993.
Mouffe, Chantal, 'Political Liberalism: Neutrality and the Political', *Ratio*

Juris: An International Journal of Jurisprudence and Philosophy of Law, vol. 7, no. 3, 1994, pp. 314-24.

Mouffe, Chantal, *On the Political*, London, Routledge, 2005.

Mouffe, Chantal, 'The Limits of John Rawls' Pluralism', *Politics, Philosophy and Economics*, vol. 4, no. 2, 2005, pp. 221-31.

Mulhall, Stephen and Adam Swift, *Liberals and Communitarians*, Oxford, Blackwell, 1992.

Nagel, Thomas, 'Rawls on Justice', in Norman Daniels (ed.), *Reading Rawls: Critical Studies on Rawls' A Theory of Justice*, Oxford, Blackwell, 1975, pp. 1-15.

Nagel, Thomas, 'Rawls and Liberalism', in Samuel Freman (ed.), *The Cambridge Companion to Rawls*, Cambridge, Cambridge University Press, 2003, pp. 62-85.

Naticchia, C., 'The Law of Peoples: The Old and the New', in T. Brook and F. Freyenhagen (eds.), *The Legacy of John Rawls*, New York, Continuum, 2005, pp. 177-94.

Newman, Stephen, 'Challenging the Liberal-Individualist Tradition in America: "Community" as a Critical Ideal in Recent Political Theory', in Allan C. Hutchinson and Leslie J. M. Green (eds.), *Law and the Community: The End of Individualism?*, Toronto, Carswell, 1989.

Nicholson, Linda J., 'Feminist Theory: The Private and the Public', in Carol C. Gould (ed.), *Beyond Domination: New Perspectives on Women and Philosophy*, Totowa, Rowman & Allanheld, 1984, pp. 221-32.

Nickel, James W., 'Does Basing Rights on Autonomy Imply Obligations of Political Allegiance?', *Dialogue: Canadian Philosophical Review*, vol. 28, no. 4, 1989, pp. 531-44.

Nicolacopoulos, Toula, 'Radicalism Without Vision: Chantal Mouffe's Affiliation to Liberal Democracy', in process

Nicolacopoulos, Toula, *In Memory of a Vision, Volume 2*, Seddon, re.press, forthcoming.

Nicolacopoulos, Toula, 'What's Wrong with "Exporting Liberal Pluralism"? On the Radical Self-denial of Contemporary Liberal Philosophy', *Philosophical Inquiry*, vol. XXIX, no. 1-2, 2007, pp. 89-111.

Nicolacopoulos, Toula and George Vassilacopoulos, *Hegel and the Logical Structure of Love: An Essay on Sexualities, Family and the Law*, Aldershot, Ashgate, 1999.

Nicolacopoulos, Toula and George Vassilacopoulos, *From Foreigner to Citizen: Greek Migrants in White Australia and Social Change 1897-2000 (Greek)*, Melbourne, Eothinon Publications, 2004.

Nicolacopoulos, Toula and George Vassilacopoulos, 'Philosophy and Revolution: Badiou's Infidelity to the Event', in Paul Ashton, A. J. Bartlett, and Justin Clemens (eds.), *The Praxis of Alain Badiou*, Seddon, re.press, 2006, pp. 367-85.

Nicolacopoulos, Toula and George Vassilacopoulos, 'The Ego as World: Speculative Justification and the Role of the Thinker in Hegel's Philosophy', in Paul Ashton, Toula Nicolacopoulos, and George Vassilacopoulos (eds.), *The Spirit of the Age: Hegel and the Fate of Thinking*, Seddon, re.press, 2008, pp. 252-91.

Nielsen, Morten Ebbe Juul, 'Limited Neutrality', *SATS: Nordic Journal of Philosophy*, vol. 6, no. 1, 2005, pp. 110-27.

Nien-he, Hsieh, 'Rawlsian Justice and Workplace Republicanism', *Social Theory & Practice*, vol. 31, no. 1, 2005, pp. 115-42.

Nino, Carlos Santiago, 'The Communitarian Challenge to Liberal Rights', *Law and Philosophy*, vol. 8, 1989, pp. 37-52.

Nino, Carlos Santiago, 'Moral Constructivism', in *The Ethics of Human Rights*, Oxford, Oxford University Press, 1991.

Noddings, Nel, *Caring: A Feminist Approach to Ethics and Moral Education*, Berkeley, University of California Press, 1984.

O'Hagan, Timothy, 'Four Images of Community', *Praxis International*, vol. 8, no. 2, 1988, pp. 183-92.

Okin, Susan Moller, *Justice, Gender and the Family*, New York, Basic Books, 1989.

Okin, Susan Moller, 'Humanist Liberalism', in Nancy L. Rosenblum (ed.), *Liberalism and Moral Life*, Cambridge, Harvard University Press, 1991, pp. 39-53.

Okin, Susan Moller, 'Gender Inequality and Cultural Differences', *Political Theory*, vol. 22, no. 1, 1994, pp. 5-24.

Okin, Susan Moller, 'Political Liberalism, Justice, and Gender', *Ethics*, vol. 105, no. 1, 1994, pp. 23-43.

Okin, Susan Moller, '"Forty Acres and a Mule" for Women: Rawls and Feminism', *Politics, Philosophy and Economics*, vol. 4, no. 2, 2005, pp. 233-48.

Parekh, Bhikhu C., *Rethinking Multiculturalism: Cultural Diversity and Political Theory*, 2nd ed., Basingstoke, Palgrave Macmillan, 2006.

Pateman, Carole, *The Problem of Political Obligation: A Critical Analysis of Liberal Theory*, New York, Wiley, 1979.

Pateman, Carole, 'Feminist Critiques of the Public/Private Dichotomy', in Stanley I. Benn and Gerald F. Gaus (eds.), *Public and Private in Social Life*, London, Croom Helm, 1983, pp. 281-303.

Pateman, Carole, *The Sexual Contract*, Cambridge, Polity, 1988.

Pateman, Carole, *The Disorder of Women: Democracy, Feminism and Political Theory*, Cambridge, Polity Press, 1989.

Pateman, Carole, 'The Fraternal Social Contract', in *The Disorder of Women: Democracy, Feminism and Political Theory*, Cambridge, Polity Press, 1989, pp. 33-57.

Peffer, R. G., 'Marxist and Leftist Objections to Rawls' *Theory of Justice*:

A Critical Review', in *Marxism, Morality, and Social Justice*, Princeton, Princeton University Press, 1990, pp. 361-415.
Pettit, Philip, *Republicanism: A Theory of Freedom and Government*, Oxford, Oxford University Press, 1997.
Pettit, Philip and Chandran Kukathas, *Rawls: A Theory of Justice and its Critics*, Cambridge, Polity, 1990.
Phelan, Shane, *Identity Politics: Lesbian Feminism and the Limits of Community*, Philadelphia, Temple University Press, 1989.
Plant, Raymond, *Modern Political Thought*, Oxford, Blackwell, 1991.
Plumwood, Val, *Feminism and the Mastery of Nature*, London, Routledge, 1993.
Pogge, Thomas W., *Realizing Rawls*, Ithaca, Cornell University Press, 1989.
Poole, Ross, *Morality and Modernity*, London, Routledge, 1991.
Quijano, Anibal, 'Coloniality of Power, Eurocentrism and Latin America', *Nepantla: Views from the South*, vol. 1, no. 3, 2000, pp. 533-80.
Rancière, Jacques, *On the Shores of Politics*, trans. Liz Heron, London, Verso, 1995.
Rasmussen, David M., 'Universalism vs. Communitarianism: An Introduction', in David M. Rasmussen (ed.), *Universalism vs. Communitarianism: Contemporary Debates in Ethics*, 1st MIT Press ed., Cambridge, MIT Press, 1990, pp. 1-10.
Rasmussen, Douglas B. and Douglas J. Den Uyl, *Liberty and Nature: An Aristotelian Defense of Liberal Order*, La Salle, Open Court, 1991.
Rawls, John, *A Theory of Justice*, Cambridge, Harvard University Press, 1988.
Rawls, John, 'Law of Peoples', in S. L. Hurley and Stephen Shute (eds.), *On Human Rights: The Oxford Amnesty Lectures*, New York, BasicBooks, 1993, pp. 41-82.
Rawls, John, *Political Liberalism*, New York, Columbia University Press, 1993.
Rawls, John, 'Reply to Habermas' Reconciliation Through the Public Use of Reason', *Journal of Philosophy*, vol. 92, no. 3, 1995, pp. 132-80.
Rawls, John, *Collected Papers*, Samuel Richard Freeman (ed.), Cambridge, Harvard University Press, 1999.
Rawls, John, 'The Idea of Public Reason Revisited', in Samuel Richard Freeman (ed.), *Collected Papers*, Cambridge, Harvard University Press, 1999, pp. 573-615.
Raz, Joseph, *The Morality of Freedom*, Oxford, Oxford University Press, 1986.
Rea, Bruno, 'Rights and the Communitarian Ideal', *Idealistic Studies*, vol. 18, no. 2, 1988, pp. 107-22.
Rehg, William, 'Discourse Ethics and the Communitarian Critique of Neo-Kantianism', *Philosophical Forum*, vol. 22, no. 2, 1990, pp. 120-38.

Reidy, David A., 'Rawls on International Justice: A Defense', *Political Theory: An International Journal of Political Philosophy*, vol. 32, no. 3, 2004, pp. 291-319.
Richard, Bellamy and Hollis Martin, 'Liberal Justice: Political and Metaphysical', *The Philosophical Quarterly*, vol. 45, no. 178, 1995, pp. 1-19.
Robert, B. Thigpen and A. Downing Lyle, 'Liberalism and the Neutrality Principle', *Political Theory*, vol. 11, no. 4, 1983, pp. 585-600.
Roemer, John E. and Erik Olin Wright, *Equal Shares: Making Market Socialism Work*, London, Verso, 1996.
Rorty, Richard, 'Postmodernist Bourgeois Liberalism', *The Journal Of Philosophy*, vol. 80, no. 10, 1983, pp. 583-9.
Rorty, Richard, *Philosophy and the Mirror of Nature*, Princeton, Princeton University Press, 1986.
Rorty, Richard, *Contingency, Irony, and Solidarity*, Cambridge, Cambridge University Press, 1989.
Rorty, Richard, *Essays on Heidegger and Others: Philosophical Papers Volume 2*, Cambridge, Cambridge University Press, 1991.
Rorty, Richard, *Objectivism, Relativism, and Truth: Philosophical Papers Volume 1*, Cambridge, Cambridge University Press, 1991.
Rorty, Richard, 'The Priority of Democracy to Philosophy', in *Objectivity, Relativism, and Truth: Philosophical Papers Volume 1*, Cambridge, Cambridge University Press, 1991, pp. 175-96.
Rorty, Richard (ed.), *The Linguistic Turn: Essays in Philosophical Method*, Chicago, University of Chicago Press, 1992.
Rosenblum, Nancy L., *Another Liberalism: Romanticism and the Reconstruction of Liberal Thought*, Cambridge, Harvard University Press, 1987.
Rosenblum, Nancy L., 'Repairing the Communitarian Failings of Liberal Thought', in *Another Liberalism: Romanticism and the Reconstruction of Liberal Thought*, Cambridge, Harvard University Press, 1987, pp. 152-86.
Rosenblum, Nancy L. (ed.), *Liberalism and Moral Life*, Cambridge, Harvard University Press, 1991.
Ryan, Allan, 'Liberalism', in Robert E. Goodin and Philip Pettit (eds.), *A Companion to Contemporary Political Philosophy*, Oxford, Blackwell, 1997, pp. 291-311.
Sandel, M. J., *Liberalism and the Limits of Justice*, Cambridge, Cambridge University Press, 1992.
Scanlon, T. M., 'Rawls on Justification', in S. Freeman (ed.), *The Cambridge Companion to Rawls*, Cambridge, Cambridge University Press, 2003.
Scheffler, Samuel, 'The Appeal of Political Liberalism', *Ethics*, vol. 105, no. 1, 1994, pp. 4-22.
Schmitz, Kenneth L., 'Community: The Elusive Unity', *Review of Metaphysics*, vol. 37, no. 2, 1983, pp. 243-64.
Seidman, Steven, 'Identity and Politics in a "Postmodern" Gay Culture:

Some Historical and Condeptual Notes', in Michael Warner (ed.), *Fear of a Queer Planet: Queer Politics and Social Theory*, Minneapolis, University of Minnesota Press, 1993, pp. 103-42.
Selznick, Philip, 'The Idea of a Communitarian Morality', *California Law Review*, vol. 75, no. 1, 1987, pp. 445-63.
Shapiro, Ian, *Political Criticism*, Berkeley, University of California Press, 1990.
Simmons, A. John, *Moral Principles and Political Obligations*, Princeton, Princeton University Press, 1979.
Simon, Caney, 'Consequentialist Defences of Liberal Neutrality', *The Philosophical Quarterly*, vol. 41, no. 165, 1991, pp. 457-77.
Smith, Steven B., *Hegel's Critique of Liberalism: Rights in Context*, Chicago, University of Chicago Press, 1989.
Spragens, Thomas A., Jr., 'Reconstructing Liberal Theory: Reason and Liberal Culture', in Alfonso J. Damico (ed.), *Liberals on Liberalism*, Totowa, Rowman & Littlefield, 1986, pp. 34-53.
Tapper, Marion, 'Can a Feminist Be a Liberal?', *Australasian Journal of Philosophy*, vol. 64, 1986, pp. 37-47.
Taylor, Charles, *Hegel and Modern Society*, Cambridge, Cambridge University Press, 1980.
Taylor, Charles, 'Overcoming Epistemology', in Kenneth Baynes, James Bohman, and Thomas McCarthy (eds.), *After Philosophy: End or Transformation?*, Cambridge, MIT Press, 1987, pp. 464-85.
Taylor, Charles, 'Reply to de Sousa and Davis: Human Agency and Language', *Canadian Journal of Philosophy*, vol. 18, 1988, pp. 449-58.
Taylor, Charles, *Sources of the Self: The Making of the Modern Identity*, Cambridge, Cambridge University Press, 1989.
Taylor, Charles, *Human Agency and Language: Philosophical Papers 1*, Cambridge, Cambridge University Press, 1992.
Taylor, Charles, 'Inwardness and the Culture of Modernity', in Axel Honneth, Thomas McCarthy, Claus Offe, and Albrecht Wellmer (eds.), *Philosophical Interventions in the Unfinished Project of Enlightenment*, Cambridge, MIT Press, 1992, pp. 88-110.
Taylor, Charles, *Philosophy and the Human Sciences: Philosophical Papers 2*, Cambridge, Cambridge University Press, 1992.
Taylor, Charles, 'Charles Taylor Replies', in James Tully and Daniel M. Weinstock (eds.), *Philosophy in an Age of Pluralism: The Philosophy of Charles Taylor in Question*, Cambridge, Cambridge University Press, 1994, pp. 213-57.
Taylor, Charles, 'Justice After Virtue', in John Horton and Susan Mendus (eds.), *After MacIntyre: Critical Perspectives on the Work of Alasdair MacIntyre*, Cambridge, Polity, 1994, pp. 16-43.
Taylor, Charles, 'The Politics of Recognition', in Amy Gutmann and Charles

Taylor (eds.), *Multiculturalism: Examining the Politics of Recognition*, Princeton, Princeton University Press, 1994, pp. 25-73.

Taylor, Charles, 'Cross-Purposes: The Liberal-Communitarian Debate', in *Philosophical Arguments*, Cambridge, Harvard University Press, 1995.

Taylor, Charles, *Philosophical Arguments*, Cambridge, Harvard University Press, 1995.

Taylor, Charles, 'Invoking Civil Society', in Robert E. Goodin and Philip Pettit (eds.), *A Companion to Contemporary Political Philosophy*, Oxford, Blackwell, 1997, pp. 66-77.

Therborn, Göran, 'After Dialectics: Radical Social Theory in a Post-Communist World', *New Left Review*, no. 43, 2007, pp. 63-114.

Tomasi, John, 'Kymlicka, Liberalism, and Respect for Cultural Minorities', *Ethics*, vol. 105, no. 3, 1995, pp. 580-603.

Tong, Rosemarie, *Feminist Thought: A Comprehensive Introduction*, London, Unwin Hyman, 1989.

Vassilacopoulos, George, *A Reading of Hegel's Philosophy*, Ph.D., La Trobe University, Melbourne, 1993.

Vattimo, Gianni, *Nihilism and Emancipation: Ethics, Politics and Law*, Santiago Zabala (ed.), trans. William McCuaig, New York, Columbia University Press, 2004.

Waldron, Jeremy, 'Theoretical Foundations of Liberalism', *Philosophical Quarterly*, vol. 37, no. 147, 1987, pp. 127-50.

Waldron, Jeremy, 'When Justice Replaces Affection: The Need for Rights', *Harvard Journal of Law & Public Policy*, vol. 11, no. 3, 1988, pp. 625-47.

Walhof, Darren R., 'Friendship, Otherness and Gadamer's Politics of Solidarity', *Poltitical Theory*, vol. 34, 2006, pp. 569-93.

Wallach, John R., 'Liberals, Communitarians, and the Tasks of Political Theory', *Political Theory*, vol. 15, no. 4, 1987, pp. 581-611.

Wallerstein, Immanuel Maurice, *The Decline of American Power: The US in a Chaotic World*, London, New Press, 2003.

Walzer, Michael, 'Philosophy and Democracy', *Political Theory*, vol. 9, no. 3, 1981, pp. 379-99.

Walzer, Michael, *Spheres of Justice: A Defence of Pluralism and Equality*, Oxford, M. Robertson, 1983.

Walzer, Michael, 'Liberalism and the Art of Separation', *Political Theory*, vol. 12, no. 3, 1984, pp. 315-30.

Walzer, Michael, 'The Practice of Social Criticism', in *Interpretation and Social Criticism*, Cambridge, Harvard University Press, 1987, pp. 33-66.

Walzer, Michael, 'Three Paths in Moral Philosophy', in *Interpretation and Social Criticism*, Cambridge, Harvard University Press, 1987, pp. 1-32.

Walzer, Michael, 'The Communitarian Critique of Liberalism', *Political Theory*, vol. 18, no. 1, 1990, pp. 6-23.

Weinstock, Daniel M., 'Modernité et morale (Book Review)', *The Journal Of*

Philosophy, vol. XCIII, no. 1, 1996, pp. 41-8.

Wenar, L., 'The Unity of Rawls' Work', in T. Brook and F. Freyenhagen (eds.), *The Legacy of John Rawls*, New York, Continuum, 2005, pp. 22-33.

Wittington, Keith E., 'In defence of Legislatures', *Political Theory*, vol. 28, no. 5, 2000, pp. 690-702.

Wolff, Robert Paul (ed.), *Political Man and Social Man: Readings in Political Philosophy*, New York, Random House, 1966.

Wollstonecraft, Mary, *A Vindication of the Rights of Woman*, London, Dent, 1985.

Wright, Erik Olin (ed.), *Approaches to Class Analysis*, Cambridge, Cambridge University Press, 2005.

Yeatman, Anna, 'The Personal and the Political: A Feminist Critique', in Nancy Fraser and Paul James (eds.), *Critical Politics: From the Personal to the Global*, Melbourne, Arena Publications, 1994, pp. 35-58.

Young, Iris Marion, 'Politics and Group Difference: A Critique of the Ideal of Universal Citizenship', *Ethics: An International Journal of Social, Political, and Legal Philosophy*, vol. 99, 1989, pp. 116-21.

Young, Iris Marion, *Justice and the Politics of Difference*, Princeton, Princeton University Press, 1990.

Young, Iris Marion, 'Gender as Seriality: Thinking About Women as a Social Collective', in Steven Seidman and Linda J. Nicholson (eds.), *Social Postmodernism: Beyond Identity Politics*, Cambridge, Cambridge University Press, 1995, pp. 187-215.

Žižek, Slavoj, 'Introduction: Between the Two Revolutions', in Slavoj Žižek (ed.), *Revolution at the Gates: A Selection of Writings From February to October 1917*, London, Verso, 2002, pp. 1-12.

About the Author

Toula Nicolacopoulos lectures in Philosophy at the School of Communication Arts and Critical Enquiry, La Trobe University. She has co-authored two books with George Vassilacopoulos, *Hegel and the Logical Structure of Love: An Essay on Sexualities, Family and the Law*, Aldershot, Ashgate, 1999 and *From Foreigner to Citizen: Greek Migrants in White Australia and Social Change 1897-2000* (Greek) Melbourne and Pireas, Eothinon Publications, 2004. With Paul Ashton and George Vassilacopoulos she has co-edited, *The Spirit of the Age: Hegel and the Fate of Thinking*, Melbourne, re.press, 2008. She has also published essays on liberalism, multiculturalism, ethnicity and minority discourses, race and critical whiteness theory, Hegel and Badiou.

www.ingramcontent.com/pod-product-compliance
Lightning Source LLC
Chambersburg PA
CBHW022053160426
43198CB00008B/214